LSU Bowl Games

LSU Bowl Games

A Complete History

NEAL GOLDEN

McFarland & Company, Inc., Publishers

Jefferson, North Carolina

LIBRARY OF CONGRESS CATALOGUING-IN-PUBLICATION DATA

Names: Golden, Neal, author.
Title: LSU bowl games : a complete history / Neal Golden.
Other titles: Louisiana State University bowl games
Description: Jefferson, North Carolina : McFarland & Company, Inc.,
Publishers, 2021. | Includes bibliographical references and index.
Identifiers: LCCN 2021006101 | ISBN 9781476683119 (paperback : acid free paper) ∞
ISBN 9781476641980 (ebook)
Subjects: LCSH: LSU Tigers (Football team)—History. | Louisiana State
University (Baton Rouge, La.)—Football—History.
Classification: LCC GV958.L65 G65 2021 | DDC 796.332/630976318—dc23
LC record available at https://lccn.loc.gov/2021006101

BRITISH LIBRARY CATALOGUING DATA ARE AVAILABLE

ISBN (print) 978-1-4766-8311-9
ISBN (ebook) 978-1-4766-4198-0

THE FRONT COVER PHOTOGRAPH
(foreground) LSU quarterback Joe Burrow, 2018 (Tammy Anthony Baker);
(background) Tigers football team on the field before the 1907 Bacardi Bowl
in Havana, Cuba (*Gumbo* yearbook, Louisiana State University)

Printed in the United States of America

*McFarland & Company, Inc., Publishers
Box 611, Jefferson, North Carolina 28640
www.mcfarlandpub.com*

To my late brother Rolland,
a huge LSU fan, in hopes that he watched the 2019
Peach Bowl and National Championship Game from on high.

Table of Contents

Abbreviations

E = end
SE = split end
WR = wide receiver
FL = flanker
TE = tight end
DE = defensive end
T = (offensive) tackle
DT = defensive tackle
G = (offensive) guard
MG = middle guard
NG = nose guard
LB = linebacker
LLB = left linebacker

RLB = right linebacker
ILB = inside linebacker
OLB = outside linebacker
DB = defensive back
SB = split back
CB = cornerback
WB = wingback
S = safety
FS = free safety
SS = strong safety
P = punter
K or PK = place kicker
PR = punt returner

LSU Bowl Games Facts and Figures

Record vs. Bowl Opponents

Opponent	Wins	Losses	Ties	Percentage
Arkansas	1	0	1	.750
Baylor	0	2	0	.000
Central Florida	1	0	0	1.000
Clemson	2	1	0	.667
Colorado	1	0	0	1.000
Florida State	1	0	0	1.000
Georgia Tech	2	0	0	1.000
Illinois	1	0	0	1.000
Iowa	1	1	0	.500
Iowa State	1	0	0	1.000
Louisville	1	0	0	1.000
Miami (FL)	1	0	0	1.000
Michigan State	1	0	0	1.000
Missouri	0	1	0	.000
Nebraska	0	4	0	.000
Notre Dame	2	2	0	.500
Oklahoma	2	1	0	.667
Ole Miss	0	1	0	.000
Penn State	0	2	0	.000
Santa Clara	0	2	0	.000
South Carolina	1	0	0	1.000
Stanford	0	1	0	.000
Syracuse	1	1	0	.500
TCU	0	1	0	.000
Tennessee	0	1	0	.000
Texas	1	1	0	.500
Texas A&M	2	0	0	1.000
Texas Tech	1	0	0	1.000

continued

Opponent	Wins	Losses	Ties	Percentage
Wake Forest	1	0	0	1.000
Wyoming	1	0	0	1.000
Totals	26	22	1	.541

Note: *The three BCS championship games (2003–04, 2007–08, 2011–12) and the 2019–20 College Football Playoff Championship games were not bowl games. If you include those, LSU's postseason record is 28–23–1 (.548)*

Note: *Bold indicates largest number in each column.*

LSU Coaches' Records in Bowl Games

Coach	Years	Wins	Losses	Ties	Percentage
Edgar Wingard	1907–08	1*	0	0	1.000
Bernie Moore	1935–47	1	3	1	.375
Gaynell Tinsley	1948–54	0	1	0	.000
Paul Dietzel	1955–61	2	1	0	.667
Charles McClendon	1962–79	7	**6**	0	.571
Jerry Stovall	1980–83	0	1	0	.000
Bill Arnsparger	1984–86	0	3	0	.000
Mike Archer	1987–90	1	1	0	.500
Gerry DiNardo	1995–99	3	0	0	1.000
Nick Saban	2000–04	3	1	0	.750
Les Miles	2005–16	6	4	0	.667
Ed Orgeron	2016–	3	1	0	.750
		27	21	1	

* *Wingard's victory was against Havana University.*

Note: *Bold indicates largest number in each column.*

Preface

The saga of LSU's fifty bowl games runs the gamut of emotions from national championship elation to the devastation of a last-minute loss. Included in the list of games are

- a game in a foreign country: 1907 Bacardi.
- bad weather games: 1936 Sugar, 1937 Sugar, 1938 Sugar, 1947 Cotton.
- games against Hall of Fame coaches: 1936 Sugar, 1937 Sugar, 1938 Sugar, 1950 Sugar, 1959 Sugar, 1960 Sugar, 1963 Cotton, 1965 Sugar, 1966 Cotton, 1971 Orange, 1974 Orange, 1977 Sun, 1983 Orange, 1985 Sugar, 2003 Cotton, 2010 Capital One.
- games with a first-year LSU coach: 1936 Sugar, 1963 Cotton, 1985 Sugar, 1987 Gator, 1995 Independence, 2000 Peach, 2005 Peach, 2016 Citrus.
- games the Tigers didn't want to play: 1937 Sugar, 1938 Sugar, 1960 Sugar, 1963 Bluebonnet, 1978 Liberty, 1985 Liberty, 1989 Hall of Fame.
- games with bizarre events before or after the game: 1937 Sugar, 1944 Orange, 1950 Sugar.
- rematches from the regular season: 1944 Orange, 1960 Sugar, 1997 Independence.
- games where a future star emerged: 1944 Orange, 2019 Fiesta.
- games on an unplayable field: 1947 Cotton, 2010 Capital One.
- games that won or contributed to national championships: 1959 Sugar, 2004 Sugar, 2019 Peach.
- games that featured Heisman Trophy winners: 1959 Sugar, 1960 Sugar, 1974 Orange, 2004 Sugar, 2016 Citrus, 2019 Peach.
- games that were overshadowed by a coach's departure or possible departure: 1962 Orange, 1971 Sun, 1979 Tangerine, 1987 Sugar, 2005 Capital One.
- upsets of highly-ranked teams: 1963 Cotton, 1966 Cotton, 1968 Sugar.
- first games against black players: 1965 Sugar, 1972 Astro-Bluebonnet.
- games with exciting endings: 1968 Sugar, 2005 Capital One, 2012 Chick-fil-A, 2018 Citrus.
- games against Super Bowl winning quarterbacks: 2015 Texas.

Bacardi Bowl vs.
University of Havana

*LSU invaded Cuba nine years after
the Spanish-American War*

Almendares Park, Havana, Cuba
December 25, 1907

LSU's Season

When the 1907 LSU Tigers under first-year head coach Edgar R. Wingard finished their season with a 6–3 record, the LSU president, Colonel T.D. Boyd, received an offer to play another game.

The city of Havana wanted an American football game to climax Cuba's annual National Sports Festival. LSU was invited to meet a team from the University of Havana—"the strongest eleven in Cuba"—on Christmas Day. The Havana team boasted "many former American college men who have played football in this country," including Rene Messa, who played for LSU in 1905–06. With the Havana committee promising to pay travel expenses, LSU agreed to the game.

Wingard gave his men some time off before starting preparations for the first appearance by an American college team on foreign soil. The team practiced through December 20 before leaving Baton Rouge the morning of December 21 for New Orleans where the 13 players (from a squad of 18), one coach, and two student assistants boarded the Southern Pacific steamer *Chalmette* for Havana. The team would remain in the Cuban capital until January 1. One report said, "It is very likely that a number of students will accompany the football team to Cuba, and those who do so will be allowed the privilege of remaining absent until January 5."

The undisputed star of the LSU team was 20-year-old 165-pound E George "Doc" Fenton. He was born in Scranton, Pennsylvania, in 1887 but began his college athletic career in Canada in 1904 at St. Michael's College where he played rugby (which was much closer to American football then than it is today). He then played football at Mansfield State Normal School back in his home state. He became the star receiver in 1906, the first year of the legal forward pass.

One day a well-dressed man introduced himself to Fenton after practice. "My name is Edgar Wingard. I'm the new coach at Louisiana University. How would you like to go

3

to a Southern school?" A native of the Keystone State himself, Wingard had coached the Pittsburgh football team in '06.

His first impression of the visitor being favorable, Doc promised to consider LSU. Edgar followed up with regular letters to Fenton. Then one day in the spring of 1907, Doc arrived home to find an unknown woman speaking to his mother. She turned out to be Mrs. Wingard. "As a speaker," said Doc, "his wife was just as impressive as he was. She sure impressed my mother. Before she left, I promised to go down to Baton Rouge for a visit."

So that summer, Doc headed south with another Pennsylvanian, E John Seip, whom Wingard also wanted. Fenton later recalled: "Baton Rouge was a nice little town, but I have to be honest and say the thing that really sold me was the nickel beers. We had blue laws back home…."

If he had stayed in the Northeast, Fenton would have set the football world on fire. But displaying his talents in the Deep South, he didn't make Walter Camp's 1907 All-American team. Future LSU president Troy Middleton recalled, "I saw Jim Thorpe, but Doc Fenton was better." T Marshall Gandy: "Doc could do more with a football than a monkey can with a coconut. He was the greatest field general who ever donned a uniform, a fellow who could punt on the run and catch the football one-handed. Doc was the hub of our team and we were the spokes."

While the '07 Tigers finished fourth in the 13-school Southern Intercollegiate Athletic Association, the *Atlanta Constitution* described them as "one of the best teams of the season in the southwest in points of fast, open and spectacular play."

Only eight years after the Spanish-American War, the Tigers were not necessarily

The 1907 LSU Tigers on the field before the Bacardi Bowl. L-R line: O. H. Noblet, H. E. Baldwin, R. L. "Big" Stovall, W. M. Lyles, Marshal H. "Cap" Gandy, John J. "Bill" Seip, Doc Fenton. Backfield: B. B. Handy, R. F. "Little" Stovall, R. O. Gill, C. C. Bauer. Standing in back: Coach Edgar Wingard, W. F. Ryan, H. C. Drew. Notice the small amount of padding on each player.

welcomed with open arms in Cuba. President Theodore Roosevelt had sent U.S. military forces to Cuba in September 1906 to end a civil war in the country, protect U.S. economic interests there, and ensure free elections to establish a new government. One offshoot of this "Second Occupation of Cuba" was that U.S. soldiers from Camp Columbia and sailors from two U.S. Navy gunboats provided a large crowd of vocal fans for LSU at the game. Non-military Americans in Cuba also rallied around the Tigers, to the point of offering to buy the players daiquiris when they sat down to eat in a restaurant.

Hooked on baseball since the 1870s, Cuba was also "football mad" by 1907. The Havana U. team had easily defeated every U.S. service team in the area. That's why Cuban officials turned to the U.S. for a more worthy opponent. While very few could attend the game, Tiger fans in Baton Rouge raised $2,000 for Wingard to bring to Havana to bet on the game.

Upon arriving in Havana, the LSU contingent learned that Havana officials were recruiting the biggest physical specimens available on the island to supplement the hometown college squad. However, the contract that LSU signed stipulated that Havana could not use American players not already on their team or players of African descent.

A Cuban newspaper reported: "There will be plenty of college spirit shown, and the Havana University students are practicing their yells, their college songs, and various institutions of noise making which will convey enthusiasm to the players, while the colors of the colleges will be seen on all sides."

The game at Almendares Park drew 4,200—"a crowd larger than any other ever seen before here at any public entertainment, from the highest American and Cuban officials to representatives of all classes of Cubans, were present.... Society turned out in force to see the Louisiana heroes, and on every side could be seen the 'swellest kinds' of rigs occupied by the cream of southern beauty" (*New York Herald*).

The Game

As the LSU team took the field for pregame warmups, they noticed several large glass demijohns filled with wine on the Havana sideline. Every so often, a Cuban player would run over and take a swig. Among them was a 300-pounder named A.C. Infante-Garcia, recruited to handle W.M. Lyles, LSU's 200-pound guard. Just before the kickoff, Fenton told Lyles, "Hit that guy in the stomach with your head, and he's done for." Sure enough, Lyles smashed his shoulder into Garcia's midsection on the first play from scrimmage. "The big guy spouted wine like an artesian well," recalled Fenton. "I give you my word. We nearly had to swim to get out of there." Any doubts that Lyle may have had about handling the big man were instantly dissolved. He exclaimed, "Well, I'll be damned. Let's go to work."

It didn't take long for the speed and teamwork of the LSU eleven to overwhelm the hometown crew. The Tigers tallied ten touchdowns worth five points apiece and six conversions to romp 56–0. The TD runs ranged from 20 to 100 yards. Havana never penetrated LSU territory beyond the 20. Included were a number of Fenton's signature broken-field runs and a 67-yard punt return by Seip. As usual, Fenton ended the game with his jersey in shreds. Coach Wingard may have invented the tear-away jersey. Before each game, he soaked Doc's woolen shirt in a mild acid solution to weaken the fabric and make it more difficult for tacklers to grab him above the waist.

Tigers on the goal line.

The American servicemen chanted throughout the game, "Lick the Spicks. Kill the Spicks. Rah! Rah! Rah! Louisiana!" E Pat Ryan recalled, "Every time we made a touchdown, you'd have thought there was a flock of blackbirds flying across the field. Those sailors from the *Paducah* and the *Dubuque* would toss their blue hats in the air and chant their … battle cry."

Postgame

Wingard lifted the curfew that night. The players were welcomed into homes and exclusive clubs. Locals offered the equivalent of $10 U.S. for the grey "L" skullcaps the Tigers wore off the field, a huge sum that the players gladly accepted.

Fenton, called "The Artful Dodger" in the U.S., earned the nickname "El Rubio Vaselino" (the Vaselined Redhead) from the Cuban fans. Doc finished the '07 season with 94 points and 14 TDs, both LSU records.

Years later, "Doc" Gandy recalled a second game in Havana between Christmas and the Tigers' departure January 1. "We found we could make $25 apiece. So we made up two teams from the two squads and played again. We only had thirteen, so we loaned Havana a couple of men. We still won it, something like 20–0." Of course, accepting the payment made the LSU players professionals who were no longer eligible for college play. But since no one back home found out, they continued their careers, which culminated in an undefeated season in 1908.

Sugar Bowl vs. TCU

Why didn't you kick a field goal, Bernie?

Tulane Stadium, New Orleans, Louisiana
January 1, 1936

The Tigers had a new head coach for the 1935 season because of Senator Huey Long's meddling in the football program. Huey criticized Coach Biff Jones publicly when the 1934 Tigers lost back-to-back games to Tulane and Tennessee. At halftime of the season finale, the Tigers trailed visiting Oregon 13–0. As Jones prepared to tell his squad what to do to get back in the game, Long barged into the locker room and demanded to talk to the team. Jones told him no and stood his ground. Huey said, "I'm sick of losing and tying games. You'd better win this one." Flushed with anger, Biff told him, "Senator, get this: win, lose, or draw, I quit."

An assistant on Jones's staff, Bernie Moore, had coached the LSU track team to the 1933 national championship. That achievement along with the recommendation of Vanderbilt coach Dan McGuigen convinced Huey to order Athletic Director T.P. Heard to promote Bernie.

LSU's 1935 Season

Moore's first LSU squad lost its opener to Rice, 10–7, then won the remaining nine games to win the Southeastern Conference crown. The Tigers pitched five shutouts: Manhattan (32–0 at Ebbets Field in Brooklyn), Auburn (6–0), at Georgia (13–0), Southwestern Louisiana (56–0), and at Tulane (41–0). LSU held three SEC opponents to less than 50 yards of total offense. The mathematical system of economics professor Frank Dickinson ranked the Tigers #4. The United Press International sportswriters' poll placed LSU #7.

Moore's offensive star was triple-threat tailback Ibrahim Khalil "Abe" Mickal, a native of Syria who would become LSU's first National Football League draftee. The undisputed defensive standout was end Gaynell "Gus" Tinsley. Years later, Bernie called Tinsley "the greatest lineman I ever saw, someone who could have made All-America at any position. He was so tough he made blockers quit."

As SEC champion, LSU received the bid as the host team for the second annual Sugar Bowl. They would play their second straight game at Tulane Stadium, this one on New Year's Day against TCU.

The Opponent

In his second season in Fort Worth, Dutch Meyer coached the Horned Frogs to an 11–1 record. A battle of unbeatens for the Southwest Conference championship on November 30 resulted in a 20–14 SMU victory that sent the Mustangs to the Rose Bowl and the Frogs to the Sugar for TCU's first post-season game.

Dickinson's final standings—he didn't recalculate after the bowl games—pegged TCU #8. The UPI voters had the Horned Frogs #4.

Known as an innovator in the passing game, Meyer had the ideal tailback to run his system. Sammy Baugh, future member of both the College and Pro Football Hall of Fames, threw for 1,293 yards on 101 completions and 19 touchdowns.

TCU and LSU met two common opponents. Both beat Arkansas by the identical score, 13–7. But LSU lost to Rice 10–7 while the Horned Frogs defeated the Owls 27–6.

Pre-Game Prospects

Even if the heavy rains that had fallen for three days stopped before kickoff, the field would at least be sloppy, which concerned Meyer. "It's going to be a great game. I hate for us to have to play on a slippery field, and we haven't played in the mud in two seasons. I'm afraid the wet ball will hurt our chances. Sam Baugh may be able to throw them, but the catching will be tough."

Bernie Moore also commented on the strong possibility of challenging conditions. "I feel that under such conditions, neither team will be retarded more than the other. If we are called upon to decide the game in the rain or on such a field that the ball becomes wet, muddy and slippery, there is little question that the attacks of both teams will suffer fully 50 per cent."

Neither team reported any injuries. TCU averaged three pounds more per man than LSU. However, the Tigers fielded the deeper squad, with "three first rate backfields and two lines of near equal strength." On the other side, only 16 of TCU's 27 players saw regular action.

The game would feature two first team All-American players in Tinsley and Darrell Lester, TCU's husky center who had been selected to the mythical team for the second time.

The Game

With hundreds of extra seats added to Tulane Stadium, 37,000 were anticipated for the game. But the chilly, damp weather cut the number to 35,000. That was still the largest crowd for a sporting event in Louisiana. With rain threatening, the "scalpers" took a scalping. They were almost giving tickets away at the entrance gates.

The estimated 4,000 Texans in their 10-gallon hats and high-heeled boots were easily distinguishable from the Tiger fans with their purple and gold colors displayed on coat lapels. Rain began falling late in the first half and continued throughout the rest of the contest. As the Sugar Bowl's web site says, "Considering everything, the crowd may have witnessed the finest touchdown-less game ever played, complete with multiple goal-line stands."

First Quarter

TCU showed more offense than LSU in the scoreless first quarter.

Abe Mickal dropped the kickoff into HB Jim Lawrence's hands on the two, and he returned it 15 yards. After three runs gained only a few yards, Sam Baugh, one of the greatest punters in football history, launched a rocket that J.T. "Rock" Reed tracked down on the 19 and returned to the 23. It was the first of 27 punts during the soggy afternoon.

The Tigers took to the air on their very first play. Mickal tossed down the slot to RE Jeff Barrett, but Baugh came up from his safety position to knock it down. Indispensable on both sides of the ball, Sammy would play all 60 minutes. Despite an offside penalty on the defense, LSU couldn't gain a first down. So Mickal, another excellent kicker, banged a punt to the TCU 20 where Baugh grabbed it and returned just 3 yards.

After an offside penalty nullified a completion, Baugh, who was subjected to a fierce Tiger rush all afternoon, passed to L.D. Meyer, the coach's nephew, for 16 yards to the Frog 37. Then Lawrence dashed 26 yards to put the ball on the LSU 37. Following three short line bucks, Reed intercepted the fourth down pass and returned it 7 yards to the 24.

On second-and-12, Reed bolted for 21 yards in what would turn out to be LSU's longest run from scrimmage. Two runs moved the ball to midfield to continue the momentum. But Mickal, who called his own plays, quick-kicked to the Frog seven. Continuing the game of "I don't want it, you can have it," Baugh immediately booted the ball to the LSU 35. On third-and-four, Mickal kicked into the end zone. After two plunges gained nothing, Baugh quick-kicked 68 yards to the 12. The Tigers moved out to the 33 as the period ended.

Score: LSU 0 TCU 0

Second Quarter

Rain started falling heavily late in the half and continued the rest of the game, but only a handful of fans left their seats. They donned raincoats and raised umbrellas in all sections of the stadium. Others piled newspapers and programs over their hats and shoulders and stayed and shivered.

The day's only points were put on the scoreboard in this period. The punting duel continued with LSU enjoying field position advantage. With Mickal resting to start the period, All-SEC HB Bill Crass booted into the end zone.

On the next series, George "Junior" Bowman ran back Baugh's third-down punt 3 yards to the LSU 48. Jesse Fatherree ripped off 11 into TCU territory. But the Frogs stopped three straight runs to force a punt which went out of bounds on the six.

Not taking any chances, Baugh immediately punted back to Bowman, who caught the ball at midfield and returned it all the way to the 18 to give LSU an excellent scoring opportunity. The Tigers would take the lead but not the way they wanted to. After Bowman gained two, Fatherree tried to pass but was dropped back at the 24. With better protection, Crass tossed a beautiful pass to Barrett who caught it on the seven and was pulled down on the two by Baugh to prevent a touchdown. Crass hurled himself at the TCU line, but 168-pound G Tracy Kellow and All-American C Darrell Lester stopped him at the one. Lester broke his collar bone on the play and left the game. Jack Tittle, "a midget in comparison with the giant Lester," performed admirably the rest of the way. LSU immediately challenged the new guy without success as Tittle stopped Crass short of the goal line. Facing fourth down from inside the one, Coach Moore didn't bother with a field goal try, presumably because of the wet conditions. Instead, Crass plunged one more time. When the pileup was unraveled, the officials placed the ball on the 6" line.

LSU turns over ball inches short of goal line. No. 62 is E Jeff Barrett (*Gumbo* Class of 1936).

With everyone expecting him to kick out of danger, Baugh instead tried to catch the defense off guard with a long pass. Taking the snap near the back of the end zone, he faked a punt and, as Tinsley and Barrett bore down on him, tried to throw the ball, but it slipped from his hand and dropped to the ground. The referee signaled safety.

LSU 2 TCU 0

TCU chose a place kick that traveled to the LSU 30, where Bowman caught it and ran it back 15 yards. The key break of the game occurred on the next play when Crass fumbled, and Willie Walls recovered for TCU on the LSU 40.

Finally free from the shadow of their own goal, the Frogs struck quickly. Lawrence crossed up the defense by taking a handoff on a reverse and passing to Walls to the 13. Fullback Taldon "Tillie" Manton fumbled but recovered for a loss of three. Then Tinsley threw Baugh for a yard loss. So Manton kicked a field goal from the 26 into the teeth of a brisk northern wind.

Gaynell Tinsley (24) and Red Barrett rush Sammy Baugh (45) in the end zone, causing a safety (*Gumbo* Class of 1936).

Joe Reed breaks away for a good gain (*Gumbo* Class of 1936).

TCU 3 LSU 2

Baugh recalled years later: "I held the ball, and I believe I was more nervous than Taldon was. The kick was … on the order of a line drive … at first I thought it might go wide to the right … but it stayed inside the posts." Manton had kicked the winning field goal in the Frogs' last game to beat Santa Clara 10–7. Ironically, Tillie attended LSU before transferring to TCU.

LSU punted on third down, Baugh returning it to the 43. Lawrence got loose again, this time for 15. Manton added four before Sammy hit Lawrence to the 29. An incompletion ended the half.

TCU 3 LSU 2

THIRD QUARTER

If the fans thought they had seen excellent punting in the first half, they changed their minds after halftime even as the weather and field conditions got worse. Yale coach "Ducky" Pond, one of many coaches from around the country in attendance, proclaimed the kicking the finest he ever witnessed.

With rain falling steadily, Fatherree ran the kickoff back to the 35. But Mickal quick-kicked on first down, the ball bounding all the way to the four where the speedy Tinsley downed it. Baugh immediately punted out of bounds on LSU's 45. Mickal threw to Barrett for 17 yards. After Fatherree picked up seven, Abe shot a long one that Baugh intercepted with a diving catch on the 16.

So what did Sammy do after his pick? He punted, of course, to midfield. After throwing an incompletion on second down, Abe tried another pass that settled into Baugh's hands on the 26.

After several more punts, Mickal went back in punt formation but instead crossed up the Frogs by whipping a pass to Fatherree for 21 to the LSU 45. Two plays later, Ernest Seago, a graduate of the same Temple, Texas, high school that produced Slingin' Sammy, crashed through the line for 8 yards and a first down on the TCU 45. But just as the offense was picking up momentum, Mickal chose to quick-kick to the 15. The punting duel continued for the rest of the period.

TCU 3 LSU 2

FOURTH QUARTER

The United Press reported, "The players on both sides were smeared with mud and hard to recognize as it began to grow dark." Baugh punted out on the 16. On third-and-three, Crass, in for Mickal, chose to punt, and this time the strategy paid off. Just as Baugh caught the ball, E Johnny Mihalic smashed Sammy, causing a fumble that Mihalic recovered on the Frog 32.

Facing what might be their last chance to score, LSU started with an incomplete pass. Then Crass smashed through for 14. Bill ran three more times, falling just short of the first down. TCU stuffed him on fourth down, but both teams were offside. Given another chance, the 200-pound fullback from Electra, Texas, made it first-and-goal at the eight. From there, Bowman swept to the two. Then Crass got nothing through the line. On third down, Baugh, determined to make up for his fumble, knifed through and dropped Bill for a 3-yard loss to the five. It was one of eight tackles Sam made that afternoon. Moore again ignored his players' pleas to kick the field goal. Instead, Mickal passed toward Barrett, but Manton knocked it down to end the threat.

Forced to hurry after fumbling the snap, Baugh got off his poorest punt of the afternoon, out of bounds on his 32 to give LSU another chance to take the lead. But on the first play, Crass fumbled, and Meyer fell on it for TCU back at the Tiger 46. The LSU offense would not penetrate enemy territory again. Despite the excellent field position, Baugh punted out on LSU's 18.

Running out of time, the Tigers took to the air, but two Crass passes sailed wild. So he punted on third down, Wardell Leisk stopping Baugh in his tracks on the 47. On second-and-eight, Sam burst through left tackle, then reversed his field all the way to the four where Tinsley tackled him from behind. A piling on penalty advanced the ball to the two. But here the LSU forward wall of Marvin Stewart, Seago, Justin Rukas, and Tinsley denied the Frogs the clinching touchdown. Hit hard, Manton fumbled but recovered for a 3-yard loss. Next, Lawrence gained nothing at left end thanks to Tinsley. On third down, Baugh passed into the end zone, where Bowman knocked the ball out of Walls' hands. On fourth down, halfback Vic Montgomery tried an end sweep, but Featheree dumped him for a loss of four thanks to Tinsley stripping the interference.

With LSU needing to travel 93 yards with five minutes remaining, Moore rushed Mickal into the game. But, indicative of the offensive philosophy of the day, when two runs gained little, Abe kicked to midfield. After three plays that ran the clock down but didn't move the chains, Baugh punted into the end zone. On first down with a minute to play, Mickal tried another pass, but Harold McClure intercepted. Two runs ran out the clock.

Final Score: TCU 3 LSU 2

LSU led in first downs 9–6 and in total yards 166–162. But the Tigers also led in turn-overs—three fumbles and three interceptions compared to TCU's one and one. TCU won the punt competition, averaging 48 yards to LSU's 45.

Postgame

Coach Moore asked, "Wouldn't that have been a great contest if that rain hadn't fallen? … My conclusion of the game was that the slippery field eliminated at least 50 per cent of the offensive power of both teams." But he added, "We have no alibis." Bernie apparently wasn't asked or refused to answer why he didn't try for a field goal on fourth-and-goal inside the TCU five.

Coach Meyer differed slightly from Moore on the effect of the weather. Dutch estimated that the weather eliminated 30 per cent of the teams' offenses. He called the game "the finest I've ever seen played in the rain."

Tulane coach Ted Cox, considered an authority on line play, raved, "The line play on both sides was exceptional. If I had to pick anybody out of the Frogs' line, it would be Kellow, a truly great guard. For LSU I thought Gay Tinsley, as ever, was the best lineman." Red Drew, line coach at Alabama, remarked, "I saw the greatest collection of ends I ever hope to see in one game."

Eight 1935 LSU lettermen played pro football: E Jeff Barrett, B Pat Coffee, B Bill Crass, G Wardell Leisk, B Bill May, B Joe Reed, G Justin Rukas, and E Gaynell Tinsley.

Sugar Bowl vs. Santa Clara

Bronco fans tore down the goal posts

Tulane Stadium, New Orleans, Louisiana
January 1, 1937

For the second straight year, the Tigers traveled down Airline Highway to appear in the Sugar Bowl. The opponent in the third annual New Year's Day classic would be the Santa Clara Broncos from the San Francisco Bay Area.

LSU's Season

Spurred by their new mascot, a Royal Bengal Tiger named "Mike" after trainer Mike Chambers, LSU won the Southeastern Conference Championship with a 6–0 conference record and finished 9–0–1 overall. The tie came in the second game at Texas 6–6. Bernie Moore's charges won all their other games by at least 12 points. After LSU clobbered his Bulldogs 47–7, Georgia coach Harry Mehre said, "They're on a par with Alabama's 1934 club with better balance, more speed, and more power. I've never seen a better-looking squad."

The Tigers' rock-ribbed defense, led by two-time All-American and Associated Press (AP) first team All-SEC E Gaynell "Gus" Tinsley and All-SEC G Wardell "Rube" Leisk, gave up only 34 points all year. The Tigers' 281 points—inflated by 93 against Southwestern Louisiana—led the nation.

LSU ranked #2 behind Minnesota in the brand-new AP poll, which conducted its final vote before the bowl games. Since the Big Ten banned its teams from post-season play, the Tigers had no chance to leapfrog Minnesota in those polls that re-voted or recalculated after January 1. The Tigers hoped the Rose Bowl would select them to face Washington. Instead, the Pittsburgh Panthers received the invitation to Pasadena.

The Opponent

The Broncos of first-year coach Lawrence "Buck" Shaw finished the season ranked #6 in the AP standings. His squad won seven of eight games with all the victories against West Coast teams except one. The common opponent with LSU was Auburn, whom the Tigers defeated by 13 and the Broncs by 12. Santa Clara's only loss came in their last game against TCU and its great QB "Slingin' Sammy" Baugh, the same team that had defeated LSU in the 1936 Sugar Bowl.

Shaw was known for developing outstanding lines. His defense went LSU's one better by yielding only 22 points. On offense, Buck used the "Notre Dame system" that he learned playing for Knute Rockne. In this single wing approach, the quarterback had to be the best blocker on the team. "Silver Fox" Shaw discovered that senior FB Nello "Flash" Falaschi was the greatest blocker on the squad. So he moved him to quarterback where he would get to run and pass as well as block. Buck selected 5'8" 185-pound G Chuck Pavelko to take Falaschi's place at fullback. The Broncs' front wall was anchored by All-Pacific-Coast G Dick Bassi and 220-pound T Lee Artoe.

Some oddsmakers established the Tigers as five to one favorites, thereby enraging both the Broncos and the West Coast media, who promised that Santa Clara would give a good account of themselves. All signs pointed to a defensive struggle between two opponents "boasting rugged lines and husky, hard-blocking backs."

The Broncos were widely considered the best team on the West Coast but couldn't go to the Rose Bowl because they weren't a member of the Pacific Coast Conference. National writers considered the Sugar Bowl the best matchup among the New Year's Day games.

Shaw took his team to Houston for two days of training December 29–30 before boarding a train to Bay St. Louis, Missouri, where they would conduct a light workout and spend New Year's Eve at St. Stanislaus College to avoid the revelry in the Big Easy. When Shaw stepped off the train from Houston and peered into the low-hanging clouds, he grinned. "We've had the same kind of weather from California to Louisiana." According to the AP writer, "Clouds lessened the hopes of Louisiana State, prepared to base their offensive on the kicking and passing of Pat Coffee, sharp-shooting blond-haired fullback."

Moore kept his boys in Baton Rouge until the morning of the game. The night before, he sent them to a movie, then told the press: "We're ready. We have no injuries and will have no alibis. We're going to do our best and, if we lose, Santa Clara will just be the better team." Bernie planned to use Bill Crass, "noted 'mudhorse' fullback," in the event of a soggy field.

The front that passed through on New Year's Eve brought rain that continued until just before kickoff. That was not good news for LSU. Coach Moore said, "A slippery ball would hurt our chances, for we have counted heavily on our passing attack to open up that big Santa Clara line."

The Game

Another record crowd of 38,483 saw the teams battle on "the rain-softened turf" of Tulane Stadium.

First Quarter

The Broncos scored two quick touchdowns in the first period on the sluggish Tigers. After an exchange of punts, Santa Clara began its second possession at the LSU 44. HB Don De Rosa, unable to find an open receiver, started around Gus Tinsley's end, reversed his field, shed E Bernie Dumas in the backfield, and ran to the 32. After an incompletion, Falaschi called his "favorite scoring play." Pavelko took the snap, hit into the line but handed the ball to Flash. He raced back in a wide arc and threw 21 yards to HB Manuel "Mexican" Gomez, a "little ball of dynamite," who outran "Slick" Morton into the end zone.

Santa Clara 7 LSU 0

The second touchdown was set up by a great punt. Pavelko booted 51 yards out of bounds on the one. Crass tried to reciprocate but got the ball only to the 28. On third and four, Tinsley tackled Falaschi for a 7-yard loss. Undaunted, Pellegrini fired a 30-yard touchdown pass on fourth down to E Norman Finney with four minutes remaining in the opening period.

Santa Clara 14 LSU 0

Second Quarter

The Tigers had to stage a goal line stand to keep the Californians from scoring again. Gomez intercepted a pass from Pat Coffee on the LSU 40 and returned it to the 18. Everett Fisher ran twice for a first down at the four. The Tigers dug in and stopped Fisher for no gain. Then Tom Gilbert pushed to within a half yard of the goal line. Falaschi tried to go over and slipped across the goal line, but the officials ruled his knee hit at the 2' line. On fourth down, Gilbert tried a shovel pass to Gomez who was nailed on the three and fumbled. Dick Gormley recovered for LSU.

With Santa Clara threatening to score again, Rock Reed changed the momentum when he intercepted a pass and raced 26 yards to the LSU 40. Crass passed to Mihalic for 12 yards over the middle for LSU's initial first down of the game. Then Tinsley showed the Californians why he was an All-American. Gaynell twisted to take Crass's 5-yard pass in the right flat, reversed his field, shook off several tacklers, picked up his interference, and raced to pay dirt. Guy Milner converted.

Santa Clara 14 LSU 7

LSU's Guy Milner (66, in white jersey) carries the ball (*Gumbo* Class of 1937).

Guy Milner is tripped by Manuel Gomez with Charley Pavelko (7) in hot pursuit (*Gumbo* Class of 1937).

Shaw had prepared for the wet conditions to give his team a fresh start for the second half. He arranged with the coaches at sister Jesuit college Loyola right next door to Tulane to supply his men with fresh shoes to replace their mud-caked pairs. Shaw also had his squad change into their dry practice uniforms for the final 30 minutes.

THIRD QUARTER

Santa Clara extended its lead back to 14 on an unusual play three minutes into the period. LSU received the kickoff with hopes of building on the momentum from the end of the first half. But a wild exchange of turnovers ensued. First, Coffee fumbled, and Dick Bassi recovered on the Tiger 32. Then Morton intercepted one of DeRosa's tosses. However, Coffee turned the ball over again with an errant throw that Gomez snared and ran back 35 yards before Morton nailed him at the 15. Pavelko plunged for three, and Flash sneaked for eight and a first down. After three plays went nowhere, "Mississippi" Smith from Picayune, 60 miles from New Orleans, took the ball on an end around on fourth-and-goal at the four. When pinched by two tacklers, Smith tossed the ball forward. Falaschi leaped, grabbed the pigskin, and nose-dived over the goal line. Afterwards, the Broncos insisted it was a well-rehearsed pass, not a fumble. Mishandling the PAT snap, Falaschi improvised and passed to Smith for the extra point.

Santa Clara 21 LSU 7

FOURTH QUARTER

LSU tacked on a touchdown in the final period when the Bronco second stringers got careless. After Santa Clara was penalized for unnecessary roughness to its 10, Jules

Perrin, strongly rushed by Dumas, shanked a punt out of bounds on the 20. Milner rambled up the middle for six only to fumble backwards, LSU recovering for a loss of three. Moments later, with the ball on the 16, Crass threw to Reed on the nine, and he outran Perrin for six points. Milner added the extra point.

Final Score: Santa Clara 21 LSU 14

Santa Clara fans tore down one of the goal posts to celebrate their upset victory. They offered to pay for the goal posts beforehand, but Sugar Bowl officials told them to help themselves.

"Slick" Morton stops a Bronco as Bill Crass (38) assists (*Gumbo* Class of 1937).

Postgame

Moore didn't offer the wet field as an excuse. "We just met a better ball club today than ours, that's all. Everyone on that Santa Clara team was good."

Shaw praised his warriors. "I thought our boys … played their best game of the season. Our team certainly surprised me with its great blocking and precision passing."

Years later, Shaw would recall: "That was a day I'll never forget. LSU was supposed to have the greatest team in its history, and we were such underdogs that hardly any odds were posted."

Seven of the 1936 Tigers played pro football: B Pat Coffee, B Bill Crass, T Ben Friend, G Wardell Leisk, B Bill May, B Joe Reed, and E Gaynell Tinsley. Tinsley would be inducted into the College Football Hall of Fame in 1956, two years after Coach Moore.

Sugar Bowl vs. Santa Clara

You don't often win committing five turnovers

Tulane Stadium, New Orleans, Louisiana
January 1, 1938

LSU's Season

The Tigers' 1937 campaign was defined by one game, the 7–6 loss at Vanderbilt that ended LSU's 13-game SEC winning streak. The Commodore TD came on a "hidden-ball" play, with a lineman picking up the ball after it had been laid on the ground by the blocking back. The score was the first points allowed by LSU all season and one of only four touchdowns for the year. The 9–1 record was remarkable considering that 13 of the first 22 players from the 1936 team graduated.

Senior TB/S Charles "Pinky" Rohm excelled on both sides of the ball. Sophomore Young Bussey led the second string in Coach Bernie Moore's system of substituting eleven-man units en masse. Both Rohm and Bussey were considered among the finest passers in the country. Another sophomore, E Ken Kavanaugh, gave promise of filling the shoes of the great Gaynell Tinsley, now in the National Football League.

The Opponent

The Sugar Bowl wanted to pit 9–0 Alabama against either 9–0 Pittsburgh or 7–0–1 Fordham for the fourth edition of the game. However, Bama wanted to go to the more prestigious Rose Bowl as did Fordham. Pittsburgh's players voted not to accept any bowl invitation. Tired of waiting for the Rose Bowl to make its choice, the Sugar turned to the same schools as the year before: 9–1 LSU, #8 in the final AP poll, and 8–0 Santa Clara, tied with Notre Dame for 9th. A bowl spokesman called the matchup "the finest intersectional football attraction attainable."

Like the Tigers, the Broncos lost more than half their starting lineup from the 1936 team. Yet Coach "Buck" Shaw ran his two-year record at Santa Clara to 16–1. The defense surrendered only nine points, 18 less than LSU, although the Tigers played a much stronger schedule. Another similarity between the teams was the substitution of a full team of 11 on a change of possession or the end of a quarter. The Broncos fielded a staunch line and a versatile backfield led by sophomore sensation Jack Roche.

Coach Moore had a serious morale problem on his hands. If the LSU players were not happy about going 85 miles down the road to the Sugar Bowl for the second straight time the year before, they were even less enthusiastic for trip #3, especially against the same foe. However, Moore proclaimed the day before the game that his team was more "mentally ready" than they had been for either of the two previous bowl games. Following his 1937 Sugar Bowl script, Moore kept his 37-man squad in Baton Rouge until the morning of the game.

LSU's line averaged 200 pounds per man, five more than the Broncos' forward wall.

The Tigers ruled as a slight favorite although the arrival of California fans with money to bet caused the odds to drop from 8-to-5 to 6-to-5. Fifteen hundred coaches who gathered in New Orleans for their annual meeting were polled concerning the outcome of the Sugar Bowl. Those who responded favored LSU by a 3-to-1 margin.

The Game

The weather was bad for the third straight year. A crowd of over 40,000 sat through a light drizzle throughout the first half with temperatures in the 50s. They saw the defensive struggle you'd expect from two teams who gave up a total of 36 points between them in 18 games.

First Quarter

Santa Clara ran its plays from the Notre Dame box, the entire backfield shifting left or right just before the snap. Facing a five-man line most of the game, the Tigers' single wing attack had difficulty moving the ball as Santa Clara implemented its plan of taking out the interference to expose the ball carrier. When the Tigers punted after their first possession, HB Orv Hanners kicked the rolling ball as he tried to pick it up, bobbled it again on the second try, and Barrett Booth recovered for LSU at the SC 29.

Rohm immediately hit HB Guy Milner down the middle for 12 yards. Then Pinky slashed to the four for another first down. Two plays later, Milner pushed to the one. On third down, Guy tried a sweep, but T Al Wolff tackled him from behind for no gain. On fourth down, Rohm rammed up the middle but met a wall of defenders a half-yard short of the goal line.

As teams often did in those days, the Broncos punted out of danger on first down. Starting from the SC 37, the Tigers went backwards. On third-and-13, Rohm quick-kicked over the goal line. The teams continued exchanging punts, the Tigers enjoying the field position advantage until Chuck Pavelko intercepted Milner's pass right before the end of the period.

Score: LSU 0 Santa Clara 0

Second Quarter

Both teams sent in new elevens as the slow rain continued. Santa Clara's second team would soundly outplay their LSU counterparts throughout the afternoon. Even though there were only 2 yards to go for a first down, the Broncos punted on third down. Young Bussey ran back the kick 15 yards to the 20. Runs by Jabbo Stell and Bussey moved the chains. But after several failed reverses and a penalty, Young quick-kicked.

From their 34, Santa Clara ran just one play and quick-kicked back. But the ball slid off the side of Bruno Pellegrini's foot and went out of bounds on his 47. Could the Tiger second team finally capitalize on good field position? The possession started promisingly when Bussey's pass to E Ken Kavanaugh was ruled complete at the 34 because of interference. But the Tigers bogged down, and Bussey tried to punt only to have T George Locke block the kick. G Jerry Ginney picked up the ball and tried to lateral the hot potato to no one in particular. The ensuing scramble resulted in Bronco Ray McCarthy diving on the ball at the LSU 38.

That proved to be the break the Broncos were waiting for, but they didn't capitalize right away. Gaining only 3 yards on three snaps, SC punted, Rohm returning to the 12. A holding penalty on the first snap moved LSU back to the one. With the Tigers in maximum protect formation, Bussey launched a punt to the LSU 45. Jim Barlow took the ball on the run and sped back 15 yards before any defender could get near him until Jimmy Cajoleas brought him down on the 21.

Given an even better chance to score, the Broncos began badly when Kavanaugh tossed Bruno Pellegrini for a 9-yard loss. Then Pellegrini took a handoff and ran left before turning and lofting a pass back to McCarthy, who caught the ball amid two Tigers on the 12 before Bussey downed him on the nine. The same play had worked against the Tigers on the same field a year earlier. Two runs put the pigskin on the four. With the defense massing for another plunge, Pellegrini took the snap and threw quickly to E James Coughlan who slipped into the left flat, took the ball on the one, and fell into the end zone while being tackled by LB Roy Joe Anderson. Pellegrini's PAT kick sailed wide.

Santa Clara 6 LSU 0

Bussey returned the kickoff to the 30. On second down, he tried to punt, but G Russ Clark shoved his chest into Young's foot, the ball bounding out on the 33. LSU called time-out to allow the rest of its B team to enter the game. On a no-interference play, McCarthy

Bruce Pellegrini throws to James Coughlin for the only touchdown of the game (*Gumbo* Class of 1938).

broke loose around right end for 15 yards as his mates went the other way. But the Tigers drew the line there. On third down, Pellegrini tried the same run-left-toss-right play that had set up the TD. This time the wet ball slipped through Barlow's fingers. So Bruno tried a field goal from the 15 that went wide.

After the Tigers went backwards from the 20, Pinky dropped back to punt on third-and-21. But a bad pass from center caused him to get off a poor punt that sailed out on the 10. Fortunately, the Broncos were penalized for roughing the kicker. Given new life, Rohm fired a low bullet that Larry King caught for 10 yards. On third and six, Rohm faded to pass but, not finding a receiver, got away to the LSU 46 as the half ended.

Santa Clara 6 LSU 0

The rain stopped during the intermission. However, the teams still had to contend with the wet field.

Third Quarter

Santa Clara's second string kicked off to LSU's B unit. On third and 13, Bussey punted. Hanners, making up for his earlier bobble, picked up the ball on his 37 and raced back 10 yards. Pellegrini ran the same play he had used twice earlier but to the opposite side. Rolling right behind two blockers, he tossed a long pass to Pavelko running all alone down the left side. Chuck had to wait for the ball at the 25, giving Slick Morton enough time to make a TD-saving tackle at the 19. The way the Bronco defense was playing, LSU could not afford another score. Two runs that netted only a single yard and two failed passes turned the ball over. After Bussey's long pass to Kavanaugh slipped through his fingers, LSU punted to the Santa Clara 43. King made the key play that disrupted the Broncos' possession when he spilled FB Bill Gunther for a 6-yard loss.

On their next possession, the Broncos reached the LSU 20 thanks to passes of 21 and 13 yards. But the SC advance ran out of gas when Morton came up fast from his safety position to drop Hanners for a 2-yard loss on a third down sweep, and Pellegrini's pass under pressure fell incomplete.

Bussey faded deep and fired a pass to midfield for Kavanaugh, who made a flying leap but could not quite reach the oval. That typified the Tigers' frustration as they ended the period with only 10 yards of offense and no first downs compared to 63 yards and two firsts for Santa Clara.

Santa Clara 6 LSU 0

Fourth Quarter

The first units returned for both sides. Rohm sailed a sensational 56-yard quick kick that went out of bounds on the nine. LE Ogden Bauer tore through and grabbed the ball carrier and twisted him down just short of the goal line. The Broncos lined up in tight punt formation, and Barlow boomed a punt to Rohm at the Tiger 45. He ran free until the coverage caught him at the 32.

That set up the most crucial sequence of the game for LSU. After a 2-yard gain, Rohm threw two incompletions. He then pooched a coffin corner punt that barely went into the end zone. When Santa Clara was penalized for offside, the Tigers decided not to punt but instead go for the first down. With Rohm back in punt formation, Morton, lined up as right wing back, spun around on the snap, took a handoff from Rohm, and headed around the left side on the soggy field. He cut back and set sail for the goal line before Norman Ginney dove and tripped him at the three. The small Santa Clara contingent began to envision losing the game 7–6. Rohm tried to skirt right end but was thrown for a 7-yard loss by Roche. It was the key defensive play of the afternoon because it caused LSU to take to the air, with bad results. Pinky took the snap and fired a quick pass over the middle to Bauer breaking over the goal line. But Roche struck again, knocking the ball down. LSU tried something a little different on the next snap. Rohm lined up at left wing back but immediately came back and took a handoff and sailed a pass over Bauer's head in the end zone. That gave Santa Clara possession at the 20.

But the Tigers weren't finished. Following the common viewpoint of the era–I'd rather give you the ball in your territory than keep it deep in mine–Santa Clara punted to the LSU 47. Following Rohm's 11-yard run, Ginney made another fine play, throwing Pinky for a 2-yard loss. On the next snap, the Tiger tailback wanted to pass but ran instead, gaining just one. On fourth down, Rohm was hit as he threw, and Jim Smith intercepted, racing to the LSU 45 where he lateralled to McCarthy who continued to the 38.

In a decision that could not have pleased Coach Shaw, Barlow shot a pass down the middle that was almost intercepted by Morton. After Barlow gained eight on a reverse, he

Pinky Rohm almost breaks loose for a touchdown (*Gumbo* Class of 1938).

Guy "Cotton" Milner sets sail for the goal line before being tripped up at the three. Other Tigers are Roy Anderson (72), Bernie Dumas (37) and Gordon Lester (17) (*Gumbo* Class of 1938).

provoked his coach's ire again when he started an end run. As he was hit, he tried to lateral, but the ball hit Kavanaugh, who covered it on the 34.

With plenty of time for a last-ditch effort, Rohm ran for six, then hit King for a first down at the SC 43. Two plays later, Pinky connected with Ken down the middle to the 32. But the pattern that prevailed throughout the game continued. The Bronco defense never allowed the Tigers to string together consistent gains. Milner tried a reverse, but one gold-clad blocker couldn't stop three red shirts. The result was a 4-yard loss. Following an offside against the Tigers, Pinky connected with Kavanaugh to make it third-and-three. But Rohm was dropped for a 3-yard loss, then had his long pass intended for Kavanaugh batted down. The Broncos took over on their 28 with three minutes remaining.

Shaw rushed in eight of his first stringers while Bussey came in for LSU. In a decision that bewilders us today, the Broncos punted instead of eating some time off the clock. Bussey took to the air right away but, with a rusher in his face, his pass to Kavanaugh fell short into the hands of Hanners who returned to the SC 44. This time the Broncos didn't punt right away. The possession ended when a fourth down run turned the ball over at midfield with only 20 seconds left.

Out of timeouts, LSU took the 5-yard penalty to plan a desperation effort. Bussey shot a pass to Guy Milner, who broke loose before being tackled in bounds on the 30. As soon as he hit the ground, Milner shouted for time, but no official heeded his plea, and time ran out.

Final Score: Santa Clara 6 LSU 0

The statistics told a misleading tale. LSU garnered 12 first downs to just four for the Broncos. The Tigers also led in yardage 156–90. Santa Clara committed five turnovers, three interceptions and two fumbles. The Bengals threw the ball 21 times but completed only eight.

Postgame

Moore was brief. "It was a tough one to lose. Oh, hell, there's nothing to say." Jubilant Buck Shaw praised the Tigers and the hospitality of the city of New Orleans.

Notre Dame coach Elmer Layden gave this summation of the contest. "It was probably the line of Santa Clara that decided it. Their blocking and tackling and charging were fine."

Villanova coach Clipper Smith said it was an unusually well-played game under adverse conditions. "I thought the outstanding feature was the all-around line play of both teams. … Pinky Rohm and Ken Kavanaugh are two exceptionally fine players."

University of Detroit coach Gus Dorais: "It was a fine climax to the football season to have such a splendid game played here under the conditions. As usual, the breaks decided it. LSU got a break on a dropped punt but failed to score. Santa Clara got hers on an intercepted pass and made good. The speed and fine blocking made the game worthwhile."

Three 1937 Tigers played pro football: B Young Bussey, T Ben Friend, and E Ken Kavanaugh.

Orange Bowl vs. Texas A&M

*Steve Van Buren spearheaded
LSU's first bowl victory*

Orange Bowl, Miami, Florida
January 1, 1944

With World War II draining college-age manpower, only four of the twelve Southeastern Conference schools fielded football teams in 1943: LSU, Tulane, Georgia, and Georgia Tech. This reflected a national trend in which 150 colleges abandoned football that season. Those who did compete usually played fewer than the ten games allowed each team.

Bernie Moore's LSU squad consisted of two groups of players. (1) Those who had been rejected for military service for some reason. For example, star RB Steve Van Buren failed his army physical because of defective vision. (2) Students too young for the draft who could play for a year before entering the service. LSU lacked the Navy V-12 training program that provided manpower for teams at other schools. The purpose of the program was to train future officers by providing them with a bachelor's degree as a steppingstone to obtaining a commission as an ensign. The Navy allowed the participants to play sports.

LSU's Season

Led by Van Buren, the Tigers compiled a 5–3 record, going 2–2 in the SEC. How could LSU end up 2–2 in the SEC when there were only three other opponents? Simple—they played Georgia twice, once in Tiger Stadium to open the season (34–27 victory) and again in Athens (27–6 triumph). Another of the victories came at the expense of LSU's Army Specialized Training Program team. The Army program had a different purpose from the Navy's V-12 program. The primary goal of the ASTU was to turn out technically-trained personnel and not officers. Two Tiger losses came to Georgia Tech (42–7) and Tulane (27–0), both of whom had the Navy V-12 program. One of the Green Wave's stars was Dub Jones, who played for LSU in 1942 before joining the V-12 program at Tulane. Dub's son Bert would quarterback the Tigers from 1970 to 1972.

LSU's other defeat occurred against Texas A&M, another V-12 school, in Baton Rouge. Having won their first two games, the Tigers entered the contest ranked #17 in the

Associated Press poll. Called by the AP writer of the game report as "an eleven man track team in football toggery," the young Aggies, dubbed the "Kiddie Corps" by the press, beat the larger Tigers 28–13. Van Buren didn't enjoy the success he had in the first two games. His best work came when he started to pass, then ran, including a 38-yard jaunt down the sidelines for a touchdown. The key difference in the game was A&M's passing prowess: 110 yards to 37 for LSU.

The five bowls that existed at the time–Rose, Sugar, Orange, Cotton, and Sun—faced slim pickings. The Sugar Bowl, which had chosen an SEC team seven of its first nine years, selected Georgia Tech to face Tulsa. With Van Buren the drawing card, the Orange Bowl arranged a rematch between LSU and 6–2–1 Texas A&M.

Opponent

It was amazing that Texas A&M could beat anyone in 1943 after a whopping 77 members of Homer Norton's 1942 squad entered the military during the summer, leaving him with only four players. So he threw out a wide net on campus, asking, "Are there 11 men in the student body who can play football?" The student newspaper made its own pitch. "It is time for the twelfth man to rise up from the student body and offer his services to the corps. This is a necessary action to take in order that varsity sports will continue at Texas A&M. Turn out, twelfth man."

One-hundred-thirty-five students responded. Of the 75 Norton chose, only one had played college football. The rest were freshmen. The average age was 17.5. Sportswriters called the Aggies "a glorified high school football team." But some had not even played in high school.

Coach Moore was pleased with the bowl bid. "All we hoped to do when the season started was keep football alive," he said. As 14-to-15-point underdogs, the Tigers hoped to exact revenge on the Aggies and win their first bowl game after three failures.

Moore and his staff knew they had to do something different from the first meeting to help Van Buren get loose. So they moved 165-pound WB Joe Nagata to fullback. They didn't do this because of Nagata's blocking. The plan called for Joe to take direct snaps from center in LSU's version of the Notre Dame box. Joe stepped forward, pivoted left or right, and handed the ball to Van Buren. The intent was to freeze the linebackers for a moment to give Steve an extra step. Nagata would occasionally keep the ball and run up the middle.

The Aggies would play without the nation's top receiver in terms of yardage, Marion Flanagan. He had injured a knee in the Thanksgiving game against Texas.

Traveling to Miami for the game was no simple matter thanks to wartime regulations that gave priority to troop movements. With trains not an option, the Tigers benefited from the largesse of Baton Rouge banker Lewis Gottlieb. He purchased eighteen used cars to transport the players. He later sold the cars at his automobile agency.

The Game

An overflow crowd of 25,203, not counting servicemen let in free, saw the action, and listeners around the world heard Ted Husing's call on Armed Forces radio.

FIRST QUARTER

Moore wasted little time in deploying his new offensive scheme. The result was two touchdowns before A&M awoke. After neither team went far on its first possession, the Bengals started at their 41 with a brisk wind at their back. The Tigers pulled one of several fancy plays they had prepared for the rematch. Van Buren passed 15 yards to Carroll Griffith who, as he was being thrown to the ground, lateralled to E Charley Webb who continued to the A&M 32. Two plays later, Steve faked a pass and skirted left end to the 15. But the Aggies resisted fiercely, and the Tigers found themselves facing fourth down at the 11. Moore sent in QB Charley Barney with instructions to run another special play the Tigers had prepared. Nagata took the snap and handed to Griffith running left. Griffith then put the ball into the hands of Van Buren heading the opposite way. Steve raced untouched around across the goal. The extra point attempt failed due to a fumbled snap.

Score: LSU 6 Texas A&M 0

When LSU got the ball back, Van Buren unleashed a 51-yard quick kick that "Red" Burnitt unwisely tried to pick up only to fumble it. Webb wrestled it away from him at the A&M 22. On third-and-eight, Barney reentered the huddle with more instructions from the sideline. Van Buren rolled right, stopped, and passed across the field to Burt Goode who snagged the ball as he crossed the goal. Steve's PAT try failed.

LSU 12 Texas A&M 0

With Van Buren taking a rest, the Aggies wasted little time getting back in the game. Starting from their 30, they unleashed the aerial attack that had knocked the Tigers for a loop in Baton Rouge. Three straight completions and a roughness penalty put the ball on

Steve Van Buren (on the 33 yard line) throws to Carroll Griffith (on the 47), who will lateral to Charley Webb (on the 50) to set up LSU's first score (*Gumbo* Class of 1944).

the LSU 20. TB Jim "Babe" Hallmark passed to Burnitt, who made a nice grab just inside the end zone to atone for his earlier miscue. Bing Turner added the point.

LSU 12 Texas A&M 7

SECOND QUARTER

When they got the ball back, the Aggies picked up where they left off on their previous possession. Burnitt took a flat pass and rambled to the LSU 30, but a Tiger tackler took the ball away from him. After failing to gain a first down, the Tigers lined up in punt formation. Van Buren took the snap and, with several rushers storming in, took off over the right side on a meandering run during which he broke three tackles. He ran out of gas, slowing to a walk at the A&M 25 where he was easily tackled. Steve stayed down for a while before leaving the game. Red Knight took over at tailback and got off a perfect pass to Griffith who raced to the four where the safety made a touchdown-saving tackle. After trying each end, the Tigers went up the middle twice but were stuffed a yard from the goal on fourth down.

A&M immediately punted out of danger, Van Buren returning to midfield. The Tigers pushed to the 15 before running out of downs. After a clipping penalty pushed them back, the Aggies again punted from their end zone, Steve returning to the 16. But after four downs, the Aggies reclaimed the ball at that spot. Staying on the ground, the Lone Star boys ran out the clock.

LSU had dominated the period but had no points to show for it.

LSU 12 Texas A&M 7

Van Buren breaks into the clear. Other Tigers are Joe Nagata (11), James Lewis (65), Bill Schroll (35), and Martin Rinaudo (41) (*Gumbo* **Class of 1944**).

Third Quarter

On the third snap after the kickoff, Big Steve showed his All-American form by breaking loose for 62 yards through the entire Aggie team. This time he converted.

LSU 19 Texas A&M 7

Down by 12 again but with a strong breeze at their backs, A&M took to the air and moved to the LSU 48 before having to punt. On the first play, Nagata fumbled and Aggie Butch Butchofsky recovered on the 25. On third down, Hallmark shot another one to Marion Settegast for a touchdown. Turner booted the point to reduce the margin to five again.

LSU 19 Texas A&M 14

The fray settled into a defensive battle. Neither side came close to scoring the rest of the period with the Aggies passing or trying to pass on most downs while the Tigers, with poor field position, stuck to the ground. A&M's best chance came when LSU punted from the end zone to the 30 as the third quarter ended.

Fourth Quarter

The period started with a turnover fest. After an A&M pass to the 12, Bill Schroll intercepted at the six to end the threat. The next time the Aggies got the ball, Hallmark overthrew the receiver down the middle right into the hands of Knight, who returned to midfield to give the Tigers their best starting position of the half. Red completed a pass to Griffith to the 22. But the gold-clad eleven could push no further. Even with the Tigers playing back to defend against the pass, Hallmark completed several long tosses that carried the Aggies to the LSU 41. But the advance ended when Diego Pardo intercepted the next try and returned to the 44. Two plays later, LSU fumbled, and A&M recovered on their 47.

Facing now or never, Hallmark tried to pass but was plastered and fumbled, an Aggie falling on the ball for a 15-yard loss. Another long pass sailed too high into the arms of Knight who returned into A&M territory before fumbling the ball back to the Aggies. What today would be called a sack put A&M in a hole at the eight. Another desperation pass resulted in Schroll's second pick. He lateralled to Nagata who raced to the 22. One more run finally ended the game and gave Bernie Moore his first bowl victory in four tries.

Final Score: LSU 19 Texas A&M 14

LSU won the statistical battle. First downs were square at seven apiece, and the Texas cadets gained 199 yards passing to 100 for LSU. But the rushing numbers told the story. The Tigers stuffed A&M to the tune of -15 net yards while amassing 210 themselves. Displaying the skills that would earn him a spot in the Pro Football Hall of Fame, Van Buren gained 160 of LSU's 181 yards. The Aggies filled the air with aerials, 32 of them, but completed just 14.

Postgame

"Were we good enough to please the customers?" asked Moore. "That kid Van Buren was terrific. If Steve had been playing on a team of mature players, he'd have gotten a lot more recognition last fall. But that's not taking anything away from the other boys. For kids, they did fine." Asked how this game compared with the regular season encounter with the Aggies, Bernie said his boys "played a 50% better game." While acknowledging that A&M missed Flanagan, the LSU coach added, "Our kids were hot. They played a great game."

When the Aggies entered their dressing room, some threw their helmets against the wall and slumped on the benches. A couple cried unashamedly. "We have absolutely no alibis," said Coach Norton. "It was a fine game, and we gave the crowd a great show. We have no apologies for anything, and we lost to a great team." Homer refused to use Flanagan's absence as an excuse. "My boys are just kids, but they played a great game." He praised Van Buren. "We knew how good he was, and we were trying to stop him, but he was just too good. We had been up against him before, and I tried to tell you folks he was great. But I guess you saw for yourself."

Postscript

The Tigers' trip back to Baton Rouge was even more challenging than the one to Florida. As the convoy headed home, the group ran out of gas rationing stamps. So the coaches begged each gas station they stopped at to let them buy one gallon of gas. One of the cars broke down. "It took a couple of days to get it fixed," recalled Nagata. "But we enjoyed swimming in the Gulf of Mexico while we were waiting."

Nagata would soon become a military hero. The Japanese-American fought in Europe with the 442nd regiment, composed entirely of Nisei. The unit became the most decorated of the war. Nagata won the Bronze Star and the Infantry Combat Medal. After his discharge, he returned to LSU and finished his degree.

Van Buren was the only 1944 Tiger to play pro football. He was inducted into the Pro Football Hall of Fame in 1965.

Cotton Bowl vs. Arkansas

*How do you gain 15 first downs
to one and not win?*

Cotton Bowl Stadium, Dallas, Texas
January 1, 1947

Radio broadcaster John Ferguson, who called LSU games from 1946 to 1987, insisted that the best Tiger team he covered was the first one. "That team, filled with returning war veterans, was six deep everywhere. Believe me, pound for pound, as far as pure talent, this was the champion Tiger team." To illustrate the talent on the 1946 LSU roster, twelve players would play in the National Football League or the new All-America Football Conference. And halfback Joe Glamp is not one of them. After lettering in 1942, he entered the military. When he returned from the war, he surveyed the talent Bernie Moore had assembled and decided he had a better chance to make the Pittsburgh Steelers, the perennial doormats of the NFL. His choice proved wise as he started for three years for the Steelers.

LSU's Season

The 1946 Tigers finished 9–1. The veterans could attend school without a football scholarship because of the G.I. Bill. That freed scholarship money for the youngsters. The loss came to Georgia Tech in the fourth game, 26–7 at Tiger Stadium. Unfortunately, that defeat cost the Tigers a share of the SEC crown as the Georgia Bulldogs defeated Tech 35–7 to finish 10–0.

The Tigers were led by junior quarterback Y.A. Tittle, a member of the United Press All-SEC team, and a deep corps of running backs led by Jim Cason and Dan Sandifer. G Wren Worley made the Associated Press all-conference eleven while T Walter "Piggy" Barnes earned a spot on sportscaster Bill Stern's All-America team. LSU ranked #8 in the final AP poll, which was conducted before the bowl games.

The Opponent

John Barnhill finished his first season as Arkansas coach with a 6–3–1 record. The 16th-ranked Razorbacks went 5–1 in the Southwest Conference to share the championship with Rice. UA's lone league loss came at Texas 20–0. With the 8–2 Owls accepting a bid to the Orange Bowl, Arkansas took the conference's Cotton berth.

Coach Moore had a problem motivating his team for the Cotton Bowl, which guaranteed LSU $62,000. First of all, the players had their hopes set on a shot at Georgia in the Sugar Bowl to show they were better than the SEC champions. But the Crescent City bowl chose North Carolina and its star halfback "Choo Choo" Justice as the Bulldogs' opposition.

Before practice could begin for the bowl game, Moore and Athletic Director Thomas "Skipper" Heard had to deal with an insurrection by the older players, who wanted $600 each to play in Dallas. When the administration flatly denied the request, the squad met before practice and took a vote on whether to play in the Cotton Bowl. When a close vote favored striking if their demands weren't met, the players refused to practice and returned to their dormitory, expecting someone from the athletic department to come and talk to them. Tittle, who opposed the plan, recalled, "Nobody came to us. They just let us sleep on it. Eventually, a counterproposal appeared: $100 a man if LSU won the Cotton Bowl. That was enough to end the walkout."

The Tigers flew to Dallas on four separate flights. Moore, preferring to stay earthbound, made the trip by automobile. Newspaper stories focused on E Clyde Lindsey, who got married the day before the team left for Dallas. Not distracted, Clyde would play all 60 minutes New Year's Day.

On the eve of the game, Moore admitted knowing little about Arkansas. "We not only didn't scout each other but have little information from others who saw our teams in action. One fellow wrote from Oklahoma that he could give me the lowdown on Arkansas, but I didn't know him, so I didn't take advantage of the offer." Bernie knew that Arkansas had a fast team led by the running of Clyde "Smackover" Scott and the pass receiving of big Alton Baldwin, a four-year letter winner and second-team All-American end.

The oddsmakers made LSU a 10-point favorite. Both squads reported no significant injuries.

A United Press article the day before the game proclaimed: "Weather forecasts were that it would be cold and cloudy but that no rain or snow was expected." Unfortunately, that prediction didn't pan out. The game day report said: "Sub-freezing temperatures and a blanket of snow today furnished a frigid setting for the 11th Cotton bowl football game…. The condition of the field remained an unknown quantity until the huge tarpaulin protecting it from Tuesday's snow was removed shortly before the kickoff."

The LSU cheerleaders took 600-pound Mike the Tiger in his cage on their trip to Dallas but, fearing the effect the icy weather would have on him, decided to leave him in a warehouse in Shreveport. "He's too old—eleven years—to risk catching pneumonia," said T. Kelly McKnight.

Nevertheless, the Cotton Bowl went on as planned. Thirty-eight thousand of the 45,000 ticket holders showed up. They sloshed through foot-deep snow in the aisles and sat in a misty rain that eventually turned to sleet to watch what came to be known as "The Ice Bowl" 30 years before Dallas's own Cowboys played in another "Ice Bowl" in Green Bay for the NFL Championship. Some spectators set fires in the stands to keep warm.

Moore sent trainer Jules Roux to the store to buy long underwear for the players and several charcoal heaters, which were placed on the sideline. For the only time anyone could remember, the Tiger linemen all wore gloves. LSU procured several oil drums, filled them with charcoal, and started a fire to produce heat on the sideline. AD Heard brought in 25 bales of hay to spread in front of the bench to keep the players' feet warm. Assistant coach Harry Rabenhorst remembered that "the cold brought tears to everyone's eyes. I went up to Bernie one time and, sure enough, the tears had frozen on his cheeks."

On the sidelines patches of snow that had melted, froze again, then melted and froze a second time covered all but the playing field, which had been protected by tarpaulins. Game time temperature was reported as 29 degrees. Fur coats, raincoats, blankets, parkas, umbrellas, cowboy boots, and galoshes were the basic costumes of the spectators. Both Louisiana Governor Jimmie Davis and Arkansas Governor Ben Laney shivered in the stands. Two Arkansas bandsmen wore the flaring bells of their sousaphones as rain hats. A stylishly-clad brunette from the Bayou encased her lovely legs in brown paper bags.

The Game

Never before or since has an LSU team so dominated its opponent yet failed to win.

- First downs: LSU 15 Arkansas 1
- Yards Rushing: LSU 255 Arkansas 54
- Passing: LSU 17–5–0/271 Arkansas 4–0–1/54
- Fumbles Lost: LSU 2 Arkansas 3
- Penalties: LSU 8–50 Arkansas 1–5
- Punting average: LSU 9–30.4 Arkansas 11–36.0

In the only statistic that counts, LSU and Arkansas tied 0–0. The Razorbacks stopped the Tigers inside the 10 three times.

A major reason Arkansas gained only one first down is the poor field position they constantly faced. Even in good weather, coaches in that era preferred to punt the ball on first or second down from deep in their own territory rather than risk a fumble or interception.

FIRST QUARTER

The game began in a light sprinkle that gradually increased to a steady drizzle. The *Arkansas Gazette* article on the game said, "Arkansas won the toss and chose the South Pole—rather, south goal—and Louisiana decided to kick off." After an exchange of punts, Arkansas started a possession on its 20. Freshman fullback Leon "Muscles" Campbell pounded over center, bounced off LB Shelton "Buck" Ballard, and gained 18 yards for what would turn out to be the Hogs' only first down of the day. After T Walter "Piggy" Barnes dropped Campbell for a gain of one, Aubrey Fowler quick-kicked to the LSU three. Gene "Red" Knight immediately punted back, Fowler returning to the Tiger 37. However, the Razorbacks could go no further than the 29 and punted into the end zone. Little did anyone know that Arkansas had achieved its deepest penetration of the game and would gain only 18 more yards for the afternoon. As one writer put it, "The rest of the game found the Porkers too busy warding off Tiger thrusts to even think about putting on a drive." Sandifer, Ray Coates, and Rip Collins combined for two first downs to the Arkansas 48. With the rain coming down harder, Tittle tossed a third-and-13 screen pass to Rip for 12 yards. With LSU going for it on fourth-and-one, Tittle's handoff to Red fell

The LSU ball carrier is stopped deep in Arkansas territory as Hubert Shurtz (79) trails the play (*Gumbo* Class of 1947).

loose, and John Hoffman recovered for UA on their 42. But two plays later, Hoffman fumbled right back, Tittle recovering at the LSU 48.

Score: LSU 0 Arkansas 0

SECOND QUARTER

Cason, Al Heroman, and Knight pounded the line for a first down on the UA 38, but the Hogs forced a punt by smothering Heroman for a 5-yard loss on a Statue of Liberty play. One account of the game contains a sentence at this point that explains a difference in the 1946 rules from today's regulations: "Knight got off a great punt which rolled to the Arkansas three, but Jeff Adams raced in and fell on the ball, thus making it an automatic touchback..."

But Barnhart didn't want the ball deep in his own territory. So Fowler quick-kicked to the LSU 40 to implement a plan the Hogs would follow all day. Knight plunged for 16, but again Arkansas threw the Tigers back, and on fourth down Charles Lively blocked Knight's punt. Baldwin, wearing a pair of brown carpenter's gloves like many of his teammates, picked up the ball near the LSU sideline and set sail for the Tiger goal, but "little Jim Cason dove right over a blocker and pulled him down from behind on the LSU 44 to save a very probable touchdown."

The Razorbacks couldn't take advantage of the good field position. After an incompletion, Scott fumbled the ball on a reverse, and Lindsey recovered for the Tigers on the 45. When LSU went three-and-out, Fowler tried to find Bud Canada down the right sideline, but Tittle intercepted and returned to the UA 16 to give LSU a great chance to score right before halftime. Y.A. chose to pass twice unsuccessfully, the second being knocked down by Scott in the end zone. Cason took a lateral around right end for 7 yards, but on fourth-and-three from the nine, Knight fell inches short, and Arkansas took over on their seven. Fowler immediately tried to punt out of danger, but Cason took it on the 42 and returned beautifully back to the 19.

With another chance to get on the scoreboard, the Tigers sputtered again. After two runs gained five, Tittle tried a pass to Lindsey, who fumbled the ball into a Razorback's hands, but the play was called back and LSU penalized for offsides. With the rain slacking a bit, Sandifer gained 10 on a double reverse to make it fourth-and-five. This time Knight pushed past the first down marker to the eight for first-and-goal with 40 seconds left in the half. But the Tigers let another scoring opportunity slip away. First, the defense dropped Knight for a 2-yard loss. Then LSU was penalized 5 yards for excessive time-outs. On the last play, Tittle threw incomplete in the end zone.

LSU 0 Arkansas 0

THIRD QUARTER

The rain picked up again, rapidly changing to sleet. LSU took the kickoff but didn't keep the ball long. Knight quick-kicked on third down to Fowler, who returned 28 yards to the LSU 44, where the punter took him down. When three runs gained only eight, Holland kicked out on the eight.

From there, the Bengals surged all the way to the Arkansas 18. Coates and Sandifer pounded out most of the yardage. With the Razorback linebackers continuing to play wide, Ray ripped off a gain of 18 while Dan burst for 19. Three snaps later, Knight banged for a first down at the 21. But the Hogs dug in again, stuffing Red for no gain and holding Sandifer to two before Coates tried a pass that went awry. On fourth down, Kenny Holland batted Tittle's pass out of Sandifer's hands at the goal line.

Bill Schroll tries flying over the line. No. 61 is Harvey Core (*Gumbo* Class of 1947).

After Fowler kicked out, Moore sent in some fresh backs. Zollie Toth cracked the line for 18 to the UA 47. But on third down, Cason fumbled a lateral, and James Minor recovered a yard short of midfield. The Razorbacks could gain only eight, and Fowler kicked yet again, this time to Cason who ran it back to the 26 as the period came to a close.

LSU 0 Arkansas 0

Fourth Quarter

Would the beleaguered Arkansas defense repel the Tigers for 15 more minutes? Toth plowed over right guard for a first down. Then Tittle connected with Mel Lyle to the 28, but the play was nullified by offensive interference on Sam for pushing his defender. Two snaps later, Scott fumbled a punt and Fred Land recovered for LSU at the UA 41. But when the Tigers went backward from there, Collins punted dead on the nine.

Not surprisingly, Arkansas kicked right back, Coates making a fine return to the UA 41. LSU then started still another march into the red zone. Sandifer for six, Collins for 16, and Coates for 10 put the pigskin on the nine. After gaining zilch at right guard, Rip pushed to the six. Tittle then flipped a pass to Jeff Adams, but Scott drove him out of bounds on the one. It would prove to be a game-saving tackle because on fourth down, Toth banged into the middle of the line only to be stopped a foot short by a gang of Razorbacks.

Not bothering to run several plays to at least take time off the clock, Arkansas kicked out, Dale Gray returning 8 yards to the 31. With six minutes left, Moore now had fresh legs in the backfield in the persons of Gray and Willard Landry to mount what might be a final push. On second down, Landry fumbled, but Adams recovered for a first down on the 20. Willard slipped through left guard for 9 yards, then hit the same hole to make it first-and-goal on the nine. Once again, the embattled Razorbacks drew the line. Running left behind Barnes and Fred "Skinny" Hall, Gray got four, then Toth made two as the clock ticked under three minutes. But Landry was dropped for a 2-yard loss as he tried to turn left end. Moore finally decided to try a field goal. Holly Heard lined up at the 15, but Coates' chilly fingers couldn't corral the snap. Heard picked up the pigskin but was swarmed under on the 16 as the Arkansas fans roared.

This time, the Razorbacks tried to run some clock, but the effort almost backfired. On second-and-six, Fowler fumbled but recovered for a 10-yard loss. So Aubrey booted out of bounds on the LSU 49 with 1:35 on the clock.

Having to pass now, Tittle misfired to Lyle. Then Scott broke up a long one aimed at E Ray Bullock. After another throw to Lyle failed to connect, Moore decided not to go for it on fourth down. Instead, Tittle punted to Fowler who was stopped in his tracks on the 12. Fowler ran for seven on the last play of the game.

Final score: LSU 0 Arkansas 0

Coates gained more yards than Arkansas as he romped for 61 on seven carries. The media selected Tittle as LSU's outstanding player, with Baldwin the top Razorback.

Postgame

An Associated Press article included this passage: "Arkansas and Louisiana players shivering in the dressing rooms after the game all commented on Dallas weather, for the most part unprintable." Coach Moore called it "the worst football weather I've seen in 35 years of coaching. Of course, it affected the passing, ball handling, and receiving, both for us and for Arkansas."

Barnhill: "My boys played a great defensive game. LSU's trap play through the middle of the line was the only thing that gave us any real trouble." He ranked LSU right up there with the better Southwest Conference teams he had faced.

Postscript

The Cotton Bowl Committee decided to present a trophy to each side. At the banquet for the teams that night, Barnhill won the coin toss and departed Dallas with the original Cotton Bowl Trophy. LSU would have to wait for a duplicate to be ordered and shipped to Baton Rouge. Each player on the two teams went home with a new wristwatch.

Despite the weather, the game grossed the largest gate in Cotton Bowl history, more than $150,000. So each school could expect to get the $60,000 it was promised.

Twelve lettermen on the 1946 LSU team played pro football: G Walter Barnes, E Jeff Burkett, B Jim Cason, T Ed Champagne, B Ray Coates, B "Rip" Collins, T-G Fred Land, B Dan Sandifer, LB-FB Bill Schroll, T Hubert Shurtz, QB Y.A. Tittle, and E Abner Wimberly. Tittle was elected to the Pro Football Hall of Fame in 1971.

Sugar Bowl vs. Oklahoma

*The clock struck midnight
for the Cinderella Tigers*

Tulane Stadium, New Orleans, Louisiana
January 2, 1950

Bernie Moore shocked LSU fans when he retired as head coach following the 1947 season to become Commissioner of the Southeastern Conference. His replacement was one of his assistants, former Tiger All-American end Gaynell "Gus" Tinsley. Tinsley was as surprised as everyone else that he was selected since he had no head coaching experience at the college level. His first season ended with a 3–7 record, including a 46–0 thrashing by Tulane in the annual finale.

LSU's Season

So not much was expected of the 1949 Tigers. They were picked to fight with Auburn for last place in the Southeastern Conference. To start with, LSU's daunting schedule included three opponents that would win their conference championships that year: Rice (Southwest Conference), North Carolina (Southern), and Tulane (SEC). On the bright side, eight of the ten games would be played in Baton Rouge.

By the end of the season LSU was referred to as the "Cinderella Team of the South." The key to the unexpected success was the defense, which surrendered only 74 points in ten contests led by all-SEC T Ray Collins. The result was an 8–2 record, including an upset that ended North Carolina's 20-game winning streak plus victories over Rice and Texas A&M from the Southwest Conference. The season ended with a 21–0 revenge triumph against Tulane that propelled the Tigers to #9 in the final AP poll—the highest ranking of any SEC team—and made them the Sugar Bowl's choice instead of the 7–2–1 Green Wave.

Some strings had to be pulled first. The SEC had a rule that a member team must win at least 75 percent of its league games to be eligible for bowl competition. LSU's 4–2 conference mark fell .083 short. LSU Athletic Director T.P. "Skipper" Heard began phoning conference members the day before the Tulane game to lobby for the rule to be waived should the Tigers win their final contest. Within a few hours of the victory, the SEC unanimously waived the rule.

40

The Opponent

Bud Wilkinson's Oklahoma Sooners, champions of the Big Seven Conference for the third straight year, finished second in the final AP poll to another undefeated team, Notre Dame. Led by 13 seniors, the Sooners came to New Orleans with a 20-game winning streak that included a 14–6 victory over North Carolina in the 1949 Sugar Bowl. The speedy Sooners ran the Split T formation. Senior QB Darrell Royal satisfied Bud's call for a split T QB "who is smart, who can pass, and who can run." LSU had never played a team that ran the split T.

Led by swift HB George Thomas and burly FB Leon Heath, OU ran up 3,202 yards rushing to just 556 for their opponents. The Sooners spread their backs more than in the standard T but didn't split the linemen any more than LSU did. Wilkinson alternated lines in half quarter intervals with each group playing both ways. His biggest problem was motivating his team, which didn't seem excited about a second straight trip to the Sugar Bowl.

A former LSU player, on his own or at the behest of his alma mater, gave Bud what he needed to fire up his squad. Two days before the game, Walter "Piggy" Barnes, a former LSU lineman currently playing for the Philadelphia Eagles, was caught secretly observing OU's closed drills in Biloxi, Mississippi. Barnes insisted he wasn't scouting for LSU but rather for his NFL team. Wilkinson told reporters, "I was very agitated at the discovery. We had worked a month on a new offense for the Sugar Bowl and had rehearsed several times the special defense we will use against LSU." When Bud arrived at the annual Sugar Bowl dinner, he refused to shake hands with an LSU assistant coach, proclaiming, "I don't shake hands with spies."

The Game

In weather more befitting early fall than winter—clear with a high of 70 degrees—82,289 fans jammed Tulane Stadium.

First Quarter

An eight-point underdog, the Tigers started like they had played all season long, battling the mighty Sooners on even terms in the first 15 minutes. The LSU line actually outperformed Wilkinson's alternating units. The teams went three-and-out on their first three possessions. Finally, the Tigers gained the initial first down when QB Charlie Pevey threw a jump pass to HB Billy Baggett, who raced to the OU 36. But the next four plays gained only 7 yards. The Sooners moved the chains on their second snap when Thomas swept left end to the 40. On third-and-four, Thomas fumbled when hit by E Armand Kitto, and G Dick Bradley recovered for the Tigers on the OU 45. The program listed Kitto at 170lb, but that was generous. He was closer to 155.

Lee Hedges threw a halfback pass to Mel Lyle who made a fine catch at the 34. Then Pevey tossed to Baggett to the 19. But the defense rose up, and the Tigers soon faced third-and-16. Pevey misfired on two passes in the end zone to stop the threat.

The OU possession started strong when Thomas gained seven and Heath eight for a first down at the 40. But three more runs netted a mere yard. So Royal, getting a good roll, kicked out on the 14. Not chancing a pass deep in their own territory, the Tigers ran the ball three times, and Kenny Konz punted to the OU 46. Thomas gained four as the period ended. Konz had been the hero of the Tulane upset when he returned a punt 92 yards for a touchdown and intercepted three passes.

Score: LSU 0 Oklahoma 0

SECOND QUARTER

The Sooners drove deep into LSU territory thanks to some adjustments. Royal said, "Our drop-back passes were completely useless because they knew exactly what was coming. The passes I did complete were a new set of plays that we didn't practice." On third down, Lindell Pearson took a pitchout and threw to Robert Goad behind the defenders on the eight to set up first-and-goal as Konz made a touchdown-saving tackle. Thomas sliced for 3 yards before being swarmed. With LSU employing an eight-man line, G Jim Shoaf and HB Jimmy Roshto stopped Pearson on the four. Thomas tested the center of the defense again but gained just one. On fourth down, Royal tried a keeper at left end but was stopped inches short of the goal line by Collins.

Taking no chances, Konz immediately punted against the wind to the 45, Buddy Jones returning 8 yards. With even better field position this time, the Okies were not to be denied. On third down, Pearson took a pitchout and threw down the middle to Thomas, who pivoted the other way and ran into the end zone.

Oklahoma 7 LSU 0

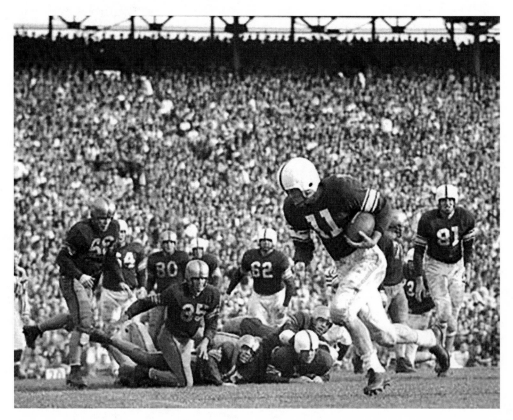

Oklahoma QB Darrell Royal keeps around Dick Bradley (69), Jim Lyle (80), Armand Kitto (85), and Chester Freeman (15) (photograph from tiptop25.com).

Lyle took the bouncing kick on the 35 but, carrying the ball loosely, fumbled, and OU recovered on the 37. Royal went for the jugular right away, but Roshto and Freeman knocked down his long pass. After Ebert Van Buren, younger brother of Steve, stuffed Heath, Thomas took a pitch to the 21. Then Pearson tossed a perfect pass to Thomas standing in the end zone. With a defender closing in, George dropped the ball. But that merely delayed the inevitable. Heath gained six and Pearson seven for a first down on the eight. The Sooners again dodged a bullet when Thomas fumbled a lateral, but Royal recovered on the six. Billy West stopped Heath after a 1-yard gain. Then Thomas took a pitchout and sped around left end for the touchdown.

Oklahoma 14 LSU 0

Neither team could sustain a drive the rest of the half. Konz ended OU's deepest penetration by intercepting Pearson's halfback pass on the two.

Oklahoma 14 LSU 0

Third Quarter

After a short kick, LSU started on the 45. With a chance to get back in the game, the Tigers went backwards thanks to Jim Owens' 10-yard sack of Pevey. So Konz kicked to the 14. Then came the killer. On the first play, Heath sprinted straight through the middle of the line behind a trio of blockers all the way to pay dirt. The 86-yard run was the longest in Sugar Bowl history at that point. Kitto recalled, "I chased Heath all the way. They say on a long run like that, a bear will jump on the runner's back. Well, I just kept waiting for the bear to jump on him, and instead he jumped on me. I carried that bear all the way down."

Oklahoma 21 LSU 0

The game then descended into a turnover exchange. LSU backup QB Carroll Griffith fumbled, and OU recovered on the nine. On the first play, Pearson lobbed a pass into the end zone that Konz intercepted—his fifth pick in two games. Behind good blocking, he ran up the left sideline, sidestepped tacklers, then headed to the middle of the field on a sensational return to the LSU 31. Zollie Toth, unused in the first half, ran twice for a first down on the 41. Then the third consecutive turnover occurred when Baggett fumbled into OU hands on the 44. But Royal fumbled right back, Kitto grabbing the pigskin. Pevey threw a long pass to E Aubrey Anding, who grabbed the ball in stride just before stepping out on the OU 28. But Tiger hopes were dashed on the next play when Buddy Jones cut in front of Pevey's pass down the middle on the 15 and returned to midfield to make it five straight possession-ending turnovers.

In three plays, the Sooners gained a first down at the LSU 38 thanks to Thomas and Pearson, but OU soon had to punt. With LSU unable to move the Sooner line, Konz dropped back to punt. Ken Tipps partially blocked the kick, and the ball rolled out on the LSU 40. The defenses dominated the next several possessions, and the period ended with LSU having gained a net of 40 yards with only two first downs.

Oklahoma 21 LSU 0

Fourth Quarter

LSU tried an end around, but Lyle fumbled when hit hard, putting OU in business

Kitto (85), Freeman (15), Bradley (69), and other Tigers swarm Lindell Pearson (photograph from tiptop25.com).

on the 14. It took the Sooners just three plays to score, Royal doing the honors from the four.

Oklahoma 28 LSU 0

On LSU's next possession, Griffith hit E Warren Virgets two straight times to the 29. But Clark stepped in front of the next pass, delivered while falling backward under duress, and returned it to the 29. On second-and-five, Heath raced to his second touchdown without a hand laid on him.

Oklahoma 35 LSU 0

The rest of the game continued the comedy of errors. Lyle took the short kickoff on the 30 and gave Tiger fans a thrill by running down the sideline to the end zone. But the officials ruled he stepped out on the LSU 35. Three plays later, Griffith threw right into the hands of Owens, dropping off the line, on the OU 35. The big end ran 10 yards before he lateralled to Charles Dowell, who continued to the LSU 38. However, the Sooners were penalized back to their 45 for a forward lateral. Still in the game, Heath got 5 yards, then, on the next snap, broke away to the LSU 40, where he fumbled, and Konz recovered. Three plays later, Jones intercepted Pevey's jump pass on the OU 40 and returned it 16 yards. It was Charlie's third turnover of the afternoon. But backup QB Claude Arnold and Heath couldn't make connections on a handoff, Red Baird covering the ball for LSU for the 14th and final turnover of the afternoon.

Still perturbed by the spying incident, Wilkinson didn't take out his regulars until three minutes remained in the game.

Final Score: Oklahoma 35 LSU 0

Tinsley was unstinting in his praise of Oklahoma. "We were beaten by a better ball club, which was primed to play an outstanding football game. I think Oklahoma is the best team we have faced this year, and they have one of the greatest backfields and lines I

Leon Heath blocks for Clendon Thomas as Kitto chases (photograph from tiptop25.com).

have ever seen. It was a case of playing a superior football team, and although I feel that they were helped on some occasions, they played a flawless game, and we feel badly that we didn't make a closer contest of it."

Wilkinson was gracious after the game. "If we played LSU a dozen times, we'd never play that well against them again or score that many points. They're too good a team."

Six 1949 Tigers played pro football: HB Billy Baggett, T Ray Collins, DB Ken Konz, LB Joe Reid, RB Zollie Toth, and LB Ebert Van Buren.

Sugar Bowl vs. Clemson

*It wasn't supposed to be this tough
for the nation's #1 team*

Tulane Stadium, New Orleans, Louisiana
January 1, 1959

LSU's Season

The prognosticators didn't think much of LSU's prospects for 1958. The *Birmingham News* put LSU at #8 in the 12-team SEC. After all, the Tigers had not been overly impressive in 1957, finishing 5–5 after a 4–1 start. However, junior RB Billy Cannon exuded confidence. "It will be between us and Ole Miss." What did Cannon know that the sportswriters and coaches didn't?

Thirty-four-year-old Paul Dietzel, on the hot seat after winning only 11 of 30 games his first three seasons as head coach, installed a whole new offense during spring practice. Iowa coach Forrest Evashevski spent hours with the LSU staff explaining the Wing-T he used. Dietzel liked the system because it took advantage of the Tigers' speed at every backfield position. Basically a T formation with single wing principles, the Wing-T set one halfback next to the fullback behind the quarterback but often stationed the other halfback just outside one end where he could come inside for crossbucks and reverses or sprint out for passes. No team in the Southeast had played against the formation.

Dietzel also embraced the weight training that Alvin Roy had originated in Baton Rouge. The result was stronger, faster players who would not fade late in the season.

LSU's recruiting class of 1956, the finest in school history, were now juniors and ready to strut their stuff in '58. Add to their number FB-K Tommy Davis who was back from the Army.

Dietzel concocted an ingenious way to circumvent the NCAA's limited substitution rules, which mandated that a player who started a quarter could leave the field once and return during that quarter, but a player who did not start the quarter could not return until the next quarter. So Paul put his best eleven players on the White team, which started each game and played both offense and defense. The Chinese Bandits were defensive specialists while the Go Team played exclusively on offense.

Everything came together to produce a 10–0 season. The unranked Tigers rose to #3 in the Associated Press (AP) poll by winning their first five games. The closest contest was a 13–3 victory over Alabama in Bear Bryant's first game as head coach of his alma mater.

A 10–7 triumph over Florida vaulted LSU to #1 and set up a battle of unbeatens with #6 Ole Miss. Before the first packed house in the newly-enlarged 68,000-seat Tiger Stadium, LSU shut out the Rebels 14–0.

After a 50–18 romp over Duke, the Tigers survived their closest call of the season on a soggy field in Jackson that negated LSU's speed advantage. A missed extra point proved to be the difference over Mississippi State, 7–6. Then a record SEC crowd of 83,221 fans jammed Sugar Bowl Stadium for the annual finale against Tulane. The outmanned Green Wave hung with the Tigers the first half, trailing only 6–0. But LSU exploded for 56 points in the final 30 minutes to cement the SEC title as well as the national championship as determined by the final AP poll and the UPI Coaches poll. Dietzel also won the Coach of the Year awards from the AP, the College Football Coaches Association, and the Football Writers Association while Cannon made every All-America team. Four additional Tigers earned All-SEC honors: E Billy Hendrix, C Max Fugler, QB Warren Rabb, and HB Johnny Robinson.

The Opponent

As SEC champs, the Tigers earned the host spot in the Sugar Bowl against another band of Tigers from the Atlantic Coast Conference. Clemson's 8–2 record earned a #12 AP ranking.

The two head coaches couldn't have presented a bigger contrast. Forty-nine-year-old Frank Howard, an Alabama native, was a "slow-talking, tobacco-chewing, quick-quipping country boy who relished the role of underdog." Frank believed in old-fashioned Southern football: run the ball and play good defense.

The nationwide disparagement of the matchup gave Howard fodder to stir up his troops. "Anybody knows a hungry Tiger is more dangerous than a fat Tiger," said the veteran of 19 seasons at Clemson. "Our players wanted this opportunity to meet them"—the first time the school had ever played the nation's #1 team. He added, "The biggest problem right now is to get everybody well." In particular, he needed a healthy QB Harvey White since he kept the ball often in Howard's option attack from an unbalanced T formation.

Dietzel worried about the opponent's size advantage. "Clemson plays hard, tough football. I look for them to try to overpower us, outmuscle us. They'll try to beat us up badly and wear us down. … We'll be giving away 15 pounds per man in the line." Remembering the game in Jackson, the LSU head man worried about rain on New Year's Day. With the point spread rising to as much as 17 in some quarters, Dietzel warned his team against overconfidence.

The Game

Overcast skies and some mist early New Year's morning portended an uncomfortable afternoon. But the sun came out an hour before the kickoff and helped the temperature reach a high of 50 degrees. A sellout crowd of 82,000 saw a game much closer than pundits predicted. The slippery grass bothered both teams but especially the Bayou Bengals.

First Quarter

The opening period featured some fine punting by both teams with LSU generally holding the advantage. Clemson went three-and-out on its opening possession. On LSU's second play, Cannon burst for 15, but Clemson held, and Billy punted to the 25. After two more punts, Clemson gained its initial first down when HB Bob Morgan broke loose for 21 yards. But the purple-shirted Tigers couldn't move the chains again and punted to the 20.

Dietzel sent in the Go team, his offensive specialists. On second down, Tommy Davis got free for 15 yards to the 40. Two snaps later, QB Durel Matherne hit E Scotty McClain with a fine pass all the way to Clemson's 30. HB Don Purvis gained five as time expired. In the story of his life, Cannon summarized what the Tigers felt about their opponent at this point. "They were good, better than we expected. … The Clemson defense was as good as any we'd played all season."

Score: LSU 0 Clemson 0

Second Quarter

LSU's foray into Clemson territory ended when Matherne and Donnie Daye botched a handoff, and a defender recovered on the 22. Staying with its game plan of off-tackle slants, Clemson rammed for a first down by a hair on the 32—the first of four close calls on the afternoon. But Charlie Horne soon went back in punt formation. A high pass from

J. W. Brodnax halts the Clemson back as Johnny Robinson (34) and Bo Strange (72) assist (*Gumbo* Class of 1959).

center threw off his timing, and the ball went off his ankle to the 28 to give LSU another excellent scoring opportunity.

Two plays, including a Rabb-to-Cannon pass, moved the pigskin to the 12. But three passes failed, and Tommy Davis came on with the kicking tee. But the Tigers decided to pull a fake. Rabb took the snap as the holder, jumped up, and tried another aerial that sailed over the head of Cannon who was all alone in the end zone. "We had been practicing the play," Davis explained. "We figured they would all come in and that we could make a touchdown on it."

After Clemson went three-and-out, Rabb connected with E Mickey Mangham for 25 yards to the 32. Then Warren kept around end for 13, hurting his hand on the tackle. Rabb gained three more before FB Red Brodnax burst through right tackle to the eight. Cannon added six on two runs to put the ball on the two. Clemson called timeout to devise a goal line defense, but luck prevailed over design. As Brodnax plunged into the end zone, he fumbled the ball, and Doug Cline recovered for a touchback. "I thought I was over," Brodnax insisted after the game.

Rabb left the game and did not return. "I didn't know my hand was broken until I came out before the half. I think it got hit with a helmet." With Bandit QB Darryl Jenkins out of action due to a pregame injury, Dietzel had one experienced signal-caller at his disposal, the Go team's Matherne. Not only was he less talented than Rabb, but Dietzel didn't want to risk getting him hurt. So no rollouts were called, removing an effective option from the offense.

Set back by a holding penalty, Clemson had to punt, Purvis returning 19 yards to the 42. But incompletions led to Cannon kicking over the goal line. Clemson gained 8 yards in three plays to run out the clock. The halftime score shocked the nation.

LSU 0 Clemson 0

THIRD QUARTER

Cannon returned the kickoff 32 yards to the 39. But a third-down incompletion forced Billy to uncork a beautiful 50-yard punt to the six only to have the play called back

"Red" Brodnax fumbles at the goal line. No. 64 is Larry Kahlden, and 85 is Billy Hendrix (*Gumbo* Class of 1959).

and LSU penalized 15 yards for holding. Still not throwing its first pass of the day, Clemson used straight-ahead, no-frills T-formation power to drive for four first downs from its 28 to LSU's 27. But a hard tackle forced George Usry to lose the ball, and Tiger T Bo Strange fell on it. LSU couldn't move the defense led by future New Orleans Saints T Lou Cordileone. So Davis boomed a 53-yarder to the 10, Morgan getting thrown back to the eight on the return.

LSU finally got the break it was looking for four plays later. With Clemson in punt formation, backup C Paul Snyder launched a misguided snap that bounced off the leg of the upback, and T Duane Leopard recovered for LSU on the 12. The Tigers had to resort to trickery to penetrate the Clemson goal line. After gaining just three on two runs, Cannon took a pitchout from Matherne to the right and shot a perfect pass to Mickey Mangham in the end zone. Billy converted. "I threw it and prayed," said Cannon about the scoring pass. "I was looking for Robinson, but they had him covered. Then I spied Mickey and let it go." Billy added years later, "The version of the play we decided to run was a fake screen to the right. I was delighted because it would give me the chance to throw. If the defense read the play, I could still run it. The two ends … fake blocked then ran their patterns into the end zone. As soon as I cleared the outside of the offensive tackle, I could see both receivers were totally uncovered. … Scott McClain (the other end) stayed mad at me for forty years. He always tells me, 'I was wide open, and I could have been the star,' and I tell him, 'Yeah, but if I'd have thrown it to you, would you have caught it?'"

Clemson moved out to their 48 before the horn sounded.

LSU 7 Clemson 0

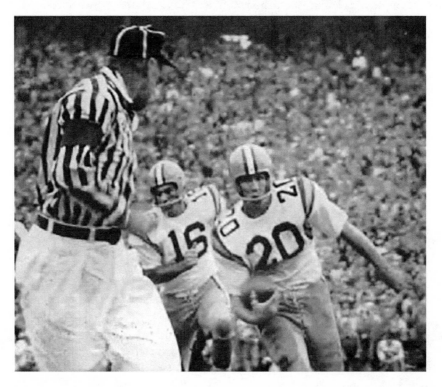

Billy Cannon sweeps left end as Durel Matherne (16) looks for someone to block (*Gumbo* Class of 1959).

FOURTH QUARTER

Two-hundred-ten-pound FB Rudy Hayes smashed for a first down on the LSU 48. But four plays later, Usry barely missed another first down to turn the ball over on the 39. Once again, Howard's defense caged the Rabb-less Bengals, and Cannon punted to the 17.

Dietzel sent in the rested Chinese Bandits. But they were no match for the burly Clemson offense. Lowndes Shingler ran for 12, then White threw his first pass of the game, a completion to E Wyatt Cox for another first down, and just like that Clemson reached their 47. Soon after, White hit Sam Anderson for another 12 yards, then threw again to Anderson for 11 to the 40. Aided by a 5-yard penalty, the Carolinians gained another first down on the 28 with 3:40 to play. On the sideline, Howard decided to go for two if his boys scored. After two runs gained four, Clemson suddenly changed its strategy. White threw an incompletion to make it fourth down. He then flipped a screen pass to Usry, who appeared to have running room. But the throw was low, and he dropped the ball. With the collective sigh of LSU fans audible all the way to Baton Rouge, the white-clad Tigers took over with a minute and a half to play and ran out the clock.

Thus did LSU win its first Sugar Bowl in five tries to complete the most successful gridiron campaign in school history.

Final Score: LSU 7 Clemson 0

Six 1958 Tigers played pro football: DL Mel Branch, FB J.W. Brodnax, HB Billy Cannon, K Tommy Davis, QB Warren Rabb, and HB Johnny Robinson. Robinson was inducted into the Pro Football Hall of Fame in 2019.

Sugar Bowl vs. Ole Miss

*The Tigers didn't want
the rematch, and it showed*

Tulane Stadium, New Orleans, Louisiana
January 1, 1960

LSU began the 1959 campaign ranked #1 in the nation in the Associated Press Poll. Who could blame the 60 voters who put the "hat" on the Tigers? Paul Dietzel lost only four players from the three platoons of his undefeated 1958 team.

LSU's Season

Billy Cannon stands at the 10-yard line on Halloween Night before 68,000 fans in frenzied Tiger Stadium. LSU trails Ole Miss 3–0 with ten minutes left in a matchup of the #1 and #3 teams in the nation. The Tigers have done nothing offensively against the stout Rebel defense. Coach Paul Dietzel has a rule that you don't field a punt inside your 15-yard line. But Billy thinks, "If I can get my hands on this one, I'm going to take it back." Sure enough, as if guided by his guardian angel, the ball bounces right to him on the 11, and he sets sail on perhaps the most famous run in college football history—89 yards through seven would-be tacklers to the end zone. But the thrills aren't over. The Tigers have to stop the Rebels on fourth down at the one with less than a minute to play to preserve the 7–3 victory and their #1 ranking. Cannon's punt return clinched the 1959 Heisman Trophy for him.

Fast forward one week. Cannon lines up in his LHB position as LSU attempts a two-point conversion trailing Tennessee 14–13 in Knoxville with 13:44 left in the game. The Vols had scored on a 54-yard interception return and a 29-yard drive after a fumble recovery. Billy takes the handoff and drives over right tackle. He disappears under two Vol tacklers inside the one. The line judge runs in shaking his head, ruling Billy short. He wrote in his autobiography, "I will go to my grave believing I went across into the end zone, but when the play was over, the linesman waved his arms that no, I hadn't. The most sickening feeling I've ever had was … knowing I'd crossed the goal line with the ball, albeit by inches or less than a foot, and seeing the referee saying no." Later in the period, Cannon loses a fumble at the Tennessee 20 to end LSU's deepest penetration the rest of the way.

The Tigers had roared through their first six games, allowing only six points and shutting out four foes to extend their winning streak to 18 games, longest in the nation. Beating Ole Miss seemed to clinch a second straight national championship for the Tigers until the Tennessee loss derailed those plans. Cannon recalled, "We lost our chance for the national championship. We were not number one again. We were fifty guys, coming back tired, disgusted, not pointing fingers but upset about the mistakes we'd made. I think on that trip home, the fire burned out."

The Tigers won their remaining two games but, in Cannon's words, they were flat, anti-climactic, hollow victories. Having gone to the Sugar Bowl the year before, the LSU players looked forward to a new venue for their bowl game.

As soon as LSU dispatched Tulane in the annual finale, the Sugar Bowl offered the Tigers an official invitation. Reportedly, the Sugar Bowl also invited Ole Miss, but the Rebels couldn't formally accept until after their game with 2–6 Mississippi State the following Saturday.

LSU put off any decision until a meeting of players at 6:30 p.m. the following Monday. LSU was rumored to be considering an offer from the newly-founded Bluebonnet Bowl at Houston. However, that fell through when TCU, an LSU victim during the regular season, accepted an invitation after their final game.

The Baton Rouge *Morning Advocate* published this Monday morning: "Although nothing has come from LSU on the subject, the word is that LSU doesn't want a rematch with the Rebels and, secondly, the players aren't keen about the New Orleans junket. The 85-mile trip from Baton Rouge to New Orleans isn't much of a holiday for the players, or at least that's the way off-records reports have it. And then too, many of the players feel that almost six weeks of remaining in training … is sacrificing too much for a bowl date."

Cannon's biography contains this passage: "Coach Dietzel and athletic director Jim Corbett called the team together, so the players were told, to vote on whether or not to accept the invitation. 'Corbett knew we didn't want to go,' Billy recalled, 'and he knew if he tried to force us to go, it would be a wasted trip. We weren't dummies. We'd played the game defensively as well as we could,' Billy said of the regular-season Ole Miss game, 'and had gotten lucky and won the game offensively. … We ended up voting on the proposal three times. The first time we voted no. Then Corbett offered us ten tickets each that they would sell for us,' a financial incentive for the players, 'and when we voted no a second time, they let all the red-shirts … vote. … The third time … it passed by three or four votes.'"

Dietzel's autobiography contains this passage: "At the end of the season, the Sugar Bowl Committee 'double banked' us. They invited Ole Miss to the bowl and then publicly announced that they were daring LSU to accept the challenge and replay the Rebels. The players and coaches all wanted to go to a different bowl, but because of tremendous political pressure, LSU accepted the challenge to play Ole Miss in the Sugar Bowl. An old saying among coaches is 'Never replay a team you've already beaten in the same year.' That adage would be drummed into my mind forever. I would never allow myself to repeat that mistake again."

The Opponent

The Rebels easily defeated their instate rival 42–0 and gleefully accepted an opportunity to get a shot at the only team that beat them during the season. The game would be the first rematch in Sugar Bowl history.

Ole Miss boasted an even better defensive record than LSU—just 27 points surrendered vs. 29 for the Tigers. While the Rebels didn't play as strong a schedule as the Bayou Bengals, Ole Miss's final margin of 284 points against just 29 for the opponents showed the strength of the team many called Johnny Vaught's best in his 13 years in Oxford.

Comparative scores did not bode well for LSU.

LSU 9 @Kentucky 0	Ole Miss 16 @Kentucky 0
@Tennessee 14 LSU 13	Ole Miss 37 @Tennessee 7
@LSU 27 Mississippi State 0	Ole Miss 42 @Mississippi State 0
@LSU 14 Tulane 6	@Ole Miss 53 Tulane 7

Lawrence Wells wrote in *Ole Miss Football* (1980): "By 1959, Johnny Vaught had established a dynasty at Ole Miss. Tom Swayze's recruiting program had become a well-tuned machine functioning at peak efficiency. Talent was evident two and three men deep at nearly every position. Senior quarterback Bobby Franklin … directed an attack that featured 205lb fullback Charlie Flowers…, and halfbacks Bobby Crespino and Cowboy Woodruff. … An excellent kicking game was provided by specialist Bobby Khayat."

Vaught's beautiful offense centered around the quarterback-fullback duo. It featured variations in motion with flankers that kept the defense guessing. He liked quarterbacks who could throw the sprint out pass as well as the traditional drop back pass.

LSU came out of the grueling season with injuries to key players.

- Halfback Wendell Harris would not play with a broken arm.
- Quarterback Warren Rabb would play with a "tender" knee.
- Starting halfback Johnny Robinson broke his right hand in practice nine days before the Sugar Bowl. The cast was removed two days before the game.

Bookmakers rated Ole Miss a seven-point favorite, marking the first time all season that LSU was cast in an underdog role. The Sugar Bowl would be the final game for 19 LSU seniors who had arguably participated in the finest three years of LSU football.

Football writers wondered whether the teams would stick to the strategies that had propelled each to a 9–1 season or come up with new approaches. Would LSU pass more than they did in Baton Rouge? Would Vaught run more wide stuff than in the first game?

The Game

The weather forecast of occasional rain and gusty winds came to pass. Temperature was 49 degrees at kickoff. The field was wet everywhere and muddy in places as the crowd of 81,500 gathered.

First Quarter

Billy Cannon returned the kickoff to the 23. But LSU could not make a first down, and Cannon's punt rolled dead of the Rebel 44. Going to the air immediately, Bobby Franklin hit FB Charlie Flowers for a 12-yard gain. Flowers made consistent gains for a first down at the LSU 24. Then Franklin shot a pass that Rabb intercepted on the LSU five,

Charlie Flowers (41) slips away from Don Purvis (23), while Cowboy Woodruff (32) grins in glee (*Gumbo* Class of 1960).

where he slipped down. Later in the period, Ole Miss started a drive from their 39 after a Tiger punt and pushed to the 16 as the period ended with fourth-and-five.

Score: LSU 0 Ole Miss 0

SECOND QUARTER

On the first play, Bob Khayat missed a 33-yard field goal into a 14 mph wind. A short time later, the Rebs were back in business at their 41. Emile Fournet dropped George Blair for a 7-yard loss. But Franklin got that back and more with a 24-yard pass to the LSU 32. Flowers gained nine, then three for another first down. Two plays later, Franklin rolled around right end for eight. On third-and-one, Flowers banged into the line but fell a foot short of the first down. So the All-American fullback tried again but hit a solid wall of Tigers and went nowhere. For the third game in a row, LSU had stopped the Rebels on fourth down inside their own 15.

Once again stymied by the stalwart Reb defense, Cannon punted to Blair, who made a fair catch on the 45. Rebel E Johnny Brewer explained that he was personally assigned to follow Cannon on every play. "Everywhere he went, I went," said Johnny.

LSU's defensive specialists, the Chinese Bandits, took the field and caused havoc immediately. E Mel Branch and T Tommy Lott threw new QB Jake Gibbs for a loss. Then Gibbs tried a long pass that Darryl Jenkins intercepted on the 10 and returned 15 yards. The Bandits stayed in on offense but went three and out. Gaynell Kinchen got off a bad punt that went out of bounds on the 45.

LSU got a big break that could have been bigger when Roy Winston snagged Blair's fumble in midair with open field ahead of him, but he stumbled and fell to the muddy turf. Scooter Purvis gained what would be LSU's only first down rushing for the day. But the drive stalled, and Cannon punted out of bounds on the Ole Miss 37 with 1:10 to go in the half. It looked for all the world like the teams would head to their locker rooms deadlocked 0–0.

Gibbs carried on the first play and fought for extra yardage. The Tigers became overeager in piling into him, drawing a personal foul penalty to the LSU 43. After backup HB Jerry Hall caught a pass for no gain, Ole Miss suddenly broke the scoreless tie. Halfback Cowboy Woodruff came in with a play from Vaught. Flanked out, he split the two deep Tiger defenders and, angling left, pulled in a perfect pass from Gibbs at the 10 and ran in untouched with Cannon in vain pursuit. Just like that, Ole Miss penetrated the LSU goal line for the first time since 1957. It was also the first TD pass against LSU all season. Franklin booted the PAT.

Ole Miss 7 LSU 0 (0:38)

Rabb fumbled and Ole Miss recovered. But the Rebs could run only one play before the half ended.

After the game, LSU assistant coach George Terry explained the scoring play. "They just got four men deep on three defenders. They sent a man down and out on each side, Woodruff up the middle and another man as a flare. We only had three men deep, and each had a man covered, but Gibbs hit the open man. We just didn't rush hard enough on the play. They shouldn't have had that much time to get four men deep. They tried the same play five or six times in the game, and it never did work again."

Ole Miss 7 LSU 0

Third Quarter

Inspired by their late first half touchdown, the Rebels took the kickoff and stormed 64 yards to a second one in nine plays. Runs by Woodruff and Franklin gained a first down a yard past midfield. Bobby, on his way to the MVP trophy, completed three straight passes, 16 yards to Blair, 12 yards to Bobby Crespino, and a beautiful 18-yard aerial to E Larry Grantham at the left corner of the end zone. Khayat added the point.

Ole Miss 14 LSU 0 (12:22)

Play was confined between the 35-yard stripes the rest of the period. The Go Team gained one first down on a 12-yard pass from Durel Matherne to FB Earl Gros.

Fourth Quarter

Starting from their 25 where Cannon's punt rolled dead, the Rebels drove to their third touchdown. The yardage was gained mostly on the ground against the White Team. Flowers started with a 12-yard smash. Then, on third-and-one, Blair skirted right end to the LSU 45. After Dietzel sent in the Chinese Bandits, LSU nearly got a big break when Branch hit Franklin hard as he tried to pass and batted the pigskin into the air. A couple of Tigers stretched out for the ball with plenty of open space in front of them, but it fell to the ground. Undeterred, Bobby connected with Dewey Partridge for 19 yards to the 26.

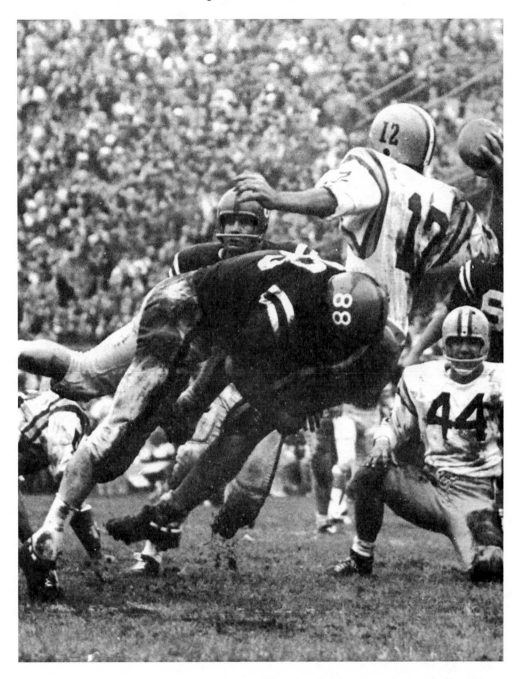

Larry Grantham crashes into Warren Rabb as Donnie Daye watches (*Gumbo* Class of 1960).

Then he tossed to Flowers who rambled to the eight. Blair gathered in a swing pass in the right flat and squirmed over the goal with a Tiger hanging on.

Ole Miss 21 LSU 0 (9:17)

The Bandits tried their hand at offense starting from the 28 after the kickoff. Matherne connected twice with E Scotty McLain to give LSU its first penetration of enemy

Billy Cannon snags a pass (*Gumbo* Class of 1960).

territory. Cannon came in and punched out 4 yards to the 34. But the angry Rebels pushed the Bengals back to their 42 where the ball went over on downs.

The Tigers continued to fight hard and kept Ole Miss from threatening the rest of the game.

Final Score: Ole Miss 21 LSU 0

The statistics testify to Ole Miss's domination.

First downs: Ole Miss 19 LSU 6
Rushing: Ole Miss 140 LSU -15
Passing: Ole Miss 15–27–2/223 LSU 9–25–1/89

Cannon netted a measly 8 yards on six carries. LSU set a dubious record with its fifth loss in six Sugar Bowl appearances.

Postgame

Coach Dietzel shook his head in bewilderment. "Vaught just prepared his team better than I did for the game. I'll take full responsibility for anything that happened out there today. We have no excuses. They were that much better. … I was very proud of our boys. They fought to the hilt."

Athletic Director Jim Corbett, who had forced the Tigers to play the game, said, "LSU in no way regrets playing this game here today. We're just sorry we didn't win."

RABB: "We gave 'em another chance, and, boy, did they make the best of it. Losing to a team as good as Ole Miss isn't bad, but losing by that kind of score is tough to take."

CANNON: "There aren't any excuses when you lose 21–0. We just got kicked good and proper by a better team today."

Many Tigers agreed that the touchdown pass with less than a minute to play in the first half was the turning point. Fugler said, "That took a lot of starch out of us. ... Ole Miss was a better ball club today than when we played them earlier. But we just made too many crucial errors."

Coach Vaught: "The condition of the field today was not as bad as it was when we played in Baton Rouge. ... Our attack is built on the option outside and to throw. In the first meeting, we couldn't throw as much as we would have liked. ... This is the greatest Ole Miss team I have coached. ... The boys wanted the other one as bad as this one."

In his autobiography, Dietzel wrote this about the 1960 Sugar Bowl: "Our team was not easily motivated for the game. Why should they be, since they had already beaten the Rebels? I don't think our players ever developed a real interest in the game. ... From the beginning, I felt that it was a mistake to replay Ole Miss. As it turned out, agreeing to play in the Sugar Bowl was a serious failure on my part. But I also thought it was wrong for some folks at LSU to insist that we play in that game. ... It was a sour note to end a fine year. When all was said and done, LSU concluded its 1959 season ranked number four."

Eight 1959 Tigers played pro football: DE Mel Branch, HB Billy Cannon, FB Earl Gros, HB Wendell Harris, DB Tommy Neck, QB Warren Rabb, HB Johnny Robinson, and LB Roy Winston. Robinson was inducted into the Pro Football Hall of Fame in 2019.

Orange Bowl vs. Colorado

*LSU said farewell to Paul Dietzel
with a dominating victory*

Orange Bowl, Miami, Florida
January 1, 1962

Tiger fans had to endure a rebuilding year in 1960 after the loss of 20 seniors who had led LSU to a 20–2 record their last two seasons, including the national championship in 1958. The 1960s young Tigers with 18 sophomores in the first 33 tied three-TD-favorite Ole Miss in Oxford, then won their last four games to finish with a 5–4–1 record. It wasn't good enough to get to a bowl game but nevertheless boded well for the future. The defense gave up only 50 points in ten games, but the offense averaged just 10.5 points per game. The undisputed star of the team, the next Billy Cannon if you will, was sophomore HB Jerry Stovall, who excelled on both sides of the ball and as a kick returner.

LSU's Season

LSU ranked #5 in the Associated Press 1961 preseason poll. And who could quarrel with the voters when Coach Paul Dietzel returned 24 starters from his famous three-unit combo of White team, Go team, and Chinese Bandits?

But the season didn't start well at all. In Houston, 73,000 fans saw Rice defeat the Tigers 16–3. In the home opener the following week against Texas A&M, LSU trailed 7–2 in the fourth quarter before HB Wendell Harris tight roped down the sideline for the go-ahead score. Georgia Tech came to town ranked #3 but returned home a 10–0 loser. Victories over South Carolina, Kentucky, and Florida moved the Tigers up to #6 and set up another classic battle with #2 Ole Miss. For the third time in four years, the annual matchup had national implications. The Rebels had not crossed LSU's goal line in regular season play since 1957. Adding to the visitors' motivation, the Tigers had spoiled perfect seasons for Johnny Vaught the last two years. Ole Miss dominated the statistics but lost again because they scored only once in the six times they crossed midfield while LSU scored twice in its three trips into enemy territory.

The Tigers took care of business in their remaining three games to finish 9–1 and #4 in the final AP poll. The players voted to accept an invitation to play in the Orange Bowl against the Big Eight Conference champion.

The Opponent

Colorado defeated all seven of its conference opponents to earn the school's first Big Eight championship and the trip to Miami. Thirty-one-year-old coach Everett "Sonny" Grandelius had been an All-American halfback at Michigan State and served as an assistant there to Duffy Daugherty. The Buffs entered the AP Top Ten in Week 4 and moved as high as #6 before finishing #7. The offense was well-balanced—1,919 yards on the ground compared to 1,182 through the air. The Buffaloes would field the bigger team. All four starting backs tipped the scales at no less than 190 pounds.

As LSU began preparations for the bowl game, an event 1,400 miles from Baton Rouge would change Tiger football forever. On December 9, Army dismissed head football coach Dale Hall. The announcement of the firing stated that Hall would be replaced by "the finest coach available." That implied that West Point would break with its tradition of restricting the head coaching post to academy graduates. That opened the door for potential candidates who served as assistants at Army during legendary Coach Red Blaik's tenure, including Dietzel, who coached at West Point in 1953–54 before coming to LSU.

When asked whether he was interested in the West Point job, Dietzel told reporters, "I am very happy here and plan no change." However, he had in fact been contacted by the Academy athletic director. Dietzel then reported the contact to LSU Athletic Director Jim Corbett and asked if getting out of his contract would be a problem. Jim replied (according to Dietzel), "If you want to go, there's no way we would want you to stay. It wouldn't be good for either of us."

Meanwhile, the Tigers returned to the practice field for 12 days of drills before leaving for Miami December 26. Once in Florida, the Tigers followed the same routine they used all season the week of each game. The main difference for Dietzel was fending off the constant questions about the Army job as national articles listed him as one of the top three candidates. "My one thought is to get ready for Colorado," he insisted, "and that's all I'm worried about." Nevertheless, the Dietzel Departure story gained momentum as the game approached.

Two New Orleans newspapers and a TV station reported that Dietzel would sign a contract with West Point that would pay him $20,000 a year, a raise of $1,500 over his LSU salary. Reporters noted that Dietzel no longer denied the reports as he had been quick to do several weeks earlier.

Despite the distraction, the Tigers were favored by as many as 17 points by some oddsmakers. The game was billed as a classic matchup of Speed vs. Power. The headline over the January 1 article on the game in the *Chicago Daily News* proclaimed, "THREE L.S.U. SQUADS FACE ONE OF COLORADO." The burning question was whether the incessant talk of Dietzel going to Army would prove to be a distraction for his players.

The contest was notable for the LSU players in that "it was the first time we played against black guys," as T Fred Miller recalled. "We were just keyed up and happy and saying these guys (Colorado) can't beat us," he added.

The Game

Two teams from far away failed to fill the Orange Bowl. Attendance was announced as 68,150. Spectators needed raincoats and umbrellas as the game was played in a steady drizzle—a first for an Orange Bowl game.

First Quarter

LSU won the toss and elected to receive. It proved to be a good choice as the Tigers drove to the first score of the game. QB Jimmy Field skirted right end for 10 yards on third-and-six to keep the drive alive. Two plays later, Field threw his first pass, completing to HB Jerry Stovall for 7 yards into Colorado territory at the 46. On third-and-one, Jerry got just enough up the middle to move the chains. Field then tossed to HB Wendell Harris, who made a one-handed reception for 14 yards and another first down at the 30. Stovall got three before FB Earl Gros smashed through left guard for a first down on the 17. But a delay of game mark off on the next series proved too much to overcome. When Field's third-down pass to E Jack Gates was broken up in the corner of the end zone, Harris booted a 30-yard field goal.

Score: LSU 3 Colorado 0 (6:59)

The Buffs' first possession started badly when Bill Harris fumbled the kickoff on the three and had to fall on it at the nine. When two plunges gained only three, Coach Grandelius lived up to his pledge, "we will never kick on third down" with disastrous results. QB Gale Weidner's pass was almost intercepted by E Bob Flurry. So Chuck McBride dropped back to punt. He juggled the snap, giving junior LB Gary Kinchen time to block the kick through the end zone.

LSU 5 Colorado 0 (5:01)

The Go Team came out to receive the free kick, which QB Lynn Amedee caught on a fair catch at the LSU 45. Dietzel's offensive specialists started strong, ripping off two first downs to the 34. Ray Wilkins' 8-yard sweep and Amedee's pass to HB Bo Campbell for eight were the key gains. But two Buffaloes sacked Lynn on third-and-six at the 39. So Stovall came in and punted dead on the 18. The period ended with Field dumping the CU ball carrier for a 6-yard loss.

Score: LSU 5 Colorado 0

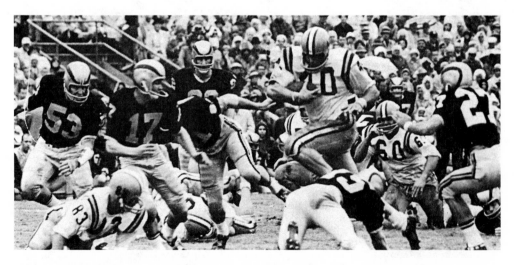

FB Earl Gros tears through the Colorado defense. No. 60 is Roy Winston, and 83 is Gene Sykes (*Gumbo* Class of 1962).

SECOND QUARTER

Colorado couldn't overcome second-and-16 and punted, Harris signaling for a fair catch at the CU 47. Two plays later, the downtrodden Buffaloes took the lead. Field rolled right and, under a heavy rush, threw off balance. LB Loren Schweninger picked off the wobbly toss and sped untouched down the sidelines 50 yards to pay dirt.

Colorado 7 LSU 5 (12:54)

Dietzel sent in the Go Team, and they quickly regained the lead, driving 82 yards in eight plays. LB Joe Romig stopped Bo Campbell after a gain of four, but a personal foul penalty moved the ball to the 37. Amedee converted a third-and-four by tossing a swing pass to his man-in-motion, Ray Wilkins, who raced all the way to the 20. Following Charles Cranford's 2-yard gain, Harris sped around the left side for 17 yards to the one. After the defense stuffed Cranford for no gain on first down, Charlie made one of his patented leaps over the line for the touchdown. The Tigers went for two, but Amedee's pass to TE Billy Truax was broken up.

LSU 11 Colorado 7 (8:57)

Starting from their 20, the Buffaloes gained three first downs, the first two on passes,

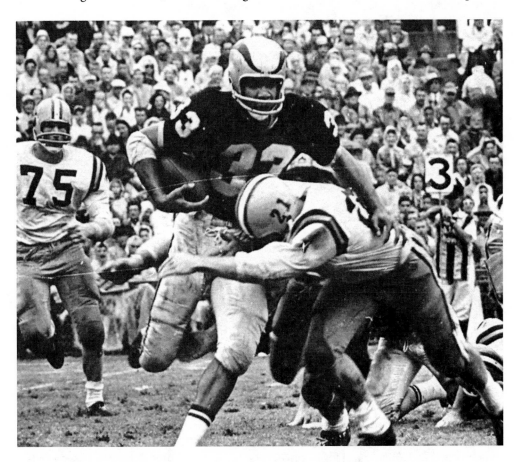

Jerry Stovall tackles Ted Wood. No. 75 is Don Estes (*Gumbo* Class of 1962).

to put the ball on the LSU 38. But the Chinese Bandits, with some White team players mixed in, drew the line there, aided by an illegal procedure penalty.

After a punt into the end zone, the Tigers went three-and-out. To make matters worse, LSU was penalized for a personal foul on the punt return to set up the Buffs at the Tiger 44. But the defense ended any CU momentum before it started. Two incomplete passes and T Fred Miller's stop for no gain set up a field goal try by Jerry Hillebrand from the 44 that fell short.

The White team drove from the 20 to the 45 to run out the clock.

LSU 11 Colorado 7

The halftime statistics showed LSU's dominance: First downs 11–3; yards rushing 103–15; yards passing 67–32

Third Quarter

The Buffaloes needed to take the kickoff and, using any adjustments made at halftime, get their offense clicking. Starting from the 20, Weidner threw two passes. The first was broken up by Harris, and all-American E Hillebrand dropped the second. Under pressure again, McBride barely got off a punt that traveled only 18 yards to the CU 43. From there, LSU moved smartly to another touchdown. On second down, Gros dragged defenders for 18 yards to the 22. Three plays later, facing third-and-nine, Field rolled right to the nine. Then he kept the ball again over left tackle into the end zone. Harris booted the extra point.

LSU 18 Colorado 7 (10:34)

Giving up on running the ball, Weidner threw three straight passes, completing just one for 4 yards. So LSU started from their 32 after the punt. The only way the Buffs could get back in the game was to get turnovers. And they got one when Claude Crabb snagged Amedee's long pass at the CU 40. But they couldn't capitalize. On fourth and less than a yard, Grandelius gave the signal to go for it. But Ted Woods fumbled, and LB Sammy Odom recovered at the CU 49.

Amedee's completions to Campbell for 18 and Wilkins for eight sparked a Go Team drive that reached the 19. But a holding penalty forced the Tigers to go to the air. Three straight incompletions led to Stovall's beautiful punt that went out of bounds on the five.

When three plays gained only 4 yards, McBride dropped back for his second punt from the end zone. It was hard to imagine it could be any worse than the first one, which led to a safety, but it was. E Gene Sykes blocked the kick and fell on the ball in the end zone.

LSU 25 Colorado 7 (0:26)

Fourth Quarter

With the issue no longer in doubt, Weidner had no choice but to pass. After three incompletions, LSU received the punt near midfield. But the Tigers gave the ball right back, Woods recovering Gros' fumble at the CU 42. Weidner took advantage of the second chance to penetrate the LSU 35 for the first time all day. With plenty of time to throw, he connected with Hillebrand for 13 yards, then 12. After running a draw to slow the rush, Gale threw twice to E John Meadows to put the pigskin on the 11. But two incompletions

Gene Sykes recovers the blocked punt for a touchdown. No. 23 is Bo Campbell, and 81 is Danny Neumann (*Gumbo* Class of 1962).

and an offside penalty set CU back. Going for it on fourth down, Weidner went to his best receiver, Hillebrand, but Field broke it up.

From the 16, the Go Team ate up more clock, gaining three first downs on 11 runs and an Amedee completion to Campbell for 12. Finally, from the CU 30, Lynn was again bitten by the interception bug as Bill Harris snagged his second pick. But more errant throws by Weidner, on his way to setting an Orange Bowl record with 39 passes attempts, forced McBride to boot.

Neither team threatened the rest of the way.

Final Score: LSU 25 Colorado 7

Postgame

Dietzel: "I didn't think they could run on us, but they could throw the ball real well. We didn't lay our hands on Weidner all day. He is a real good passer and had fine protection. I don't believe we were nearly as sharp today as we were during the season. We weren't spectacular … but we got the job done." On the topic on everyone's mind: "Concerning my moving to Army, I put it out of my mind until the Orange Bowl game was over. I'll now give it my full consideration. … I have no further comment."

Lynn Amedee: "They are built like pros. I've never seen a team so big. Our fullbacks were blocking real well to help our outside stuff."

Jimmy Field: "I gave 'em a really cheap TD. I knew we would have to score again in the second half but felt we could and could hold them."

C/LB Roy Winston: "I thought they had a big, tough line. I believe their line was just as good as any SEC line although they weren't as fast and didn't have the depth."

Coach Grandelius: "LSU is a fine football team. I can't take anything away from them. They did a fine job on that rollout pass and run. Our linebackers were just not quick enough to stop them. … Their three teams didn't wear us down. We just made too many mistakes."

Postscript

On January 5, the LSU Board of Supervisors released Dietzel from his contract obligations and authorized AD Corbett to negotiate for a new coach. Jim promoted defensive assistant Charlie McClendon, who was being wooed by his alma mater, Kentucky. Dietzel flew to New York and signed a contract with Army January 6.

A dozen 1961 Tigers played pro football: OL Don Estes, LB Dennis Gaubatz, RB Earl Gros, DB Wendell Harris, DL Fred Miller, LB Mike Morgan, DB Tommy Neck, DL Bobby Richards, HB Jerry Stovall, DB Gene Sykes, TE Billy Truax, and LB Roy Winston.

Cotton Bowl vs. Texas

"The Battle of Identical Twins" went the Tigers' way

Cotton Bowl, Dallas, Texas
January 1, 1963

LSU's Season

All eyes were on Charlie McClendon for his first season as head coach. With NCAA rules still limiting substitutions, Mac employed the same three-unit system that Paul Dietzel invented for the 1958 season. Led by the runner-up in the Heisman Trophy voting, all-purpose back Jerry Stovall, the Tigers tied Rice and lost to Ole Miss, which finished the season a perfect 9–0.

Stovall averaged 4.1 yards per carry, led the team in pass receiving yardage with 213, averaged a fantastic 41.6 yards on kickoff returns, led in scoring with 66 points, and averaged 37 yards on 50 punts.

The Tigers continued their tradition of playing rock-ribbed defense. The White team, which played both ways, and the Chinese Bandits defensive unit pitched five shutouts during the season. The Tigers surrendered only 34 points in ten games, tops in the nation. Nearly half of those points, 15, were scored by Ole Miss. LSU finished the regular season with a streak of 16 straight games without allowing a TD on the ground.

When the season ended, Coach McClendon gathered the team together and told them, "Fellas, we are invited to the Cotton Bowl, and we're here to vote on it." Little did Mac know that the team had some resentment from the Orange Bowl the year before in Paul Dietzel's last game as LSU coach. As senior FB Steve Ward recalled, "We worked our butts off in the prebowl workouts under Coach Dietzel and came to realize it was more like spring training than a reward to go to a bowl. Also, [us] single guys got the shaft at the Orange Bowl, because all the married guys on the team got to bring their wives." Also, there wasn't much the players could do on the Miami Beach strip. "It was … quite expensive, and we were quite broke." Little did Mac know that the single players had gotten together and voted not to go anywhere. "Coach Mac almost had a heart attack when the show of hands indicated that the majority didn't want to go." Team captain Fred Miller met with Mac and Athletic Director Jim Corbett and demanded spending money and lighter practices. "It must have worked," Ward said, "because [we] got a $250 'laundry check' before we left for Dallas, and we worked out in shorts and shoulder pads for most of the prebowl practices."

The Opponent

Walter Robertson of *The Dallas Morning News* called the 1963 Cotton Bowl "the Battle of the Identical Twins." He explained that the two teams "are about as close to carbon copies in their philosophies for winning football games as two teams can get. Basically they both believe that the best formula for winning is to possess the football a considerably greater portion of the game than the opponent; that if you must give up the ball, give it up at such a position on the field where the opponent can do little with it except maybe eat it…." So he predicted that the game "will be no shoot-em-up, with footballs ricocheting around the floor of the Cotton Bowl cavern like Dodge City at high noon." He cited Texas coach Darrell Royal's famous saying: "When you put that football in the air, three things can happen—and two of them are bad." And who could argue with success? The two teams had lost only one game between them in 1962 with two ties. Texas (9–0–1) was ranked #4 in both the Associated Press and Coaches Polls following its first undefeated season since 1923. LSU (8–1–1) was #7 in the AP and #8 in the Coaches poll.

LSU was rated a two-point favorite. Royal on the point spread: "I don't think anybody should be favored, but two points would indicate that the oddsmakers think it's about as close as any game might be." McClendon was also puzzled. "I don't see how we could be favored since we are back of Texas in the rankings, they are undefeated, and we have lost one game."

The teams had four common opponents during the season. LSU outscored the common foes 70–9, a 61-point margin. Texas outscored them 76–26, a difference of 50.

Two of the four coaches of common opponents registered a prediction about the Cotton Bowl. Abe Martin of TCU took Texas because it had a better defense. Tommy O'Boyle of Tulane chose LSU because it had more experience. Hank Foldberg of Texas A&M and Jess Neely of Rice refused to pick a winner but agreed it would be an even game. The two lines were almost equal in size. LSU averaged 214 pounds per man across its forward wall while Texas averaged 210.

Texas was by far the fastest opponent the Tigers had played. So the coaching staff created a couple of plays to make the Longhorns' speed work to LSU's advantage. One play looked like a sweep to one side but turned into an off-tackle play to the other side. The other started as a quarterback sprint-out that morphed into a pass to an end cutting across the middle. Go Team QB Lynn Amedee recalled, "They were our bread and butter. Every time we needed something, we got it from those plays."

The Tigers gained a psychological edge after arriving in Dallas that would motivate them in the game. "We felt slighted in Dallas," recalled T Fred Miller. "The press, at the functions, almost everything, it was Texas, Texas, Texas. It was almost as if we were there just so the Cotton Bowl could fill out its ballgame."

The Game

Tiger fans flocked to nearby Dallas in much greater numbers than had traveled to

Miami for the Orange Bowl the previous season. A capacity crowd of 75,500 attended on an overcast 50 degree day.

FIRST QUARTER

The first half lived up to the expectation of a low-scoring defensive battle. LSU won the toss and elected to receive. The Tigers gained one first down before having to punt. On the first Texas play from scrimmage, DT Fred Miller broke through to drop HB Tommy Ford for a 5-yard loss. Coach Mac said afterwards, "You could hear it (the collision) over on the sidelines. That kind of set the tone for the rest of the day." Playing old-fashion Southern football, Royal had Ernie Koy punt on third-and-13. And what a punt it was. The pigskin hit the ground and took off like a jackrabbit toward the LSU goal line, coming to rest on the 12. The amazing 72-yard boot was not even a Cotton Bowl record since Kyle Rote had banged one 84 yards for SMU in 1949.

Runs by Jerry Stovall and Danny LeBlanc gained a first down on the 25. Several plays later, the Tigers took the first gamble of the game when they went for it on fourth and short. QB Jimmy Field stayed under center in punt formation and sneaked for the first down at the 36. With the Go Team taking over, LSU moved the chains again on a 12-yard aerial from QB Lynn Amedee to Charles Cranford at the 48. But the drive bogged down and the rest of the period plus the early minutes of the second quarter descended into a punting duel between Stovall and Koy. Jerry had kicks of 42, 49, and 57 yards during the afternoon. Royal sometimes ordered punts before fourth down when deep in his own territory.

Score: LSU 0 Texas 0

SECOND QUARTER

The sun that came out during the first minutes of the period shown a little more brightly on LSU than Texas. After four punts, Texas found themselves at their 14 after a

Jimmy Field stumbles on a keeper. Other Tigers are Dennis Gaubatz (53), Rodney Guillot (72), and Danny LeBlanc (26) (*Gumbo* Class of 1963).

clipping penalty. From that point, the Southwest Conference champs made their most powerful showing of the first half, reeling off four first downs before being stopped. Senior QB Johnny Genung surprised the Chinese Bandits by hitting Joe Dixon in the left flat. With blockers coming out, Joe stepped inside for a 17-yard gain to the 31. Ford zipped for 11 yards, and Genung completed two flat passes to make it first-and-10 at the LSU 45. After an incompletion, the Longhorns pulled a play designed to counter the Tigers' quick pursuit. Genung handed to a halfback who turned and gave it back to him. Johnny then rolled out and connected with 6'4½" SE Charley Talbert for 15 more. At that point, LB Ruffin Rodrigue made it his personal mission to stop the onslaught. He made successive tackles, one on Koy after a gain of three and the second crashing Ford to the ground after only 2 yards. The sophomore from Thibodaux then tipped Genung's third down slant-in pass intended for Talbert high in the air. It landed beyond everyone. "The Texas quarterback was throwing right over my head at him," explained Ruffin. "I leaped up and managed to get half my hand on the football." So shoeless kicker Tony Crosby, who made only two field goals during the regular season, tried one from the 32, but it fell short and to the left. Texas's penetration to the 25 would be their deepest of the game.

With 5:12 left, the Go Team took over on the 20 and started a march that showed Amedee's versatility. An interference penalty on his third down pass gave LSU a first down at the 39. After Bo Campbell rammed for three, Lynn rolled left and tossed a swing pass to Ray Wilkins for another first at the 49. On third-and-five, the senior from Baton Rouge hustled away from the rushers for 6 yards when he couldn't find an open receiver. On fourth-and-one at the Texas 46, McClendon rolled the dice and won when Cranford dove over the right side to the 40. With time ticking down, Amedee converted another third down by calling one of the plays installed for the game. He sprinted to the right, stopped, and fired to TE Billy Truax over the middle for 22 yards to the 12. McClendon explained after the game, "The complicated defenses that Texas was throwing against us–I believe they were stunting more than usual—forced us to throw the ball more." Following two short runs with time running out and no timeouts left, McClendon sent in Field with the kicking tee on third down. Amedee booted a 23-yard field goal to give the

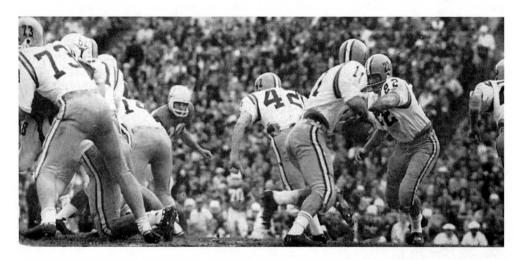

Lynn Amedee fakes to Ray Wilkins as Charlie Cranford blocks. No. 73 is Ralph Pere (*Gumbo* Class of 1963).

Tigers a 3–0 lead at the half. A Longhorn got a finger on the ball, which cleared the cross-bar in a circular motion instead of end over end.

LSU 3 Texas 0

THIRD QUARTER

LSU got the big break of the game on the kickoff when Gene Sykes and Dennis Gaubatz (the only Texan on the LSU team) slammed returner Jerry Cook, causing a fumble that the ubiquitous Amedee, who kicked off, recovered on the UT 37. On second-and-seven, Field rolled left and fired an 11-yard pass down the middle to LE Gene Sykes. Following a short run to the 22, Jimmy rolled right but, spotting an opening to his left, took off downfield. HB Joe Dixon had a shot at him against the sideline, but Jimmy sidestepped him and continued for his first touchdown of the season. "I was looking for Steve Ward," Field said, "but they had him well covered. For a minute, I was going to keep going to my right, but when I looked and saw nothing to my left, I took off."

LSU 10 Texas 0 (13:06)

The Steers roared back, moving on the ground to a first down at the LSU 45. Two plays later, Genung spotted WR Ben House open just inside the sideline for a first down at the 38. But the Longhorns could move no further, and Koy punted into the end zone.

After Stovall's 57-yard punt rolled dead on the 14, Texas pushed out near midfield. But Tiger G Jim Turner batted Tommy Wade's pass into the air, and Rodrigue intercepted on the LSU 47. Field passed to Stovall for 12. A few plays later, E Jack Gates made a great diving catch to make it first-and-goal at the seven. But Cook and NG Johnny Treadwell teamed up to stop Stovall for a loss of 5 yards around right end. Another loss set the Tigers back as the period ended.

LSU 10 Texas 0

FOURTH QUARTER

LSU squandered the scoring opportunity and turned the ball over on downs on the 24. With UT fans wondering why all-conference FB Ray Poage got no carries all afternoon, Texas penetrated LSU territory to the 32. But a reverse handoff from QB Tommy Wade to Cook went awry, and LB Buddy Hamic covered the ball on the LSU 29. "He still had the ball under his arm," said Buddy, "but he didn't have a firm grip on it. I jerked it away from him, and then he tried to fight to get it back." Cook said, "Somebody kicked me in the head, and I went one way and the ball went the other. They were hitting pretty hard."

From there, the Go Team got going again. Danny Neumann made a good catch in traffic of Amedee's pass for 16 yards to the LSU 48. Swivel-hips Campbell boomed over right tackle for 10. Stovall came in and lined up at wingback in the gap between left end and tackle. He took a handoff and glided around right end for 14. After two plays gained six, Amedee hurled a strike down the middle to Truax for 14 yards to the eight. On third-and-seven, Amedee lofted a perfect strike to Billy in the end zone. However, an official detected an ineligible receiver downfield, setting LSU back to the 20. It was the Tigers' only penalty of the afternoon. After an incompletion, Amedee booted a 37-yarder to break the Cotton Bowl distance record that he himself had set earlier. "I never thought the ball would make the crossbar," recalled Lynn. "There was a little breeze blowing in from the end zone. … I don't believe I cleared it by more than two feet." It was Lynn's seventh three-pointer in 10 tries for the season, an outstanding percentage in that era of straight ahead kicking.

LSU 13 Texas 0 (4:58)

The highlights of the remaining minutes were Koy's 69-yard punt and Stovall's interception of a Wade pass to allow the Tigers to run out the clock on their second straight bowl victory.

Final Score: LSU 13 Texas 0

Because of his passing, kicking, and fumble recovery, Amedee was voted the game's Outstanding Back in a landslide.

Postgame

Captain Miller presented the game ball to Coach McClendon, who had been given a victory ride on the shoulders of his players at the end of the game. Mac said, "They gave me the first one (after the victory over Texas A&M in the season opener) and they gave me the last one." He pointed to the end of the first half and the opening of the second as the turning point. "Those final seconds of the first half with the field goal and the touchdown opening the third quarter put 10 points on the scoreboard for us. … I never felt safe until we got through 60 minutes of football.… I was especially proud of our 18 seniors. They gave us the leadership again today that they've consistently given all year, and it was a pleasure to coach such a dedicated group of young men."

Amedee on his award: "I'm proud to accept this on behalf of my teammates who made it possible.… I think it was the best game our team played all season. What defense we were playing. And did you see Jimmy (Field) on that touchdown run? He faked the pants off of 'em."

Royal acknowledged the thorough whipping his Longhorns received. "LSU is truly a great team. We're disappointed, but I don't feel that it is a disgrace to lose to the kind of team that beat us. … I just didn't expect them to pass and catch like that. Their passing was tremendous, and their receiving was great." He admitted he couldn't remember when a team dominated his squad as LSU did. "When you fumble and get passes intercepted like that, you're gonna be dominated."

G-LB Johnny Treadwell, winner of the trophy for Best Lineman, called LSU "the best football team we've played against since I've been at the University of Texas."

Six 1962 Tigers played pro football: S White Graves, T Dave McCormick, E Doug Moreau, LB Mike Morgan, G Remi Prudhomme, and E Billy Truax.

Bluebonnet Bowl vs. Baylor

*SEC's top rushing team vs.
nation's top passing team*

Rice Stadium, Houston, Texas
December 21, 1963

Charlie McClendon's second Tiger team was forced to emphasize the ground game when their outstanding dual-threat quarterback was lost for the season while the Baylor Bears rode the coattails of the best passing combination in the nation.

LSU's Season

Coach Mac had an important decision to make before the season started because of a new NCAA rule. The Rules Committee continued the trend toward returning to unlimited substitutions and so-called "two-platoon football"—with important restrictions. The 1963 regulation allowed unlimited substitution on second and third downs and on first down if possession of the ball hadn't changed on the previous play. In all these cases, the clock had to be stopped. At all other times—and these were precisely the times when unlimited substitutions could do the most good (punts and change of possession)—each team could send in only two men.

McClendon decided to stick with the three-team system he had inherited from Paul Dietzel. Of the 34 players who would see action under that system, 16 were sophomores. Included among them were three backs whose recruitment brought excitement to LSU fans a season after Jerry Stovall departed for the NFL: QB Pat Screen (New Orleans), HB Joe Labruzzo (Lockport), who ran the 100-yard dash in 9.6 wind-assisted seconds, and FB Don Schwab (Thibodaux).

An injury in the fourth game changed the trajectory of LSU's season. After beating Texas A&M, the Tigers lost to an experienced Rice team in Houston. Bobby Dodd, the coach of LSU's next opponent, Georgia Tech, sang Screen's praises as "probably the best running quarterback we'll see this year." Pat scored the game's only touchdown as the Tigers held on 7–6.

Disaster struck in Miami the next week. In the LSU offense, the quarterback often led the blocking after making a pitchout. With the Tigers clinging to a 3–0 lead, Screen pitched the ball to Danny LeBlanc for a power sweep. When Pat blocked the Miami end,

"I felt a sharp pain and knew right away something was wrong. If I moved my arm just a little, my shoulder hurt." X-rays revealed a separated shoulder that ended his season. Go Team QB Billy Ezell moved up to Screen's spot and led victories over Kentucky and Florida by a combined 35 points. The 5–1 Tigers now faced #3 Ole Miss on CBS-TV. Only a four-point underdog, the Tigers were overwhelmed by the Rebels 37–3.

Could the Tigers regroup for the last three games? They trailed TCU 14–7 at halftime the following week but rallied behind Labruzzo, playing despite multiple injuries, to win 28–14. Next, the Tigers trailed Mississippi State in Jackson 7–0 after the Bulldogs scored with only 1:25 left in the game. But Ezell rallied the Tigers with a whirlwind 51 yard scoring drive. E Doug Moreau caught the 6-yard scoring pass with 0:14 on the clock. McClendon decided to go for two, but Ezell's pass to E Billy Truax went awry.

The Tigers needed to win their annual finale with Tulane to have a chance for a bowl bid. The day before the game, President John F. Kennedy was assassinated. As the home team, LSU chose to play the game. Fifty-five thousand spectators watched two uninspired teams play a lackluster game that the Tigers won 20–0.

LSU received an invitation to play Baylor in the Bluebonnet Bowl. Truax recalled, "We had a team meeting before accepting that bowl bid, and Mac asked us if we wanted to go, and most of us said no. We were tired. Ole Miss had beat the hell out of us, which was embarrassing." Nevertheless, Athletic Director Jim Corbett accepted the bid for LSU's first appearance in a bowl game that was not played on New Year's Day.

The Opponent

Baylor finished 7–3 like LSU. One of the few teams running a pro-style attack with two split receivers, the Bears boasted one of the NCAA's finest passing offenses. Senior QB Don Trull led the nation in completions, passing yards, and total touchdowns. His favorite target was junior All-American WR Lawrence Elkins. Trull, who audibled on at least half of Baylor's plays, entered the bowl game with a streak of 66 passes without an interception. Elkins caught an NCAA-record 70 passes for 873 yards and eight TDs. WR James Ingram snagged 40 for 537 yards and four TDs.

The pivotal game of the season for the Bears was the annual clash with Texas November 9 in Austin. With first place in the Southwest Conference at stake, the Longhorns prevailed 7–0 thanks to an interception in the end zone of a Trull pass for Elkins in the final minute.

Coach John Bridgers followed the professional style of two-platoon football, with one eleven playing offense and the other unit entering the game on defense at the first opportunity. Trull and FB Dalton Hoffman played offense only.

LSU and Baylor met three common opponents during the season.

- LSU lost to Rice by the same score by which the Bears beat the Owls: 21–12.
- LSU beat Kentucky 28–7 while the Wildcats defeated Baylor 19–7 in a game that Elkins missed because of injury.
- Both teams thumped TCU handily: LSU 28–14, Baylor 32–13.

LSU, which had been hampered in its preparation by rains in the Baton Rouge area, flew to Houston Thursday, two days before the game, only to be greeted by heavy rains Friday. Rice officials covered the stadium turf for two days so the footing for the game would be excellent.

LSU's plan called for the SEC's top rushing team to control the ball to keep Trull & Company off the field. McClendon explained, "Baylor has few pass routes, but they execute the pass play as good as anyone. … We will use varied defenses trying to halt Trull. We will rush sometimes, drop back and hope to double-team Elkins…"

Bridgers also praised LSU as "physically the strongest team we will meet this year. They have good athletes, are well coached. … They have had the best defense that I know of for the past six years, and we believe that their running attack is the best they've had in a number of years."

Baylor entered the fray as a two-point favorite.

The Game

A shivering crowd liberally estimated by bowl officials at 50,000 watched in damp 37° weather as the LSU defense shut out the Bears until wearing down in the final period.

First Quarter

The Tigers executed their game plan well in the first period, holding the ball for 18 plays to Baylor's nine. After an exchange of punts, LSU started from the Baylor 43 and moved smartly to pay dirt. After running for 5 yards on first down, QB Billy Ezell flipped to TE Billy Truax on a swing pass down the sideline for a first down at the Baylor 25. No one could know that would be LSU's only completion of the afternoon. After Don Schwab gained four up the middle, Ezell ran for a first down at the 10. Schwab got two before HB Buddy Soefker took a reverse around the left side into the end zone. Doug Moreau ran his PAT record to 16-for-16.

Score: LSU 7 Baylor 0 (7:18)

Don Schwab runs after taking the handout from Billy Ezell (11) (*Gumbo* Class of 1964).

Billy Ezell fakes a pass (*Gumbo* Class of 1964).

The Bears gained one first down before having to punt. After stopping the Tigers, the Bears started their first real threat with HB Tom Davies gaining 14 on a draw play to the LSU 46. FB Dalton Hoffman got nine, then three for another first down.

LSU 7 Baylor 0

SECOND QUARTER

The Bears dominated the period, running 26 plays to LSU's four, but failed to score. On third-and-15, Trull hit Ingram for 30 yards to the 21. But Remi Prudhomme broke through and tossed Don for an 11-yard loss, and DT Milton Trosclair tackled Elkins for a loss of seven. So Eddie Whiddon punted to the four where Ingram caught the ball in the air, which drew a 15-yard penalty.

Facing eight- and nine-man lines but refusing to pass, LSU went three-and-out. So Neumann punted to the Baylor 42. Trull led the Bears downfield against the Chinese Bandits, connecting with Pickett for four, then Elkins for 14 to the LSU 40. Two plays later, Hoffman picked up 12 but fumbled, and DB Dwight Robinson recovered at the 26.

When Neumann shifted field position with a punt to the Baylor 18, Trull got his offense moving again. Four completions made it first-and-10 at the LSU 34. With the defense reeling from the aerial circus, Hoffman picked up 10 for another first down at the 24. Two snaps later, Trull ran down the middle for 11 to the eight. But again the Tigers rose up and repelled the threat, starting with an 8-yard sack. After an incompletion in the end zone, the Tigers chased the quarterback all over the field before he managed to drop a pass over the middle to Hoffman to restrict the damage to a 3-yard loss. Baylor lined up for a field goal, but holder Trull instead got up and passed to Davies, who was dropped for another 3-yard loss with just four seconds left in the half. Trull had already broken the Bluebonnet Bowl record of 11 completions in a game.

LSU 7 Baylor 0

THIRD QUARTER

Baylor continued to wear down the valiant LSU defense, running 21 plays to just nine for the Bengals. After an exchange of punts, the Bears stormed upfield from their 16. Trull completed a pass for 14, but Elkins lost six on a pitchout. No problem as Trull found

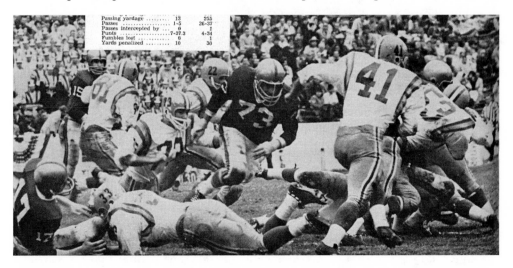

Mike Vincent breaks loose against the Bears. No. 81 is Danny Neumann, 33 is Buddy Soefker, 22 is Joe Labruzzo, and 53 is Bill Bass (*Gumbo* Class of 1964).

Ingram for 18 and a first down at the 41. Hoffman's 8-yard run and a sneak by Trull moved the chains into Tiger territory at the 48. With LSU double covering Elkins all afternoon, Trull found Ingram for 11 on third-and-seven to the 34. Davies bulled for 14 on a draw to the 20 before Trull hit Hodge with a 10-yard pass. Pickett brought the Green and Gold fans to their feet when he swept to pay dirt, but the elation was short-lived as Baylor was penalized for holding to the 22. After an incompletion, Soefker stepped in front of a Trull heave at the 10 and returned it 7 yards to repel yet another onslaught.

But the defense had little time to rest since the Tigers went three-and-out and punted to the 32. This time, the Bears were not to be denied. Runs by Hoffman and Bobby Mitchell gained a first down. Then, on third-and-14, Don kept the drive alive with a 31-yard completion to Ingram, who eluded E Kenny Vairin. Mitchell gained seven to the 22.

LSU 7 Baylor 0

FOURTH QUARTER

After a run for another first down, Ingram took a throw to the five. Trosclair registered his second sack of the afternoon to give Tiger fans hope for another goal line stand. But Trull took the next snap and fired to Ingram for a 7-yard TD. Ingram explained afterwards, "I had to use double fakes the entire game and hook back to get open. I also had to use delayed patterns."

Baylor 7 LSU 7 (13:10)

After more LSU offensive ineptitude, Neumann booted 39 yards to the 30. Trull moved his team from there to the winning TD. On third-and-three, the Trull-Elkins connection gained a first down at the 43. Then Don slipped past a gang of defenders for 11 into LSU territory. Two runs made it first-and-10 at the 36. Two plays later, Trull flipped to Elkins for 15 to the 19. Then Don went to his other flanker, Ingram, for nine. However, Mitchell lost three. But that setback was only temporary. On the next play, Dandy Don threw to Ingram at the one, and the elusive receiver squirmed over to give Baylor its first lead of the day.

Baylor 14 LSU 7 (5:20)

The Tigers needed a big play badly, and Labruzzo gave it to them. He took the kickoff on his three and raced up the middle into the clear, then broke to the sideline to the Baylor 25 where the kicker, the speedy Elkins, pulled him down. Afterward Trull said, "That kickoff return really scared me. I thought he was gone." Elkins: "I literally ran out of my shoes to catch him. I don't think my legs have ever carried me as fast." Labruzzo explained, "Willis Langley threw a good block to get me started. I saw daylight and just started running for it. When I cut toward the sideline, I didn't see anyone in front of me. I thought I was gone. But then I saw Elkins coming up out of the side of my eye. ... He must be quite a runner. Now I know how our poor defensive backs felt all day covering that guy."

After throwing only two passes the whole game, Ezell took to the air three times without success. After LeBlanc gained three on first down, Truax was wide open at the goal line, but Billy overshot him. When the fourth down pass slipped off Schwab's fingertips, Tiger hopes went down the drain. Baylor had time to penetrate LSU territory yet again, reaching the 32. Running out the clock on the last play of the game, Trull got off the cold ground flexing his right arm to throw a scare into the Baltimore Colts and Houston Oilers, both of whom had drafted him in the two competing pro leagues.

Final Score: Baylor 14 LSU 7

Trull, completing a personal best 26 passes, easily won the game's outstanding back award while Ingram took home the most valuable lineman trophy after setting Bluebonnet Bowl records with 11 receptions for 163 yards.

The game was not nearly as close as the score indicated. The first down discrepancy was an incredible 27–4 in favor of Baylor. The Bears gained 430 yards to just 116 for the Tigers.

Postgame

McClendon: "Baylor just had the football too much. They did a real fine job of executing their plays. We didn't play our game at all, and Baylor's defense was excellent. They controlled the ball and probably had it more than twice as much as we did" (80 plays to 37).

Labruzzo on Trull: "He's the greatest passer I've played against.... I've never seen anyone like him—not even in movies."

Bridgers was carried into the locker room on his players' shoulders. "I don't think I've ever been as proud of a bunch of boys." He described his team's performance as "the finest football game that I have ever seen a Baylor team play. ... Trull showed why he is great. LSU is one of the finest teams we have played, but we got them off balance. ... Nobody was ever guarded any better than Elkins today. ... We did some ball control of our own today with our throwing. This wasn't our game plan the way we had to pull it out, though. Our game plan was to get ahead and stay there."

McClendon shouldered his way into the locker room to congratulate his opposite number. "John, our boys are all saying what a great bunch of boys you have, as players and as persons. It hurts to lose, but it's not quite as hard when it's to a team like Baylor. I've told my sophomores they'll never have to worry any more in their whole lives about seeing any more or better passes."

Trull modestly praised his teammates. "Our entire team played a great game. The wind or wetness didn't bother us at all. ... I think it ought to be pointed out that our defense today did the greatest job it's ever done."

Seven 1963 Tigers played pro football: S White Graves, OL Dave McCormick, TE Doug Moreau, LB Mike Morgan, OL Remi Prudhomme, DL George Rice, and TE Billy Truax.

Sugar Bowl vs. Syracuse

"Their pursuit was terrific"

Tulane Stadium, New Orleans, Louisiana
January 1, 1965

The 7–2–1 Tigers earned their seventh trip to the Sugar Bowl while Syracuse finished 7–3 to gain a bowl bid for the sixth time in school history.

LSU's Season

Charlie McClendon continued with his three-unit system for 1964 although there was less two-way playing by the White Team. Charley Pevey, who today would be called the offensive coordinator, abandoned his tight formation offense in favor of a more wide-open pro look. One of the three backs who previously lined up behind the quarterback moved to a flanker. Junior Pat Screen provided both a passing and running threat from under center. He also handed off or pitched the ball to a pair of junior running backs, Joe Labruzzo and Don Schwab. Don led the SEC in rushing with 683 yards.

The new offense produced only 12 points in the first two games, but that was enough to win both thanks to the stout defense: 9–6 over Texas A&M and 3–0 at Rice. The new attack produced 47 points in the next two contests to slay North Carolina 20–3 and Kentucky 27–7.

For the second year in a row, Billy Ezell took over at quarterback when Screen suffered an injury. A frustrating 3–3 tie with Tennessee when Doug Moreau missed three field goal attempts inside the 30 preceded a thrilling 11–10 triumph over Ole Miss thanks to a two-point conversion in the final minutes.

Ranked #8 nationally, LSU renewed its series with Alabama that had lain dormant since 1958. The #3 Crimson Tide handed the Tigers their first defeat of the season, 17–9 in Birmingham. After beating Mississippi State (14–10) and Tulane (13–3), LSU accepted the Sugar Bowl invitation. But the regular season wasn't over. Florida's October 3 visit to Tiger Stadium had been postponed because of Hurricane Hilda. Led by sophomore QB Steve Spurrier, the Gators chewed up the Tigers 20–6.

The Opponent

Ben Schwartzwalder had been Syracuse's head coach since 1949. His 1959 team, led by great RB Jim Brown, finished 11–0 to earn the #1 ranking in the final Associated Press poll.

Competing as an independent, the Orangemen lost their opener at Boston College, then rattled off four victories in a row, the most notable being a 39–0 rout of UCLA and a 21–14 triumph at archrival Penn State. A transcontinental trip to Oregon State resulted in a 31–13 loss. After defeating Pittsburgh, Army, and Virginia Tech to run their record to 7–2, Syracuse accepted the bid to the Sugar Bowl. Then the Orangemen lost their final game, 28–27 to West Virginia. That, coupled with LSU's loss to Florida, robbed the South-vs-East matchup of much of its luster.

Syracuse was led by "the finest one-two punch the East had seen since the days of Glenn Davis and Doc Blanchard" at West Point. Sophomore HB Floyd Little wore the same #44 that had identified two previous Orange greats, Brown and Heisman Trophy winner Ernie Davis. Floyd gained 828 yards on 149 carries during the 1964 season. Yet that total didn't lead the team. That distinction went to senior FB Jim Nance, who ran for 951 yards. The Orangemen averaged almost 200 more yards of rushing per game than passing. Floyd and Nance scored 25 touchdowns between them—14 more than LSU scored as a team. Stopping either one of their bruising ball carriers would challenge any defense. Stopping both would take a super effort from the Chinese Bandits.

Participation of the two African American backs in the Sugar Bowl had been made possible a year earlier when the U.S. Supreme Court ruled that Louisiana's law requiring racial segregation at public athletic events was unconstitutional. Freed from that restraint, the Sugar Bowl could scan the entire nation for the best opponent for the Southeastern Conference host team.

The Game

LSU was installed as a 5½ point favorite. A crowd of 60,000, the smallest for a Sugar Bowl since 1939, gathered on a sunny day to watch the first gridiron meeting of the Tigers and Orangemen.

FIRST QUARTER

Baton Rouge *Morning Advocate* writer Bud Montet wrote, "The Tigers played the first half with their usual disinterest in Sugar Bowl proceedings." LSU received the kickoff, but a 15-yard penalty back to the 11 forced a punt to midfield by Gerald "Buster" Brown. Syracuse surprised the Tigers by moving regular QB Walley Mahle to halfback with Rich King under center. The Orangemen immediately drove to the first points of the game. King hit Mahle for 9 yards before Jim Nance and Mahle combined for seven on the ground, and Floyd Little gained another nine to make it first-and-ten at the 25. Little then broke loose for 18 yards to the seven where DB Jerry Joseph hauled him down. However, a 15-yard penalty forced Syracuse to settle for their first field goal of the season—a 23-yarder by Roger Smith.

Score: Syracuse 3 LSU 0 (9:12)

The Orangemen sprang another surprise on the Tigers on defense. LSU T George Rice said after the game, "We had trouble blocking the first half mainly because they were in a goal-line defense most of the half ... and we didn't expect it all over the field like that." After another 15-yard penalty stopped the Tigers, Brown booted to the Syracuse 42 where Charley Brown fumbled, and C Richard Granier recovered for LSU. But the Tigers could not capitalize, and Buster booted to the three. On first down, 250-pound T George Rice burst through and tackled Little in the end zone for a safety. Floyd said afterward, "That guy must have come out of the ground." Rice explained, "Their tackle was pointing to the outside. I figured they were going wide, so I gambled and shot the gap."

Syracuse 3 LSU 2

Neither team could move on the next three possessions. So Brown came in for his fourth punt. This time, disaster struck. Dennis Reilly broke through and blocked the punt off Buster's foot. Brad Clarke picked up the ball at the 30 and sped untouched to the end zone. Smith booted the PAT. Reilly explained after the game: "That end lined up a bit too wide, and I got through before he could come in.... Brad scooped it up and ran faster than he has in a long time." Brown explained, "They had a defensive stunt on. The snap was a little high, and I had to reach for it. I don't remember even seeing the man until he blocked it."

Syracuse 10 LSU 2 (0:04)

George Rice tackles Floyd Little for a safety. No. 11 is Billy Ezell, 81 is Beau Colle, 50 is Richard Granier, 67 is Remi Prudhomme, and 70 is Charles Simmons (The Historic New Orleans Collection, Gift of the Sugar Bowl).

SECOND QUARTER

After the teams exchanged three-and-outs, LSU gained the initial first down of the quarter on three runs by HB Gawain DiBetta. QB Pat Screen connected with FB Don Schwab for 15 more to the Syracuse 38. Then a 13-yard sack brought Buster in again for a punt to the two. Four plays later, LSU got the ball back at the Syracuse 43. But the Tigers again failed to exploit the advantage. After two incompletions, Screen's third aerial ended up in the hands of DB Ted Holman, who returned 13 yards to the 35. With LSU stifling his running game, King tried two passes that failed. So he rocketed a punt 60 yards to the Tiger 11, Labruzzo returning to the 16. Little Joe ran for eight and Schwab for 11 to get a quick first down, but it wasn't long before Brown kicked again. Two plays later, the horn ended the half. LSU had 77 yards of total offense, two more than Syracuse. The offenses accounted for only three of the 12 points on the scoreboard.

Syracuse 10 LSU 2

THIRD QUARTER

After Syracuse's opening drive was derailed by a 15-yard penalty, LSU finally cranked up a touchdown drive. The 75-yard march featured runs by Labruzzo and Schwab as well as a crucial 9-yard pass from Ezell to Joe for a first down. When a holding penalty pushed

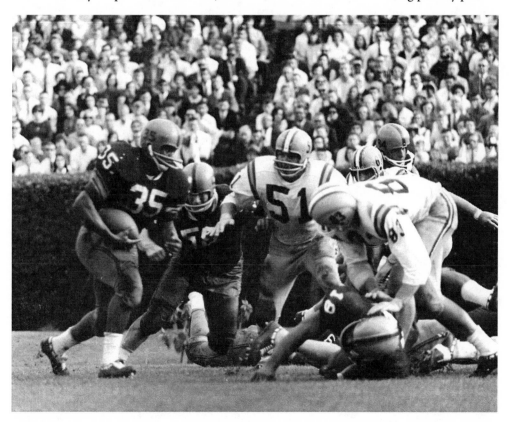

Ruffin Rodrigue (51) and Beau Colle (81) converge on Jim Nance (The Historic New Orleans Collection, Gift of the Sugar Bowl).

the Tigers back from the Syracuse 40 to their 43, Brown began warming up his leg again. But on the next play, Ezell called "I-26-wide-and-go," which sent Moreau out as the lone receiver. In the opening period, Doug had beaten DB Will Hunter by 15 yards on the same play, but Ezell overthrew him. This time Billy faked a throw down the middle, then lofted the ball to Moreau who was 10 yards behind the secondary at the 25. The Tiger flanker caught the ball in stride and raced to pay dirt. "I just ran towards the sidelines, faked, cut out and was wide open," said Moreau. "Most teams in the Southeastern Conference give you the short passes, but Syracuse was just the opposite. They played us tight up close but loose in the deep secondary." Ezell explained, "It looked like they were playing Doug tight. I asked him and decided to see if the safety man might go for a fake." LSU went for two and succeeded on Ezell's pass to Labruzzo running a wheel route out of the backfield.

Syracuse 10 LSU 10 (7:35)

Syracuse stayed on the ground, moving from their 22 to the LSU 34. Included was Nance's longest run of the day—20 yards to the LSU 45. After the Tigers threw Little for a 6-yard loss, Mahle, back at quarterback, hit E Jim Cripps at the 19. Facing third-and-five, Mahle tried a pass that DB White Graves plucked out of the air at the five. "I saw Little open at the goal line, and I watched the cornerback," said Mahle. "Whoever intercepted the ball must have had good pursuit because I never did see where he came from." Schwab gained five on the final play of the period.

Syracuse 10 LSU 10

FOURTH QUARTER

The Tigers moved out to the 26 before having to punt. A clipping penalty on the return put Syracuse back at their 20. On third down, the Orangemen tried some trickery. King pitched to Mahle who lateraled to Nance for 13 yards. But Syracuse soon had to punt. On LSU's possession, Screen, who was scheduled to undergo an operation on his knee three days after the game, broke around right end and scampered down the sideline for 23 yards to the Tiger 48. "Their end made a fool out of me on the previous play," said Screen. "I rolled right, and he gave me a shoulder fake. I thought he was coming up, and I flipped the ball back to DiBetta. But he went right for Gawain and dropped him for a loss. The next time, I was determined not to go for another fake. I just rolled right and ran." On third-and-13, Pat fired down the middle to Labruzzo, who caught the ball a split second before being grabbed by a defender for 36 yards to the Syracuse 19. Joe explained, "I ran that route three times, and I was wide open each time. Once the pass was underthrown, another time it was overthrown, and the last time it was right on the mark." Already in field goal range, the Tigers gained only eight on three plays. So after a timeout, Moreau, who had been limping after a collision on the previous play, booted a 28-yard field goal out of Ezell's hold. Not only did it give the Tigers the lead, but it also tied the NCAA record of 13 three-pointers in a season. "The angle didn't bother me," said Doug. "The kick felt good when it left my shoe. Then, before I looked up, Billy screamed, 'It's good!' We were in a similar situation in the Mississippi State game. I was a little bushed from running routes, and I didn't get a chance to rest before trying the field goal and missed. This time we called time out so that I could take a breather. It worked."

LSU 13 Syracuse 10 (3:55)

Doug Moreau kicks the winning field goal. No. 42 is Don Schwab, 78 is George Rice, and 84 is Billy Masters (*Gumbo* Class of 1965).

Trailing for the first time, Syracuse converted a third-and-three on a draw play to Nance to their 45. When King failed to connect on three straight passes, the Orangemen had to go for it on fourth down, but another incompletion turned the ball over to LSU at the 45 with 1:42 on the clock. Two Schwab runs gained a first down at the 35. Schwab for five and Ezell for seven moved the chains again and cemented the victory.

Final Score: LSU 13 Syracuse 10

Doug Moreau easily won the Miller-Digby Outstanding Player Award. The victory gave Charlie McClendon the distinction of being the first coach who had played in the Sugar Bowl to come back as head coach and win.

Postgame

The Tigers held Nance to 70 yards and Little to 40, their lowest combined total all year. Still, T Remi Prudhomme, one of LSU's six seniors, called the Syracuse tandem "the best we've ever faced. In fact, they were the only thing that kept them in the game." He added in response to a question, "No, playing against Negroes for the first time didn't bother me. They were just another bunch of football players as far as I was concerned."

In the Syracuse locker room, Coach Schwartzwalder said, "Their punting game beat us." But he also expressed disappointment in his offense. "We didn't have it when it counted. Anytime we hold 'em to 13 points, you've got to blame it on the offense when we lose."

Nance praised the Tiger defense, which held the nation's top offense without a touchdown. "Their pursuit was terrific…. Every time I thought I was in the clear, a whole bunch of white shirts players surrounded me." Little explained why he carried the ball only eight times. "The coach figured they would key on me, so he had me line up as a flanker most of the time. But I did run the pass route many times, and it tired me considerably. I was open every time I ran a route. Our quarterbacks just couldn't get the ball to me." Nance and Little agreed that LSU showed no prejudice. Both said all comments from the Tigers were favorable.

Rich King: "LSU has a good ball club. They hit hard and gave me several good licks during the game. All in all it has been a wonderful trip. But I'm sorry we let them come back and win. The coach had told us it might be rough, and that Moreau's toe might be disastrous."

Postscript

LSU T George Rice: "I remember the banquet that night after the game we were sitting there wondering if the black players would sit next to us. I guess we were nervous because we weren't sure how to act. People had told us so many things. Floyd Little and Jim Nance came and sat next to us, and they were the best guys I have ever met. The one white guy in the group was the worst. I thought, *This is not a bad deal after all.* … It was … a great awakening for me."

Eight 1964 Tigers played pro football: OL John Demarie, DE Tommy Fussell, S White Graves, E Billy Masters, OL Dave McCormick, TE Doug Moreau, OL Remi Prudhomme, and DL George Rice.

Cotton Bowl vs. Arkansas

"The sickest I've ever been in coaching."

Cotton Bowl, Dallas, Texas
January 1, 1966

Despite a disappointing 7–3 record, the Tigers received a bid to play undefeated Arkansas in the Cotton Bowl.

LSU's Season

Snakebitten coach Charlie McClendon had lost his starting quarterback four seasons in a row. So he gave talented sophomore Nelson Stokley playing time so that he could take over should senior Pat Screen go down again.

The Tigers began the season #8 in the Associated Press poll and rose to #5 after victories over Texas A&M and Rice. But a loss at Florida dropped them out of the rankings before they moved back into the Top Ten with three straight victories. Then McClendon's quarterback plan took an unexpected twist when Stokley suffered a knee injury in the 23–0 loss to Ole Miss that ended LSU's second stay in the AP Top 10. The season cratered the following week with a 31–7 home loss to #5 Alabama.

Screen rallied the troops for a 37–20 triumph over Mississippi State and the third 62–0 rout of Tulane. LSU Athletic Director Jim Corbett, helped by SEC Commissioner Bernie Moore, LSU's coach for its first five bowl games, brokered an invitation to the Cotton Bowl for the 7–3 Tigers.

The Opponent

Coach Frank Broyles's eighth Arkansas team completed its second straight undefeated season to run their winning streak to 22 games. After leading the nation in scoring defense in 1964, the '65 Razorbacks boasted the top scoring offense in the nation (32.4 points per game). They finished second to undefeated Michigan State in both the AP and UPI Coaches regular season polls. The Southwest Conference champions defeated two LSU opponents, Texas A&M and Rice, by identical 31–0 scores. The talented Hogs boasted two All-Americans in OT Glen Ray Hines and DT Lloyd Phillips. They also filled ten of the 23 spots on the all-conference team. It's no wonder that the Razorbacks were eight- to 10-point favorites.

During the weeks of bowl preparation, Coach Mac dressed his scout squad in red jerseys all bearing the number 23 as a constant reminder of his team's goal of preventing the Porkers' 23rd consecutive victory. Mac privately felt confident that his offense would be able to run on the Arkansas defense, which surrendered more than 400 yards in a tight 27–24 win over Texas.

Arkansas and Texas fans and media complained that LSU wasn't worthy to play in the Cotton Bowl. Beating a three-loss team would not help the Razorbacks climb to the top spot in the final AP poll, which was postponed until after the bowl games for the first time. But Coach Broyles knew the Tigers were a formidable foe. "Charley McClendon's sitting behind a rock with a great football team. Don't let that 7–3 record fool you." But his admonition fell on deaf ears, as several incidents after the Tigers arrived in Dallas illustrated. The Hog faithful mocked the Tigers by yelling "LS-Who?" One arrogant writer asked McClendon, "How bad do you expect your team to lose?" As the LSU players walked through the lobby of their hotel, a woman with a red Porker hat shouted, "Look. They're going to show up for the game."

The Game

A record 76,200 spectators gathered for a rematch of the 1947 Cotton Bowl on a day so overcast the stadium lights were turned on by the 1 p.m. kickoff.

First Quarter

The teams sparred through the first half of the period. After Arkansas punted into the end zone, Pat Screen started at quarterback for LSU. He directed an offense that was slightly different from the one Arkansas saw on film. Joe Labruzzo, the speedy 5'9" 170-pound tailback, lined up deeper than usual to give him a split second longer to choose a path based on the defensive alignment. But Labruzzo's first impact came on a 19-yard reception from Screen. However, a holding penalty disabled the drive. So Buster Brown punted to the Arkansas 13.

The Hogs moved from there to the game's first score. The biggest of the 11 plays were two completions by junior QB Jon Brittenum. The first covered 29 yards to HB Harry Jones. The second came from the LSU 19 to WR Bobby Crockett, who snagged the ball at the 14 and tight-roped down the sideline to the end zone. Ron South converted.

Score: Arkansas 7 LSU 0 (3:35)

When the defensive target of the touchdown pass, junior CB Jerry Joseph, returned to the LSU sideline, he told secondary coach Bill Beall, "I can't handle Crockett by myself. It's just not possible. This guy is just too good." So Beall said LSU would go to a "bracket" defense on the perimeter. Joseph would still cover Crockett but would "follow" him in his routes instead of trying to stay with him step for step. "As soon as the receiver turned," Joseph recalled, "you turned." Joseph would also receive help from S Sammy Grezaffi, LSU's fastest player.

So far, the game was proceeding as predicted. A turning point in momentum came on Arkansas' next possession, which carried into the second period.

Arkansas 7 LSU 0

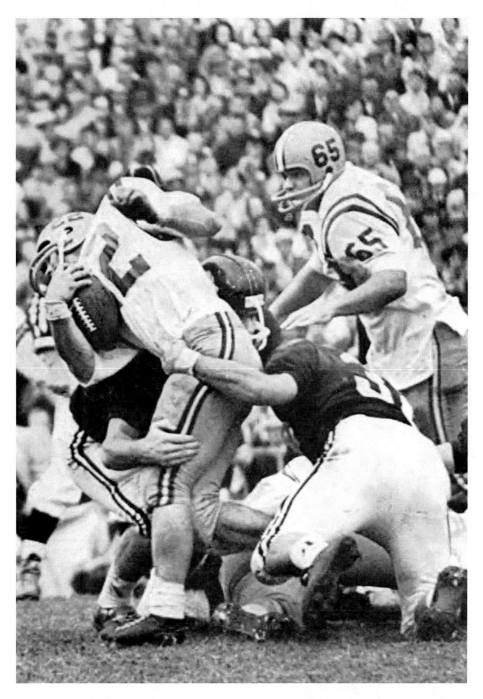

Joe Labruzzo fights for yardage as John Aaron (65) blocks (*Gumbo* Class of 1966).

SECOND QUARTER

A 14-yard pass from Brittenum to Jones with a 15-yard penalty tacked on put the Razorbacks at LSU's 25. But the Tigers forced a field goal attempt from the 41 that went awry.

Nelson Stokley's knee had been so questionable that the Tigers hadn't counted on him playing at all. But needing a spark, McClendon sent him in. Nelson quickly fired an 18-yard strike to FB Don Schwab to the 47. After runs by Stokley and Jim Dousay moved the ball 5 yards past midfield, disaster struck. Nelson didn't get up after running a sweep and had to be carried from the field. To make matters worse, a clipping penalty pushed LSU back to their 40. So Screen faced first-and-25 as he put his helmet back on. After running for 11, he got 14 more on a pass to 6'5" TE Billy Masters, who alertly caught the ball after it bounced off a defender. Pat explained later, "We found that the linebacker would be firing in, and so we'd run the play." Dousay then crashed 2 yards to the 33 for an improbable first down. Pat kept handing the ball to Dousay, Labruzzo, and Masters, usually behind 240-pound LT Dave McCormack and 220-pound LG Don Ellen as well as FB Danny LeBlanc. The target was Arkansas' RT Jim Williams, who weighed only 205. Little Joe wiggled his way for 12 yards to a first-and-goal at the seven. Going with the hot hand, Screen handed to Labruzzo three more times for two, four, and then the touchdown. Doug Moreau's kick tied the game.

Arkansas 7 LSU 7 (4:15)

Williams said after the game, "They were double teaming me most of the time in the

Jim Dousay drags a Razorback with him. Allen LeBlanc (76) and Phil Johnson (54) look for someone to block (*Gumbo* Class of 1966).

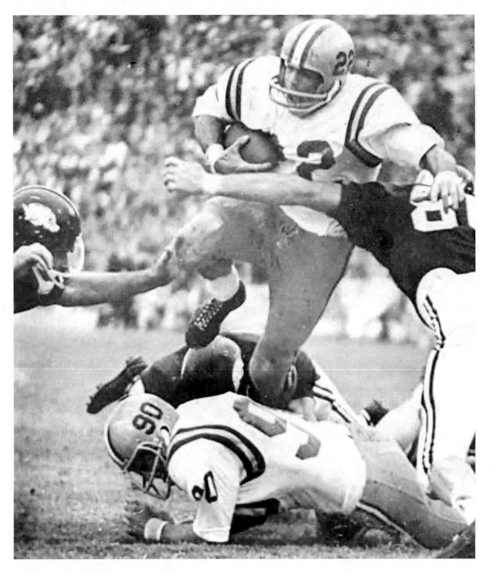

Joe Labruzzo scores his second touchdown, leaping over Lonny Myles (90) (*Gumbo* Class of 1966).

first half. And when they weren't, that big tackle, McCormick, would just stand up, and I couldn't see what was going on."

Arkansas suffered a setback one play after the kickoff when Brittenum left the field with a shoulder stinger after throwing a block. On third down, backup QB Ron South fumbled a handoff, and LB Bill Bass recovered at the 34. Smelling blood, Screen went to the air, hitting Moreau for 13. Then the Tiger offense got monotonous again. Why mess with success? Labruzzo hit left tackle for three, then 12 more. His next plunge put the pigskin at the two. Arkansas was waiting for him on the next snap, stopping him at the one. When Joe took it again, he was hit twice but wiggled, twisted, dug his cleats in, and eventually crashed into the end zone on the 16th play of the drive.

LSU 14 Arkansas 7 (0:18)

Screen explained the LSU strategy. "We had two good blockers on the left side in McCormick and Ellen, and we also were running away from their big tackle Lloyd Phillips."

LSU assistant coach Doug Hamley said he never experienced anything like what happened at halftime. "We couldn't hold the team in the dressing room. They got up four times and tried to leave, but Coach McClendon had to hold them back because the bands were still on the field."

THIRD QUARTER

A light drizzle started during halftime and continued intermittently the rest of the game. Brittenum returned for the second half but not Stokley. The Razorbacks dipped their toes in LSU territory before having to punt, Bobby Nix's boot being downed at the two. Four plays later, Brown kicked out to the LSU 49.

Intent on tying the score, Arkansas slashed to the LSU 15. On the next play, speedy Jim Lindsay took a deep pitchout and raced laterally across the field. LSU's defensive end on that side, Ernie Maggiore, was being blocked but as he went down, he spun his body around and threw his legs across Lindsey's path, tripping him for a 6-yard loss. Brittenum slipped down at the 28 on second down and then missed on a pass. So South tried a field goal from the 36 that fell short.

Arkansas' halftime adjustments thwarted the Tiger running game in the second half. As Williams explained, "I started stunting more to the right and the left after the half, and

Billy Masters runs behind the blocking of Danny LeBlanc (26), Joe Labruzzo (22), and John Aaron (65) (*Gumbo* Class of 1966).

we stopped them more." LSU gained field position when the teams traded punts the rest of the period. Nix's effort traveled just 19 yards to the LSU 46. The period ended with no Tiger first downs.

LSU 14 Arkansas 7

FOURTH QUARTER

With Dousay hacking away for short yardage, the Bengals moved relentlessly to the two before facing fourth-and-goal. Moreau was asked to convert a chip-shot field goal from the nine to put the Tigers two scores ahead. But the holder of the national record with 14 field goals in 1964 missed it. Doug said afterward, "No excuses. The angle wasn't particularly hard. Nervousness didn't have anything to do with it."

Given new life, the Razorbacks started moving again. Brittenum fired passes to Crockett for eight, 16, and 18 yards—three of his Cotton Bowl-record ten receptions during the afternoon. Following Bobby Burnett's 18-yard blast up the middle to the LSU 36, Jon tried another bomb to Crockett, but CB Joseph, who had been the target of the previous completions, intercepted at the 20 with 4:39 left on the clock. Jerry said afterward that the Tigers shifted from a man-to-man pass defense to half man-to-man and half zone in the second half to contain Crockett. "He'd been going wide on me. I decided the next time he came down wide, I was going to cut in front of him. He did, and I cut in front…. All of a sudden, there was the ball, and I caught it."

The Tigers ate up almost two minutes before having to punt. Brown boomed a 49-yarder to the 11. The Hogs didn't go down easily. Brittenum filled the air with passes in a last gasp drive that carried to the LSU 24 before time ran out.

Final Score: LSU 14 Arkansas 7

Joe Labruzzo, who carried the ball 21 times for 69 yards, won the Outstanding Back Award, and Dave McCormack took home the Outstanding Lineman Award.

Postgame

When the Tigers reached their locker room, they shredded a red jersey bearing No. 23. Coach Mac, standing on a trunk to be heard over the jubilation, told them, "The rest of your lives, you won't ever forget what you did today."

Talking to the press, he proclaimed the victory his greatest thrill since his playing days at Kentucky when the Wildcats snapped Oklahoma's 32-game winning streak in the 1951 Sugar Bowl. "Fellas, we beat a good football team. … We slowed them down and made them play our type of game. I told you writers before the game that we couldn't match their speed, and we couldn't. But we played control ball and came up with the big play. Our kids followed instructions right to the end. … We didn't have a fumble or pass interception. There were times when it looked like we should pass, but we weren't going to put the ball into the air and give them the chance for that interception. They'll kill you. … I just told Pat Screen before the game, 'Let's go after them with everything we've got.' He said, 'Coach, I think I'm ready.'"

Labruzzo said, "This is the greatest victory since Lockport beat Larose. … Arkansas is every bit as good as everyone says they are. It was the breaks that did it. Our line made the difference. This is the best that they have ever blocked. … The turning point was when we recovered that fumble right before the half and scored the second time."

LT Dave McCormick: "Don Ellen and I were doubling back and forth all day on Williams. I can't take anything away from him. I did better than I anticipated against Williams, but he's a tremendous player."

DT George Rice was impressed with the Razorbacks. "They ran like I thought they would. They were quick, real quick. They remind me of Alabama. … The coaches did an excellent job of scouting them. Arkansas did everything that I had expected them to do, except for that reverse and the screen pass. We didn't even know they had the reverse, and Arkansas never has run a screen."

Dejected Arkansas coach Frank Broyles had little to say. "It hurts. They just beat us. … I thought we had a chance until that interception. … We knew LSU could run good, and they did. They hurt us on key downs passing, and they blocked real good. … That Labruzzo is a real good runner. He and the entire LSU team are to be congratulated." Broyles said QB Jon Brittenum was favoring his injured shoulder in the second half. "But he still did a great job." Years later, the College Football Hall of Fame coach recalled the '66 Cotton Bowl as "the sickest I've ever been in coaching."

DT Jim Williams proclaimed McCormick as "the greatest tackle I've ever faced. If anyone ever deserves to be All-American, he does." Several Razorbacks commented that LSU was not only the best team they had played but the hardest-hitting. They congratulated the Tigers on their cleanly contested, hard-earned victory. WR Crockett summed it up. "We went out there and played, and played hard, and we just got beat. They had a heck of a football team."

The final AP poll placed the Razorbacks at #3. LSU catapulted to #8.

Seven 1965 Tigers played pro football: OL John Demarie, DE Tommy Fussell, LB John Garlington, TE Billy Masters, OL Dave McCormick, TE Doug Moreau, and DL George Rice.

Sugar Bowl vs. Wyoming

*"LSU kept sending in players
with nice clean jerseys"*

Tulane Stadium, New Orleans, Louisiana
January 1, 1968

Despite three losses and a tie in 11 games, LSU received an invitation to the 34th Sugar Bowl. Their opponent was a cinderella team from out west that sported a 4–0 record in bowl games.

LSU's Season

The Tigers dedicated their 1967 season to the memory of Athletic Director Jim Corbett, who died at age 47 from a heart attack in late January. Starting in 1954, he built LSU into a perennial football power.

QB Nelson Stokley underwent his third operation in two years in the spring. Entering his senior year, he had played only eight full games at quarterback the previous two seasons. Given that the Tigers were coming off a 5–4–1 season, lost seven defensive starters, and faced a tough schedule, *Playboy* magazine forecast a 2–8 record.

With a new split-back offense that employed wide receivers on both sides, the Tigers staged a dramatic 75-yard drive to score with 0:29 left to defeat Rice 20–14 despite giving up 454 yards to the Owls. The defense tightened the screws the following week in a 17–6 triumph over Texas A&M. With Steve Spurrier graduated after going 3–0 vs. LSU, the Tigers traveled to Gainesville and whipped the Gators 37–6. Next, another Florida team, Miami, came to Baton Rouge and dealt the Bengals their first defeat, 17–15. Following a 30–7 romp at Kentucky, the Tigers went almost a month without another win. They lost to Tennessee 17–14, tied Ole Miss 13–13, and fell at home to Alabama, 7–6, in a fray that had no scoring until the final period. LSU cemented its bowl bid with a 55–0 romp over Mississippi State and a 41–27 victory over Tulane. The Tigers' 6–3–1 record was misleading since they were only 10 points away from a perfect season.

The Opponent

Wyoming of the Western Athletic Conference fashioned a dream season spearheaded by the nation's #1 rushing attack. The 10–0 record was even more remarkable considering that the Cowboys hosted only four home games. Their victims included both Arizona and Arizona State as well as Colorado State, Brigham Young, and Utah. As the nation's only undefeated, untied team, Coach Lloyd Eaton's club ranked #6 in the final Associated Press poll. Nevertheless, the oddsmakers installed LSU as a six-point favorite.

The Cowboys led the nation in rushing defense (42.3 yards per game) and total defense (185.2 yards per game). The sparkplug of the offense was RB Jim Kiick, who would join with FB Larry Csonka to form the duo dubbed "Butch Cassidy and the Sundance Kid" for the undefeated 1972 Miami Dolphins.

Coach Charlie McClendon was impressed by the Cowboys. "They have the kind of speed and quickness that makes for a good football team. They have been behind and came on to win. Our best defense would seem to be control the ball."

Coach Eaton felt the weight of representing his conference in a major bowl. "We feel we play fine football in the Western Athletic Conference, and we feel that in the future the major bowls will be looking to our conference for team selections."

The Game

The crowd of 78,963 gathered on a chilly, overcast day for a game played on a field still muddy from rain the day before. They saw Wyoming dominate the first half and LSU the second thanks to the efforts of the Most Valuable Player, who didn't take the field until the third period.

FIRST QUARTER

The Tigers got two scoring opportunities but were kept at bay by the fired-up Cowboy defense. After speedy Sammy Grezaffi, battling the flu, returned the kickoff to the 26, QB Nelson Stokley missed on two passes sandwiched around a 2-yard run. It was the start of a dreadful first half for the senior signal-caller in which he completed only one of nine attempts. "My hands were wet and muddy," Stokley said after the game, "but most of the time I was just throwing off balance and not getting the ball to my receivers in the first half."

Wyoming took Mitch Worley's punt at its 35 and moved into LSU territory. QB Paul Toscano, fighting the butterflies while playing before the largest crowd of his career, rolled left and threw on the run to WR Hub Lindsey for 16 yards to the 26. But the next three plays gained only five. So All-American K Jerry Depoyster tried a field goal that was blocked by DT Fred Michaelson, LSU recovering at the Wyoming 46. Depoyster said, "I saw him come through near the center and couldn't do anything about it. That was only the second one I've had blocked this year."

With Wyoming's fine CBs Vic Washington and Dick Speights halting pitchouts and sweeps, Tommy "Trigger" Allen gained only 8 yards on three runs before Stokley tried a fourth-down sweep that lost three. But the Tigers were back in business two plays later when Toscano's pass went through the hands of WR Gene Huey to senior LB Benny Griffin, who returned 3 yards to the 32. When three plays netted only 2 yards, Roy Hurd came on for a 45-yard field goal try that fell short.

The Cowboys then started a 70-yard scoring march that continued into the next period. The biggest gains came on a 31-yard Toscano pass to TE George Anderson, Kiick's

13-yard run, and Toscano's keeper around the left side for 19 yards to the one where DT Donnie Bozeman hauled him down.

Score: LSU 0 Wyoming 0

SECOND QUARTER

Wyoming broke the scoreless tie on the first play when Kiick broke away from a host of Tigers into the end zone. Depoyster booted the PAT. Wyoming 7 LSU 0 (14:50).

On LSU's next possession, Stokley gained 19 yards on a broken play when he didn't have time to pass. But four plays later, Worley punted. CB Gerry Kent intercepted a Toscano pass at his 43 and returned to the Cowboy 40. But four running plays failed to produce a first down.

Tom Williams and Kiick took turns running the ball on a methodical march that reached the LSU 32 before Toscano finally threw a pass. Anderson snagged it for a first down at the 13. But the Tigers dug in, holding Kiick to 5 yards and Toscano to one before Kent knocked down a pass in the end zone. So Depoyster kicked a 24-yard field goal.

Wyoming 10 LSU 0 (2:58)

LSU needed to make a couple of first downs to at least run out the clock, but they couldn't even do that as DT Larry Nels threw Stokley for a 13-yard loss. So Wyoming got the ball back at midfield after the punt return. Kiick carried three times to move the ball to the 32. With time running out, Depoyster boomed the ball through the uprights for a Sugar Bowl record 49-yard field goal.

Nelson Stokley runs out of the pocket in second quarter action (*Gumbo* Class of 1968).

Wyoming 13 LSU 0

Some Tiger fans booed as their muddied warriors left the field. LSU ended the half with but a single first down and only 38 yards of offense. Wyoming had 11 first downs and 215 yards.

C Barry Wilson: "The field turned up a little sloppy, and it upset our plans to block Wyoming low. Because we weren't able to get solid footing, they merely pushed us off and got to the ball-carrier. They were also able to put a lot of pressure on Nelson. At halftime we decided to take advantage of their pursuit by starting to the outside and then running back against the grain."

THIRD QUARTER

Grezaffi returned the kickoff 32 yards to the 35. The Tiger possession started promisingly with Allen taking a pitchout for 11 yards into Wyoming territory. But on third down, Stokley missed badly on a pass down the middle. That forced a punt to the 16. Griffin and All-SEC DE John Garlington tossed Toscano for a 19-yard loss to bring in Depoyster, who rocketed a punt 60 yards to Grezaffi, who returned six to the LSU 31.

The LSU offense went from bad to worse. Stokley misfired on another pass, was tossed for an 8-yard loss, then couldn't complete a short toss to RB Kenny Newfield. So the overworked Worley kicked 45 yards to the 32. Sidestepping a blitzer, Toscano fired to Huey for 35 yards to the 31. After Kiick gained four, Wyoming was penalized back to the LSU 39 for holding. Kiick took a 10-yard swing pass to get back most of the penalty yardage. Then Garlington made another key play, breaking up the third down pass. Enter Depoyster for another 46-yard field goal attempt. He missed this time.

The Tiger offense changed when McClendon inserted his fourth tailback of the day, sophomore Glenn Smith, conspicuous in his clean white jersey and bright gold pants. With five other reserves in the lineup, the Tigers moved 80 yards for their first points of the day. Smith's first gain came on a 39-yard pass from Stokley to the Cowboy 39. "We caught their inside halfback napping," Smith explained. "I started out as if to run a flat route and then cut deep on a post route." Next, Glenn gained six, and FB Harold Stephens got one. Then Stokley threw to WR Tommy Morel down the middle at the goal line, but a trio of Cowboys converged to knock the ball out of his hands. On fourth down, Nelson hit RB Jim West for a badly needed first down at the 12. On the next snap, Stokley used his feet to scamper around left end to make it first-and-goal at the two. Smith carried twice, gaining a yard each time to finally put LSU on the board. Hurd kicked the point.

Wyoming 13 LSU 7 (2:10)

The Tigers soon got the ball back when Wyoming missed a first down by half a yard on three running plays. Grezaffi returned the punt 13 yards to the LSU 48. Newfield's 2-yard run ended the period. Wyoming 13 LSU 7

FOURTH QUARTER

Taking advantage of the fact that DT Nels was out with an injury, the Tigers kept running the same play. "We call it a 'G' play," explained Smith. "Their defensive tackle and end were pursuing so fast that I was able to cut back and go up the middle, and our line

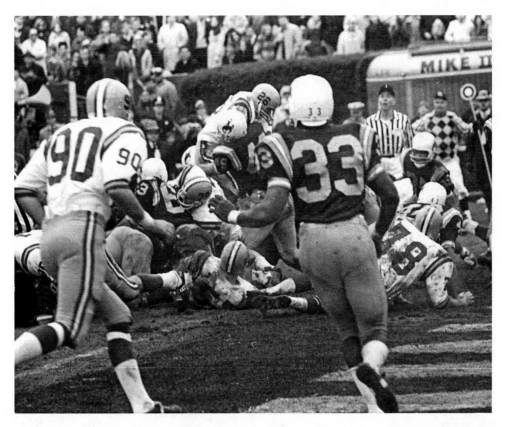

Glenn Smith goes over the top for LSU's first touchdown. No. 90 is Lonny Miles, 72 is Bill Bofinger, and 78 is Joe Reding (The Historic New Orleans Collection, Gift of the Sugar Bowl).

did a heckuva job blocking." Wyoming LB Bob Aylward explained the changes that LSU made on offense that allowed Smith to find running room. "We figured if we'd stop their option play, we could stop 70 per cent of their offense. In the second half, they came on with draws and traps, and we let down."

Embodying Vince Lombardi's mantra "Run to daylight," Smith picked up six yards at right tackle, then nine more at the same spot. Stokley changed the rhythm by rolling left and pitching to Morel, who stretched for the ball over the sideline with his feet in bounds for a first down at the 24. Keeping the momentum going, Stokley called his own number twice on either side of a 1-yard run by Smith. Nelson gained six around right end and seven the opposite way to move the chains to the 10. The Cowboys tried to draw the line there, holding Smith to three at right guard, then -1 on a pitchout. So Stokley fired to Morel in the end zone between two defenders for the tying touchdown. As he had done multiple times during the season, Hurd missed the extra point.

Wyoming 13 LSU 13 (11:39)

After several punts, Kiick tried a halfback pass, but DE Tommy Youngblood dropped back in front of the receiver and picked it off at the Tiger 36. But the Bengals couldn't move because Stokley missed on a third down pass to Morel. So Worley booted to the 32.

On the first play, Griffin snared his second interception of the day and returned it 24 yards to the Wyoming 31. This time, the Tigers capitalized on the turnover. Smith roared through a big hole up the middle and angled to his right for 16 yards and a first down at the 15. After Glenn got two more, Stokley rolled left and found Morel open at the goal line.

LSU 20 Wyoming 13 (4:32)

Tom Williams put the Cowboys in a hole by fumbling the kickoff out of bounds at the 14. Toscano kept for 13 yards at right end. Then four more runs moved the pigskin to a first down at the 39. After a pass to Kiick gained 10 and another to Williams got four, the turnover bug bit Wyoming for the fifth time. Showing the skill that would earn him a ten-year NFL career, Garlington hit Toscano with a driving tackle, forcing a fumble that John covered at the Wyoming 43.

With LSU staying on the ground to run out the final 1:37, the Cowboys used their remaining timeouts and forced the Tigers to punt to the 18 with 39 seconds left.

Just as LSU fans breathed a sigh of relief that the Tigers had clinched the hard-earned victory, a freak play nearly upset the apple cart. With the ball on the Wyoming 31 after a sideline pass to Kiick, Toscano tossed a long pass to WR Vic Washington at the Tiger 35. A trio of defenders went up for the ball with the receiver but succeeded only in deflecting it into the hands of TE Anderson who had alertly trailed the play. He set sail for the goal with no one in his path. Fortunately, CB Barton Frye had raced over from the other side of the field and made a game-saving tackle at the 17 with less than ten seconds left. "I was just kinda running for my life," said Frye. "I don't recall what was going through my mind, but I knew I had to catch him. I thought we'd have an interception, and I was just coming across as the deep cover man when their end picked off the ball on the bounce."

With time for at most two plays, Toscano threw the ball away when he couldn't find an open receiver just in time to stop the clock with one second showing. An illegal procedure penalty on the play moved the ball back to the 22. Those five yards made a difference as the Cowboy quarterback hit Huey in stride cutting across the middle at the 10. Kent and several other Tigers converged and swarmed him under at the five as the clock reached 0:00. "I would have given half a year's salary for 10 more seconds," lamented Coach Eaton.

Final Score:
LSU 20 Wyoming 13

Glenn Smith won the Most Valuable Player Award thanks to

Barton Frye makes his game-saving tackle of George Anderson (The Historic New Orleans Collection, Gift of the Sugar Bowl).

gaining 74 yards—one less than Kiick—on 16 carries with two touchdowns, all in the second half.

Postgame

Coach McClendon was still shaky following the thrilling ending. "I tell you my heart was in my throat right there at the end. Frye made a great defensive play for us. That last long gain of theirs seemed like an eternity. I can't say enough good things about our team today. Although we were down 13–0 at the half, our kids never lost their poise and came back just like they've been doing all season. There was no doubt that the running of Glenn Smith gave us a great lift in the second half. He gave us the momentum we needed." Mac added, "There were many Tiger heroes today. The defense gave us many opportunities to score, and our number two offensive line did an excellent job in helping us move the ball in the second half."

New Orleans native Smith explained his motivation. "If Wyoming had beaten us, I wouldn't have been able to go home."

Coach Eaton rued his team's missed opportunities. "Dropped passes and interceptions hurt our offensive drives in the last half. And the Tigers got stronger and stronger. They played a good game, but we did not play our best ball. The muddy field surely hurt their ground attack, and I know it hindered our passing. We would have thrown more if it had been a dry day." He also cited LSU's depth as a factor. "LSU kept sending in players with nice clean jerseys, and we just ran out of gas in the second half. We were worried about Jim Dousay and Tommy Allen but had paid very little attention to Glenn Smith in preparing for the Tigers. He gave LSU a tremendous lift in the second half. He deserved the Most Valuable Player award."

Toscano agreed that the field conditions hurt his play. "The ball was wet, and I overthrew my receivers many times. I guess I was a bit nervous too." Toscano was frustrated that so little time was left after the long gain on the deflection. "I wish we could have run several more plays as I'm confident we would have scored. Then we could have gone for two points and perhaps won."

Jerry Depoyster was downhearted that he missed the 38-yard field goal attempt in the third quarter that would have put the Cowboys up 16–0. "It just missed being good. That would have given us a comfortable lead." He added, "I hope our losing will not give the impression that we are not a good football team. I think we gave a good account of ourselves."

Only three 1967 Tigers played pro football: LB John Garlington, RB Eddie Ray, and OL Godfrey Zaunbrecher.

Peach Bowl vs. Florida State

"What is the Peach Bowl going to do for an encore?"

Grant Field, Atlanta, Georgia
December 30, 1968

LSU and Florida State were invited to play in the inaugural Peach Bowl. The game matched two head coaches who had been assistants on Paul Dietzel's staff in Baton Rouge in the 1950s—Charlie McClendon of LSU and FSU's Bill Peterson.

LSU's Season

LSU finished the regular season with a 7–3 record and the #19 ranking in the final Associated Press poll. The Tigers' conquerors were Miami 30–0, Archie Manning and Ole Miss 27–24, and Alabama, 16–7. The victories included four over Southwest Conference foes—Texas A&M (13–12), Rice (21–7), Baylor (48–16), and TCU (10–7), in addition to traditional foes Kentucky (13–3), Mississippi State (20–16), and Tulane (34–10).

Dan Hardesty of the Baton Rouge *State Times Advocate* described the 1968 Tigers as "oft-criticized and sometimes booed...." Southpaw junior QB Mike Hillman led the Tigers with 787 passing yards after taking over for the injured Freddie Haynes in the last four games. The leading rusher was Kenny Newfield (441 yards), closely followed by Tommy Allen (398 yards).

The Opponent

The independent Seminoles finished the regular season 8–2. The losses were to Florida, 9–3, when the Gators held Bill Peterson's aerial circus to 17 fewer points than they scored in any other game that season. The other loss also came at home to Virginia Tech 40–22. The key victories were 24–14 at Maryland, 48–7 at North Carolina State, and a 40–20 upset of Houston.

The Seminoles were also led by a junior quarterback, Bill Cappleman, who had the best season of any FSU passer: 162-for-287 for 2,410 yards and 25 TDs. His main target, All-American Ron Sellers, broke the national record for career pass receiving yardage with 1,496 on 86 receptions.

When defensive assistant Bill Beall left after the regular season to become head coach at Baylor, McClendon assumed the responsibility of preparing the secondary for its biggest test of the season. "They do an exceptional job of throwing the ball, and we're just going to have to be in the path of what they throw," said Mac. "Our defense is going to have to rise to the occasion."

Florida State ruled as a touchdown favorite.

The Game

The 35,545 fans that came to Georgia Tech's Grant Field on a cold, rainy night (42° with wind gusting to 25 mph) were rewarded with a game that caused the UPI reporter to ask: "What is the Peach Bowl going to do for an encore? The first annual Peach Bowl was a dilly...."

FIRST QUARTER

The Tigers got off to a miserable start that carried into the second period. The opening kickoff bounced along the slippery turf to upback Mark Lumpkin, who dropped it. John Crowe recovered for FSU at the LSU 31. A flag was thrown as the ball was snapped on the next play, causing some Tigers to relax momentarily. FSU's leading rusher, FB Tom Bailey, didn't relax at all. He raced down the sideline for a touchdown that stood because the penalty was against LSU.

Score: Florida State 7 LSU 0 (14:46)

Each of the Tigers' first three possessions ended with a turnover. Hillman, who confessed after the game that he "got butterflies and was throwing too softly" in the beginning, sparked a promising drive starting with a pass to Bob Hamlett for 11 yards with 15 more added for roughing the passer. Next Mike connected with his favorite receiver, Tommy Morel, to the FSU 22. But on third-and-11, a heavy rush forced Hillman to throw wildly down the middle, and Bill Lohse made a diving interception at the 13. After forcing a three-and-out, the Tigers got the ball back at their 46. Aided by another 15-yard penalty and a Hillman-Morel connection for 13 yards, LSU reached the FSU 22. FB Kenny Newfield romped to a first down on the 10. But on the next snap, Newfield fumbled the pitch, and Dale McCullers claimed the ball for the Seminoles at the 15.

The Tigers' next possession began with a 20-yard run by Maurice LeBlanc to the FSU 36. However, he fumbled when hit, and Mike Page grabbed the ball for the Seminoles. To add to the Tiger woes, Gerry Kent, LSU's regular season defensive MVP who had worked for a month to cover Sellers, was injured on a punt return and lost for the evening. Barton Frye, hero of the 1968 Sugar Bowl, switched over from the other side of the field to help Don Addison and Buddy Millican double-team Sellers the rest of the way. The All-American would snare only one reception in the first half. As McClendon explained after the game, "the injury changed our defensive strategy and forced us to rush the passer more." The strategy worked. As Coach Peterson admitted afterward, "Nobody has gotten to our passer like LSU did."

After the teams exchanged punts, Florida State started from their 25. Cappleman, back to pass, ran behind an array of blockers to the LSU 41. Then Phil Abraira snared a pass to the 24.

Florida State 7 LSU 0

Second Quarter

On the second play, Cappleman used Sellers to clear out several defenders and tossed to Bull Gunter coming out of the backfield into the open area down the right sideline for a 21-yard touchdown. The PAT try sailed wide, which would have a ripple effect as the game progressed.

Florida State 13 LSU 0 (14:50)

Three straight possessions resulted in no first downs for either team. That's when trouble started for FSU. Cappleman was sacked for a loss of six to the 14. Then a double reverse that lost seven and an incompletion forced a punt that resulted in what both coaches called the turning point in the game. Craig Burns fielded Bill Cheshire's weak punt at the 39, wiggled his way through the first wave of Seminoles, and rolled into the end zone.

Florida State 13 LSU 7

A holding penalty and sacks on consecutive plays forced another Seminole punt. Starting from their 33, the Tigers moved to the FSU 16 behind Hillman's passing—22 yards to Newfield—and Maurice LeBlanc's running. But the Garnet and Gold defense rose up and pushed the Tigers back to bring on Mark Lumpkin for a 32-yard field goal.

Florida State 13 LSU 10

Bill Thompson's pick of a Cappleman pass gave LSU possession on their 42. E Bill Stober snagged passes for 18 and 20 yards to make it first-and-10 at the FSU 20. But the next three plays gained only nine. Following a delay of game penalty, Lumpkin's attempt to tie the score sailed wide from the 24 in the last seconds of the half.

Florida State 13 LSU 10

After the game, Mike Hillman revealed an adjustment he made at halftime to deal with the rain. "I was a little afraid to really turn the ball loose in the first half because it was wet. But during halftime, my receivers told me to throw it, and they'd catch it."

FSU made a change in hopes of giving Sellers more success in the second half after he caught only one ball in the first 30 minutes. "We made a position switch on Ron," said Peterson. "We moved him from flanker to split end. That way, there were two men going out together against the two men who stayed with Sellers all the way." Ron would catch seven the rest of the way.

Third Quarter

LSU came out in clean jerseys and dominated the third quarter, holding the potent Seminole offense to just one first down. Sacking Cappleman for a 12-yard loss to the 18, the Tigers forced a punt. The Tigers drove 51 yards to the go-ahead touchdown. The key play was a 28-yard pass from Hillman to Tommy Morel, who made a spectacular catch with CB Mike Page all over him. From the 12, Mike then rifled another bullet to the two to Hamlett, who dragged two defenders over the goal line.

LSU 17 Florida State 13 (10:54)

The Seminoles still couldn't move, but a fine punt put LSU on its 19. LeBlanc's running moved the pigskin to the 43 but no further. Quickly forcing another punt thanks to a sack inside the 10, the Tigers, using a nine-man front on kicks, pressured Cheshire into a 22-yarder to the FSU 45. Little Freddie Haynes, playing only briefly, completed a short pass and made a 5-yard run before Hillman returned with a play from the sideline that resulted in a 25-yard strike to Morel to the 11. Two plays later, Mike found Stober all alone in the back of the end zone.

LSU 24 Florida State 13

FOURTH QUARTER

The Seminoles needed a spark, and their passing duo provided it. Cappleman threw for most of the yardage on a 72-yard, 13-play TD drive. Sellers snagged passes for 11 yards and 14 for a first down at the LSU 12. On third down, an interference penalty made it first-and-goal at the two. After the Tigers stuffed a run for no gain, Cappleman tossed into the left flat, Ron making a leaping catch at the side of the end zone. Frye hit him hard in midair, and it appeared to some that Sellers came down out of bounds, but the officials ruled otherwise. FSU went for two, but Burns picked off the pass.

LSU 24 Florida State 19 (10:35)

Another short kickoff proved poison for the Tigers. A clothesline tackle caused RB Glenn Smith to lose the ball to Ron Wallace on the LSU 37. After a penalty, Cappleman hit E Jim Tyron for 31 yards, then tossed the ball to Sellers, who caught it falling over backward for another first down at the 12. On fourth-and-two from the four, Cappleman blooped a pass into the end zone to Sellers, who stretched his 6'4" frame over Frye's 5'11" to put FSU back in front. This time FSU completed the two-point conversion pass. Cappleman rolled right, turned, and threw back to Chip Glass wide open in the left side of the end zone.

Florida State 27 LSU 24 (6:15)

The Tigers responded with a relentless drive deep into FSU territory. First, Jim West returned the short kickoff 19 yards to the 39. On LSU's first offensive snap of the period, LeBlanc gained four, then three before Hillman connected with Stober for 14. But after Maurice got another seven on two runs, the Tigers went backward thanks to a 15-yard holding penalty. That set up the most talked-about play of the game for LSU. Hillman threw toward Morel who made a miraculous catch despite being sandwiched by two defenders for a first down at the 18. Two snaps later, the lefty quarterback faked a handoff, put the ball on his hip, and rolled right. With the defense still expecting him to pass, Mike kept on running until he went out of bounds at the three. LeBlanc needed only one try to knife into the end zone. It was a thrilling end to the senior's injury-plagued career. He explained, "That play was designed to make a first down or two points after a touchdown. But the play went so well we decided to use it then. Give the credit to our offensive line. They knocked them down like bowling pins all night."

LSU 31 Florida State 27 (2:39)

Trailing by four thanks to multiple missed PATs, the Seminoles needed a touchdown. Cappleman passed for two first downs, but Addison nailed the receiver after only a 1-yard gain on the next completion. Facing pressure up front and tight coverage, Bill misfired on his next two throws. On fourth down from the LSU 44, he put the ball on Sellers' hands a step from the sideline at the 20. But Frye leaped and tipped it away at the last moment. Asked how much hand he got on the ball, Barton replied, "This much," sticking up a little finger and laughing. "I knew they'd be throwing the ball to him, and I had to be ready. … That Sellers is the best. He's just great."

Final Score: LSU 31 Florida State 27

Hillman won the Offensive MVP award for completing 16-of-29 for 229 yards and two touchdowns. DE Buddy Millican took home the defensive trophy.

Postgame

Coach McClendon quoted his 10-year-old son, who came to his side after the game and yelled, "Daddy, we just get tough in the second half, don't we?" Charlie added, "I'm proud of this squad for coming up with a real big win. This coaching staff won't ever forget it. We did a good job on Sellers early in the game, but he came back to prove what a great player he is. It took a tremendous effort on the part of our entire squad to win this one, and we made adjustments well during the game. … I think we beat them at their own game [passing]."

Mike Hillman had extra motivation for the game. "My father is in the hospital with cancer.… I hope this helps him. … I played this one for him." He explained why he threw the ball so well in the rain. "I grew up and played high school ball in Southern Louisiana, and we get plenty of rain there. So I'm used to this."

Coach Peterson was philosophical in defeat. "Good football teams win the close ones, and LSU is a good football team. I was proud of the way our kids kept coming back." However, "we just couldn't get any consistency on offense." He also said, "I was worried at the half that we wouldn't be able to keep up with their substituting, and they wore us down late."

Two 1968 Tigers played pro football: RB Eddie Ray and OL Godfrey Zaunbrecher.

Orange Bowl vs. Nebraska

Irresistible force vs. immovable object

Orange Bowl, Miami, Florida
January 1, 1971

The Tigers finished the 1969 season 9–1 and ranked #8 in the AP poll. They expected to play #1 Texas in the Cotton Bowl. However, that plan was derailed when #9 Notre Dame decided to end its self-imposed bowl ban and play the Longhorns for the national championship. In the meantime, the Sugar Bowl committee invited Ole Miss to play #3 Arkansas. The LSU squad decided to ignore invitations from the Sun and Bluebonnet Bowls and stay home for the holidays.

LSU's Season

With the NCAA allowing an eleventh game in the regular season, the 1970 Tigers finished 9–2 to earn a bid to the Orange Bowl to play Nebraska.

As the Tigers began preseason practice, senior Buddy Lee and junior Butch Duhe vied for the starting quarterback position to replace Mike Hillman, who had graduated. But Duhe died suddenly of a brain hemorrhage. That tragedy opened up playing time for sophomore Bert Jones, whose performance on the freshman team the year before prompted observers to rank him as the school's best passing talent since Y.A. Tittle.

The Tigers stumbled out of the starting gate with a 20–18 home loss to Texas A&M on a desperation 79-yard pass-and-run with 13 seconds left. LSU rebounded with four straight wins over Rice, Baylor, Pacific, and Kentucky. Then came a big test—the first visit by an LSU team to Auburn since 1908. Thirteen-point underdogs, the visiting Tigers defeated Shug Jordan's squad 17–9. LSU completed an Alabama daily double the next week with a 14–9 victory over the Crimson Tide in Birmingham. After an easy home win over Mississippi State, LSU traveled to South Bend for their first-ever meeting with the Fighting Irish, who were ranked second behind Texas and sported the #1 offense in the country. Despite outweighing the Tigers at almost every position, the Irish struggled to move the ball. Notre Dame finally moved close enough to kick a 24-yard field goal in the fourth quarter for the game's only points.

Impressed by the Tigers' effort in South Bend, the Orange Bowl invited LSU to meet the Big Eight champion on condition that the Tigers win their last two games. By agreeing, LSU put itself in an Orange Bowl-or-nothing situation.

They defeated Tulane 26–14, but the Green Wave ended the LSU's streak of 12 straight games without allowing a rushing touchdown. The Tigers closed with Ole Miss in a game moved to the first Saturday of December for television. LSU completed an undefeated SEC season to win the conference championship by belting the Rebels 61–17 to finish #5 in the AP poll. Charlie McClendon was voted SEC Coach of the Year.

For the second straight year, the Tiger defense, led by three all-SEC players, DT John Sage, LB Mike Anderson, and All-American DB Tommy Casanova, allowed only one opponent to reach the 100-yard mark in rushing. In his two years on the varsity, Casanova had played some offense as well as defense. Called "an athlete of infinite grace," Tommy intercepted seven passes, returned punts for 491 yards and kickoffs for 334 yards as well as rushing for 302 yards. McClendon described him as "one of the most gifted athletes I ever had. There's no question he could have been an All-America running back and really could've jazzed up our offense. But I needed him more on defense."

The Opponent

Bob Devaney's ninth Nebraska team completed an undefeated season with the only blemish being a 21–21 tie at USC. Devaney rotated two quarterbacks—Van Brownson and Jerry Tagge—in every game. Nevertheless, led by sensational sophomore RB Johnny "The Jet" Rodgers, a future Heisman Trophy winner, the Cornhuskers averaged 37.2 points per game. They hung 51 points on Kansas State, 54 on Iowa State, and an amazing 65 on Oklahoma State.

After arriving in Miami, Devaney, the winningest coach in college football, expressed his concern about the long lapse since his team's last game on November 21. A member of the UPI Coaches Board, Devaney said, "I feel we're the best now, and I've been voting for us for No. 1 in the poll. If we're beaten in this game, then I would have to say LSU is the best in the country."

Tagge explained Nebraska's game plan as "keeping LSU off balance. We want to run when they think we're going to pass, and pass when they think we're going to run." He praised the Tigers. "They do a good job of disguising the defensive secondary. You never really can tell whether they're in a man-to-man or a zone defense, and if it's a zone, it's hard to tell what type. That means the passer … has less time to spot his primary and secondary receivers."

McClendon's Tigers had beaten three straight undefeated bowl opponents—Texas in the 1963 Cotton Bowl, Arkansas in the '66 Cotton Bowl, and Wyoming in the '68 Sugar Bowl.

By the time the Orange Bowl kicked off in the evening, the Cornhuskers had added incentive but also added pressure. Notre Dame knocked off #1 Texas in the Cotton Bowl, and Stanford upset #2 Ohio State in the Rose Bowl. That opened the door for #3 Nebraska, a touchdown favorite, to win the national championship.

The Game

A record crowd of 80,699 and millions more watching on NBC saw a game billed as the irresistible force, Nebraska's offense averaging over 400 yards per game, versus the immovable object, LSU's rushing defense, #1 in the nation for the second straight year.

First Quarter

Speedy Johnny Rodgers returned the kickoff 27 yards on the polyturf to the 39. QB Jerry Tagge came out throwing, flipping to TE Jerry List for 16 yards. After two runs netted only a yard, DT John Sage broke through to nail Tagge for a 12-yard loss and force a punt.

LSU suffered a setback on their first offensive series when leading rusher Art Cantrelle, who had personally outgained nine of 11 opponents, sprained his ankle and was lost for the evening. Chris Dantin filled the gap admirably and would finish as the game's leading rusher with 79 yards. Finding the beefy Huskers' forward wall a tough nut to crack, LSU went three-and-out.

From the LSU 47, Tagge tried a bomb to List, but Tommy Casanova and Craig Burns broke it up. After a motion penalty, Tagge hit SE Guy Ingles for a 13-yard gain that fell 2 yards short of the first down. So Jeff Hughes punted into the end zone.

With the Huskers stuffing the ground game, QB Buddy Lee, playing with an injured thumb, completed a 16-yard pass to TE Jay Michaelson. Two plays later, the 6'4" junior from Zachary LA, connected with WR Andy Hamilton, the national leader with 22.3 yards per catch, at the Nebraska 43. But Dantin fumbled, and DT Dave Walline pounced on the pigskin at the 44.

Nebraska quickly moved into Tiger territory. Tagge found List for 17 yards. Then Jerry got 13 on a draw play. HB Joe Orduna carried for the first time, gaining a first down at the 22. After an incompletion, Tagge was on target to List to the eight. Following another errant pass, Sage dropped Tagge for a 7-yard loss. On third down, a pass to Rodgers gained only five. So Paul Rodgers booted a 26-yard field goal.

Score: Nebraska 3 LSU 0 (2:41)

The Tiger offense didn't stay on the field long. Larry Jacobson blasted Lee on first down, causing a fumble that DE Willie Harper recovered on the 15. This time, the Cornhuskers would not be denied their touchdown. Orduna swivel-hipped to the three, then knifed over on the next play.

Nebraska 10 LSU 0 (2:06)

Sophomore Bert Jones took over at quarterback for LSU, but the Tigers went backwards thanks to a 16-yard sack. To make matters worse, Wayne Dickinson's punt went off the side of his foot for only 28 yards to the LSU 39. However, the Cornhuskers could not take advantage of the excellent field position.

Nebraska 10 LSU 0

Second Quarter

The Tigers again went backward against the "Blackshirts" defense. So Dickinson punted from the end zone. After signaling for a fair catch, Rodgers fumbled the ball, and G Jimmy Elkins was Johnny-on-the-spot at the LSU 40. Nothing came of the turnover except improved field position. When the Cornhuskers regained possession, Devaney sent in Van Brownson at quarterback. On third down, he tried his first pass, but senior DB Bill Norsworthy made his sixth interception of the season at the LSU 43. The Tigers managed to pick up one first down on a 16-yard screen pass to third-string TB Del

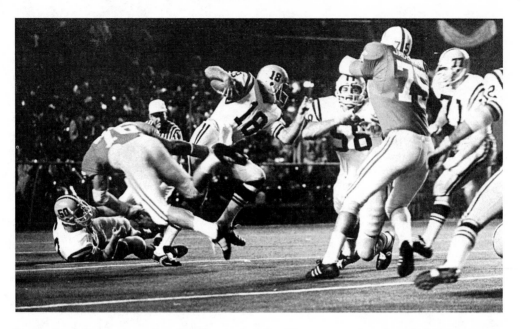

Buddy Lee tries to escape Dave Walline (76). Other Tigers are Jack Jaubert (50), Phil Murray (58), and John Foret (71) (*Gumbo* Class of 1971).

Walker, but two plays later, SE Al Coffee, the SEC record holder in both the 220 and 440 sprints, was trapped for a 12-yard loss.

Following an exchange of punts, LSU finally got on the scoreboard. Lee completed a 22-yard pass to Hamilton to the 48. After a 5-yard penalty, Buddy hit Hamilton twice more for 17 and six to the 34. Lee kept twice for four and 11, then passed to Andy again to the 10. But DE Willie Harper changed the momentum by dumping Buddy for a 10-yard loss. An incompletion brought in Mark Lumpkin for a successful 36-yard field goal try. A flag had Tiger hearts skipping a beat, but the call was defensive holding. McClendon elected to keep the points.

Nebraska 10 LSU 3 (0:54)

Third Quarter

LSU looked like a different team as they drove from their 20 to a second field goal. Dantin burst through a big hole at right tackle for 25 yards. On third down, the Tigers got a break when interference on a pass to SE Gerald Keigley put the ball at the Nebraska 32. Chris zipped for another 17, then slipped and lost two. Lee kept for nine before throwing incomplete on third down. So Lumpkin booted a 25-yard field goal.

Nebraska 10 LSU 6 (11:43)

Nebraska seemed determined to run the ball more after an almost even run-pass ratio in the first half. They moved from their 20 on five straight runs by Orduna and Tagge and were about to cross into Tiger terrain when Norsworthy snared his second pick of the evening to give LSU possession on their 48. On second down, Lee fired to Hamilton to the 36. But a short run and two incompletions brought in Dickinson, who punted into the end zone.

Nebraska moved smartly into LSU territory, the big gainer being a 26-yard pass to Rodgers who eluded LB Lloyd Frye. Tagge then kept around right end to the 41. But that's as far as the Big Red got, and Hughes punted out of bounds at the nine. Jones, called the "Ruston Rifle," threw long to his cousin Hamilton incomplete at midfield. Walker burst up the middle to the 25 only to have the gain erased by a clipping penalty. On the next snap, Walker got loose again for a first down at the 21. But the Tigers soon had to punt.

Tagge ripped off 11 on a keeper, but that would be the longest gain of the possession. With Lee at the controls, LSU moved 75 yards to take the lead. On third down, Buddy fired down the middle to Hamilton, who caught the ball on his knees at the 46. Then Lee ran a keeper for just a yard but 15 was added for piling on. Buddy again threw low down the middle, this time to Ken Kavanaugh, Jr., who made a diving catch at the 26. Lee found Coffee open behind the secondary for a touchdown on the last play of the period. Lumpkin's PAT try failed.

LSU 12 Nebraska 10

Al Coffee scores LSU's touchdown (*Gumbo* Class of 1971).

FOURTH QUARTER

Nebraska began from the 33 after fielding Lumpkin's bouncing kick. Tagge said after the game that Devaney told him to "run anything I wanted." But the coach added that he didn't necessarily have to throw deep. "We thought we could beat them deep," Tagge said, "but it didn't work out that way." Jerry overcame an offside penalty by rolling left for 13 yards to the 48. Next came the play that still irks Tiger fans. Orduna ran straight ahead into a pile of players. He lost the ball, and LSU recovered. But somehow Nebraska retained possession. Did a premature whistle blow before the fumble? Replay showed he lost possession before reaching the ground. After a 5-yard pass to FB Dan Schneiss, Ordona flew around left end only to be tripped by Casanova at the 37. A quick flip to Rodgers gained almost 10. Tagge sneaked to the 25 to move the chains. DE Buddy Millican made a nice play on the next snap, jumping up to keep Tagge from passing, then tackling him for a gain of just two. I-back Jeff Kinney circled out of the backfield into the cleared out zone in the middle to take Tagge's pass to the five. After Kinney gained two, Tagge sneaked twice, reaching the ball over the goal on the second one.

Nebraska 17 LSU 12 (8:50)

Jim Benglis blocks Willie Harper into punter Wayne Dickinson (*Gumbo* Class of 1971).

LSU gained two first downs on Lee's third-down pass to Coffee to the 27 and two runs by Dantin to the 39. But three straight incompletions not only brought on the punt team but also sent Lee to the bench with an injured elbow. Sophomore sensation Harper continued to be LSU's nemesis as he broke through and got a hand on Dickinson's punt, which went sideways out of bounds at the LSU 43. After the game, Dickinson said that Harper did not touch the ball, and Coach McClendon echoed that sentiment. However, the officials didn't call roughing the kicker because Harper was blocked into the punter.

With an excellent chance to add to their lead, Nebraska converted two third downs. Tagge rolled left and, with multiple Tigers in his face, flipped to List for a first down at the 25. Then Orduna ran twice behind All-American LT Bob Newton for a first down at the 13. Just when LSU's chances seemed hopeless, Sage smacked Orduna, causing a fumble. This time it counted when MLB Richard Picou recovered at the 13 with 4:09 on the clock.

With Jones back under center, Danton gained five before Bert hit Keigley, who stepped out of bounds for a first down at the 26. Knowing LSU had to pass, Nebraska brought pressure and sacked Jones twice. What play do you call on third-and-30? For Jones, it was a no brainer. Throw to your cousin, who stepped out of bounds at the 38. First down! Then a quick out pattern to Hamilton gained six. But that man Harper struck again, taking the ball from Jones as he wrestled him down to give Nebraska possession at the 43 with 1:15 showing.

Tagge fell down, and LSU used a timeout. Kinney gained four before another time-out. For some reason, Tagge ran an option play. DE Arthur Davis knocked the ball loose, and Millican recovered with 0:52 on the clock. Escaping pressure, Jones threw downfield to Hamilton, but Bob Terrio intercepted at the 38. Taking no more chances, Tagge fell down twice.

Final Score: Nebraska 17 LSU 12

Nebraska's 132 rushing yards were the most anyone gained on LSU all season. Also, the Cornhuskers scored two rushing touchdowns against a team that allowed only two all season.

Devaney's players carried him on their shoulders to midfield to shake hands with Coach McClendon. All the Cornhuskers had their hands raised with one finger extended in celebration of the top ranking in the final polls.

Postgame

Coach McClendon said, "They were a head taller than us, and we found it hard to find the ball." He added, "Chris Dantin played a fine game for us, but it sure is a shame your #1 tailback is out after two plays. ... I just felt like if we could have been able to do anything, anything at all in the first half, it would have been a little different situation. If I had to lose, though, it couldn't have happened to a nicer guy. He's a real fine man and fine coach. Don't you think I'm happy with losing, though. That hurts." Mac also said that the strength of the Nebraska quarterbacks was "unbelievable. We were all over them several times and just couldn't bring them down."

LB Mike Anderson felt that eight days of regimentation in Miami Beach affected the Tigers' performance. "It was a change from what LSU had done before when a more relaxed approach was taken. It wasn't much of a fun trip, and I think our performance showed it."

Devaney felt his squad had a strong claim to be #1. "I think even the Pope would vote us No. 1." He also praised the Tigers. "LSU is … a very good team. I would have to classify them with Southern Cal, which tied us earlier in the year." Big Red FB Schneiss bragged, "We ran on them. That's something nobody else could do all year."

LSU finished #7 in the final AP Poll.

Four 1970 Tigers played in the NFL: DB Tommy Casanova, WR Andy Hamilton, QB Bert Jones, and DT John Wood.

Sun Bowl vs. Iowa State

"Governor, don't leave. I need to talk to you."

Sun Bowl, El Paso, Texas
December 31, 1971

The Tigers' first appearance in the Sun Bowl was also their first-ever clash with Iowa State.

LSU's Season

Tiger fans anticipated the 1971 season because the home schedule included a legendary team making its first visit to Baton Rouge—Notre Dame. The slate also called for LSU to play another Midwest team for the first time—Wisconsin on the road.

The opener provided another intersectional game as Colorado came to Tiger Stadium. The Tiger unit that led the nation in rushing defense the previous two years would have to be rebuilt since Ronnie Estay was the only member of the four-man front returning. Still, no one foresaw what the Buffaloes did. Charlie Davis rushed for 174 yards, the most any runner had ever gained against LSU, in the 31–21 victory. Strong-armed 6'3" junior Bert Jones, the heir apparent at quarterback, threw three interceptions. That caused Coach Charles McClendon to change to junior Pat Lyons, a 5'10" scatback who could run the option play. The Tigers won the next five, including a 38–28 shootout at Wisconsin in which Lyons set an LSU single-game total offense record (304 yards) and a 48–7 romp over Florida. Then along came Archie Manning, who almost single-handedly led the Ole Miss Rebels to a 24–22 upset in Jackson. Alabama rubbed salt in the wounds the following week, 14–7.

LSU's eighth straight triumph over Mississippi State cleared the decks for the long-awaited visit of the 8-1 #2 Fighting Irish. McClendon decided to start Jones, who connected with his cousin, WR Andy Hamilton, for two touchdown passes of more than 30 yards. But the game is best remembered for three goal-line stands by the Tigers against the much bigger Irish. Final score: LSU 28 Notre Dame 8. During the third quarter, an announcement was made that LSU had accepted an invitation to meet Iowa State in the Sun Bowl. The Tigers celebrated with a 36–7 romp over Tulane the next week.

The Opponent

Former Tennessee All-American tailback Johnny Majors took over the Iowa State football program in 1968. In his fourth season, he led the Cyclones to two milestones—their first poll ranking, #17 in the UPI Coaches Poll—and first bowl appearance. After winning only one Big Eight Conference game each of Majors' first three years, the '71 team finished 4–3 in the conference and 8–3 overall. The losses were to #1 Nebraska, #3 Oklahoma, and Colorado, which was #5 when it played ISU. The Cyclones' signature victory was a 54–0 drubbing of Oklahoma State. The ball-control offense was built around "the greatest rusher in Cyclone history," junior TB George Amundsen, who gained 1,149 yards. 6'3" senior QB Dean Carlson threw for 1,643 yards and 11 TDs.

Majors praised the Tigers' "tremendous defensive quickness. They showed that against Notre Dame." Another source of concern was LSU's depth. McClendon typically used upward of 50 players in each game. Coach Mac, whose team was a two-touchdown favorite, conceded the underdog Cyclones had the psychological edge. "Iowa State certainly will be fired up even more than usual for this opportunity. Naturally, we're looking forward to our first appearance in the Sun Bowl, but it's just not the same as Iowa State feels."

Majors expected a low-scoring game while Mac predicted a high-scoring affair. After all, his Tigers led the SEC in offense with 387.5 yards per game, and their 4,263 total yards set a school record. Even though Jones finished the season as the starting quarterback, McClendon refused to name a starter for the bowl game. In the words of Marty Mule, "Jones was as headstrong as he was talented, and it was clear he thought he knew more about offensive football than his coaches. Bert spent a lot of time in McClendon's doghouse."

Mac and the rest of the coaches tried their best to keep the players from heading across the Rio Grande River to Juarez to enjoy the night life. The Tigers were also hit with a major distraction while eating breakfast the morning of the game. A report reached El Paso that Texas A&M had offered McClendon a million dollar deal to become their coach. Mac confirmed to a reporter that an offer had been made but was upset that his squad might learn of it. He also said he wanted to talk to Louisiana Governor John McKeithen before making a decision. Due to bad weather, McKeithen arrived in El Paso just in time to make the kickoff.

The Game

El Paso and Sun Bowl officials were embarrassed by the weather. After all, the city had claimed 430 straight days of sunshine at least part of the time. Still, the game drew a Sun Bowl record 33,320 fans who shivered in damp, high 30s weather. To add insult to injury, rain fell throughout the first half. Governor McKeithen lamented, "I've never been so cold in my life."

FIRST QUARTER

LSU got a break on the second play of the game. HB George Amundson fumbled the wet ball, and CB John Nagle recovered at the ISU 34. But the Tigers could not convert the turnover into points. They made one first down, but a 10-yard sack was too much to overcome. Ronnie Estay, perhaps the only defensive tackle in the nation who also punted, booted out at the Cyclones 11.

Iowa State started strong with QB Dean Carlson keeping around left end for nine and Amundsen gaining four more. But the turnover bug bit again when LB Lloyd Frye pounced on FB Dennis McDonald's bobble at the 26. But facing fourth-and-seven, LSU settled for a 39-yard field goal by Jay Michaelson.

Score: LSU 3 Iowa State 0 (9:25)

The Cyclones' woes continued on their next series when punter Keith Keown got a bad snap and barely got off a kick that traveled just 9 yards to the ISU 39. McClendon decided to give Paul Lyons and the second-stringers a shot at moving the ball. They gained one first down on TB Del Walker's burst over left guard to the 25. But a short run and two incompletions brought Michaelson back onto the field for a successful 39-yard field goal.

LSU 6 Iowa State 0 (6:01)

The Cyclone offense finally got going enough to flip the field. Carlson's 15-yard aerial to TE Keith Krepfle with a 15-yard defensive penalty tacked on moved the ball past midfield for the first time. But a holding penalty led to a punt that pinned the Tigers at the four.

LSU moved out to a first down at the 15. Two plays later, TB Chris Dantin broke into the open but fumbled. DB George Campbell caught the ball in the air and ran to the LSU 20. Two runs by Amundsen and an incompletion ended the period.

LSU 6 Iowa State 0

Second Quarter

Reggie Shoemake kicked a 32-yard field goal on the first play.

LSU 6 Iowa State 3 (14:56)

The teams exchanged punts with the Cyclones enjoying a field position advantage. With ISU at their 45, S John Staggs broke through and tossed Carlson for a 14-yard loss. Three plays later, LSU had the ball on their 12 after another punt. On third-and-two, Jones and Hamilton teamed up for the game's most spectacular play. Bert fired a rocket to Andy at the ISU 35, and the speedy receiver ran all the way to the three where he was hauled down by S Dave McCurry. That tackle proved crucial because the Tigers could not punch it in. The Cyclones stuffed RB Art Cantrelle three times before Jones tried a sneak that was stopped inches from the goal line. Afterwards, Majors told his team, "That goal line stand was the greatest I have seen in many years of football."

When LSU got the ball back, Jones found Hamilton again to the 16, but a flag for holding wiped out the gain. Two plays later, the half ended in frustration for the Tigers while the Cyclones went to the locker room buoyed by their goal-line stand.

LSU 6 Iowa State 3

Third Quarter

The Tiger offense finally came alive, taking the kickoff at the 37 and driving to the first touchdown of the game. After two first downs on a run by Dantin and a 12-yard pass to Hamilton, Jones whipped a 37-yard touchdown pass to Cousin Andy who was all alone at the goal line. "In the second half, we decided to throw more," Bert explained.

LSU 13 Iowa State 3 (12:27)

The Cyclones swiftly moved into LSU territory on a Carlson-to-Krepfle pass. Three plays later, the scoreboard showed first-and-10 at the 31. But on third down, Nagle got his second turnover, picking off Carlson's pass at the 25 and returning it to the 37. With a chance to add to the lead, the Tigers went three-and-out. But so did the Cyclones. Tommy Casanova got loose on a punt return of 32 yards to the LSU 45. The teams then exchanged turnovers. First, LB Matt Blair picked off Lyons' pass. Then ISU tried a dipsy-do that worked beautifully. Carlson pitched out to Amundsen, who threw back to Carlson. Dean raced to the Tiger 40 where he fumbled, and Frye made his second recovery of the game.

Jones engineered another scoring drive, going three-for-three: 12 yards to FB Allen Shorey, 14 to Hamilton, and 21 to Keigley for the six.

LSU 19 Iowa State 3 (3:20)

The plucky Cyclones struck back quickly, moving 77 yards in only four plays. Carlson to Amundsen for 17 plus a 15-yard penalty to the LSU 46. Carlson to SE Ike Harris for 13. Two snaps later, Dean found FB Larry Marquardt for a 30-yard scoring pass. Going for two to pull within eight, ISU tried a pass, but Staggs batted the ball away.

LSU 19 Iowa State 9 (1:49)

The Cyclones needed a turnover and got it when Shorey fumbled, and McCurry recovered. Keeping the momentum going, Carlson hit Krepfle with a short pass, and the big tight end fought his way to the three before Staggs dragged him down. The Tigers dug in, holding Amundson to a yard before Casanova tackled Marquardt for a yard loss.

LSU 19 Iowa State 9

Fourth Quarter

After Carlson gained nothing on a keeper, ISU went for it on fourth down. Carlson passed over Frye to Krepfle for the touchdown. The Cyclones went for two to pull within two, but Casanova intercepted Krepfle's left-handed pass.

LSU 19 Iowa State 15 (14:08)

Needing to respond, the Tiger offense went backwards thanks to a 16-yard sack. Iowa State took over at their 30 after the punt with a chance to take the lead. Carlson faded to pass but threw the ball away under heavy pressure. The referee called grounding and put the pigskin on the 16. Three plays later, Casanova was hit as he fair caught the punt. The penalty put the Tigers in business at the Cyclone 30. Facing third-and-five, Jones tossed a screen pass to TE Ken Kavanaugh, Jr. The son of the Tiger great of the 1930s raced to the six. After a no-gain run, Bert pitched to TE Michaelson in the end zone to regain a two-score lead.

LSU 26 Iowa State 15 (8:58)

Starting from their 11, ISU moved quickly to their 48 on an 18-yard Carlson-to-Harris pass and an interference call. But S Norm Hodgins grabbed Dean's next throw and returned it 15 yards to the LSU 47. Smelling blood, Jones fired a third down pass to Hamilton for a first down at the ISU 29. Runs by Shorey, Walker, and Jimmy LeDoux and Walker again put the ball at the six. Jones then faked a dive handoff and sprinted around left end into the end zone to put the game away. The conversion gave Michaelson as many points as the Iowa State team.

LSU 33 Iowa State 15 (3:05)

Near the end of the game, with an LSU victory in hand, Governor McKeithen decided to go down to the sideline and congratulate the Tigers. McClendon had never learned that the governor had reached El Paso. So when he saw him, Mac thought, *How lucky can a man be?* He said, "Governor, don't leave. I need to talk to you."

Final Score: LSU 33 Iowa State 15

Bert Jones, who accounted for four touchdowns, was named the Most Valuable Player.

Bert Jones high-steps into the end zone (*Gumbo* Class of 1972).

Postgame

McClendon talked to the governor on the way to the dressing room and "quickly got everything squared away." Several members of the Board of Supervisors joined a huddle in a corner of the locker room. A few minutes later, the governor told a reporter, "I'm confident Coach Mac will remain at LSU." Naturally, the press asked McClendon about the Texas A&M offer. But he dodged the issue. "I do not want to talk about it, and I still have a lot of coaching to do at LSU."

"This was some kind of aggressive football game," said Charley. "There were an awful lot of mistakes in that first half by both teams, and I knew we were in trouble when we couldn't do anything more than get two field goals, which I always hate to settle for. However, we came out in the second half, made some adjustments, and seemed to put it all together. We got a little ragged there in that half for a few minutes but came back and did a great job. ... Jones and Hamilton were just great.... Our seniors, all 16 of 'em, made me extremely proud. ... They're the winningest group we've had in my 10 years as head coach. They've won 27 games in three seasons."

Johnny Majors told his troops: "I know you're disappointed, but let me tell you that, with as much adversity as you had, you have to be proud. ... With the score 19–3, you never lost your poise. You fought back. You are a real football team and don't ever forget it."

McClendon called a press conference. "I'm going to be at LSU. It is nice that my name was rumored to be considered to be football coach at Texas A&M, but I am committed to LSU."

LSU stayed at #11 in the final AP poll.

Six 1971 Tigers played in the NFL: LB Warren Capone, DB Tommy Casanova, WR Andy Hamilton, DB Norman Hodgins, QB Bert Jones, and DT John Wood.

Astro-Bluebonnet Bowl
vs. Tennessee

A tale of two halves

Astrodome, Houston, Texas
December 30, 1972

A 9–1–1 record earned LSU a trip to the Astrodome for their first post-season meeting with the Tennessee Volunteers.

LSU's Season

Led by senior QB Bert Jones, the Tigers won their first seven games to move up to #6 in the AP poll. Included was the second win in the home-and-home series with Wisconsin, the first Big Ten team to play in Tiger Stadium. The Badgers gave the Bengals quite a battle through the first half before LSU's superior fire power and strong running game prevailed in the second half, 27–7. A tough 12–6 victory at Rice preceded the 35–7 blasting of #9 Auburn for Coach Charlie McClendon's 84th victory, a school record. Jones also tied a record in the game, matching Y.A. Tittle's career total of 23 scoring passes.

The seventh victory was both the most exciting and most controversial. Trailing Ole Miss 16–10 in the final minute, Bert led a desperate march that reached the 10 with 0:04 remaining. An incompletion in the end zone seemingly ended the game, but the clock read 0:01. As soon as the ball was snapped, the horn went off. Jones fired to RB Brad Davis at the left flag. He caught the ball and fell into the end zone. The PAT gave the Tigers an improbable 17–16 win.

The winning streak ended the next week at Alabama, 35–21. After beating Mississippi State, LSU accepted an invitation to the Bluebonnet Bowl. Then they failed to score a touchdown in the final two games, a 3–3 tie in a rainstorm at Florida and a 9–3 squeaker at Tulane.

Jones threw for 1,426 yards to make not only all-SEC but also five all-America teams, more than any other quarterback. He finished fourth in the Heisman voting.

The Opponent

The final Associated Press regular season poll ranked Tennessee #11, one slot below the Tigers. Coach Bill Battle was rewarded with a contract extension and a raise after winning 30 games in his three years in Knoxville. Sophomore Condredge Holloway, the first African American to start at quarterback at an SEC school, surpassed the magic 1,000-yard mark in total offense, passing for 807 yards and running for 266.

"A roaring start, a bit of a sag in the middle, and a steamrolling finish carried Tennessee's footballers to a 9–2 record." The two losses came to the same two teams that had defeated the Vols the year before, Auburn and Alabama. And in both instances, the Big Orange was just a play or two away from victory.

Scores against common opponents provided mixed messages. LSU beat Auburn 35–7 after the Plainsmen toppled the Vols 10–6. UT downed Ole Miss 17–0 while LSU edged the Rebels by only one. Kentucky fell to both UT and LSU by ten. Alabama bested the Vols by seven and LSU by 14.

LSU had experienced little success against Tennessee over the decades, winning only one of the 15 meetings with two ties. Tennessee entered the bowl game as a slight favorite. The problem with facing an unorthodox quarterback like Holloway is that you have no one on your squad who can simulate his skills in practice.

The game in the Astrodome marked the first indoor game for both teams. The 13 senior Tigers had a special incentive to beat the Vols. A victory would give them a school-record 28 wins in their three-year career. However, the squad overall was disappointed that their 9–1–1 record did not earn them a bid to a New Year's Day bowl game.

The Game

The Vols dominated the first half, and the 52,961 in attendance saw them withstand a furious LSU comeback.

FIRST QUARTER

The Tigers started strong, taking the opening kickoff and marching to a field goal. QB Bert Jones gained the initial first down with his feet, running up the middle on third down to the LSU 40. Several snaps later, TB Chris Dantin took a pitchout around end for 16 yards to the UT 40. On second-and-seven, Jones hit TE Chuck Williamson for 18 yards to the 19. But the defense stiffened. So Rusty Jackson booted a 29-yard field goal.

Score: LSU 3 Tennessee 0 (9:56)

DB Eddie Brown returned the kickoff 40 yards to the 40. Facing third-and-seven, elusive QB Condredge Holloway escaped the Tiger rush and raced 12 yards for a first down at the LSU 45. Two runs by FB Steve Chancey moved the chains to the 32. On the next third-and-seven, Holloway burned the Tigers again, breaking loose from another strong rush to the 18. Two plays later, TB Haskell Stanback caught a pass and broke three tackles to the six. From there, Holloway hit TE Jimmy Young for the touchdown.

Tennessee 7 LSU 3 (5:03)

Eddie Brown set up the second Vol score when he took a Jackson punt and ran 47 yards behind great blocking to the LSU 24. After completing a 9-yard pass to Stanback, Holloway scored from the 15 on a busted play. He tried to handoff to Stanback, but

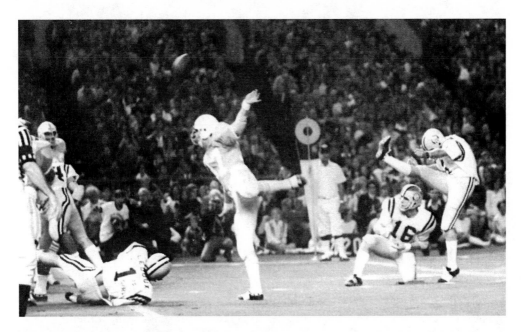

Rusty Jackson kicks a field goal to end LSU's opening drive as Paul Lyons holds. No. 1 is Jimmy LeDoux (*Gumbo* Class of 1973).

the running back slipped down. So Condredge pulled the ball back and streaked to the end zone.

Tennessee 14 LSU 3 (3:51)

With Paul Lyons at quarterback, LSU got one first down at the 41. But Lyons' long pass was intercepted by DB Tim Townes, who returned 29 yards to the LSU 44. Holloway hit FB Bill Rudder to the 22. But a 15-yard penalty on the next play made the Vols' task more difficult. Holloway hooked up with WR Dennis Chadwick for nine to end the quarter.

Tennessee 14 LSU 3

SECOND QUARTER

An 11-yard pass set up third-and-five, but a screen pass was stuffed for a gain of one. So barefoot soccer-style kicker Ricky Townsend booted a 33-yard field goal.

Tennessee 17 LSU 3 (13:47)

When Jones couldn't move the Tigers. So Jackson came on to punt. But one of his blockers was pushed back into him. The bounding ball was recovered by Vol Hank Walter at the Tiger 42.

When a 15-yard holding penalty on LB Warren Capone moved the pigskin to the 22, Tiger fans wondered what else could go wrong. But Capone went from goat to hero by intercepting Holloway's pass and returning 9 yards to the 23. That broke Condredge's streak of seven straight completions.

The beleaguered Tiger defense didn't get much rest. Another three-and-out brought them back on the field. Runs by Stanback of 12 and 18 yards put the Vols back in LSU territory at the 40. Three runs made it fourth-and-one. Coach Bill Battle said go for it, and Stanback rewarded his confidence by gaining two. Then on third-and-five, the versatile Stanback caught a pass for 13 to the 10. Holloway then darted through the right side into the end zone where he danced before happy teammates bowled him over and bounced him around as orange shakers and cowboy hats waved in the stands.

Tennessee 24 LSU 3 (6:10)

Aided by a 15-yard penalty, the Tigers pushed 2 yards into Vol territory but soon faced fourth-and-one. McClendon opted to punt. The Bandits forced a three-and-out to give LSU good field position at their 45 and a chance to score before the break. But it was not to be, and the teams traded kicks the rest of the half. Tennessee outgained LSU 232–80 and led in first downs 14 to five.

Tennessee 24 LSU 3

After the game, McClendon gave this assessment. "We were too cautious the first half. Then we tried to throw, and that got us into trouble." He added, "I never saw us miss as many tackles. We felt we had to contain Holloway, and we did as far as sweeps were concerned, but he went right up the middle on us. We decided we'd play our own game in the second half, just run from the strong set and take the ball game right at them."

THIRD QUARTER

The Tigers came out a different team. After making some halftime adjustments, the Chinese Bandits held the Vols to a measly 16 yards during the third period and their first possession of the fourth quarter.

Brad Davis gains yardage up the middle as Chuck Williamson (85) blocks (*Gumbo* Class of 1973).

CB Mike Williams, one of LSU's first two Black players with RB Lora Hinton, took UT's first punt of the evening and raced 36 yards to the UT 33. The energized offense drove to their first touchdown. FL Gerald Keigley gained 12 on two reverses with Dantin gaining seven in between. Chris gained three for a first down at the 12. On third-and-eight, Jones threw incomplete to WR Jimmy LeDoux in the end zone. But LSU finally got a break when Townes was called for interference to make it first down at the one. After Davis lost a yard, Jones kept around right end for the touchdown.

Tennessee 24 LSU 10 (7:12)

Quickly forcing a punt, the rejuvenated Tiger offense moved from their 18 to the UT 42 thanks primarily to Davis's 15-yard run and 12-yard reception. LSU then overcame a 5-yard penalty when Jones kept on an option play to the 27.

Tennessee 24 LSU 10

FOURTH QUARTER

Two carries by Steve Rogers moved the sticks to the 14. But DE Carl Johnson, who would win the Defensive Player of the Game award, tossed Jones for losses of six and eight. Juan Roca's field goal try from the 34 fell short.

After S John Staggs, LSU's leading tackler in the game, tossed Chancey for a 3-yard loss on third down, the Vols punted to the LSU 40. On the first play, Lyons pitched out to Davis, who sped 28 yards down the right sideline for a first down at the 32. After Jim Benglis got four, Lyons kept for nine to the 19. Benglis picked up nine, and two plays later Davis blasted over right guard for the touchdown.

Tennessee 24 LSU 17 (7:26)

Needing to run some clock, the Vols managed one first down on Holloway's 10-yard run before punting to the LSU 25 with 4:48 left. After two Davis runs, Jones hit TE Brad Boyd with a 35-yard pass to the UT 45. Two plays later, Benglis was on the receiving end of Bert's aerial to the 21. With visions of one of the great comebacks in LSU history filling the imaginations of Tiger fans, the orange-clad defense drew a line on the artificial turf. Jones lost a yard, then threw two incompletions. With a field goal not an option, Jones threw to Keigley, but Conrad Graham batted the ball out of his hands with 1:55 remaining. McClendon said the Tigers would have gone for two had they scored. "We already had the play set up."

The Vols picked up a first down in two plays, which enabled them to kill the clock.

Final Score: Tennessee 24 LSU 17

Jones finished his last game at LSU with only seven completions in 19 attempts for just 90 yards—one of his worst performances since becoming the starter as a junior. Holloway, the game's Offensive MVP, went 11-of-19 for 94 yards and carried 19 times for 74 more.

Postgame

Coach McClendon: "This was almost two separate ball games. I've been talking about pride this week, and you saw some. I can't express how proud I am of this Tiger comeback. There wasn't anybody in this stadium who thought we had a chance at halftime, but what we did in the second half sort of makes you appreciate what football is all about."

Coach Battle: "Momentum is a crazy thing, and you can't explain what made it swing from Tennessee to LSU. Maybe we tried to play it too conservatively in the second half."

Condredge Holloway: "They just whipped us in the second half. It wasn't us—it was them."

Ten 1972 Tigers played pro football: LB Ken Bordelon, LB Warren Capone, RB Brad Davis, LB Bo Harris, DB Norm Hodgins, P Rusty Jackson, QB Bert Jones, RB Steve Rogers, DB Mike Williams, and DT John Wood.

Orange Bowl vs. Penn State

Crusade for Eastern football

Orange Bowl, Miami, Florida
January 1, 1974

The Tigers made their fourth trip to the Orange Bowl to face Penn State for the first time.

LSU's Season

With Bert Jones in the NFL, the keys to the LSU offense were passed to junior Mike Miley, a blue-chip recruit from Metairie LA. "Miracle Mike" combined the passing ability of Jones with the foot speed of Paul Lyons. He led the Tigers to nine straight victories and the #7 ranking in the AP poll. The highlight was a 33–29 triumph at South Carolina against Paul Dietzel's Gamecocks. That was followed by a 51–14 shellacking of Ole Miss in a game in which the Rebels vowed revenge for the last-second win they felt was stolen from them the year before.

The clash with Alabama was moved to Thanksgiving night on ABC-TV. LSU had accepted a bid to play Penn State in the Orange Bowl while the #2 Tide were also 9–0 and headed for a Sugar Bowl date with #1 Notre Dame. The Tigers executed their game plan of controlling the ball, running 77 plays to Bama's 53 and leading in first downs 21–11. But Bear Bryant's club scored on passes of 29 and 77 yards and a 19-yard run on the first play after a fumble recovery to win 21–7.

LSU then traveled to New Orleans for the annual season finale with Tulane, which, at 8–2, had its best team in decades. The 14–0 Green Wave triumph ended the school's 25-year non-winning streak against the Tigers.

Brad Davis, one of four tailbacks that McClendon regularly deployed, rose to #5 on the all-time LSU rushing list, surpassing such legends as Jimmy Taylor and Jerry Stovall.

The Opponent

The Penn State Nittany Lions roared through eleven games for their third undefeated season in Joe Paterno's eight years as head coach. Their closest games were 35–29 over North Carolina State, 19–9 at Air Force, and 20–6 at Stanford.

Like the Tigers, PSU depended on a rushing game more than passing. 6'2" 215-pound TB John Cappelletti became the first Penn State player to win the Heisman Trophy after rushing for 1,522 yards on 286 attempts with 17 touchdowns. He also took home the Maxwell Award. Paterno unabashedly called Cappelletti "the best college player I've ever been around." Better than Franco Harris, he was asked? "Franco is a fine player. But John is faster than Franco and every bit as powerful." He added, "John doesn't have that Jetstream speed, and he isn't so wide that you can't wrap your arms around him. But what you can't do is tackle him. He sticks his head in there and bounces off people." LSU Coach McClendon said Cappelletti "reminds me a little bit of Billy Cannon. He's bow-legged, has that balance, and you don't knock him down."

QB Tom Shuman completed 51.6 percent of his passes for 1,375 yards and 13 touchdowns. Paterno considered him one of the best ball handling quarterbacks he'd coached.

G Mark Markovich recalled years later that "we were not the greatest collection of athletes. But we were a group of intelligent guys who decided to work together as a team and accomplished some extraordinary things."

Despite starting the season #7 in the AP poll and going undefeated, the Lions did not move any higher than #6 in the final regular season poll. So they wanted to show the world they were a top five team by beating the Tigers. "The polls are one of those things we've made up our minds we can't change," said Paterno, "so we've stopped worrying about it." Joe added, "If it's a high scoring game, we won't win it. LSU's defense is too good for us to figure on a lot of scores."

Cappelletti said, "Every game Penn State plays seems to be a crusade for Eastern football. Maybe there haven't been enough good football teams in the East, but I feel that's changing…."

The Tigers were also on a crusade of sorts. Freshman DT A.J. Duhe said, "Our seniors don't want to leave school with three straight losses." One of those seniors, All-American MLB Warren Capone, added, "I don't even like to think about it."

Tiger fans hoped that McClendon's spotless record against undefeated teams in bowl games would hold up against the powerful Lions. LSU had upset Texas and Arkansas in the Cotton Bowl and Wyoming in the Sugar Bowl.

The Game

The smallest Orange Bowl audience since 1948—60,477—gathered on a beautiful winter evening in South Florida. The artificial turf was still damp from a rain shower two hours before kickoff.

FIRST QUARTER

LSU gave their followers high hopes with one of their most impressive drives of the entire season. Freshman S Robert Dow gave the Tigers great starting position when he returned the opening kickoff 46 yards to the 49. As usual, Brad Davis was the workhorse, gaining 39 yards on five of the nine running plays, including a 16-yard jaunt to the 13. But he was hit hard on his last carry to the three. So Steve Rogers replaced him and, on his first play, raced through a big hole opened by RG Tyler Lafauci and RT Richard Brooks into the end zone. Rusty Jackson booted the PAT. LSU 7 Penn State 0 (11:11).

With first downs hard to come by, the game settled into a punting duel for most of the period with Penn State gradually gaining better and better field position thanks in part to Dow fielding a punt on his nine rather than letting it bounce into the end zone. Players on both sides slipped on the damp Poly Turf surface that Cappelletti called the worst he had ever played on.

Figuring LSU would key on Cappelletti, Penn State ran the fullback more often than the tailback. Bob Nagle ripped off the longest run of the quarter—17 yards. The Heisman winner gained just six on six carries. Coach Mac explained, "I told my guys, 'Wherever he goes, go with him. If you don't stop Cappelletti, you're in trouble.'" MLB Warren Capone said, "When they got the ball, we just went to our regular pursuit angles. We just did a good job. It's as simple as that."

Starting from midfield with 4:23 on the clock, the Lions, aided by a personal foul penalty against LSU on a punt, drove deep enough for Chris Bahr to boot a 44-yard field goal.

Score: LSU 7 Penn State 3 (1:25)

The Tigers finally gained another first down in the last minute when freshman TB Terry Robiskie rambled 17 yards to the 44. Neither team completed a pass during the quarter with LSU not even attempting one.

LSU 7 Penn State 3

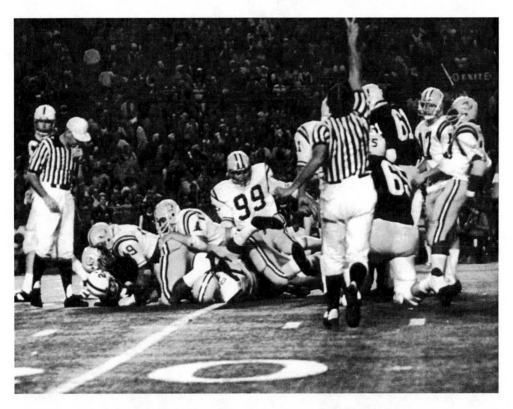

LB Thielen Smith tackles RB John Cappelletti as Kenny Bordelon (99) assists. No. 17 is Frank Racine (*Gumbo* Class of 1974).

Second Quarter

Sparked by QB Bill Broussard's 12-yard scamper, LSU reached the PSU 37 before bogging down. So Juan Roca tried a 54-yard field goal that DE Dave Graf blocked, and the other DE Greg Murphy recovered on LSU's 35. But a holding penalty set the Lions back, forcing a punt. Dow made a fair catch at the nine for the second time.

Four snaps later, Jackson boomed a 56-yard punt that Gary Hayman, the NCAA punt return leader, fielded while back-pedaling on his 27. He slipped on the turf as he caught the ball but put a hand down to catch himself, then broke into the clear. But the nearest official ruled that Hayman's knee hit the ground and blew the play dead. Television replay showed that neither knee was down. However, Penn State scored on another spectacular play anyway. Shuman sailed a long pass down the middle. WR Chuck Herd, on the dead run several strides behind DB Dale Cangelosi, stretched his left hand as far as he could, caught the ball in that one hand, pulled it in, and kept going for a 72-yard touchdown. Herd said afterward, "Frankly, I thought the ball was out of reach. It hit my left hand, and I cradled it." On the sideline, McClendon was awed by the catch. "I believe he had glue on his hands. I don't think he thought he had it himself for a minute."

Penn State 10 LSU 7 (8:19)

LSU went three-and-out; so Jackson punted again. This time Hayman didn't slip, returning 36 yards to the LSU 26 where Jackson dumped him. After a pass was almost intercepted by outstanding CB Mike Williams and a 4-yard screen pass, the Lions ran the ball seven straight times. Cappelletti finally found some daylight on runs of seven and eight. On his fourth carry of the drive, he leaped over from the one. Matt Bahr's PAT kick hit the upright.

Penn State 16 LSU 7 (2:19)

LSU seemed content to run out the clock. But a roughing the kicker penalty moved the ball to the 41. So the Tigers unleashed their passing attack and moved deep into Penn State territory. Flare passes to Davis moved the chains to the PSU 48, where LSU called its first timeout with 0:41 remaining. Miley rolled right and scrambled out of bounds at the 30. Mike then fired a pass to SE Ben Jones, Bert's brother, who made a diving catch at the 17. Timeout LSU. With a field goal in their back pocket, the Tigers blew the scoring chance by mismanaging their time. Miley threw to Davis to the nine. LSU called their last time out at 0:11. Mike threw to Brad again, but he was downed immediately at the four. The first down stopped the clock with two seconds left. When the referee marked the ball ready for play, Miley tried a "clock play" to the sideline, but time ran out as the ball sailed out of bounds. Explaining the second-to-last play, Miley said, "I was going to throw it to Brad or out of bounds. Brad was open so I threw it to him, but they covered him real quick." McClendon added, "The man that got him wasn't supposed to be there. It was a good defensive play."

Penn State 16 LSU 7

Paterno, who said before the game, "I haven't seen anybody run any harder than Davis," may not have been surprised that Brad outgained Cappelletti in the first 30 minutes. The LSU junior had 54 yards on 13 carries. Despite being without their starting outside linebackers—Gary Champagne didn't dress out, and Bo Harris was injured early in

Mike Miley slips on the turf (*Gumbo* Class of 1974).

the game—the Tigers held the PSU star to just 21 yards on 11 attempts. LSU led in statistics but not on the scoreboard: 11–5 in first downs and 170–146 in total yardage.

Third Quarter

Penn State's opening possession went nowhere. So Brian Masella came in to punt only to have the snap sail over his head. He slipped down as he picked up the ball in the end zone for a safety.

Penn State 16 LSU 9 (13:07)

After the free kick, the teams traded back-to-back turnovers. The Tigers made a first down at the PSU 47 on runs by Miley and Davis. Then a bad pitchout to Brad was recovered by LB Doug Allen at the PSU 45. On the next play, Shuman's pass bounced off Hayman's hands to Williams, who returned to the LSU 40. But another errant pitch and a sack forced a punt on fourth-and-25.

The teams traded punts until PSU got close enough to try a field goal. The Lions ripped off two first downs to reach the LSU 31, but a sack by DE Ron Daily took the steam out of the advance. Broussard led the Tigers to one first down but no more. Cappelletti finally got loose for a long gain when he took a screen pass and rambled 40 yards to the LSU 22. But the defense stuffed three of his runs to bring out Bahr, who missed from the 28.

Penn State 16 LSU 9

Fourth Quarter

After a punt exchange, PSU got the ball on LSU's side of the field when DT Randy Crowder dropped into coverage and snagged a Miley pass at the 42. But on fourth-and-four, Bahr missed again, falling short from the 43.

LSU finally got moving, traveling from their 20 to a first down on the PSU 34 on Miley's 15-yard pass to SB Richard Romain and runs by Mike and Robiskie. But three more carries gained only seven to set up fourth-and-three at the 27. LB Doug Allen was waiting for LSU's bread-and-butter option play and tackled Davis for a 4-yard loss when he took the pitchout.

After three more punts, the Tigers had one last desperate chance from their 23 with 1:06 remaining. Miley connected with TE Brad Boyd for 21 yards, but LSU ran out of downs at their 45.

Final Score: Penn State 16 LSU 9

The Tigers won several battles but not the war. They succeeded in corralling Cappelletti, holding him to his lowest total of the season, 50 yards on 26 carries. Davis gained 70 yards on seven fewer carries. LSU had more first downs (18–9), rushing yards (205–28), and total yards (274–185). But the Nittany Lions got the big plays—the 72-yard TD pass and the 36-yard punt return to set up the other touchdown.

Postgame

McClendon summed up the game like this: "We played well as individuals but did not play well as a team." Charley refused to compare bulky Penn State with quick Alabama because of the difference in makeup of the teams.

Asked who he thought was No. 1 in the nation, Paterno replied, "I just conducted the Paterno Poll, and Penn State is No. 1." Joe gave LSU's swarming defense the credit for his team's 28 net rushing yards rather than the wet Poly Turf. "LSU was the quickest and toughest team over a long period that we played all year." Cappelletti "had very little running room, but when he got room, he gained yardage. LSU's linebackers played very tight, and they read all Cappy's good plays so well." Cappelletti agreed with his coach's assessment, saying that the Tiger linebackers "were always coming, and they plugged the holes very quickly. They were tough to run on."

Paterno explained why his defense allowed no more points after LSU's opening drive. "The kids made their own adjustment. They just weren't coming off the ball fast enough. I had warned them about quickness in practice, but they didn't believe me until they got in there. When you come from cold weather to a warm situation, you lose your tempo."

Ten 1973 Tigers played pro football: LB Ken Bordelon, LB Warren Capone, RB Brad Davis, DL A.J. Duhe, LB Bo Harris, DB Norm Hodgins, P Rusty Jackson, RB Terry Robiskie, RB Steve Rogers, and DB Mike Williams.

Sun Bowl vs. Stanford

Top passer vs. top rusher

Sun Bowl Stadium, El Paso, Texas
December 31, 1977

Three straight seasons without a bowl game and a combined record of 15–16–2 put Coach Charles McClendon's job in jeopardy. With his four-year contract set to expire after the 1977 season, the Board of Supervisors voted to retain him only if he accepted a two-year contract.

LSU's Season

"As fine a runner as I have ever seen; enormously strong, quick, and competitive." McClendon was speaking of LSU's sensational junior TB Charles Alexander. The pride of Galveston, TX, running behind an offensive line that dubbed themselves the "Root Hogs," broke several SEC records during the '77 season including most yards gained (1,686) and most yards per game (153.3) and was named a first team All-American by the UPI, Kodak Coaches, and Football Writers of America. No less an observer than assistant coach Jerry Stovall, the runner-up in the Heisman voting in 1962, was constantly awed by Alexander, who ran a 4.3 40-yard dash. "Alexander the Great" helped the Tigers, loaded with freshmen and sophomores, compile an 8–3 record and end the school's three-year bowl drought.

The season began on a sour note as the Tigers lost on the road at Indiana 24–21 after blowing a comfortable 21–10 lead. "Help Mac Pack" signs were in full bloom for the home opener against Rice. The Tigers bounced back—and how—clobbering the Owls 77–0 in the wildest scoring display since 1936. But skeptical Tiger fans were still not sold on this team. Florida, ranked #9 nationally, would be the true test. LSU sprinted to a 29–0 lead before the Gators had broken a sweat. The 36–14 rout was the first victory over Florida since 1973.

Next came a visit to Vanderbilt. During the three-season dry spell, McClendon's men had won only one road game and tied one in 14 tries. The sleepy Tigers fell behind 15–0 midway through the third period before exploding for 28 unanswered points to earn LSU's first out-of-state victory since 1973. Impressed UPI voters ranked the Tigers #11, but that momentum didn't carry over to the homecoming game the following week against the finest Kentucky team in that school's history. A succession of errors turned a 13–7 Wildcat lead into a 33–7 runaway.

The Tigers righted the ship the next two weeks, flattening Oregon 56–17 and rallying from a 21–0 deficit to upend Ole Miss in Jackson 28–21. The next Saturday, though, the #18 Tigers couldn't gain any offensive traction against #2 Alabama and tumbled 24–3. After dominating Mississippi State for decades, LSU had dropped three straight to the Bulldogs. The Bengals squeaked out a 27–24 verdict when Mike Conway kicked a 28-yard field goal in the waning minutes. Next came the annual clash with Tulane. With a Sun Bowl invitation hinging on the outcome, the Tigers once again started slowly, falling behind 17–7 at the half. But once again, Mac's squad came out inspired after intermission to pull out a 20–17 victory. In the regular season finale, the Tigers annihilated Wyoming 66–7. The 365 total points for the season were the second highest ever by an LSU team.

The Opponent

Forty-six-year-old Bill Walsh, a veteran college and pro assistant coach, took the reins of the Stanford program in 1977. The future three-time Super Bowl champion and Pro Football Hall of Fame coach led the Cardinals to an 8–3 record, good enough to tie for second in the Pac-8 conference and earn the school's first bowl invitation in six seasons.

Known as a passing game guru, Walsh improved senior QB Guy Benjamin's play to the point where the Cardinals led the nation in passing, and Benjamin was awarded the Sammy Baugh Trophy, given each year to the best passer in college football. Senior receiver James Lofton caught 57 passes for 1,010 yards and 14 touchdowns to earn second team All-America honors. Lightning fast Darrin Nelson became the first freshman running back in conference history to rush for more than 1,000 yards in a season. He also caught 50 passes for 524 yards.

One San Francisco columnist wrote, "Walsh is the ideal coach for Stanford…. The man has done a remarkable job [making] the most of what he has…. Walsh has been able to utilize the talents of his best players to compensate for the weaknesses of the team, and the Cards are playing better than anybody could have expected."

Despite LSU ranking last in the SEC in pass defense, oddsmakers made the Tigers a slight favorite. McClendon praised his young team. "They play with reckless abandon and refuse to quit. Four times this year, we came back to win in the second half. A young team like this usually tends to quit, but this is a wild bunch."

The Game

At the 43rd Sun Bowl, 31,318 gathered for the 11:30 a.m. kickoff on New Year's Eve. The weatherman ordered a bright clear day with temperature in the 50s—much nicer than the Tigers experienced on their previous trip to El Paso six years earlier. Even though both coaches held closed practices during the week, each team followed the offensive script it had used the entire season. One team ran up and down the field while the other passed up and down the field. Charles Alexander broke the bowl rushing mark, and Guy Benjamin smashed the passing mark. In the end, the passers won out.

FIRST QUARTER

The Tigers made one first down after taking the kickoff when FB Kelly Simmons, usually consigned to blocking for TB Charles Alexander, picked up 15 yards on a draw up the middle. After Bobby Moreau punted 49 yards, Guy Benjamin came out chunking. He hit Marty Smith for 12, then Nelson for seven. Undeterred when CB Willie Teal dumped Nelson for a 7-yard loss, Benjamin called a screen to Darrin that was good for 13. Then Guy went to his #1 receiver, 6'3" James Lofton, a future NFL Hall of Famer, for another 13 yards and a first down at the LSU 49. When the West Coast gunslinger missed on a long pass, the Cardinals had to punt.

The Tigers marched 80 yards in nine plays for the game's first score. Two Alexander runs gained 14. After picking up another four, he broke over left tackle and raced 53 yards to the six. "My favorite play was student body right and anything off tackle," recalled Charles. "You had three options off tackle. You could bounce it, you could go where the hole is supposed to be, or you could cut it back." On third down from the three, QB Steve Ensminger tossed a scoring pass to SB Mike Quintella.

Score: LSU 7 Stanford 0 (3:56)

After Stanford went backwards on their next series, the Tigers looked like they would add to their lead even with Alexander taking a rest. Three runs moved to the 34. But an errant pitchout took the steam out of the drive. Moreau sliced a punt out of bounds at the Stanford 33.

LSU 7 Stanford 0

SECOND QUARTER

Stanford tied the score on the third play of the period. After Nelson picked up 10 and then five to the LSU 41, Lofton got a step ahead of Teal on a post pattern, pulled in Benjamin's pass in stride at the five and careened into the end zone.

LSU 7 Stanford 7 (14:03)

A bad snap and an offensive pass interference hampered the next LSU possession. After Moreau punted to the Stanford 42, the Cardinal moved to the 19 because of a 16-yard pass to Nelson and a 15-yard penalty. When the Tigers held, Ken Naber booted a 36-yard field goal.

Stanford 10 LSU 7 (8:18)

With alternate QB David Woodley at the controls, LSU embarked on a relentless 17-play, 80-yard drive to retake the lead. Alexander carried six times for 34 yards, Simmons added 21 on three carries, Woodley got seven on two carries, and Jerry Murphree gained seven more. David completed just one pass, but it was a crucial one—13 yards to SE Carlos Carson for a first down at the Stanford 25. Finally, from the nine, Alexander broke to the left, cut up the middle, and eluded two tacklers into the end zone.

LSU 14 Stanford 10 (0:56)

Despite having less than a minute on the clock, Stanford moved far enough for Naber to try a 60-yard field goal that missed as the horn sounded.

LSU 14 Stanford 10

Gordy Ceresino (95) tackles Charles Alexander (David Madison/1977 Sun Bowl/Getty Images).

THIRD QUARTER

Stanford rolled 80 yards in 12 plays to retake the lead. Benjamin went four-for-seven, including two 18-yard completions to WR Bill Kellar. He hit Lofton for 11 yards to the 11. On fourth-and-one from the two, Coach Walsh called a play that would be a staple of the "West Coast Offense" he would popularize in the NFL. Lofton went in motion across the formation. Benjamin rolled right and tossed to James as the lanky receiver crossed the goal line.

Stanford 17 LSU 14 (10:19)

The Tigers reeled off three first downs to move across midfield. Ensminger connected with Kelly Simmons for 11 to the LSU 35. Two plays later, Kelly gained five to move the chains to the 46. On third-and-three, Steve kept for four to the Stanford 43. But DB Rick Parker picked off Ensminger's long pass at the 10. Steve said afterward, "I should have run and was starting to when (TE) Clif Lane came back."

Benjamin got the Cardinals out of the hole by bootlegging around right end for 21 yards to the 32. Hampered by a 5-yard penalty, Stanford punted out at the LSU 47. Taking advantage of the field position, LSU drove close enough for a field goal try. The key play was an Ensminger-to-Simmons pass for 16 yards to the Cardinal 35. A third down incompletion brought in Moreau, who missed a 49-yard field goal attempt. Benjamin went right back to work, hitting Lofton for 18, then Kellar for 14 to the LSU 48. But a 15-yard penalty clipped the Cardinal wings.

Stanford 17 LSU 14

FOURTH QUARTER

Starting from the 29 after the punt, LSU moved briskly into Stanford territory. Alexander sped around right end to the 46. Four straight runs made it first-and-ten at the 17. But on second-and-eight, Steve lost four trying to pass. Then he tossed an interception into the hands of John Pigott to deprive the Tigers of a chance to at least tie the score. Asked about the decision to pass twice in a row after the running game had moved 66 yards, Alexander replied, "We don't question coaches' calls. It's their job. We have the best offensive coordinator in the country, Coach Lynn Amedee, and it wasn't him that threw the interceptions or missed the blocks. We just didn't execute."

LSU held the Cardinals, forcing Brad Fox to punt. But S Jackie Casanova, Tommy's younger brother, fumbled, and Stanford recovered at the LSU 49. The Tiger defense did itself proud when DE Kent Broha sacked Benjamin for a 10-yard loss. Then a penalty back to the 23 brought on the punting unit. With a chance at a good return, Chris Williams fumbled, but Rusty Brown recovered for LSU at the 32.

With Woodley under center, an 11-yard reverse to Quintella started the possession, but three runs netted -5 yards. So Moreau booted to the Stanford 21 with 4:42 on the clock. Wanting to at least eat up some time, the Cardinals got much more. Held in check for most of the game, Nelson showcased the skills that would win him election to the College Football Hall of Fame. First, he sprinted 15 yards to the 36. After three runs to the LSU 35, Benjamin tossed a flare pass to Nelson on the sideline, and the fleet receiver outraced the defenders to pay dirt.

Stanford 24 LSU 14 (1:27)

LSU didn't give up. A combination of runs and Ensminger passes, the last one to SB Marcus Quinn for 13 yards, made it first-and-10 at the Stanford 40. After an incompletion, Steve threw to Carson sprinting into the end zone, but Carlos dropped the ball with a second left to play. On the final snap, another desperation pass was intercepted in the end zone.

Final Score: Stanford 24 LSU 14

Alexander was voted the Most Valuable Player for gaining 197 yards on 31 carries with a touchdown.

Postgame

Coach McClendon sighed, "Our passing game, whew!" Asked about the three interceptions, he replied, "That's part of the danger of putting the ball in the air. We're a better passing team than we showed." He added, "I don't think you can find two more evenly matched teams." The statistics bore him out. First downs were 21–21. Total yards favored LSU by only 375–372. The Tigers ran 86 plays to Stanford's 63 and held the ball 10:40 longer than the Cardinals. But LSU "won" the wrong statistic: four turnovers to none.

Mac praised his star running back. "I can't be happier with Charley's effort. There's no telling what he would have had in yardage if we hadn't had to pass at the end. Only one came easy (the 53-yard run), and the rest he had to twist and turn and come up with key first downs."

Alexander said he wasn't expecting the MVP trophy. "Not with the kind of game Benjamin had and him being on the winning team. I thought he would win it." Would or should? "I thought he would. I'm happy to have it. I'm not going to take it over there and give it to him."

McClendon was asked why Woodley didn't play more since Ensminger seemed to be having an off day. "We divided their time at first. Woodley's game was pretty even, but we put Ensminger back in because he has run the two-minute offense better and more often." Ensminger said, "I was throwing good except for the first one. I didn't play that bad. They were just good."

Coach Mac summarized the Sun Bowl experience this way. "We were just glad to be here. You don't have as good a time when you lose. But it's been a good year, and I think next year we can have a conference contender, I hope. We'll be a good sound team."

Coach Walsh left no doubt that he considered Alexander quite a back. "This is the best defensive game we played this season. The main thing was tackling number four (Alexander), but we didn't bring him down every time." Bill thought penalties hurt his running game but praised his quarterback. "Without any doubt, Benjamin is the best quarterback in college football. This is one of his best games ever considering he had no interceptions."

Stanford LB Gordy Ceresino earned the Outstanding Lineman trophy for his 18 tackles and four assists. "This is our biggest win because 50 million people (an overstatement) were watching, and I believe most people think of Stanford football players as intellectual, high class pussycats. Today we showed everybody we can play real football. Stanford is on the rise. The only thing that could be better would be to win the Rose

Bowl next year." Gordy also praised LSU's star back. "Alexander is a lot faster and stronger than I thought. After films, I looked at him as a tall, frail back. But if you don't hit him, wave bye-bye."

Ten 1977 Tigers played pro football: RB Charles Alexander, WR Carlos Carson, RB Hokie Gajan, TE Greg LaFleur, DB Marcus Quinn, DB Willie Teal, LB Lyman White, LB Blake Whitlatch, CB Chris Williams, and QB David Woodley.

Liberty Bowl vs. Missouri

One good half isn't enough

Liberty Bowl Memorial Stadium, Memphis, Tennessee
December 23, 1978

Carl Maddox retired as athletic director after eleven years. His controversial replacement was Paul Dietzel, who had coached LSU to the pinnacle of college football in 1958 and two more top five finishes in '59 and '61. But after promising, "I'll never leave LSU," he took the head coaching job at Army. Ironically, Paul became the athletic director at Indiana in 1975, and his Hoosiers upset the Tigers to start the '77 season.

LSU's Season

Charley McClendon's 17th season as head coach was expected to be his last in accordance with the two-year extension he received after the 1976 season. With nine returning starters on offense, including All-American TB Charles Alexander, and five on defense, LSU ranked #13 in the preseason AP poll. Juniors Steve Ensminger and David Woodley continued to alternate at quarterback.

With the opening of the west upper deck at Tiger Stadium, a record crowd of 78,534 saw the Tigers even the score with Indiana 24–17. Next came an unimpressive 13–11 squeaker over Wake Forest and a 37–7 thumping of Rice in Houston during which Alexander broke the school record for career total offense.

The first real test came the next week in Gainesville, and LSU passed it with flying colors, dominating the Gators 34–21. The momentum of that road victory carried over to the first half at home against Georgia the next week. But the Bulldogs overcame a 17–7 halftime deficit to win 24–17. The Tigers rebounded with easy road wins over Kentucky and Ole Miss.

Next came the annual loss to Bear Bryant's Crimson Tide. Alexander's Heisman hopes suffered a big setback when he gained only 46 yards. It would not be the last time that a Tiger running back's Heisman hopes died at Bryant-Denny Stadium.

An announcement the following week made the rest of the season anti-climactic. Dietzel told the press that McClendon's contract would be extended one more year through the 1979 season after which "I will recommend a new head football coach ... the best available from the ranks of proven head collegiate football coaches." The extension would allow Charley to fulfill a longtime dream to serve as president of the American

Football Coaches Association. Also in that news-filled week, the Liberty Bowl extended LSU an unconditional invitation.

Alexander gained only 57 yards in a 16–14 loss to Mississippi State that dropped the Tigers out of the Top 25. Did the McClendon announcement have an effect on the lackluster performance? "I don't think so," said SB Mike Quintella. "We just didn't play worth a damn."

The Tigers defeated Tulane 40–21 and Wyoming 24–17 to finish with an 8–3 record. Alexander finished fifth in the Heisman voting, four places higher than the year before.

The Opponent

First year coach Warren Powers led Missouri to a 7–4 record and their first bowl game in five seasons. His tenure couldn't have started any better—a 3–0 victory at Notre Dame. The other signature win came in the last game of season, a wild 35–31 triumph at Nebraska. The Tigers of the Big Eight Conference had two common opponents with LSU. Both beat Ole Miss, Mizzou by 45–14 and LSU by 30–8. Both lost to Alabama, Mizzou by 38–20 and LSU by 31–10. For his quick turnaround in Columbia, Powers was voted the Walter Camp Coach of the Year.

His outstanding offensive player was 6'5" 245-pound All-American TE Kellen Winslow, who led all Mizzou receivers with 29 catches for 479 yards—a 16.5 yards average. The future Pro Football Hall of Famer credited Powers' shifting the offense from the power-I to the veer for his increases in receptions and yardage. "Last year in the power-I, most of my receptions were short shots, mostly because of a new quarterback." Now QB Phil Bradley "knows our offense, and we can run the deeper routes, and the veer is much

Charles Alexander goes over the top against Wake Forest (*Gumbo* Class of 1979).

quicker-hitting for the backs. We don't have to spend all that time getting beat up on the blocking assignments." Bruising 6'3" 225-pound sophomore James Wilder led the ground attack with 873 yards while smaller but more elusive Earl Gant gained 789.

The defense was led by co-captain LB Chris Garlich, the leading tackler and an honorable mention All-American, and 6'3" 240-pound DT Steve Hamilton, whom Chris called "an animal." Garlich spoke for his team when he said he was "real excited about it (the bowl). It's a great chance for us since we've never been to a bowl game." As for LSU, "I know they have a great back in Alexander. He's the one we're going to have to concentrate on stopping a lot. However, we've played against some tough teams this year and fared pretty well against them."

Hamilton also looked forward to playing the SEC Tigers. "I feel they are strong offensively since they have such good running backs. They have a big line and are strong up front…. And, they have an All-American back, but basically we're looking at holding them up and shutting them down. We stopped Notre Dame and Nebraska, and we know we can play defense." FL Leo Lewis summarized the team's attitude. "It's an important game for the whole state of Missouri. This is a good time to prove Missouri is back."

The two teams had nearly identical rushing statistics with Mizzou having a slight edge 244.6–243.5. But the Black and Gold Tigers surpassed LSU in passing, 169.6 yards per game to 131.7. As usual, LSU's strong suit was its defense, which led the SEC, holding opponents to 283.8 yards per game.

Missouri was favored by seven points, but LSU could find hope in the fact that the underdog had won nine of the last ten Liberty Bowls.

The Game

A record crowd of 53,064 watched the Tiger fight on a sunny 55° afternoon. They saw the Bayou Bengals continue their trend of playing just one good half.

FIRST QUARTER

Each team scored on its first possession. Running more option plays than they did during the regular season and getting off the ball fast and hard, Missouri embarked on a relentless 75-yard, 13-play drive that showcased QB Phil Bradley's dual threat capability and the running of James Wilder and Earl Gant. On successive plays, Bradley rolled out and ran for a first down, then passed to Carl Downer for 18 more to the LSU 45. Facing fourth down and less than a yard on the next series, Coach Powers said go for it, and Gerry Ellis gained just enough. With LSU contesting every yard, Mizzou faced a third-and-one. But Wilder knifed through left tackle for 9 yards to move the chains to the LSU 16. After a gain of three, Gant took a pitchout around right end to the pylon.

Score: Missouri 7 LSU 0 (8:43)

LSU surprised Mizzou by putting both quarterbacks, Steve Ensminger and David Woodley, in the backfield. But when two plays gained only a yard, Ensminger went to the sideline. Woodley then rolled out for a first down at the 38. Charles Alexander took a handoff through a big hole at left tackle for 23 yards to the Missouri 39. Ara Parseghian, the former Notre Dame coach doing color commentary for the ABC telecast, explained the contrasting styles of the teams' top runners. Alexander had quick feet and made defenders miss whereas Winder ran straight ahead and powered through tacklers. After two runs gained six, Woodley rolled left and found SB Mike Quintella for 16 yards. The defense then blitzed on two of the next three snaps, dropping Woodley for a loss and disrupting two pass attempts. So with the wind at his back, Mike Conway booted a 37-yard field goal.

Missouri 7 LSU 3

The Big Eight Tigers started moving again. Wilder skirted left end for 13, and Bradley tossed 10 yards to Downer. Gant galloped 24 yards on a reverse to the LSU 25. After Ellis gained 11, all-SEC DE John Adams and sophomore DT Benjy Thibodaux sacked Bradley at the LSU 23. So Jeff Brockhaus tried a field goal that sailed wide.

When LSU went three-and-out, Bill Whitaker returned Adams' punt 20 yards to the LSU 48. Gant's 5-yard run ended the quarter. Mizzou led in first downs 9–3, yardage 138–51, and time of possession 10:58–4:02.

Missouri 7 LSU 3

SECOND QUARTER

Facing fourth-and-seven, Missouri sent in Brockhaus to punt. LSU rushed ten men but failed to block the punt, which went into the end zone. LB Craig Hensley crashed into Brockhaus to give Mizzou a first down at the 30. Given new life, Mizzou continued to their second touchdown. Showing his versatility, Wilder gained 13 on two runs and took a flat pass for three more to the 14. The Bengals had done an excellent job on Kellen Winslow, shutting him out to this point. But on second-and-12, Bradley rolled right and threw to the big tight end at the eight, where he sidestepped CB Willie Teal and ran into the end zone.

Missouri 14 LSU 3 (11:13)

LSU's possession showed promise when Woodley tossed 26 yards to Quintela to the 46. But the next three plays netted -3 yards. After a punt exchange, the Bengals took over at their 38. Woodley tried to hit Quintela again, but the ball went off Mike's hands to DB Eric Wright at the 34.

The defenses continued to dominate. Two more punts set up Missouri at the LSU 49 with 3:29 left, enough time to add to their lead. Three Wilder runs made it fourth down with a foot to go. Mizzou went for it. Bradley rolled right and threw to Gant who raced all the way to the seven. A penalty on LSU on the play put the pigskin at the 3½. Wilder took a handoff and ran through two defenders into the end zone. The PAT try failed.

Missouri 20 LSU 3 (1:21)

In the final minute, Ensminger's pass was tipped by Wright and intercepted by Eric Berg to give Mizzou another shot at the LSU 48. The Bengals finally got a break when Bradley's 18-yard keeper was negated by a penalty. Undaunted, the Mizzou signal-caller hit WR Leo Lewis for 25 yards, then raced to the 15 on the next snap. However, a 15-yard penalty brought back the run, and the half mercifully ended for LSU.

Missouri 20 LSU 3

The halftime statistics showed Missouri running 49 plays in 18:38 of possession time to LSU's 33 and 11:22. Benjy Thibodeaux said after the game, "We got a lot more fired up the second half. We had too many breakdowns, and it seemed like we would hold them two downs and lose on the third." Woodley expressed a similar frustration for the offense. "It seemed like we would get three plays, then a mistake."

Third Quarter

Needing to assert themselves to have any chance of catching Mizzou, the LSU offense drove 80 yards to their first touchdown behind an all-senior offensive line led by all-SEC RT Robert Dugas. Alexander broke free for gains of 15 and 19 to make it first-and-10 at the Missouri 43. On third-and-four, Woodley hit SE Carlos Carson to the 28. Two Alexander runs and a keeper by Woodley gained a first down at the 13. After another 6-yard gain by Charles, FB Hokie Gajan burst through the center of the line to make it first-and-goal inside the one. Alexander launched himself into the end zone for his 14th touchdown of the season. Mike Conway's PAT kick was blocked.

Missouri 20 LSU 9 (9:37)

Missouri couldn't control the ball the second half the way they did in the first 30 minutes. After the game, Bradley hinted at some displeasure with the second half play selection. "We played conservatively in the second half. Let's put it that way." But another reason was the improved play of LSU's defense after the break. Kent Broha, LSU's senior defensive tackle, explained, "We got more adjusted to what they were doing during the second half. I could have even called out some of their plays, by the formation or the way a back was cheating up a step, things like that. The first half I guess we were too busy feeling out the man over us." McClendon added, "We made some adjustments, but the greatest one was just coming off the line. We just weren't doing that in the first half."

Missouri's first possession after the LSU touchdown ended with CB Brent Elkins intercepting a long pass on his knees at the two. Elkins had replaced starter James Britt when the freshman suffered a broken jaw on Missouri's opening drive. A safety by trade, Elkins said, "I've never played a down of cornerback in my life." But LSU's defense didn't get a long rest because two plays later, Mizzou returned the favor when Whitaker picked off Woodley's pass at the LSU 40.

Starting from the 20 after forcing another punt, LSU gave Missouri a dose of their own medicine by keeping the ball the rest of the period. Alexander did most of the heavy lifting with runs by Woodley and Gajan mixed in.

Missouri 20 LSU 9

Fourth Quarter

LSU had all the momentum until the turnover bug bit them again on the first play of the period. Playing a second-and-nine from the Missouri 25, Woodley took the shotgun snap and scrambled to the right. He fumbled when hit by NG Norman Goodman, and Berg recovered for Missouri. LSU put the quarterback under center the rest of the game although McClendon admitted, "The fumble was not caused by the formation but after the play developed." Offensive coordinator Lynn Amedee, who suggested the shotgun snap, explained his reasoning. "We felt they would blitz, but still we could get Woodley outside on a sprint and get away from their line quicker. We needed a big play. I think Mike Quintela was open, too, but he (Woodley) didn't see the blitz coming. We felt all along we could throw on them because other people have. And they play ball control, so we felt we needed to try to get quicker."

After two punts, Bradley and Company started from their 39, but a holding penalty proved to be too much to overcome. So Chris Williams fair caught the punt at the LSU 33 with 7:29 on the clock.

The Bengals started a promising drive led by Ensminger, the better passer of the two quarterbacks. With the Mizzou secondary playing loose, Steve hit Quintana and Carson on quick out patterns to move to midfield. Then Carlos snagged another to the 34. But if you live by the pass, you might die by the pass. Kurt Peterson repelled the threat when he stepped in front of a sideline attempt with 5:27 remaining.

LSU held and started another march deep into Missouri territory. Woodley's 15-yard scramble with a personal foul penalty tacked on moved the ball to the Mizzou 42. Then David converted three straight third downs by passing to Carson to the 21, then the nine, then the one. But Missouri forced LSU to take the full four downs to score. David faked to Alexander diving into the line and kept the ball over the left side into the end zone. The two-point conversion pass fell incomplete.

Missouri 20 LSU 15 (1:33)

A black shirt Tiger grabbed Conway's squib kick just before a white shirt Tiger arrived. With LSU using its last two timeouts, Missouri ran the ball four times, including on fourth down. Powers explained afterward, "They had a better chance of blocking a punt than throwing a home run."

Taking over with only 17 seconds left, Woodley threw to Carson, who was tackled inbounds. Time expired before LSU could run another play.

Final Score: Missouri 20 LSU 15

Alexander gained 133 yards on 24 carries to earn LSU's outstanding offensive player award while sophomore DT Benjy Thibodeaux, with seven unassisted tackles and eight assists, received the defensive trophy.

Postgame

Coach McClendon summarized the game like this. "Turnovers and mistakes, particularly when we roughed their kicker, killed us in the first half. With all those turnovers (four interceptions and a fumble), it's a wonder the score was anything like it was. … We did play a good second half. I'd have been disappointed if we hadn't."

Mac said Alexander "put on a real performance, but he didn't have a heckuva lot of help." Charley also praised Missouri's stars. "Wilder is a real tough runner, but their quarterback was most impressive. He has a lot of poise."

A dozen 1978 Tigers played pro football: RB Charles Alexander, DB James Britt, DB Clinton Burrell, WR Carlos Carson, RB Hokie Gajan, WR Orlando McDaniel, DB Marcus Quinn, DB Willie Teal, OL Mike Turner, LB Lyman White, CB Chris Williams, and QB David Woodley.

Tangerine Bowl vs. Wake Forest

*"No way possible we were going
to lose that football game"*

Orlando Stadium, Orlando, Florida
December 22, 1979

Charley McClendon's last season as LSU coach ended with an emotional bowl victory.

LSU's Season

When the 1979 schedule was revealed, all eyes focused on the third game—mighty Southern California at Tiger Stadium. When the Trojans received the #1 ranking in the preseason AP poll, anticipation reached a fever pitch.

The Tigers easily disposed of their first two opponents, Colorado 44–0 and Rice 47–3, to jump into the AP standings at #20. Out West, commentators were calling John Robinson's squad perhaps the finest USC team ever. Thirty-three players, counting redshirts, would play in the NFL. "It's quite likely," said McClendon, "this is the most talented team ever to play in Tiger Stadium." A record crowd of 78,322 roared from start to finish, inspiring their heroes to play the game of their lives. LSU led 12–3 going into the final period before the visitors rallied to pull out a 16–12 victory.

No one could have blamed the Tigers if they suffered a letdown the next week when they hosted Florida. Instead, they belted the Gators 20–3. The pattern of alternating wins and losses continued through the rest of the season. One of the losses was a nationally televised game against #8 Florida State at home. Two weeks later, the Tigers played the new #1, Alabama, off their feet on a rainy night only to fall 3–0. In Coach Mac's last home game of his career, the Tigers leveled Mississippi State 21–3. The season ended with a disappointing 24–13 loss to Tulane in the Superdome. Fortunately, LSU had already accepted an invitation to the Tangerine Bowl.

The Opponent

In their second season under head coach John Mackovic, the Wake Forest Demon

Deacons compiled an 8–3 record, good for fourth place in the Atlantic Coast Conference. It would be the school's third bowl game and first in thirty years.

The Deacons' top victory was a 22–21 squeaker at Georgia, where LSU would lose 21–14 a few weeks later. They also defeated another SEC team, Auburn, 42–38.

Wake gained 58 percent of their yardage through the air. QB Jay Venuto passed for 2,432 yards to earn the Atlantic Coast Conference Player of the Year award. One thousand of those yards went to WR Wayne Baumgarner. The workhorse of the ground game was RB James McDougald with 1,177 yards.

After his own running game was a season-long disappointment, McClendon predicted, "You're gonna see the ball in the air quite a bit." The Deacons fanned five receivers across the field 75 percent of the time. "I know we can cover five people but not six, and I know there are that many coming out of the backfield," said Jolly Cholly. He also promised to rotate more players than was his custom. "Some people have done a little better job since we've regrouped" for the bowl game.

The '79 Tigers finished the season with the reputation of being a one-dimensional passing team. Mackovic pointed out that LSU threw 56 times in its last game against Tulane, more than his team ever attempted. "We've called that many," he admitted, "but we didn't get them all off."

Ticket sales showed much more interest in the game from the Wake Forest faithful than from Tiger fans. Although Wake was a much smaller school than LSU, 11,000 Deacons fans bought tickets while Tiger followers mustered only a little more than 2,000. Miffed Tangerine Bowl officials felt they were misled as to the drawing power of LSU.

The Game

Shortly before the kickoff, McClendon cleared the locker room of assistant coaches and addressed his team. "When I came here, I never thought I'd be at LSU 27 years. I knew this day would come. As you become a grown athlete, you push it back. But it's here…." With teary eyes, he continued, "I've never done anything. Anything I have you gave me, you and those assistant coaches out there. I'll give my right arm for those people. And tonight I'm asking you to do the same thing for them. There's no tomorrow. … God bless you all." When he left the players alone, they vowed to win this one for their beloved coach. LB Mark Ippolito recalls, "We loved Coach Mac. He was a player's coach and basically our dad at LSU. I don't think there was any way possible we were going to lose that football game."

The Tigers exploded onto the field and overwhelmed Wake Forest in the first half before a record Tangerine Bowl crowd of 38,666.

FIRST QUARTER

Earlier rains made the field a bit muddy, but nothing slowed down the Tiger offense, which was determined to show they could run the ball as well as pass. David Woodley directed an 80-yard march behind an offensive line that controlled the line of scrimmage. The big gainers were a quick 11-yard throw to WR Jerry Murphree, a 9-yard burst by FB Jude Hernandez, a slant pass to WR Orlando McDaniel for 10, and another reception by

Steve Ensminger runs the option play (*Gumbo* Class of 1980).

Murphree for 13 to the Wake 22. On third down from the 14, Woodley kept over left end and, aided by an excellent block by Murphree, scampered into the end zone. Donny Barthel booted the PAT.

LSU 7 Wake Forest 0 (9:08)

The Deacons overcame Lyman White's 7-yard sack of Jay Venuto to gain one first down on a 19-yard draw play by James McDougald before the march ended abruptly when SS Marcus Quinn intercepted a pass at the Wake 35. Six plays later, LSU was back in the end zone. Facing no pressure from the defense, Woodley hit SE Orlando McDaniel for 15 yards to the 20. The Tigers got a break when Woodley rolled left and, with a defender hanging onto his leg, lobbed a pass to SE Carlos Carson to set up fourth-and-two at the 12. David kept the ball at right end behind Hernandez's block for 3 yards to keep the drive alive. Then Woodley attacked the other side of the defense, cutting between two would-be tacklers at the goal line for his second six-pointer of the game.

LSU 14 Wake Forest 0 (4:14)

Facing constant Tiger pressure, Venuto continued to overthrow his receivers. So LSU got good field position at its 46 following a three-and-out punt. Steve Ensminger moved under center and handed off twice to FB Danny Soileau for first downs. Three straight quarterback keepers set up second-and-goal at the six.

LSU 14 Wake Forest 0

SECOND QUARTER

Pass interference in the end zone made it first-and-goal at the one. Freshman TB Jesse Myles tried to leap into the end zone but fell short. When he tried it again, he lost control of the ball, and DB Eddie Green recovered at the one. Needing a big play to gain some momentum, the Deacons got it when Venuto connected with streaking WR Wayne Baumgarner for a gain of 45 yards to midfield. That allowed Wake to flip the field four plays later on a punt to the 13.

With Ensminger at the controls, five straight runs moved the ball to the 37. Steve hit SE Tracy Porter at the WF 40. After FB Hokie Gajan gained seven, the Wake Forest defense made three straight fine plays, including stuffing Ensminger for no gain on third down and doing the same to Murphree on fourth down. The Deacons made one first down before a 14-yard sack by Ivan Phillips forced a punt that put LSU in a hole at the nine.

Woodley came in and made it look easy, moving the Tigers to their third touchdown in only five plays. Following a face mask penalty on the second play that moved the ball to the 30, the senior quarterback from Shreveport hit Carson to the WF 19. After an incompletion, Woodley lofted a pass to Murphree running an out and up pattern down the right side. Jerry snagged the ball on the run over the defender in the end zone.

LSU 21 Wake Forest 0 (3:28)

A strange play quickly set up the Tigers deep in Wake territory again. Albert Kirby had the ball inadvertently kicked out of his hand by one of his linemen who was on the ground, and LB Albert Richardson recovered at the 20. Intervention from on high for Mac's last game?

After Woodley connected with Lionel Wallis to the 11, the Deacons brought pressure that caused two incompletions. So LSU settled for a 31-yard field goal by Barthel.

LSU 24 Wake Forest 0 (2:53)

Kenny Duckett returned the kickoff 43 yards to the 45. The Deacons took to the air and moved quickly to the LSU 32. Then Willie Teal intercepted an ill-advised throw into the end zone.

But the Demons regained possession when Woodley scrambled to escape the rush and threw a pass that Landon King picked off at the WF 34. Coach Mackovic inserted David Webber at quarterback, and lo and behold the sophomore, who was only one-for-five passing for the season, led the Deacons to their first points. He connected with TE Mike Mullen to the LSU 47 with 0:20 on the clock, then hit FB Bob Ventresca at the sideline for 20 more. That was close enough for Phil Denfeld to kick a 43-yard field goal as time expired.

LSU 24 Wake Forest 3

McClendon later called his team's play "the best first half we've had all season." Wake coaches undoubtedly reminded their squad that they had trailed #13 Auburn 38–20 at halftime back in October before rallying to win 42–38.

THIRD QUARTER

The Deacons came out like a team reborn. Going to quick passes with the offensive line getting off the ball faster, they drove 80 yards to cut the margin to 14. Two completions by Venuto to his favorite targets, McDougald and Baumgarner, moved the ball to the 41. Then a short pass to McDougald turned into a 25-yard gain to the LSU 34. Two plays later, Jay threw long down the right sideline to Baumgarner, who turned and caught the underthrown ball in the end zone before DB James Britt arrived.

LSU 24 Wake Forest 10 (11:45)

Coach McClendon was concerned on the LSU sideline. "I'll give credit to coach Mackovic and his staff. They didn't let up when they came out for the second half, and they took the ball 80 yards for a touchdown. For a while there, I had visions of another effort like they did against Auburn when they overcame an 18-point deficit to win."

The Wake defense did their part to keep momentum on the Black and Gold side by forcing a three-and-out. So John Adams came in for his first punt of the evening. After two runs moved the chains to the WF 46, LSU dug in and forced a punt that went out of bounds on the 16.

Woodley zipped up the middle on a quarterback draw to the 38. But Gajan fumbled on the next play, Wake recovering at the 48. With a chance to pull within a touchdown, the Deacons could gain only 3 yards. So they settled for kicking LSU into a deep hole at the five.

On third-and-five, Ensminger ran a quarterback draw to the 22 to give the Tigers some breathing room. But a couple of incompletions brought in Adams, and Wake again enjoyed excellent starting position at their 46. They started moving again before another strange turnover stopped them. Venuto took a deep drop and tossed to Baumgarner over the middle to the LSU 37. McDougald gained six and Ventresca 14 more to the 17. Then LSU brought the heat, forcing Venuto to run to his right. Just before being knocked out of bounds by Adams, Jay tried to toss the ball to avoid a big loss. Instead, the pigskin went straight into the hands of DT Benjy Thibodaux at the 28.

After the game, Coach Mackovic cited the interception as a turning point. "At the half, we determined that we had to come out and play with more intensity, and I thought we did a good job early in the second half. We lost a great deal of momentum on that one play. Jay was trying to throw it. We had a halfback in that area." RB James McDougald called the turnover "the straw that broke the camel's back."

LSU 24 Wake Forest 10

FOURTH QUARTER

LSU's offense finally put more points on the board. Taking advantage of a blown coverage, Woodley threw long to Porter for 48 yards to the WF 22. But a delay of game penalty and two sacks made it third-and-22. A screen pass to Hernandez gained a few more yards to make Barthel's job easier. His 41-yard field goal gave LSU a three-score advantage again.

LSU 27 Wake Forest 10

Needing to answer, the Deacons gained one first down before Lyman White leveled Venuto for a sack and knocked him out of the game. Ensminger returned and topped off his LSU career by leading the Tigers 58 yards to put the game away if it wasn't already. Steve completed three in a row—Wallis for four, then, escaping the pressure, 18 yards to Carson, and Murphree for 11 more to the nine. After Leroid Jones gained five, Steve decided to finish the drive himself. He kept off the left side twice, lunging over the goal line on the second carry.

LSU 34 Wake Forest 10 (8:32)

When LSU got the ball back, Woodley came in for one last series of his career and sped 21 yards to the Wake 30. Four plays later, Barthel missed a 34-yard field goal attempt. But LSU got the ball back on the next play when former QB Robert Lane, now playing safety, intercepted a pass and returned it to the WF 40. With freshman Robbie Mahfouz seeing action at quarterback, three runs gained 6 yards. So Barthel tried a 50-yarder that fell short.

With second- and even third-stringers getting playing time on both sides, Wake Forest drove to the LSU 21 before giving up the ball on downs.

**Final Score: LSU 34
Wake Forest 10**

McClendon ended his 18-year tenure with a record of 137–59–7 (.692), which is still the most wins in school history by 23 over Les Miles. The victory ended LSU's four-game bowl losing streak and pushed Mac's postseason record over .500—seven wins against six losses.

LSU swept the three MVP awards. QB David Woodley won

Coach McClendon carried off after his last game as LSU coach (Gr/AP/Shutterstock.com).

the overall award while SB Jerry Murphree and DT Benjy Thibodeaux were named the offensive and defensive winners.

Postgame

Coach McClendon: "I'm going to push back and relax and take a look at things, but as far as I'm concerned, I've coached my last college game except for the all-star game (East-West Shrine Game). ... Two hours before the game, I started realizing it was the last game. And I got choked up more than once and had to get off by myself a little while." He praised his assistant coaches. "They really prepared for this game, and I asked the players to win it for them. They are very capable, and I don't expect them to have any trouble finding jobs. I plan on helping them as much as I can." He continued, "Our two quarterbacks did a tremendous job tonight. ... I thought the big difference was at the beginning when our receivers were catching the ball. They caught everything thrown at them."

LSU C John Ed Bradley said, "We broke a bunch of jinxes tonight. People said we couldn't win on the road, and we couldn't beat a good team. We did that tonight. I'm proud to end my career like that. We're going out winners."

Mark Ippolito recalls, "We won the game, but we were sad because we lost our head coach. It was a somber feeling, like a funeral."

Coach Mackovic: "We didn't play very well, but LSU had a lot to do with that. Their offense did a good job controlling the game, and their pass rush was tremendous. We dropped passes in the first half and made mistakes."

Fifteen 1979 Tigers played pro football: DB James Britt, WR Carlos Carson, RB Hokie Gajan, TE Greg LaFleur, DL Leonard Marshall, WR Orlando McDaniel, RB Jesse Myles, WR Tracy Porter, DB Marcus Quinn, TE Malcolm Scott, DB Willie Teal, OL Mike Turner, LB Lyman White, CB Chris Williams, and QB David Woodley.

Orange Bowl vs. Nebraska

"You just played the No. 3 team to a standoff"

Orange Bowl, Miami, Florida
January 1, 1983

The LSU Board of Supervisors chose Charles "Bo" Rein, the North Carolina State coach, as the successor of Charlie McClendon for the 1980 season. However, 42 days later, Rein died in an aircraft crash while returning from a recruiting trip. Athletic Director Paul Dietzel recommended 38-year-old assistant coach Jerry Stovall to succeed Rein. Jerry ranked as one of the greatest players in LSU history. His senior season, 1962, the ace running back finished second in the Heisman voting. Dietzel praised Stovall, a member of Paul's last two Tiger teams, as "young, tough, aggressive, articulate, a great recruiter with superior integrity."

Jerry's first LSU squad finished 7–4 but did not receive a bowl bid. Then his 1981 squad went 3–7–1. But his excellent recruiting paid off in '82.

LSU's Season

With 22 future NFL players on the roster—the most in school history to that point, the Tigers started with seven wins and a tie. Two exciting home-grown freshmen running backs, Dalton Hilliard from Patterson and Garry James from Gretna, helped senior QB Alan Risher direct an offense that scored 45 against Oregon State and 52 at Rice in the opening games. A 24–13 win in Gainesville vaulted the Tigers into the AP rankings at #18. After the disappointing tie with Tennessee, Stovall's squad ripped off four more wins, the last one being the first victory over Alabama in 12 years. The 20–10 beatdown in what would be Bear Bryant's last year as head coach was not as close as the score indicates. LSU gained 20 first downs to six for the Tide and held a 320–119 edge in yardage. The victory moved the Tigers up to #6 in the AP poll.

But they didn't stay in that heady stratosphere long. They fell to Mississippi State in Starkville the following week, 27–24, in what today would be called a "trap" game. The Tigers then hosted Florida State for the fourth straight season. The #7 Seminoles had beaten LSU by a combined 45 points in the three previous games. But this LSU team could match FSU's talent and scored their third win over a top ten team, a 42–14 shellacking as oranges rained down from the frenzied fans. But just as they had done after the Alabama triumph, the Tigers followed a great performance with a stinker, losing to

Tulane 31–28 to drop to #13 and diminish the luster of their meeting with #3 Nebraska in Miami.

The Opponent

Nebraska came to Miami still glowing from the 28–24 win over Oklahoma for the Big Eight Conference title and the host spot in the Orange Bowl for the second straight year. The only blemish on the Cornhuskers' record was a 27–24 last-second defeat at Penn State in the third game. Tom Osborne's offense, led by QB Turner Gill, topped the 40-point total in eight of the twelve games and ended the season #1 in the nation with an incredible average of 518.6 yards per game. Despite ankle problems, RB Mike Rozier gained a school-record 1,578 yards, which was good for third in the nation. When he was out, Roger Craig filled the void, especially in the second half of the Oklahoma game. The Huskers ran the ball 78 percent of the time. When they passed, Gill's favorite target was WR Irving Fryar, who averaged 12.3 yards per catch.

The Blackshirts, as the Husker defense was called, held opponents to 14 or fewer points eight times and ranked #13 in the country in defensive efficiency. Eleven different players snared at least one of the 16 interceptions.

LSU was as much as a two-touchdown underdog on some boards.

The Game

Only 54,407 persons of the 68,713 who bought tickets showed up on a warm, humid night, making it the smallest Orange Bowl crowd since 1947. A civil disturbance earlier in the week in a nearby neighborhood may have deterred many fans. Also many may have stayed home to watch Penn State and Georgia battle for the national championship in the Sugar Bowl.

FIRST QUARTER

The best way to slow down the Cornhusker offense was to control the ball. But the Tigers, using two tight ends with 5'8" 185-pound Dalton Hilliard as the lone set-back, went three-and-out after receiving the kickoff. With Garry James out of action with a strained groin muscle, Hilliard would have to bear the rushing load. Starting from their 48 after Clay Parker's weak barefoot punt, Nebraska made it look easy, reaching the end zone in just six plays. QB Turner Gill started with a short pass to WB Irving Fryar to the LSU 30. The rest of the yardage came on the ground. Gill kept on the option to each side to make it first-and-goal at the eight. Turner kept again to the two. Then he handed to bowling ball FB Mark Schellen (5'10", 230 pounds) who pushed up the middle for the touchdown.

Score: Nebraska 7 LSU 0 (10:57)

LSU returned to its regular I-formation and had more success on its second possession. Afterward, QB Alan Risher said, "It didn't bother us that they scored first. That's happened all season long. We knew we were going to move the ball and score points." He hit 6'5" TE Malcolm Scott on third-and-seven to midfield. Risher went to Scott again on the next play, but Malcolm fumbled. Fortunately, Hilliard was hustling downfield and just beat a Husker to the ball at the 29. After a false start penalty, Risher wanted to go to WR Eric Martin but, finding him covered, threw to Hilliard for a first down at the 16. Two plays later, DE Scott Strasburger sacked Alan at the 19. After an incompletion, Juan Betanzos kicked a field goal. However, Nebraska was guilty of roughing the kicker. Going against the adage that says never take points off the board, Stovall took the penalty to get the automatic first down at the nine. After Hilliard was dumped for a loss of three, Risher threw into a crowd in the middle of the field, and the tipped ball landed in the hands of DT Toby Williams at the seven.

Tiger fans had hardly started second-guessing their coach when Nebraska gave the ball right back. Ramsey Dardar, the nose guard in LSU's 3–4 defense who would battle all-American C Dave Rimington all evening, hit Mike Rozier, causing a fumble that FS Liffort Hobley recovered at the 11. Rozier said afterwards, "Before the game started, everybody was together. Then I fumbled the ball and that got us down a little bit."

It took six plays, but LSU tied the score. On third-and-seven, FB Mike Montz submarined to the one to make it fourth-and-inches. Stovall kept the field goal unit on the sideline. Risher didn't gain much on a sneak, but it was enough to keep possession inside

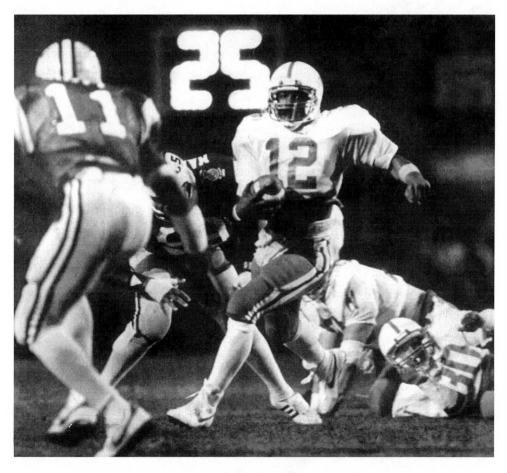

James Britt (11) blocks Turner Gill's path (*Gumbo* Class of 1983).

the one. It took two plays to gain the final inches, Hilliard crashing into the end zone behind the blocks of RG Kevin Langford and FB Montz.

Nebraska 7 LSU 7 (4:24)

Starting from the 30, the Cornhuskers alternated runs and passes to keep possession the rest of the period. A quick pass to SE Todd Brown gained a first down at the 45. A swing pass to Rozier coupled with a face mask penalty moved the pigskin to the LSU 37. A false start penalty failed to halt the advance as Gill hit Brown for 9 yards and, two plays later, connected with Fryar for another nine to make it first-and-10 at the 22. Brown snagged another pass to the 13 as the period ended.

LSU 7 Nebraska 7

Second Quarter

The Tigers ended the threat on the first play when OLB Rydell Malancon recovered Gil's fumble at the 14. Four snaps later, Fryar dropped the ball as he returned the punt, and LSU RB Gene Lang fell on it at the Cornhusker 45. Fryar complained afterward about the footballs. "They were real slick, and we couldn't hold on to them. It felt like they had plastic on them. They didn't seem to have the small dimples in them like the ones we used all season. We finally got them to change to our footballs after my fumble."

The Tigers took advantage of the break to take the lead with Hilliard doing almost all the work. First, Dalton took Risher's pass to the 21. Then he gained four more before Alan threw to him again to the three. With the Blackshirts digging in, Dalton banged into the line three times to place the ball a foot from the goal. Finally, with Nebraska figuring LSU would run to their right as they did most of the season, Risher handed to Hilliard who slanted left into the end zone.

LSU 14 Nebraska 7 (9:32)

Betanzos's sky kick backfired when FB Doug Wilkening returned it to the 41. On third-and-three, DB James Britt hit Fryar just as the ball arrived to bring on the punt team. But the snap went to Wilkening, the upback, who pushed a yard across midfield but fell an inch short of gaining the first down. Risher started with a first down pass to Scott to the 39. But after three straight incompletions, Parker punted into the end zone.

The Cornhuskers made two first downs to move into Tiger territory. First, Gill hit TE Jamie Williams for 23 yards. Rozier slashed to the LSU 47 for another first down, then powered within a foot of another one. Turner went for broke on second down but overthrew Brown at the goal line. So Gill sneaked to move the chains to the 36. The Bandits drew the line there thanks to three straight good plays. After Rozier gained nothing, LSU's all-time leading tackler, LB Al Richardson, blitzed up the middle and tackled Gill for a 4-yard loss. Then Britt knocked a pass away to prevent a big gain. So Grant Campbell punted to the nine.

Four plays later, the Cornhuskers were back in business at the LSU 42 with two minutes left in the half. Gill found Fryar down the middle to the 25—close enough to score at least three. But on third down, the Tigers pressured Gill into throwing his first interception in 83 attempts. Malancon snared it at the 15 and returned to the 28 to allow the Tigers to run out the clock.

LSU 14 Nebraska 7

Averaging almost 400 yards rushing per game, Nebraska was held to 80 on 25 attempts. They also led LSU in first downs (10–8) and total yards (186–123) but were plagued by four turnovers.

Rozier said that, at halftime, Coach Osborne "told us the nation's best offense has class, that we had to go out there and prove it in the second half." C Dave Rimington explained afterward, "We knew we could win. We've been in the same situation at the half before. We knew we were moving the ball, and we decided to stick with it. The first half, we made more mistakes than we made all year."

THIRD QUARTER

Nebraska decided to go with quick counts to prevent the LSU defense from shifting. After Jeff Smith returned the kickoff 39 yards to the 49, Rozier ran three straight times to make it second-and-three at the 23. But momentum evaporated when backup RB Craig entered. He gained only two on two carries. Stovall turned down a holding penalty on the third down carry. Osborne then made his own controversial decision, sending in the field goal unit. Old-fashioned straight-on kicker Kevin Seibel missed badly from the 30.

When LSU couldn't move, Nebraska started again at their 33. Rozier touched the ball three straight times to overcome a motion penalty and earn a first down at the 45. Then Schellen zoomed up the middle for seven. But the turnover bug bit again when Gil, with a rusher in his face, tossed an errant pitchout that ILB Lawrence Williams recovered at the 41.

LSU turned the turnover into three points. Risher threw to Hilliard on an out pattern for 15 yards. With a blitzer in his face, the senior from Slidell zipped a pass down the middle to former HB Martin, who made a spectacular diving one-handed catch at the eight. Next came a play whose significance wasn't appreciated until after the game. FB Montz ran to the one only to have an illegal procedure penalty move the ball back to the 12. That forced Risher to go back to the air without success. MG Jeff Merrell sacked him, then pressured him into two incompletions. So Betanzos kicked a 33-yard field goal.

LSU 17 Nebraska 7 (6:40)

Facing an unfamiliar situation—down 10 in the second half, the Cornhuskers moved 80 yards to their second touchdown. They got help on the second play when a late hit on Rozier put them at the 35. On third-and-two, Gill ran the option to the left, faked a pitchout, and turned upfield to the LSU 44. Backups Smith and FB Mark Moravec combined to make it fourth down and less than a yard at the 34. Gill fired to Brown to the 17. Turner said he had three options on the play, with Fryar being the primary receiver. But "they had a defensive end covering him. I could have also run, but I threw the ball to Brown because he was open." Three plays later, Gill tossed a swing pass to Rozier, who had gone in motion to the right. With no linebacker near him, Mike ran down the sideline and just made it past the pylon as Hobley hit him.

LSU 17 Nebraska 14 (1:25)

LSU's possession started auspiciously with Risher hitting Scott in stride down the middle for 25 yards to the 45. But 9 yards of the gain was immediately wiped out by DE

Tony Felici's team-leading 14th sack. Then Merrell and DT Toby Williams followed suit to end the period.

LSU 17 Nebraska 14

FOURTH QUARTER

Parker lined up to punt and made a decision that cost LSU dearly. With a lone rusher roaring in from his right, he stopped his punting motion to let the defender go by. Clay had time to get the kick away but decided to run instead. He gained 11 but needed 20. The TV announcers wondered if Parker had mistaken the stick marking the start of the series for the first down marker.

Nebraska drove 48 yards for the go-ahead touchdown. A crucial play was the pass interference call on James Britt on a third-and-five pass that gave the Cornhuskers a first down at the 35. On the next third down, Gill hit Fryar on the dead run streaking across the middle at the 20. Irving continued to the five. Rozier plunged to the one to set up Gill's jump over center into the end zone.

Nebraska 21 LSU 17 (11:14)

Eric Martin made a poor decision when he tried to run the kickoff out from a yard deep only to be tackled at the 12. Risher, only 10-for-25 passing because of relentless pressure, fired a fastball to Martin at the sideline for 6 yards. After Montz gained two, Risher's pass was almost intercepted. So Parker boomed a punt to the Nebraska 32, but he out-kicked his coverage. Fryar roared 43 yards to the 25. The Bandits dug in and allowed only 7 yards on three runs. So Seibel lined up for another field goal. Noticing that Gill was the holder, Stovall suspected a fake and noticed a Cornhusker just in bounds on his sideline. Sure enough, Gill took the snap and threw to Tim Brungardt wide open inside the 10. But the backup running back dropped the ball.

Two plays later, LSU was in trouble again. An overthrown pass bounced off the hands of S Bret Clark into the hands of CB Dave Burke lying on his back. Gill went for the home run right away, but Britt knocked the ball away from Brown at the 10. Then Rich-ardson tipped Gil's pass into the hands of LB Lawrence Williams, who returned 6 yards to the Nebraska 37.

Hilliard ran twice and took a pass to bring up fourth-and-one. LSU lined up to go for it only to commit their first delay of game penalty of the season. Risher explained, "We had a sweep called, but they came out in a defense that didn't look good. I had to get us out of the play and switch to an off-tackle power play." So Stovall sent in Betan-zos, who thrilled LSU fans by kicking a 50-yard field goal. Osborne didn't fault the strategy. "I'm sure Jerry felt they could get the ball back and maybe go for another field goal."

Nebraska 21 LSU 20 (5:05)

The Bandits had battled the #1 offense in the nation all evening. They needed one more stop to give the offense a chance to steal the victory with another field goal. Betan-zos had confidence that he could kick the winner if given a chance. But the Nebraska offensive line that boasted three future NFL players wouldn't let that happen. Rozier reached the 100-yard mark with a 15-yard scamper. With LSU burning timeouts, Mike converted two more third downs. Finally, Gill sealed the victory by passing to Fryar on third-and-eight.

Final Score: Nebraska 21 LSU 20

Postgame

Coach Stovall was pleased with his team's performance. "I told them … you just played the No. 3 team to a standoff. I told them all week we would win with 30 seconds to go on a field goal. If we had stopped them on that last drive, I think we would have." Jerry ranked Nebraska as the best team the Tigers faced all season.

Alan Risher said, "The Nebraska defense is much more physical up front than we expected. Their pass rush was rushing me all night."

NG Ramsey Dardar was not impressed with C Dave Rimington. "We kept telling the referees they were holding. The referees just laughed at us and told us to play ball. To me, he's not the greatest center. He's not as quick as some people say. (Steve) Mott from Alabama is better."

Looking tired and relieved, Coach Osborne praised his 12–1 team as "the best one I've had in my 10 years at Nebraska" and hoped they would get considered for the #1 ranking in the final polls. "I really don't think we played well enough for No. 1 consideration tonight, but when you look at the entire season, I think we're the only team that won 12 games. … But the way it will turn out, it looks like we could be No. 2. I hope we are No. 2." He said that the big factor in the game "was that we were able to hang on to the football at the end." Tom called LSU "a team of the future. … Their backs run super hard and, with their young talent, I would say their future is ahead of them. They certainly are one of the best teams we've played this year."

C Dave Rimington spoke for his 27 fellow seniors who had lost to Oklahoma and Clemson in previous Orange Bowls. "I'm so happy we won our last game. We seniors haven't been having much luck down here, but I guess the third time is the charm." The winner of the Lombardi and Outland trophies praised LSU's NG Ramsey Dardar. "I knew he would be tough. He hurt us a couple of times on pitch plays. I give him credit for his play tonight." Dave added, "No matter how hard you train, the heat and humidity kills you in a game down here. But I think we were in better condition than they were at the end. The way we were moving the ball, you could see it in their eyes that they knew something was going to go wrong."

QB Turner Gill explained, "We really didn't change anything at the half. … I was glad to see that they continued to have confidence in my passing. But you've got to give LSU credit because they stopped our running game pretty good."

Twenty-two 1982 Tigers played pro football: TE Mitch Andrews, DL Roland Barbay, DB James Britt, LB Shawn Burks, DB Jeffrey Dale, DB Eugene Daniel, DL Ramsey Dardar, DL Bill Elko, WR Herman Fontenot, RB Dalton Hilliard, DB Liffort Hobley, RB Garry James, LB Tim Joiner, RB Gene Lang, LB Rydell Malancon, DL Leonard Marshall, WR Eric Martin, RB Jesse Myles, QB Alan Risher, TE Malcolm Scott, OL Lance Smith, and OL Mike Turner.

Sugar Bowl vs. Nebraska

*"You have to play well
the entire game, and we didn't"*

Louisiana Superdome, New Orleans, Louisiana
January 1, 1985

After the Tigers fell to 4–7 for the 1983 season despite having 21 future pros on the roster, second-year Athletic Director Bob Brodhead fired Coach Jerry Stovall and hired 57-year-old Bill Arnsparger, who had been the defensive coordinator on the undefeated Miami Dolphins team that won Super Bowl VII. Former LSU LB A.J. Duhe, who played for Arnsparger with the Dolphins, praised the hire. "He's the best defensive coach in the country, pro or college. He's come up with more ideas and concepts about playing defense than any other coach I've known."

With a personality described as "flinty, demanding, devoid of soft edges and sentimentality" as well as "tough as nails," Arnsparger wasted no time in turning around LSU's fortunes.

LSU's Season

After opening with a 21–21 tie at Florida, the Tigers reeled off five wins, including a 23–3 victory at USC, to rise to #7 in the nation. Then Notre Dame came to Tiger Stadium and went home with a 30–22 victory that ended any hope of competing for the national championship. Conference road wins over Ole Miss and Alabama were followed by a 16–14 upset loss at Mississippi State, a foe that would prove to be a thorn in Arnsparger's side since their wishbone offense was unlike anything Bill faced in the NFL. The Tigers rebounded with a 33–15 beatdown of Tulane.

LSU finished second in the SEC standings, one game behind the Gators, thanks to Alabama's upset of Auburn in the Iron Bowl. However, the conference banned Florida from postseason play for recruiting violations. So the 16th-ranked Tigers took the SEC's spot in the Sugar Bowl.

Arnsparger might have been known as a defensive genius, but he and his staff also improved the offense. They turned the offensive line, known as the "Lunch Bunch" in '83, into a "Lean Machine." For example, All-American T Lance Smith played the '84 season at 265 pounds, 30 less than the year before. Improve your offensive line and you improve your offense. Junior QB Jeff Wickersham threw for 2,165 yards to break Alan Risher's LSU passing yardage record for a season. Senior SE Eric Martin set an SEC career receiving yardage record with 2,625. Junior RB Dalton Hilliard became only the third ball carrier in LSU history to break the 1,000-yard barrier in a season.

The Bandit defense was led by ILB Shawn Burks, the team's #1 tackler (108) and all-SEC FS Liffort Hobley, whose six interceptions ranked second in the conference. OLB Michael Brooks led the team in sacks with eight. He also recorded 11 tackles behind the line of scrimmage.

Unfortunately, the Tiger defense would play the Sugar Bowl without injured NG Henry Thomas, the anchor of the three-man front wall.

The Opponent

Despite losing their entire offensive backfield, including Heisman Trophy winner Mike Rozier, Nebraska extended its string of consecutive Top 10-rankings to 15 and consecutive bowl appearances to 15. The Big Red started the season at #2 but rose to the top after thumping Wyoming in the home opener. Wins over Minnesota and UCLA by a combined 70 points kept them there until they stumbled at the Carrier Dome, losing to Syracuse 17–9.

Six straight wins, all against Big Eight foes, moved them back to #1 and set up the annual confrontation with Oklahoma for the conference championship. The Sooners held the Cornhusker offense, which had averaged 35.2 points per game, to just seven to win by ten in Lincoln and earn the host spot in the Orange Bowl.

Head coach/offensive coordinator Tom Osborne had to deal with the loss of eight offensive starters. Two quarterbacks saw extensive playing time. Craig Sundberg was the better passer, completing 63.1 percent for 740 yards. Travis Turner gained 190 yards on 77 rushing attempts. The offensive workhorses were I-backs Doug DuBose with 1,040 yards rushing and Jeff Smith with 935.

The Big Red defense led the nation, allowing 203.3 yards per game and only 9.5 points per game. All-American S Bret Clark used his :04.4 speed in the 40 to intercept six passes and make 45 tackles. A pair of linebackers, sophomore Marc Munford and senior Mark Daum, led the team in tackles. Munford had 16 tackles in the finale against Oklahoma.

Osborne praised LSU's skill players as "the best we've seen this year" and singled out Hilliard as the best runner they'd faced.

The Game

On New Year's night in the Superdome, 75,608 watched the 51st Sugar Bowl game.

FIRST QUARTER

LSU made one first down on an 18-yard Jeff Wickersham bullet to Eric Martin to the Nebraska 47. But the next series ended with Clay Parker punting into the end zone. Craig Sundberg, ill with the flu earlier in the day, started under center for Nebraska. The

Huskers went three-and-out and punted to the 28. The Tigers started a scoring drive from there. On the first play, Garry James sped around left end for 36 yards to the UN 33. After the game, Nebraska DE Scott Strasburger said, "We've got a fast scout team but haven't seen any speed like LSU's before. It was incredible. But as soon as we got adjusted to how fast they were, we started to shut them down." A short pass and two runs brought up fourth-and-inches. Offensive coordinator Ed Zaunbrecher took a chance and called a naked bootleg for Wickersham. It worked as Jeff rolled around left end to the 26. Next came the first of many plays that LSU would rue after the game. Wickersham fired a beautiful pass to James who caught it a step ahead of the linebacker in the end zone. But a holding penalty negated the touchdown. Set further back by a delay of game penalty and a sack, the Tigers settled for a 37-yard field goal by Ronald Lewis.

Score: LSU 3 Nebraska 0 (4:40)

The Cornhuskers gained their initial first down on three runs by I-back Jeff Smith before a third down incompletion forced a punt. The period ended with the Tigers at midfield. They had dominated Nebraska: First downs 6–1, total yards 125–28, time of possession 9:49–5:11.

LSU 3 Nebraska 0

SECOND QUARTER

The period would bring a touchdown for LSU but also much frustration. Wickersham found Martin in the center of the field again to the 31. Then James ran a delay route underneath the dropping linebackers, took the pass in stride, and hobbled to the 13. He left the game with a groin injury. An interference penalty moved the pigskin to the two. From there, LG Curt Gore, LT John Harrell, and TE Mitch Andrews cleared a big hole for Hilliard to blast into the end zone behind FB Craig Rathjen, who had no one to block.

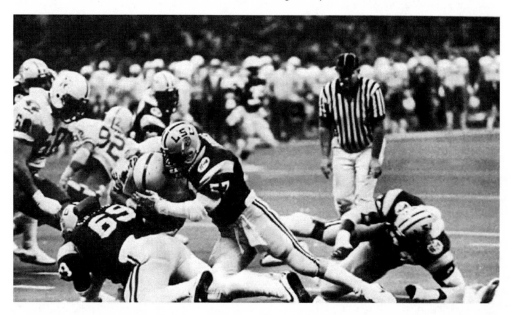

Toby Caston (69) and Shawn Burks (57) tackle a Cornhusker (*Gumbo* Class of 1985).

LSU 10 Nebraska 0 (13:11)

The senior-laden Cornhuskers took less than two minutes to answer with a six-pointer of their own. Backup RB Doug DuBose gained 53 of the 70 yards on the six-play drive. The touchdown came on a throwback screen to DuBose, who ran 31 yards untouched behind four blockers. Doug said he knew he was gone almost as soon as he caught the pass. "Craig faked a pass to the left, and I snuck out there alone. LSU's defense pursues real well, and as soon as I cut back across the grain, I knew I was heading for the end zone."

LSU 10 Nebraska 7 (10:31)

The Tigers moved into Nebraska territory on a Wickersham pass that went through the hands of a defender to FL Rogie Magee for a 50-yard gain to the 17. An incompletion was followed by a James run to the nine. But a mix up on the next snap produced a fumble that LSU recovered. So Lewis booted a field goal. But a defender crashed into him, causing Arnsparger to make a decision reminiscent of one that Jerry Stovall made two years earlier in a bowl game. Bill took the points off the board to get an automatic first down at the six. James ran off the left side and fumbled out of bounds at the one when hit. Then Garry stuck his head in at right tackle but was stopped short. But the Tigers got another break because Nebraska was offside. When the Tigers lined up, a false start penalty set them back to the five. James then tried left end but was stopped at the two. On third down, Wickersham rolled right and threw incomplete to a well-covered Fontenot. So Lewis tried a 19-yard field goal from the left hashmark. But he pushed it wide right.

The comedy of errors continued to halftime. Seven straight runs nudged Nebraska a yard past midfield. LB Michael Brooks put pressure on Sundberg as he rolled right, causing him to throw into double coverage. DB Jeffery Dale intercepted at the 31 with 2:45 left in the half. But three plays later, LSU turned it back when Rathjen fumbled after snaring a pass.

Travis Turner made his first appearance under center and promptly threw another pick. His pass bounced off the receiver's hands to DB Liffort Hobley, who took the ball on his knees at the LSU 28. As the clock ticked under a minute, the Tigers moved to the UN 48 on a pass to Andrews. But on the next play, Munford's interception ended Wickersham's streak of seven completions. The half ended fittingly with a Brooks sack.

LSU 10 Nebraska 7

The halftime statistics all favored LSU. First downs 14–7, Total yards 295–142, Time of possession 17:41–12:19. Turnovers were even at two each. The Tigers had far surpassed the average yards per *game* given up by Nebraska for the year. Wickersham shredded the nation's top defense, going 17-for-25 for 217 yards and one interception.

The Cornhuskers made several defensive changes for the second half to combat Wickersham's passing. First, they switched from the four- to a three-man front to add a secondary defender. They also had the middle linebacker drop deeper on passes. As Osborne explained, "LSU had a tendency to run short crosses and then a deep cross, 15 to 17 yards downfield. We picked it (the defensive scheme) up from the Miami Dolphins a few years ago, and I think Bill (Arnsparger, when he was the Dolphins' defensive coordinator) is responsible for that."

MLB Chad Daffer, who would play a big role in Nebraska's second half comeback, said Osborne got his team's attention in the locker room. "Coach was pretty upset at halftime. He raised his voice, and he usually doesn't. When he does, he usually gets everybody's attention."

QB Sundberg said the offense "didn't make a lot of adjustments at the half. From the beginning, they lined up like we thought they would. We took the stance that we were going to be the stronger team in the fourth quarter, whether we were ahead or not."

Third Quarter

The period brought more frustration for LSU. Nebraska gained one first down on an interference penalty on DB Kevin Guidry. But they could get no more and punted. Sammy Martin and Garland Jean Batiste started in the backfield for LSU. The move paid off when Martin cut outside left end and rambled 28 yards to the UN 48. Two more carries by the freshman from New Orleans moved the chains to the 35. But Wickersham, who was hot and cold throughout the season and within games, didn't read the deep drop of the middle linebacker and threw a pass down the middle that Daffer intercepted and returned to the 33.

Nebraska marched from there to the go-ahead touchdown. DuBose was a key factor just as he was on the first touchdown drive. Sundberg hit WB Shane Swanson for 19 yards to the LSU 37. Two straight bad plays seemed to take the starch out of the Nebraska onslaught. First, Sundberg ran the option around left end and pitched forward when across the line of scrimmage. Then he made an errant backward pitch on the opposite side. But the senior quarterback responded with two excellent plays. He rolled out and passed to TE Brian Hiemer to the nine. Then he kept around left end untouched into the end zone. The TV replay showed that the Cornhusker blocking Brooks on that edge committed two penalties that weren't called. First he held him; then he tripped him.

Nebraska 14 LSU 10 (8:14)

Trailing for the first time, LSU needed Wickersham to adjust to the new coverages. On third-and-eight, he again didn't read the middle linebacker dropping deep and threw the ball right to Daffer again. When Jeff went to the sidelines, the LSU coaches talked to him to keep his confidence up after two incompletions and three interceptions on his last five passes. Wickersham admitted after the game that "I got a little tight after I threw that second interception, and I just didn't play as well as I can. I started trying to place the ball too much."

When the teams traded punts, a personal foul on the return put LSU in business at their 36. Hilliard gave the offense the spark it needed by roaring through a big hole at right tackle 44 yards to the 20. After James got nothing, Garry took the ball to the 10 on a counter sweep that LSU borrowed from Nebraska. But with momentum building to take the lead, LSU again self-destructed in the red zone. Two runs by Hilliard placed the ball on the two. Then Wickersham faked a handout to the right, turned and flipped the ball to Magee, who was open at the left edge of the end zone. But as the ball descended into his hands for the go-ahead touchdown, Rogie stumbled and caught the ball out of bounds on his backside. So Lewis came in for another short field goal from the left hash mark. Arnsparger had told the TV sideline reporter at halftime that he regretted not taking a delay of game penalty to create a better angle on the missed field goal in the first half. So Bill did that now only to have Nebraska decline the penalty. Overcompensating for missing wide right the first time, Lewis pulled this one to the left.

Nebraska 14 LSU 10

Fourth Quarter

The Cornhuskers felt confident heading into the final period. As G Harry Grimminger said afterward, "It came down to the fourth quarter, and nobody has been stronger in the fourth quarter than us." The Big Red overcame a 7-yard sack by Brooks and continued to the touchdown that effectively put the game away. DuBose took a draw play handoff and nearly broke loose for a long gain. Guidry tackled him at the 31. Doug carried twice and took a flare pass to push across midfield by 3 yards. Sundberg rolled right and fired to TE Todd Frain to the 35. After DuBose knifed for 10, Sundberg again threw on the run to Frain slanting across at the goal line to give the Big Red a two-score cushion. LSU LB Shawn Burks said that the rollout pass "is real hell on the linebackers and the defensive backs. We broke the coverages, and that's how they scored."

Nebraska 21 LSU 10 (10:54)

LSU's next possession ended disastrously. On third-and-two, Wickersham tried a quick pass to get the first down, but DE Scott Strasburger made a great play, drifting into the flat and snagging the ball before falling to the ground at the 34. It was Jeff's fourth interception of the evening, a new Sugar Bowl record.

The weary Tiger defense couldn't reverse the momentum. After Porter ran to the 17, Sundberg, seeing CB James Pierson playing up on the line of scrimmage, called an audible that sent Frain racing past him to the end zone for his second touchdown.

Nebraska 28 LSU 10 (8:40)

Anyone who left the Dome at this point missed nothing of significance the rest of the way. With the defense knowing he had to pass, Wickersham couldn't find an open receiver and was sacked for a 10-yard loss. Yet an ABC graphic showed that LSU *still* had more yardage than Nebraska, 413–387. But the Cornhusker reserves gained enough on the LSU reserves to make the final tally 423–404 in favor of Nebraska. Sophomore Doug Powell replaced Wickersham and—guess what—threw an interception, Nebraska's fifth to go along with a fumble recovery.

Final Score: Nebraska 28 LSU 10

Postgame

Coach Arnsparger had a simple summary of the game. "We just have to have more points. One touchdown and field goal is not enough to beat a good football team." He added, "I don't think you ever have a team like Nebraska on the ropes. To beat a team like them, you have to play well the entire game, and we didn't."

Offensive coordinator Zaunbrecher said, "We didn't do anything different in the first and second halves. We made some errors. We threw the ball away, and you can't do that against Nebraska." Then he added, "It's not all Jeff's fault. It takes 11 guys. We're all in this thing together. You can't single anybody out."

T John Harrell said, "Nebraska came out and just played a helluva second half. As far as it being Jeff's fault, I think Jeff is a great quarterback, and he'll be back next year and ready to go."

Wickersham was grateful for the support from his teammates. "That's nice, but it's not the truth. I think I had a lot to do with the loss—all the interceptions and everything."

He pointed to the failed opportunities in the first half. "Not putting the ball in the end zone those two times really hurt. We got down inside the 10 two times and didn't score any points, and that's the offense's fault. It's not Ronnie Lewis' fault. We should have scored the touchdown."

Coach Osborne said that in the first half, "We were fortunate we weren't 17 down." He added, "I don't think we were tight, but we just looked lethargic. I told the team at halftime it looked like we were playing 80 percent. We didn't do anything quick." But he said that, overall, his team played their best ball of the season.

QB Craig Sundberg won the Most Valuable Player award after not being sure he could play earlier in the day. "I felt weak and tired," he said of his bout with intestinal influenza that had him vomiting just four hours before the game. "We were lucky to be in the game the first half. ... In the first half they looked like the team that tied Florida and beat Southern Cal."

Twenty-three 1984 Tigers played pro football: OL Eric Andolsek, TE Mitch Andrews, LB Michael Brooks, LB Shawn Burks, LB Toby Caston, LB Ricky Chatman, DB Jeffrey Dale, WR Wendell Davis, WR Herman Fontenot, DB Kevin Guidry, RB Dalton Hilliard, DB Liffort Hobley, RB Garry James, RB Garland Jean Batiste, DB Norman Jefferson, TE Brian Kinchen, RB Jamie Lawson, WR Eric Martin, RB Sammy Martin, DB Steve Rehage, OL Lance Smith, DT Henry Thomas, and DL Karl Wilson.

Liberty Bowl vs. Baylor

Not as close as the score indicates

Liberty Bowl Memorial Stadium, Memphis, Tennessee
December 27, 1985

LSU's Season

As you'd expect from a Bill Arnsparger–coached team, his second LSU squad excelled on defense. The Tigers averaged three sacks, seven tackles for loss, a fumble recovery, and two interceptions per game. No opponent scored more than 20 points, and the defense pitched two shutouts and held three other foes to seven points or less. LSU finished third nationally in scoring defense (10.3 points per game) and eighth in rushing defense (107.1 yards per game). The result was a 9–1–1 record and the #12 ranking in the AP poll. Florida inflicted the only loss, 20–0, in Tiger Stadium. The tie also came in a home game, 14–14 to Alabama to cost both teams a chance to tie for the league top spot. The highlight of the season was the 10–7 victory over Notre Dame in South Bend.

Offensive coordinator Ed Zaunbrecher directed a balanced attack—2,017 yards rushing vs. 2,267 yards passing. Senior QB Jeff Wickersham ended the regular season owning virtually every LSU passing record. He ranked third in Southeastern Conference history with almost 7,000 passing yards in three seasons. His favorite target was senior RB Garry James with 50 catches while sophomore WRs Rogie Magee and Wendell Davis were neck and neck for most receiving yards (473–471). Still, Wickersham took heat for the fact that he threw only five touchdown passes against nine interceptions. But Arnsparger defended him. "For the number of passes he's thrown (346), he has one of the lowest interception rates in the country." The other senior running back, Dalton Hilliard, served as "Mr. Inside" to James's "Mr. Outside," gaining 1,134 yards, almost twice Garry's total. That left Dalton only 156 yards short of Charles Alexander's LSU-record career rushing total, which ranked second behind only Herschel Walker in SEC history.

Any top-notch defense is spearheaded by top-notch linebackers. ILB Shawn Burks led the SEC's stingiest scoring defense with 113 total tackles. The other ILB, Toby Caston, ran a close second with 99. With opponents running away from him, All-American OLB Michael Brooks had only 63 tackles, but 21 of them were for losses. SS Steve Rehage led in interceptions with four while CB Norman Jefferson pilfered three.

After the last game against East Carolina, Arnsparger told the team they could vote on what bowl to go to since LSU was out of the running for one of the four major bowls.

The players had their eyes on the Aloha Bowl in Hawai'i. When Arnsparger convened the meeting, Athletic Director Bob Brodhead walked in and told the team he had already accepted the bid to the Liberty Bowl. The coaching staff, from Arnsparger down, as well as the players, resenting Brodhead's intrusion, lost much of their enthusiasm for the bowl game.

The Opponent

The Baylor Bears also hung their hats on defense. They ranked third nationally in pass defense (107.1 yards per game), 11th in scoring defense (13.2 points per game, a school record), and 13th in total defense (291.7). Junior FS Thomas Everett earned All-America honors for his 103 tackles and three interceptions. Opponents drove inside the Baylor 20 a total of 27 times but scored only 10 times.

Picked to finish in the bottom third of the Southwest Conference, the Bears won seven of their first eight games, the loss coming at Georgia 17–14 in Week 2. But their quest for the league championship was derailed by losses to Arkansas and Texas. The three losses, all on the road, were by a combined 16 points.

Grant Teaff, in his 13th season as head coach, alternated two quarterbacks, senior Tom Muecke and junior Cody Carlson, to lead his split-back veer offense. Muecke was the better runner while Carlson, blessed with a strong arm like his LSU counterpart, was the better passer. No rusher had more than 369 yards (junior Derrick McAdoo), but five gained over 200 yards.

Mississippi State with its "diamondbone" offense had given LSU fits in November, amassing 464 yards of total offense. Would Arnsparger, who hadn't faced a veer or wishbone-type offense in the pros, learn from that tight 17–15 win and blunt Baylor's option attack?

The LSU offense would play without starting C Nacho Albergamo, who suffered a broken bone in his foot. In addition, starting OLB Ron Sancho developed a high fever the night before the game that kept him out of action. Freshman Eric Hill made his first start in Sancho's place.

The game was rated a tossup.

The Game

The 27th Liberty Bowl was played before a crowd of only 40,186, the lowest Liberty Bowl attendance since 1967. The frigid weather—temperature dipping into the 30s as the night wore on with strong wind gusts—further diminished the enthusiasm of the LSU players.

FIRST QUARTER

Both teams opened the game with long drives but had no points to show for the effort. Baylor's 10-play march into LSU territory ended when OLB Michael Brooks threw RB Broderick Sargent for a 3-yard loss that forced the Bears to punt. The Tigers held the ball for nine plays until RB Garry James lost a fumble at the Baylor 40.

The defenses began living up to their billing. LSU bottled up the Bears and forced a punt from their 43. Buzzy Sawyer's missile traveled into the end zone, but a clipping penalty on Baylor forced him to kick again. He hit another long one, 51 yards. Norman Jefferson took the ball at the 21, found an alley down the left side, shook off a pair of potential tacklers, and burst into the clear down the sideline to finish the 79-yard return. "We had some good blocks, and I turned the corner," said Jefferson. "I just outran the punter." No one would have guessed that would be the Tigers' only points of the evening.

Score: LSU 7 Baylor 0 (5:17)

The Bears responded, driving 80 yards to tie the score. The big gainer came when Cody Carlson faked the option and dropped back to pass. He found SE John Simpson wide open at the LSU 20. CB Willie Bryant saved the touchdown by hauling Simpson down at the nine after a 59-yard gain. On third-and-five, SE Matt Clark made a diving catch in the end zone despite being well covered by Jefferson.

LSU 7 Baylor 7 (2:30)

Because the Tigers had too many men on the field on the extra point, they were assessed 15 yards on the kickoff. So the Bears tried an onside kick that they almost recovered at the LSU nine. Four plays later, Baylor was back in business at its 47 after Matt DeFrank's 43-yard punt.

LSU 7 Baylor 7

SECOND QUARTER

Carlson again faked an option run and passed. He connected with SE Leland Douglas for 41 yards to the three. The Tigers drew the line there. Tom Muecke took over under center but failed to gain on first down. Then Brooks blitzed and threw Muecke for a 13-yard loss. Carlson came in but fared no better as Brooks and NG Henry Thomas dropped him for a 4-yard loss. The Bear offense left the field empty-handed when Terry Syler missed a 37-yard field goal try.

LSU tried a dipsy-doodle play that almost succeeded. Wickersham handed to Hilliard who pitched it back to Jeff. He spotted TB Sammy Martin open deep in Baylor territory, but the pass was slightly underthrown, and CB Ron Francis made a fingertip interception just in front of Martin at the 14. With Muecke back at the helm, the Bears continued to pick apart the secondary. He connected with FL Glenn Pruitt for 17 and then found Simpson for another long reception of 43 yards to the eight. But once again, the Tigers thwarted the Bears. RB Randy Rutledge gained nothing on first down. Then an errant pass on second down and a gain of only two on a swing pass on third down made it fourth-and-goal at the six. Syler nailed the chip shot field goal.

Baylor 10 LSU 7 (5:36)

The defenses dominated the rest of the half.

Baylor 10 LSU 7

THIRD QUARTER

After LSU punted, Muecke, supposedly the running quarterback, connected on three passes, including a 20-yard completion to SE Matt Clark and a 10-yard connection with FL Glenn Pruitt to set up first and goal at the seven. "We weren't getting jams on their receivers at the line, and that hurt our coverage," said Brooks. "It was hard for me to get a sack. Their quarterbacks released the ball so quickly." But the Tigers staged their third consecutive goal line stand. First, S Steve Rehage broke through and nailed HB Broderick Sargent for an 11-yard loss. Muecke then threw two incompletions to bring on Syler, who booted a 35-yard three pointer.

Baylor 13 LSU 7 (8:54)

When the Bears forced yet another three-and-out, Carlson engineered a drive of his own, hitting a couple of first down passes. Backup HB Charles Perry ripped off runs of 10 and 11 yards to set up first-and-10 at the LSU 29. But the drive stalled, and Syler missed wide left from the 27.

LSU finished the period with a pitiful 7 yards of offense and no first downs.

Baylor 13 LSU 7

FOURTH QUARTER

On third-and-four at the 15, Carlson fired a strike to SE John Simpson for a touchdown. Simpson would win the offensive MVP award for his three catches for 117 yards. When Baylor decided to go for two, what happened next epitomized LSU's evening. WR Matt Clark lined up wide right. When Carlson saw no one covering Matt, he tossed him the ball. "I don't know what happened," said Clark. "I guess you'll have to ask them (LSU). I didn't run my pattern. I just walked into the end zone. That's all I had to do."

Baylor 21 LSU 7 (10:42)

The Tigers finally picked up a first down when Hilliard ran 6 yards to the 35. Wickersham followed with a 15-yard strike to SE Wendell Davis, and Dalton soon moved the chains again to the Baylor 36. But the defense bowed their backs and stopped Hilliard 2 yards short on a fourth-down swing pass at the 28 with 6:58 remaining to effectively end the Tigers' hopes for a comeback. It was LSU's deepest offensive penetration of the game.

When LSU got the ball back, Arnsparger pulled Wickersham in favor of freshman Mickey Guidry, but the change didn't make much difference. "Things were pretty much out of reach, and Mickey needs experience for next year," said Wickersham. "They were able to put a lot of pressure on me, and they did cover our receivers well."

Final Score: Baylor 21 LSU 7

Postgame

The statistics showed that the game was not as close as the score indicated. Baylor gained 489 yards, the most given up by the Tigers all year, to 192 and made 26 first downs to nine, the Tigers' lowest output of the season. The offensive ineptitude was summarized by the fact that DB Norman Jefferson was named the Offensive MVP for his punt return. Cody Carlson was named the game's outstanding player. He completed nine of 12 passes for 161 yards and two touchdowns.

Coach Arnsparger took the blame for not preparing the Tigers well enough. "Obviously I didn't do the job. We failed to take advantage of the opportunities we had. ... It is my responsibility to have us prepared to play. We were disorganized in every phase of the game." Defensive coordinator Mike Archer added, "You can't give big plays to an option team. … That's the worst defense we've played. We couldn't stop them throwing the ball."

LB Michael Brooks took exception to Arnsparger taking the blame for the defeat. "I felt we had prepared well in practice for everything they would do. I think we were ready for them; we just didn't execute." QB Jeff Wickersham agreed that the Tigers were "well enough prepared; we didn't execute…. It wasn't his (Arnsparger's) fault." Jeff said LSU "played its worst game" of the season while Baylor had "one of the best defenses we've played. They were really quick, and they showed why they are one of the top two or three pass defenses in the nation."

Baylor's final touchdown, a 15-yard pass to an unguarded receiver, typified the errors that plagued LSU throughout the game. "There were breakdowns on our part in the secondary," said CB Norman Jefferson, who was victimized on passes of 43 and 41 yards. "We came up instead of staying back. We just made too many mistakes against the option."

Steve Rehage minced no words in evaluating his team's performance. "We've never played a complete game this season. In one game, the offense has won the game, and in the next game, the defense has won the game. But in this game, both of us stunk."

Coach Teaff said, "We're pretty good defensively, and we've shut a lot of teams down." He also bragged, "We throw the ball well. That's the way we've done it all year." CB Ron Francis added, "It was our best defensive performance of the year." Baylor FS Everett said he was surprised LSU didn't throw deep more often. "I thought they would be quicker than that. On film they looked quicker." DT Steve Grumbine said early defensive pressure from DE James Lee bothered Wickersham. "Lee rattled him, and his passing was off the rest of the night. We also batted down a few of his passes, and I think we frustrated him."

Twenty-three 1985 Tigers played pro football: OL Eric Andolsek, TE Mitch Andrews, DL Roland Barbay, LB Michael Brooks, LB Shawn Burks, LB Toby Caston, WR Wendell Davis, DB Kevin Guidry, LB Eric Hill, RB Dalton Hilliard, DB Greg Jackson, RB Garry James, RB Garland Jean Batiste, DB Norman Jefferson, RB Victor Jones, TE Brian Kinchen, RB Jamie Lawson, RB Sammy Martin, DB Mike Mayes, OL Ralph Norwood, DB Steve Rehage, DL Henry Thomas, and DL Karl Wilson.

USF&G Sugar Bowl
vs. Nebraska

"It seemed like everyone wanted to kill us"

Louisiana Superdome, New Orleans, Louisiana
January 1, 1987

LSU's Season

A 9–2 season would be considered outstanding by most fan bases. But when the two losses came at home to Miami (OH), which was considered so big an underdog that there was no betting line on the game, and to Ole Miss when the Tigers were 11-point favorites, the season is a disappointment that makes fans think about what might have been. Victories over Florida and Alabama coupled with the Tide's loss to Auburn made LSU the undisputed SEC champions and earned them the host berth in the Sugar Bowl. But perhaps the most satisfying triumph was a 21–19 squeaker over Notre Dame in Tiger Stadium.

Tommy Hodson had a season unlike that of any other freshman quarterback in LSU history. His 60.8 completion percentage, 2,261 passing yards, and touchdown to interception ratio of 19:8 earned him All-SEC honors. His 19 TDs were a school record. His favorite target was junior WR Wendell Davis, who broke school records with 80 receptions for 1,244 yards and 11 touchdowns. With Dalton Hilliard a rookie in the NFL, no runner came close to the 1,000-yard mark that he surpassed the previous two years. Freshman Harvey Williams led with 700 yards.

Much was expected from a defense that returned ten starters. Despite losing All-American LB Michael Brooks in game three, the Bandits gave up just 14.1 points per game. In addition, DBs Norman Jefferson and Steve Rehage missed the first half of the season with knee injuries. Nevertheless, the secondary set a school record with 27 interceptions spread among 13 players. S Chris Carrier led with six, and CB James Pierson was close behind with four.

"Their front three is as good as any we've seen," said Alabama coach Ray Perkins before playing LSU. The trio was composed of seniors Karl Wilson, Roland Barbay, and Henry Thomas. However, Barbay would not play in the Sugar Bowl. The NCAA had mandated drug testing for all players on bowl teams, and Roland tested positive for steroids that he used to help rehabilitate his knee. Junior Tommy Clapp replaced him.

The three-year kicking jinx was cured by freshman David Browndyke, who took over midway through the season. Punter Matt DeFrank increased his average from 38.0 in '85 to 42.0 in '86.

The Tigers would play with a lame duck coach. Arnsparger announced his resignation the day after the Tulane game. He said, "it's time to step down" after 36 years of coaching, although his clashes with Athletic Director Bob Brodhead were rumored to be a major factor in the decision. Defensive coordinator Mike Archer, with strong support from the players, was named the next head coach, effective after the bowl game. It was later revealed that Steve Spurrier, the former coach of the United States Football League's Tampa Bay Bandits, was interested in the job.

The Opponent

Nebraska began the season with national championship aspirations but finished with the same record as LSU, 9–2. The losses came to conference foes Colorado (20–10) and, for the third straight year, Oklahoma (20–17). The 1987 Big Red were not that different from the '85 team that faced LSU in the Sugar Bowl. For that matter, they weren't that different from any of Tom Osborne's 13 previous Cornhusker teams.

As one Nebraska writer put it, "It isn't that Nebraska can't pass. The Cornhuskers just don't …. or, at least, they rarely do." Junior SE Rod Smith explained, "With Coach Osborne's concept of offense, to establish the run is far more important than establishing the pass. In this type of offense, you have to create opportunities to pass through the run." The offense averaged an incredible 305.5 yards per game rushing against 97.6 yards per game passing with a completion percentage of only 43.5. Forty touchdowns came on the ground and just 11 through the air. And half the passing TDs went to tight ends. Making the rushing success even more remarkable was the fact that I-back Doug Dubose, who gained 102 yards against LSU in the '85 Sugar Bowl, was lost for the season with a knee injury. Junior Keith Jones, the fastest football player in school history (:04.33 in the 40-yard dash) gained 889 yards to take up the slack. Result: A #2 national ranking in total offense.

The defense was not as good as the '84 Blackshirts. Two years earlier, 95.7 yards per game allowed rushing vs. 78.8 and 139.9 yards per game allowed passing vs. 124.5. Yet they still finished second in the nation in total defense. MG Danny Noonan anchored the line, and junior-college All-American CB Brian Davis led the secondary. Osborne called Davis "one of the more talented players we've had."

Nebraska held a 4–0–1 record against LSU, making the Huskers the only team that had played LSU at least three times that the Tigers had not beaten.

A war of words broke out between the teams when they arrived in New Orleans. Cornhusker DT Lee Jones wasn't impressed with Hodson compared with the South Carolina and Colorado quarterbacks he had faced during the regular season. "Hodson's nothing like the South Carolina quarterback (Todd Ellis), just watching the film. That guy had a lot quicker release, and he was faster. As far as his ability to play, the LSU quarterback is worse than Colorado's quarterback (Mark Hatcher). I'm not saying he's terrible. I'm just saying he's not as good as those other guys." Hodson said he admired Jones for "saying what he feels. … I've never heard another player say things like that. They're trying every kind of tactic, aren't they? They've tried the threatening tactic, now they're trying the cut-down tactic. That's always made me play better."

If the Cornhuskers were inclined to take the Sugar Bowl lightly after the disappointing end to their season, numerous incidents after they arrived in New Orleans stoked their determination. Eleven Cornhuskers were arrested in the French Quarter just hours after arriving in the Crescent City. They were warned by a police officer to stop shouting and slapping parked cars. Instead the group shouted obscenities. They were booked for disorderly conduct, charges that were later dropped. Coach Osborne responded by ordering his players to stay out of the French Quarter.

Nebraska DE Broderick Thomas got LSU's attention when he told reporters, "We're going to start our 1987 hell-raising tour against LSU. … I'm not a dirty player, but if I break your arm making a tackle, hey, that's part of football. … I don't know who their quarterback is, but I pray to God he lasts two quarters. He will get punished. … LSU expects to get hit, and I won't disappoint. I will bring the wood. If I don't get blocked, bring out the stretcher because somebody's going to need it." LSU DE Karl Wilson responded by saying, "They have a lot of big mouths. That will get us going." S Steve Rehage said he nearly "broke up" laughing after reading Thomas' comments. "They seem pretty mean to me. We might not want to show up. … If he's still talking at the end of the game, he will have accomplished something. He'll probably be the one who won't make it through two quarters." OLB Ron Sancho said, "The theory we have at LSU is we don't talk with our mouths. We talk on the field." DT John Hazard had this response. "They just don't like us. That's fine with me. We don't like them. Let's leave it at that and go on the field and fight." RB Harvey Williams added fuel to the fire when he said Nebraska will have "a bunch of convicts on the field" during the game.

Nebraska MG Danny Noonan said after the game, "People in restaurants did a lot of talking. Some people threw stuff at us when we were walking down the streets. We were treated like dirt, basically. I was here two years ago, and it was different. It seemed like there was a lot more animosity toward us this year. It seemed like everyone wanted to kill us."

Nebraska was rated a five-point favorite.

The Game

The clash between the #5 Tigers and #6 Cornhuskers drew a crowd of 76,234 to the Superdome.

FIRST QUARTER

The Tigers started with a bang. After Harvey Williams returned the kickoff 30 yards to the 33, Hodson found Wendell Davis open on a down and up on the left sideline to the Nebraska 23. On third-and-eight, Hodson, an excellent athlete who averaged 27 points per game in high school basketball, could not find a receiver. So he zipped upfield to the five. An unsportsmanlike conduct penalty moved the ball half the distance to the goal. It took him three tries, but Williams finally plunged into the end zone. David Browndyke converted. Unfortunately, that would be the last penalty-free possession by LSU in the first half.

Score: LSU 7 Nebraska 0 (12:06)

The Tiger defense also started strong, forcing a three-and-out. The offense moved into UN territory in two plays that showed shifty Sammy Martin's versatility. First, he took a flanker screen pass for 7 yards. Then the 165-pound whirling dervish from New Orleans lined up in the backfield and rambled around right end to the Nebraska 43. But the possession was thwarted by flags for a personal foul and holding. So on fourth-and-32, Matt DeFrank punted into the end zone.

Nebraska charged into Tiger territory on three straight runs and another personal foul on LSU. Two-hundred-fifteen-pound RB Tyreese Knox, starting in place of the injured Keith Jones, angled into the defense four straight times to gain a first down by half a football at the 35. But a fumble for a 2-yard loss and a third down incompletion brought out Dale Klein for a 51-yard field goal try that sailed wide left.

LSU's offense shot itself in the foot again when Hodson's pass to TE Brian Kinchen for a first down was wiped out by an ineligible receiver downfield.

Nebraska ended the period with only 36 yards of offense.

LSU 7 Nebraska 0

Second Quarter

The ragged football continued. DT Neil Smith, a New Orleanian, flushed Hodson out of the pocket to force a third down incompletion. A foolish late hit on the punt return set up Nebraska at the LSU 46. But a bad pitchout that CB Norman Jefferson recovered ended the threat. Hodson connected with Kinchen, but guess what? Holding. Two plays later, DeFrank went back to punt. A low snap delayed his stride. Seeing a red shirt looming to his left, Matt panicked and tried to run. He was hit and fumbled backwards. LSU recovered, but the ball went to Nebraska on downs at the 25. A holding penalty on the Cornhuskers kept them from making a first down. So they settled for Klein's 42-yard field goal to cut the margin to four.

LSU 7 Nebraska 3 (10:01)

The Tigers gained three first downs before bogging down. A third down pass to Williams moved the chains to the 40. Then another pass, this one to Eddie Fuller out of the backfield, eased the Tigers into UN territory at the 48. Showing his speed, Harvey cut back on an end sweep and found running room up the middle for 15 yards to the 33. But the Cornhuskers dug in there and forced a punt. After the touchback, junior Clete Blakeman took over the signal calling. He was supposedly a better passer than starter Steve Taylor. But Clete's tenure didn't last long as an intentional grounding penalty while being hit by NG Henry Thomas led to a punt that Jefferson returned 10 yards to give LSU excellent field position at the 28.

With a great chance to add to their lead, the Tigers went backwards, beginning with a false start. On second down, Hodson finally targeted Davis again on an underneath route to the 24 only to have a holding penalty wipe out the gain. Two plays later, Tommy threw long down the middle into the hands of SS Brian Washington at the 28 with 1:42 left in the half. At this point, LSU had 109 yards in offense and 90 yards in penalties.

Nebraska had enough time to take the lead. Told on the sideline to quit giving up on the pass so quickly, Taylor came back in and showed why he was the first sophomore quarterback to start the opening game of the season for Tom Osborne. Steve rolled right and fired to SE Rod Smith to the 43. Then he threw to TE Tom Banderas to the LSU 38 and to FB Ken Kaelin for seven more. Then Knox took an option pitch out of bounds at the 26 to stop the clock. Following another pass to Kaelin to the 20, Osborne called time-out with 1:07 left. When play resumed, Taylor escaped the pressure and ran to the 12. He then threw a slant that failed to connect, but a member of the busy Southwest Conference officiating crew called a suspect interference penalty on CB Kevin Guidry to put the ball at the 2½. Taylor kept the ball and stepped into the end zone over the left side with 39 seconds left. Steve later explained the surge to take the lead this way. "At the beginning of the second quarter, the line started blocking better. I was reading my reads correctly, and the backs were running well. I think we physically wore LSU down."

Nebraska 10 LSU 7

Third Quarter

Nebraska's offense was built to hold onto leads with their strong ground attack. They illustrated that on the opening possession when they drove relentlessly 78 yards in nine plays to increase their margin. Taylor went three-for-three passing, one of which went to TE Todd Millikan for 19 yards on third-and-four to the LSU 40. Two plays later, Knox roared through the left side all the way to the one before S Greg Jackson, hanging onto the runner by his shirt, pulled him down. Tyreese finished the job on the next snap.

Nebraska 17 LSU 7 (10:35)

The Tigers needed to answer to stay in the ball game. But with the TV announcers wondering when Hodson would go back to Davis, Tommy fumbled the snap on the first play. Then on third down, he threw into zone coverage down the sideline to Rogie Magee and was lucky the pass was not intercepted. A personal foul on the punt set the Big Red back to their seven. But after a Knox 12-yard run, the Tigers held and took possession at midfield.

The game was not out of reach, but the LSU offense had to get into gear. Hodson finally threw to Davis, but he was surrounded by three red shirts—incomplete. Tommy flipped to Martin to make it third-and-one. But Williams was stopped short by the length of the football, and on fourth down, RB Mickey Harris slammed into a stone wall up the middle.

Three runs, the last an 11-yard scamper by Taylor around right end, moved the chains to the LSU 42. On third-and-nine, Steve found Rod Smith at the 32, where he was leveled by Jefferson a foot short of the first down mark. No problem. Knox slammed over right tackle to the 30. But an errant pitchout and a Karl Wilson sack led to Klein trying a 52-yard field goal that was blocked by Thomas. In the scramble for the ball as it bounded toward the Nebraska goal, Henry batted it forward. It ended up going out of bounds at the 17.

With LSU in great position to pull within three points, the Nebraska forward wall rose to the occasion, sacking Hodson twice. Trash-talking DE Broderick Thomas got the first one for a loss of 15. Then Smith and MG Danny Noonan overwhelmed the offensive line for a 9-yard sack.

Nebraska 17 LSU 7

Fourth Quarter

What do you call on third-and-34? Hodson threw to Davis on a drag route for 6 yards—Wendell's first reception since the game's opening play. DeFrank got an excellent punt that went out on the four. Thus ended the Tigers' third penetration of the Nebraska 30 that ended with no points.

With a +10 turnover ratio for the regular season, LSU needed one now to get back in the game. They didn't get it but did force a punt after the Cornhuskers made one first down. The Tigers got another break when the boot traveled just 15 yards to the UN 39. Hodson started strong, hitting Magee for 8 yards, then firing a strike to Williams. But Harvey was hit as he started to run, and Nebraska recovered the fumble at the 28.

From there, the Big Red machine marched to the clinching touchdown against the worn-down defense. FB Micah Heibel blew through right tackle for 19 yards to midfield. After SE Robb Schnitzler caught a pass for 11 more, sophomore ILB Oliver Lawrence stemmed the tide temporarily with a 4-yard sack. Two plays later, though, Taylor hit Banderas to the 22 to keep the drive alive. The quick quarterback kept to the 11, Jones carried to the eight, and Taylor to the three. Steve then faked a handoff and flipped to Millikan in the end zone.

Nebraska 24 LSU 7 (6:02)

Knowing LSU had to pass, Nebraska increased the pressure on Hodson, who threw into a deep zone for Davis. CB Brian Davis picked it off and returned to the LSU 12. Three runs made it fourth-and-four at the five. Taylor kept to the one to make it first-and-goal. Then he handed to Knox who jumped over the line into the end zone.

Nebraska 30 LSU 7 (3:26)

From the beginning of the second quarter to this point in the game, LSU had made only two first downs and run 32 plays for a mere 38 yards. As the game dragged on toward the three-hour mark, chippy incidents led to several ejections. A personal foul penalty against Nebraska gave LSU back the yards it lost on an unsportsmanlike conduct foul on the previous play. Facing reserves, Hodson fired down the middle to Magee for a gain of 20 to the Nebraska 45. After two incompletions, Davis snagged his third reception of the game to the 27. On second-and-seven, Tommy threw to freshman WR Tony Moss running across the field on the 10. The 5'7" freshman spun the opposite way and ran into the end zone. Hodson lobbed to WR Alvin Lee for the two-point conversion.

Nebraska 30 LSU 15 (2:01)

Final Score: Nebraska 30 LSU 15

Henry Thomas was voted LSU's Defensive MVP thanks to his 12 tackles, the most on either side. The Tigers ended with a dubious Sugar Bowl record: 12 penalties for 130 yards.

Postgame

Bill Arnsparger finished his LSU coaching career 0–3 in bowl games. "They didn't do anything different. You could see that in the films. We didn't protect the quarterback well, and that didn't give Tommy enough time to look for the second man. … We had too many long-yardage situations. We felt like we were physically whipped in the first half. When we got in those long-yardage situations, we just couldn't keep them out. And when we did hold them out, we were guilty of holding. The second half, we had the opportunity to come back, but we couldn't do anything. Our field position was good, and then we would get sacked. Today, our players were whipped on the offensive line." Offensive coordinator Ed Zaunbrecher explained, "If we stayed in a normal situation on first and second downs, we had a chance to do the things we wanted to do. Obviously, it's very hard to overcome the things that happened out there today."

Tommy Hodson expressed his disappointment. "We wanted to come out and give them a good shot. We wanted to put down what was said before the game. Instead, we backed up everything that was said. It was frustrating." C Nacho Albergamo said, "The thing I'll always wonder is that you don't know if they were really that good or if the penalties made us that bad."

Coach Osborne summarized his team's motivation like this. "We weren't playing for the national championship; the Big Eight championship was out the window. The only thing we had left was the Sugar Bowl." He added, "Defense was exceptional today. They really held us in there. We had some bad field position. We had the blocked field goal. We had a couple times when we punted the ball out of our own end of the field and didn't have real good punts. So I think the defense did a tremendous job. … We looked at 11 films of LSU, and we were impressed by the lack of pressure that Hodson usually had. They really protected the passer well. And I really credit the defense to put as much pressure on him as we had. I think he got sacked tonight more than he had in four or five ballgames total, and certainly he had to hurry his throws a lot."

DT Neil Smith, who prepped at McDonogh 35 in New Orleans, explained, "The team wasn't pleased about the things that happened here (in the week before the game). A lot of the guys said they'll never come back. We had to give them a going away present."

QB Steve Taylor sounded a similar theme. "It was really the icing on the cake to really let Louisiana State know that we didn't come to play around, that we meant business. We didn't want the game to be close at all."

Twenty-one 1986 Tigers played pro football: OL Eric Andolsek, DL Roland Barbay, LB Michael Brooks, LB Toby Caston, WR Wendell Davis, DL Karl Dunbar, RB Eddie Fuller, DB Kevin Guidry, TE Ronnie Haliburton, LB Eric Hill, QB Tommy Hodson, DB Greg Jackson, RB Garland Jean Batiste, DB Norman Jefferson, TE Brian Kinchen, RB Sammy Martin, OL Ralph Norwood, DB Steve Rehage, DL Henry Thomas, RB Harvey Williams, and DL Karl Wilson.

Mazda Gator Bowl vs.
South Carolina
"We should have been favored"

Jacksonville, Florida
December 31, 1987

LSU's Season

The nation's youngest head coach, 33-year-old Mike Archer, had a successful first season, 9–1–1. The loss to Alabama cost the Tigers a share of the SEC title because Auburn finished with only a tie blemishing its conference record. LSU's tie came on Ohio State's first visit to Tiger Stadium.

It was hard for QB Tommy Hodson to improve on his sensational freshman season, but he came close. He completed 162 of 265 passes for 2,125 yards to again make All-SEC. A knee injury kept him on the sidelines until the final period of the loss to Alabama. With defenses keying on him, senior WR Wendell Davis couldn't match his 1986 NCAA-leading receiving yards total of 1,244, but he still had an outstanding season with 72 catches for 993 yards. TE Brian Kinchen joined Davis on the All-SEC team along with G Eric Andolsek and C Nacho Albergamo, both of whom had bulked up in the offseason after being overpowered by Nebraska's defensive linemen in the Sugar Bowl. Sophomore Harvey Williams led the rushing attack with 1,020 yards. Unfortunately, a knee injury in the finale against Tulane would keep him out of the bowl game. Senior Sammy Martin and sophomore Eddie Fuller would have to pick up the slack.

The biggest challenge on defense was replacing the front three, all of whom were in the NFL. But Tommy Clapp, Darrell Phillips, and the tandem of Clint James and Karl Dunbar did an admirable job as the Tigers gave up an average of just 15.3 points per game. The pass defense sacked quarterbacks and intercepted passes less frequently than the year before, yet was more effective due in part to tight coverage by a veteran defensive backfield led by All-SEC S Chris Carrier.

After three straight bowl losses under Bill Arnsparger, Archer adopted a different approach. The staff installed the entire package for South Carolina in Baton Rouge so that the morning workouts in Jacksonville could be used only to refine the game plan during morning workouts. That gave the team more free time in Florida. "The kids this year are more vocal in saying this is the way it should be done," Archer said after one of the workouts. "Their mental frame of mind and outlook is better."

179

The Opponent

Led by sophomore Todd Ellis, the quarterback Nebraska the year before had rated as better than Tommy Hodson, South Carolina averaged nearly twice as many yards through the air as on the ground. The "run-and-shoot" offense aimed to spread out the defense using motion to get skilled receivers in one-on-one situations. An improved running game helped the Gamecocks win eight games. Their three losses all came on the road against teams ranked #2 (Nebraska), #8 (Miami), and #20 (Georgia) in the AP poll. SC's sweetest victory was over archrival Clemson, ranked #8.

After the 13–6 loss at Georgia the third week of the season, a game in which USC failed to score a touchdown on five red zone possessions, Coach Joe Morrison installed the I-formation and Power-I to better utilize the skills of TB Harold Green. The move paid off handsomely as the 6'2" 205-pound sophomore averaged 95 yards per game to spark six straight wins before a season-ending loss at Miami (FL).

Ellis began his career in '86 by setting NCAA freshman records for passing yards (3,020), total offense (2,975), and touchdowns (20). He threw for 2,902 yards as a sophomore but continued to be interception-prone—20 picks for a total of 42 in two seasons. His favorite receiver was senior WB Sterling Sharpe with 56 receptions for 862 yards despite being double- and triple-teamed.

Defensive guru Joe Lee Dunn transformed the "Black Death" defense from a porous unit that surrendered 367 yards per game in 1986 into the nation's No. 2 overall defense in '87. He switched USC from a 4–3 reading defense to a "50" defense featuring multiple alignments and blitzes from anywhere. In one late-season two-game stretch, the Gamecocks held North Carolina State and Wake Forest to a total of -10 yards rushing. LSU would have to find a way to block senior NG Roy Hart, who led the team in sacks and tackles for loss.

Surprisingly, #9 South Carolina was favored over #7 LSU by 3½ points.

When the Tigers took the field, they saw a sea of red and black in the stands since the Gamecock fans outnumbered the Tigers faithful five to one, making this like a road game. Instead of being intimidated, they gained confidence since LSU had been 16–1–1 on the road in the last four seasons and 13–0 the last three years.

The Game

The 82,119 spectators along with the CBS television audience watched LSU end its four-game bowl losing streak and run South Carolina's bowl record to 0–7 on a perfect day for football.

FIRST QUARTER

LSU won the toss and deferred the choice to the second half. The move paid off as they got the first score of the game anyway. On South Carolina's second snap, Clint James roared through to chase Todd Ellis from the pocket. Tommy Clapp sacked him for a 20-yard loss. After an incompletion, Jimmy Young returned a low punt 11 yards to the SC 39.

On second-and-10, Tommy Hodson made a quick throw to Wendell Davis on a simple out route. He eluded the cornerback, got a block from fellow WR Tony Moss, and continued down the left sideline to the end zone. David Browndyke converted.

Score: LSU 7 South Carolina 0 (13:31)

SC's second possession showcased the talents of RB Harold Green. First, he delayed out of the backfield and took a short toss for 12 yards. Then he ran twice for another first down at the 45. On second-and-10, OLB Eric Hill's blitz disrupted Ellis's timing, allowing Karl Dunbar to sack him for a 4-yard loss. Then it was the other OLB Ron Sancho's turn to blitz. He hit Ellis as he threw the ball, which sailed into the hands of SS Greg Jackson who returned 48 yards to the 13 where WB Sterling Sharpe made a touchdown-saving tackle. An illegal procedure penalty, an incompletion, and a short completion set up third-and-nine. Hodson called for maximum protection, with both backs at his side to counter the blitz. The move allowed him just enough time to throw to Davis, who made a leaping catch at the left edge of the end zone. The Tigers already had 14 points against a defense that allowed only 10.1 points per game all season. CB Robert Robinson, who was beaten on both of Davis's touchdowns, said afterward, "I just missed a tackle on the first one and on the second, I was in position, but it was a great throw and catch."

LSU 14 South Carolina 0 (9:50)

Aided by a fumble recovery, the Gamecocks got on the scoreboard before the period ended. Mixing runs by Green with quick passes, Ellis engineered a drive that advanced to the 16. But S Chris Carrier, assigned to shadow Sharpe as he went in motion across the formation, made a beeline for the future first round draft choice as he took a pitchout and dropped him for 2-yard loss. A blitz on the next snap caused Ellis to hurry a pass to Green that ended up in the hands of CB James Pierson, who ran to midfield. However, a clipping penalty set the offense back to the 13.

On third-and-five, Hodson tossed to Davis coming across the middle. A stride after he caught the ball, he fumbled when hit and FS Brad Edwards recovered. Hoping to cut the lead in half, the Gamecocks had to settle for a field goal as Ellis continued to over-throw receivers. Collin Mackie, who was tied for the most field goals nationally, sailed a 44-yarder through the uprights.

LSU 14 South Carolina 3 (3:04)

Even with C Nacho Albergamo on the sideline after being kicked in the calf that bothered him most of the season, the Tigers found success running and passing up the middle. FB Mickey Harris, who gained only 14 yards all season, plunged twice for a total of 10 yards to move the chains. Sammy Martin ran two straight quick outs on the right sideline to make it first-and-10 at the SC 22. On third-and-seven, Hodson called another max protect and hit Davis at the four as the period ended.

LSU 14 South Carolina 3

SECOND QUARTER

Attacking from all angles, the Black Death defense dug in and held the Tigers to a 27-yard field goal by Browndyke.

LSU 17 South Carolina 3 (14:13)

Ellis started strong by hitting WR Ryan Bethea for 15 yards to the 41. Seeing Sharpe uncovered wide left, Todd flipped the ball to him, and the wingback ran straight ahead to the LSU 44. On third-and-nine, Ellis connected with WR Danny Smith for 18 yards and a first down at the 25. Soon the Gamecocks went for it on fourth-and-a foot and made it on a sneak. Two snaps later, Ellis broke the middle finger on his left hand when he rolled right and threw incomplete just as George Henriquez slammed him to the ground. The next play brought worse results. NG Darrell Phillips dropped Todd at the 32. So Mackie booted a 39-yard field goal.

LSU 17 South Carolina 6 (7:59)

The Tigers used up the rest of the period with a 17-play drive that included two fourth-down conversions. A pair of 200-pound backs, Victor Jones and Eddie Fuller, did the heavy lifting on the ground. Fuller converted the first fourth down try when he cut inside off the right side behind good blocking for 4 yards to the 30. Three snaps later, Davis made a great diving catch just short of the first down mark. So Jones nudged just across the 20 to keep the drive alive. With under a minute to play, Coach Archer began using his three timeouts. On third-and-three, Davis made another fine coach of a low pass for a first down at the four with 0:16 on the clock. With blitzers forcing him to throw quickly and off balance, Hodson again threw low, Roggie Magee snaring the ball at the two. Timeout at 0:10. Fuller took a toss around right end but got only to the one. Archer used his last timeout and sent in the field goal unit. Browndyke split the uprights with a second left.

The Tigers finished six-of-11 on third-down conversions and two-of-two on fourth down.

LSU 20 South Carolina 6

Third Quarter

LSU's decision to defer to the second half paid off as they took the kickoff and drove to their third touchdown. Martin got things started with a 49-yard return to the Carolina 47. Following Sammy's 3-yard run, Hodson threw a beautiful pass to Davis who slanted in from the left side, then back toward the pylon to take the ball over his shoulder at the five two steps behind the defender and into the end zone.

LSU 27 South Carolina 6 (12:34)

Ellis's frustration continued when his bullet down the middle to Smith for a first down on third-and-29 was negated by a holding call. The punt resulted in good field position for the Tigers at their 45. But an unsportsmanlike conduct penalty killed any hope of moving into SC territory. So Matt DeFrank brushed off the cobwebs and came in for his first punt of the afternoon.

The next minutes brought an exchange of turnovers. Three plays into the possession, ILB Darren Malbrough recovered a fumbled handoff exchange at the SC 35. But a minute later LSU made the same error to give the ball back at the 28. Ellis made his best throw of the day, hitting Smith between two defenders at the 44. Two plays later, the Gamecocks crossed midfield on a flare to Green. Ellis sneaked for a first down on third-and-one. After two incompletions, Ellis fired right to deep-dropping ILB Nicky Hazard, who returned his second pick of the year to the SC 49.

The miscues continued as a holding penalty wiped out a 36-yard catch and run by Tony Moss. Then a second bad exchange between backup C Todd Coutee and Hodson put SC in business at the Tiger 43. After converting 53 percent of their third downs during the season, the Gamecocks were only three of 10. But Ellis hit WB Hardin Brown on the run across the middle for 21 yards to the 17. Then the Tigers ended the period with sack #6, this one by Ron Sancho at the 25.

LSU 27 South Carolina 6

FOURTH QUARTER

On third-and-18, Ellis got bailed out by a pass interference call on a long incompletion. From the 10, Green burst up the middle into the end zone.

LSU 27 South Carolina 13 (14:47)

Gamecock fans came to life and got even louder when a holding penalty on first down moved LSU back to the 15. With the black shirts coming from all directions, Hodson threw two incompletions to bring on the punt unit. Sharpe returned the weak kick to the LSU 43. SC quickly moved to a first-and-10 at the 27. But Clapp came through with another sack, this one for -8. The drive ended when Ellis threw to Sharpe for a gain of just two on fourth-and-11.

One way to take the steam out of a comeback and quiet the fans is to grind out a sustained march. Other than a quick pass that Davis twisted back to grab for a first down at the 39, LSU ran the ball eight times. The biggest gain came when Martin ran past the blitzers through the left side for 21 yards to the SC 36. Sammy gained seven more before Fuller zipped for 13. Eddie pounded out 10 more on three carries to fall inches short of a first down at the six. Archer decided to take the easy points, sending in Browndyke for a 23-yard field goal.

LSU 30 South Carolina 13 (8:17)

The LSU defense needed to avoid giving up big plays and make the Gamecocks take precious minutes off the clock advancing the ball. After SC made one first down, a clipping penalty negated a 19-yard pass to Sharpe. But Ellis hit Bethea to the 47. Then Todd scrambled to the LSU 45. Another strike to Sharpe moved the pigskin to the 32. When Green carried a swing pass to the 23 and Bethea took an option pitch to the 15, it looked for sure like SC would score a touchdown. But Ellis got greedy and threw down the middle to the end zone where Jackson snagged his second interception of the game and sped out to the 43. LSU went three-and-out but at least ran

LB Ron Sancho hauls down Harold Green (*Gumbo* Class of 1988).

off more time. On the first play of Carolina's possession, Clint James registered sack #7, dropping Ellis for an 8-yard loss. A fourth-down incompletion turned the ball over to LSU with 1:32 left.

Final Score: LSU 30 South Carolina 13

The Tigers carried Archer on their shoulders for the handshake with Coach Morrison. Interviewed by CBS at midfield, Mike said his squad was motivated by the fact that South Carolina was favored despite LSU having the higher ranking. He also said his defense felt snubbed because all the talk was about the Black Death.

Hodson and Davis were voted co-MVPs for LSU while Green won the honor for SC.

Postgame

LSU's seniors topped off their careers with their first bowl victory to finish with the best three-year record in school history: 28–6–2. One of those seniors, Wendell Davis, explained how he caught nine passes for 132 yards and three touchdowns. "They lined up one-on-one. That's what a receiver dreams about. It's hard for a defender. He's got to cover you all over the field."

Tommy Hodson said, "A lot of credit has to go to Coach (Ed) Zaunbrecher for putting in a 'pickup' package to handle the blitz. Our offensive line just did a great job. We threw a lot of timing routes. There were just a few times when I had to throw with people in my face."

Senior LB Nicky Hazard echoed what Coach Archer said in the TV interview. "Not a word was said about our defense. Everything was about South Carolina's. That was a motivational factor."

Senior DL Tommy Clapp expressed his feelings succinctly. "This team will be remembered for winning 10 games and beating the crap out of the Gamecocks."

Archer: "You live by the blitz, and you die by the blitz. South Carolina died by the blitz. We had some different formations in our backfield to make sure we could get the ball off. We didn't think they could cover our receivers."

Todd Ellis gave no excuses for one of his most miserable afternoons—28-of-47 for 304 yards with a Gator Bowl record four interceptions. "They just came after me. They switched their defense up and blitzed more than we had seen, and they did it with different people. They put us into second-and-long and third-and-long situations. They forced me to throw faster than I wanted to."

Gamecock LB Matt McKernan praised LSU. "They were one of the best teams in handling our blitz. Obviously, we thought we could cover Davis one-on-one. But it was tough."

LSU ended the season ranked #5 in both the AP poll and the UPI Coaches poll.

Eighteen 1987 Tigers played pro football: OL Eric Andolsek, DL Kenny Davidson, WR Wendell Davis, DL Karl Dunbar, RB Eddie Fuller, DB Kevin Guidry, TE Ronnie Haliburton, LB Eric Hill, QB Tommy Hodson, DB Greg Jackson, RB Victor Jones, TE Brian Kinchen, RB Sammy Martin, DB Mike Mayes, OL Blake Miller, OL Ralph Norwood, RB Harvey Williams, and OL Willie Williams.

Hall of Fame Bowl vs. Syracuse

"We all could have played better"

Tampa Stadium, Tampa, Florida
January 2, 1989

It's hard to imagine a season when LSU finished as co-champion of the SEC as a disappointment, but that's what 1988 was.

LSU's Season

Mike Archer's second squad wasn't picked in the preseason to win the conference for two reasons: heavy losses to graduation, especially on offense, and a daunting schedule that included consecutive September road games against Tennessee, Ohio State, and Florida. WRs Wendell Davis and Rogie Magee, TE Brian Kinchen, RB/kick returner Sammy Martin, and All-SEC G Eric Andolsek were all in the NFL. All-American C Nacho Albergamo had graduated, and RB Harvey Williams was redshirted with a knee injury.

Nevertheless, the Tigers started at #18 in the AP poll but quickly rose to #9 following victories over Texas A&M and Tennessee, the latter being the first time LSU had ever won in Knoxville. The season reached a crescendo the following week when the Tigers led Ohio State 33–20 with less than five minutes to play at Columbus. But the Buckeyes stormed back to pull out the 36–33 victory. As often happens, one defeat led to another—a 19–6 clunker in Gainesville.

The offense continued to struggle against Auburn but managed to pull out a 7–6 home victory in the "Earthquake Game." The crowd roared so loudly when QB Tommy Hodson connected with RB Eddie Fuller for the go-ahead touchdown in the final two minutes that the seismograph in the Geoscience Building registered the rumble as an earthquake.

Four more conference victories followed, including a 19–18 squeaker in Tuscaloosa on David Browndyke's field goal in the final minute. Then the #3 Miami Hurricanes came to Baton Rouge and humiliated the Tigers 44–3 in a rainstorm. LSU took out their frustration on Tulane, 44–14.

Their 6–1 SEC mark gained the Tigers a tie for first with Auburn. Despite AU's loss in Baton Rouge, the Sugar Bowl chose the #7 Plainsmen to face #4 Florida State. #16 LSU was relegated to the Hall of Fame Bowl in Tampa against #17 Syracuse.

The Opponent

Syracuse started the 1988 season burdened by the challenge of following the most successful team since the great 1959 squad that went 11–0. The '87 Orangemen finished 11–0–1, the tie coming against Auburn in the Sugar Bowl. Fifth-year senior QB Todd Philcox had the biggest shoes to fill. Coach Dick MacPherson's option attack required a quarterback who could both run and pass. Don McPherson had filled that role ably in his four-year career, throwing for 5,812 yards and running for 1,284 more. After tossing a grand total of 10 passes in four years, Philcox had the second best statistical season by an SU quarterback. He finished fifth in the nation in passing efficiency and set a school record by completing 60.2 percent of his passes.

After a 26–9 loss to Ohio State the week before the Buckeyes beat LSU, the Orange won seven in a row, including a 24–10 triumph that ended a 16-game losing streak to Penn State. Next came the Lambert Trophy battle for eastern independent supremacy with West Virginia. The 31–9 loss left a bitter taste in the mouths of the Orangemen, but they shook off the loss and beat Pittsburgh 24–7. That gave SU double-digit wins in two straight seasons for the first time in school history.

Top individuals for Syracuse were senior DB Markus Paul, the NCAA's active leader in interceptions who broke the school career record with 19. Another senior, Daryl Johnston, was generally regarded as the best fullback in the country. His 138-yard rushing against Boston College was the most by an Orange fullback since Larry Csonka's 154 in 1967. The Syracuse seniors became the first class in school history to play in three bowl games.

The Orangemen were favored by 2½ points. The game attracted 11,000 Syracuse supporters while LSU followers numbered just 3,000. Would the disparity in attendance be an indicator of the investment of the teams in the game?

The Game

On a beautiful afternoon, 51,300 gathered to watch the rematch of the 1965 Sugar Bowl, which LSU won 13–10. The outcome was decidedly different this time.

First Quarter

Syracuse drove 80 yards in 14 plays to take a lead it never relinquished. RB James Drummond set the tone on the first play when he took an option pitch 15 yards. Drummond capped the march with a 2-yard plunge. FB Daryl Johnston said afterward, "I think coming out and scoring on that first possession gave us the confidence we could move the ball." Drummond agreed. "From that first drive when we moved the ball so well, I knew the game was ours."

Score: Syracuse 7 LSU 0 (9:18)

LSU started efficiently also, driving 41 yards to the Syracuse 35. But 5'8" WR Tony Moss stumbled while running his pattern, and QB Tommy Hodson's pass sailed over Tony's head to S Markus Paul at the 14. After forcing a punt to the LSU 42, the Tigers started moving again. FB Jay Egloff burst through for 14 yards, and Hodson hit TE Ronnie Haliburton to set up fourth-and-one at the 11 on the final play of the quarter.

Syracuse 7 LSU 0

SECOND QUARTER

During the break, Coach Mike Archer opted to kick a field goal, then changed his mind and decided to go for it. But LB Dan Bucey stuffed FB Victor Jones. "We're here to win," explained Archer. "We're here to be aggressive. If we can't make a yard, we're not going to win anyway."

The Orange drove 68 yards to set up a 38-yard field goal by Kevin Greene.

Syracuse 10 LSU 0 (8:22)

As he had done multiple times during the season, backup QB Kevin Guidry came in and led the Tigers to points. The key plays were a 26-yard pass to RB Eddie Fuller and Guidry's 8-yard scramble to the SU 36. However, Kevin injured his right shoulder on the play and left the game, never to return. Hodson came in and ran a "flea flicker." He handed to Fuller, who pitched it back to him. The pass to Alvin Lee floated to CB David Holmes at the nine. LSU had now driven deep into Syracuse territory three times with nothing to show for it. "That was a tough pass to throw coming off the bench," said Hodson. "The throw didn't feel right coming off my hand. That's rule No. 1—don't throw it inside and short on a streak."

The defense held again, and LSU got the ball back at midfield. A 9-yard pass to junior TB Calvin Windom and a 15-yard roughing the punter penalty put the ball on the 26. After Egloff lost a yard, Hodson found Moss for nine to the 19. Windom then zipped through a hole at right guard and raced untouched to the end zone. David Browndyke booted the extra point.

Syracuse 10 LSU 7 (1:52)

LSU had reason to be optimistic. They trailed in five SEC games but won them all. Defensive coordinator Pete Jenkins said, "They gave us their whole offense on the first drive. Then we really thought we had them pegged. After the first half, I really thought we were going to win."

THIRD QUARTER

The Tigers tied the score on their first drive. On third-and-four from the 37, Hodson hit Moss for 43 yards. But the drive bogged down, and Browndyke kicked a 35-yard field goal. "I thought we were going to come back," said LSU LB Ron Sancho. "They were starting to suck air a little bit."

Syracuse 10 LSU 10 (11:39)

Syracuse came right back, driving from their 33 to the LSU five in nine plays. Jenkins pointed to the next snap as a "swing play" that had a big impact on the outcome. On third-and-goal from the four, CB Jimmy Young and WR Rob Moore were bumping as soon as the ball was snapped while Moore tried to run under a lob pass. Young was called for interfering with Moore while jumping for the ball. Instead of bringing on the field goal unit, it was first-and-goal from the two. "That was robbery," said Sancho. "If anything, it should have been on the Syracuse receiver instead of Jimmy Young. That turned around the game right there." Archer said, "The ball was clearly overthrown." It took three plays, but Drummond pushed over the right side for the touchdown.

Syracuse 17 LSU 10 (5:53)

LSU's next possession suffered a body blow when Hodson was sacked for a 13-yard loss. After the punt, Syracuse drove 56 yards in ten plays to take a two-score lead.

Syracuse 17 LSU 10

Fourth Quarter

WR Deval Glover outran backup CB John Childers on an out route and made a 4-yard touchdown catch. The PAT failed.

Syracuse 23 LSU 10 (14:13)

LSU had time to come back but never got further than the SU 45 the rest of the game. The defense needed to force a turnover, but that never happened. "An option team that's pitching it and reading things as they do, there's the opportunity to turn it over, and they didn't," said Archer.

Final Score: Syracuse 23 LSU 10

Postgame

Coach Archer lamented, "We couldn't run, throw, tackle, or kick the ball off. … We didn't stop them for a loss on the option the whole game."

Tommy Hodson, whose three interceptions set a Hall of Fame record, minced no words in summarizing his team's performance. "I don't care if you drop the ball or fumble as long as you play hard. I don't think we played hard. I'm not pointing my finger at anybody. I'm just saying we didn't play hard." C Todd Coutee backed up what his quarterback said. "Some guys just weren't excited about the game. They were just here for a good time. Some people had a lackadaisical attitude the whole week. I don't know if we were here too long or what."

LSU defensive coordinator Pete Jenkins expressed his frustration. "We spent five weeks practicing against the option; it sure didn't look like it today. They just out-executed us at the corner. You've got to give Syracuse some credit because nobody worked harder than we did to get ready. They were what we expected. It just seemed like every play one of us would miss something … a call, a tackle, an assignment—something."

Senior OLB Ron Sancho had hoped to finish his career on a high note. "It seems like every time they ran the option, somebody wasn't doing what they were supposed to be doing or being where they were supposed to be." A lack of execution? "Plain stupidity," he replied. "I don't think this was indicative of the kind of defense we had this year. I loved my time at LSU. I hate this might be what people remember. We all could have played better."

SU's execution on the option left LSU's other senior OLB, Eric Hill, shaking his head. "It was a low blow for me. I couldn't figure out how to stop them, and we've faced the option before. They probably have more weapons than most SEC teams. They knew our schemes and blocked our defensive backs with a huge tight end. I'm still shocked by how they moved the ball on us."

Syracuse QB Philcox said the coaching staff crafted an offensive game plan to exploit holes in the LSU defense they had seen on film. "They figured that if we could get to the perimeter, we could be effective if we could get the pitch off."

Syracuse senior TB Robert Drummond won the MVP award after rushing for 122 yards on 23 attempts with two touchdowns. "What I did," he said, "was only because of what the offensive line was able to do. They were the cause of me getting the award. And it was pretty easy running behind Daryl Johnston." Drummond revealed the team's motivation. "Everyone ridicules us. They say, 'Syracuse are northern boys. They can't play football.' Last year (in the Sugar Bowl) … we played damn good football only to have Auburn come up to tie us. We had to play to prove something. They're an SEC team. They've got a little arrogance. We do our talking on the field."

Coach MacPherson expressed the same attitude. "Anybody who's from the south saw the north come down and play like the south. We went after them." He added, "I've said it publicly many, many times. The SEC is without a doubt the strongest conference in America, and we're trying to grow. I think people can learn how to respect Syracuse football."

Fourteen 1988 Tigers played pro football: DL Marc Boutte, DL Kenny Davidson, DL Karl Dunbar, RB Eddie Fuller, TE Ronnie Haliburton, LB Eric Hill, QB Tommy Hodson, DB Greg Jackson, RB Victor Jones, DB Mike Mayes, OL Blake Miller, OL Ralph Norwood, DB Corey Raymond, and OL Willie Williams.

Poulan Weed Eater Independence Bowl vs. Michigan State

The magic is back!

Independence Stadium, Shreveport, Louisiana
December 29, 1995

The loss to Syracuse in the 1989 Hall of Fame Bowl marked the beginning of a dark period for LSU football. No one imagined that the Tigers would go *six years* without playing in a bowl game, the longest dry spell since 1949–58 when there were only a half dozen bowls. The cumulative record for 1989–94 was 25–41, with the nadir coming in 1992 when the Tigers won only two games against nine losses—the most in school history.

Mike Archer proved unable to maintain the program at a high level and was dismissed after the 1990 season. Athletic Director Joe Dean hired Hudson "Curley" Hallman based on his coaching Southern Mississippi to a 23–11 record in three seasons highlighted by victories over national powers Florida State and Alabama on the road. Unfortunately, at LSU Curley did not have future Pro Football Hall of Famer Bret Favre as his quarterback as he did at USM. When Hallman's fourth Tiger team did not improve on 1993's 5–6 record to create the first four-year streak of losing seasons in LSU history, Dean pulled the plug.

Curley's successor was a tough sell to the Board of Supervisors, Tiger fans, and, most important of all, the players. Gerry DiNardo's head coaching experience consisted of four losing seasons at Vanderbilt, where he finished 19–25, including a 65–0 humiliation at the hands of archrival Tennessee in his last game. But he quickly won over the players and the fans by stating, "It's my responsibility ... to bring the magic back to Tiger Stadium. We've got a lot of work to do, but we've got tremendous support. It's one of the truly, truly special places in college football."

LSU's Season

DiNardo left his first Baton Rouge press conference and headed straight for Carencro, the home of his #1 recruiting target, *Parade* All-American Kevin Faulk. A running quarterback in high school, Faulk started at tailback for LSU from Game One.

The Tigers faced one of the nation's most daunting schedules, with games against four preseason top 10 teams, starting with #3 Texas A&M, a 33–17 road loss. Faulk rushed for 171 yards the following week to spark the 34–16 victory over Mississippi State. That set up the first home game of the DiNardo era against #5 Auburn. At the behest of fans, Gerry successfully petitioned the NCAA to allow an exception to its rule that the home team had to wear dark jerseys. A question on the minds of many in the second-largest crowd ever for a game in Tiger Stadium was how senior QB Jamie Howard would play against the team that intercepted him six times the year before, including three pick sixes in the fourth quarter. Clad in the revered white jerseys at home for the first time in 13 years, LSU prevailed 12–6 when CB Troy Twillie intercepted a pass in the end zone as time expired. After completing 19 of 30 passes for 220 yards and one touchdown with only one interception, Howard was carried off the field on the shoulders of teammates.

The 2–1 Tigers were over .500 for the first time since October 1990, and their #18 ranking was their first since September 1989. Following a romp over Rice, LSU tied South Carolina at Columbia in a rugged game that left the Tigers battered and bruised when they hosted Steve Spurrier's #3 Florida Gators the following week. The fact that the Tigers lost only 28–10 could be interpreted as a sign of progress.

With Howard out with a shoulder injury, LSU absorbed a disappointing 24–16 loss at Kentucky. At 3–3–1, the Tigers needed to win three of their final four games to insure a bowl bid. They started with a blowout of North Texas. After a tough 10–3 loss at Alabama, LSU finished strong, beating Ole Miss and Arkansas by a combined 66–9 with freshman Herb Tyler under center. The Tiger defense held each of their last four opponents to ten points or less.

In the 1970s and '80s, a bid to the Independence Bowl in Shreveport would not have excited the Tigers or their fans. But after the six-year drought, LSU Nation rejoiced.

The Opponent

After four straight non-winning seasons, Michigan State ditched Coach George Perles and hired Nick Saban, a 44-year-old assistant coach of the Cleveland Browns who had been on Perles' staff his first five years at MSU. Saban led the Spartans to a winning season—just barely.

Nick inherited a program facing possible NCAA sanctions for academic fraud and cash payments to prospects. He instituted much needed discipline with mandatory study halls and his brutal "Fourth Quarter" winter conditioning program.

The season couldn't have started much worse—a 50–10 home drubbing from #2 Nebraska. But four wins and a tie in the next six games created momentum that was halted by a 45–14 beatdown at Wisconsin. Next came the annual showdown with archrival Michigan. Saban had promised Spartan fans at the UM-MSU basketball game in February that, "We're going to kick Michigan's ass!" A 28–25 triumph might not meet that high standard but did end the new coach's probationary period. A win at Indiana the following week gave the Spartans the sixth win they needed to be bowl eligible. The season ended with a tough 24–20 loss at Penn State.

Michigan State's team and individual statistical rankings reflected their 6–4–1 record. The Spartans ranked eighth in the Big Ten in points per game and ninth in points allowed. Senior QB Tony Banks finished third in the league in completion percentage (60.5) but first in interceptions (15). RB Scott Greene tied for second in rushing touchdowns. The WR tandem of Derrick Mason and Muhsin Muhammad ranked fourth and fifth respectively in receptions (53 and 50).

The two 6–4–1 teams were mirror images of each other in that they both ran a "pro" I-formation offense and a 4–3 defense. As you'd expect in an SEC-Big Ten matchup, analysts predicted the team that ran the ball better would most likely win. For Michigan State, that meant containing "Thunder and Lightning," freshman RB Kevin Faulk (852 yards), the SEC Offensive Freshman of the Year, and redshirt freshman RB Kendall Cleveland (562 yards). LSU's defense finished #6 in the NCAA in points allowed (14.6 per game) but had four runners enjoy 100-yard rushing games during the season. Would they be able to contain MSU's 1,057-yard rusher Marc Renaud?

The kicking game might well determine the outcome. DiNardo said the bowl game "has two of the best return guys in the country playing against each other." Junior WR Eddie Kennison led the SEC with 13.3-yard per punt return and ranked eighth in kickoff returns (21.8 ypr). MSU's Mason led the Big Ten in kickoff yards per return with 26.3 and averaged 10.6 yards on punt returns.

The Game

Tiger fans predominated among the record crowd of 48,835. The late afternoon kick-off took place under clear skies with a temperature of 47 degrees.

FIRST QUARTER

Each team scored on its opening possession. The Spartans hit paydirt on their second play, a 78-yard pass from Tony Banks to WR Mushin Muhammad, who ran right past CB Tory James.

Michigan State 7 LSU 0 (14:13)

LSU responded with their own 80-yard drive. Key plays were a Herb Tyler strike to Eddie Kennison for 18 yards and Kevin Faulk's 40-yard scamper down the left sideline to the 19. The Tigers stayed on the ground from there. Offensive coordinator Morris Watts inserted 290-pound DT Anthony "Booger" McFarland, SEC Defensive Rookie of the Year, to do his Refrigerator Perry imitation at the fullback spot. TB Kendall Cleveland followed Booger off right tackle 6 yards into the end zone. Andre Lafleur booted his 35th consecutive PAT.

LSU 7 Michigan State 7 (12:07)

The game settled down to mostly trench warfare the rest of the period. MSU had moved out to their 40 when one of Nick Saban's disciplinary moves bit him. He didn't start four players who missed curfew earlier in the week. One of the four, LT Robert Denton, watched from the sideline as DE Gabe Northern roared past the backup and horse-collared Banks as he tried to pass. Gabe finished the play by falling on the fumble at the 26. But LSU euphoria was short-lived. Faulk fumbled right back on the next snap.

After an exchange of punts, the Spartans converted two third downs to drive deep into Tiger territory. On third-and-five, Banks shot a bullet to WR Nigea Carter to the 49. Three snaps later, MSU offensive coordinator Gary Tranquill beat the blitz by calling a screen pass to TB Mar Renaud for 21 yards to the four. But Banks pulled away from center a split second too soon on the next snap, and LB Allen Stansberry covered the pigskin at the three. Cleveland ran the ball three straight times to the 18 as the period ended.

LSU 7 Michigan State 7

SECOND QUARTER

Disaster struck the Tigers on the first play of what would be a wild 15 minutes in which 31 points were scored. OLB Carl Reaves read the eyes of Tyler and moved into the passing lane to snare his pass and rumble to the three. Spartan FB Scott Greene, chomping at the bit on the sideline during his one-quarter suspension, entered the game and drove over right tackle into the end zone on the first play. The kick was blocked by 6'6" DE Arnold Miller.

Michigan State 13 LSU 7 (14:44)

The MSU lead lasted 14 seconds. Kennison, a four-time track all-American, took the kickoff on the eight, started up the middle, then found an opening to the right and sprinted untouched to the end zone.

LSU 14 Michigan State 13 (14:30)

The Tiger lead lasted 13 seconds. WR Derrick Mason took the kickoff a yard deep in his end zone and didn't stop running until he was in LSU's end zone. The 100-yard scamper made him the all-time Big Ten leader in kickoff return yardage. The Spartans went for two and made it easily on Greene's smash through left tackle.

Michigan State 21 LSU 14 (14:17)

The MSU lead lasted 1:06. Faulk ran the kickoff back 33 yards to the 43. After Kennison took a flanker reverse 6 yards, Kevin roared through the right side, veered to the outside, and scampered 51 yards to tie the game. Four touchdowns in less than two minutes!

Michigan State 21 LSU 21 (13:11)

The game settled down with no more scoring until the end of the period. The Spartans advanced to the 41 before having to punt, downing the ball at the six. The Tigers got out of trouble when Faulk tore through the left side 68 yards to the 29. But Tyler was sacked for an 11-yard loss to force another punt. Chad Kessler dropped it nicely at the four.

Banks completed three passes to spark a march that reached the LSU 40—not quite far enough for a field goal try. So MSU punted into the end zone with 2:14 to play.

Trying to eat up some clock, LSU ran the ball three times, but Saban called two of his timeouts. So the Spartans got the ball back at their 39 with 1:02 on the clock. They made the most of their second opportunity. Two completions to Mason and a Banks scramble made it second-and-four at the LSU 34, where MSU took their final timeout. Two incompletions forced Saban to make a decision: long field goal attempt or go for it. He chose the latter, and Banks hit Muhammad on a crossing route to the 20. Two incompletions brought on Chris Gardner, who kicked a 37-yard three-pointer.

Michigan State 24 LSU 21 (0:01)

Two teams that prided themselves on their defenses gave up 558 total yards—323 for MSU and 235 for LSU. DiNardo told the Tigers to play with more intensity. "We were just short of breaking a lot of plays…. I had thought it was going to be a close game, and I felt right from the start of the game that we had the better team, but we hadn't demonstrated it in the first half."

Third Quarter

The second half, like the first, started with a bang—three touchdowns in the first 7:47. But unlike the first half, all three were scored by one team. The Tigers drove 74 yards in only three plays aided by two major penalties on the Spartans. Saban had told the media that he feared LSU's big play ability. His concern was justified as most of the yardage came on Tyler's 48-yard pass to Kennison to the MSU 11. A personal foul penalty on the play moved the ball to the five. In came big Booger to lead Faulk over right tackle into the end zone.

LSU 28 Michigan State 24 (14:27)

Saban said afterward, "We came out in the second half a little bit flat." He also expressed disappointment that "we lost our poise when things went poorly in the beginning of the third quarter." After the game, MSU DE Yakini Allen said he drew a personal foul penalty when he grabbed the face mask of an opponent who used a racial slur twice. "When I got flagged, the ref was right there listening to him." Two reporters from Michigan newspapers said an anonymous black LSU player verified that two LSU players used a racial epithet.

Taking DiNardo's halftime advice to heart, the intense Tiger defense forced a three-and-out to give the offense the ball on the 10 after the punt. But the Spartan defense responded with a three-and-out of their own. On third-and-12, the Tiger blitz overwhelmed the MSU line, and Northern pulled the ball loose from Banks while sacking him, then picked up the ball and ran 37 yards to the end zone. "In the second half, we just started flying around. We just got a lot faster. I think being off for a month, you really tend to slack off," said Northern. "The closer I got to the goal, I thought somebody was going to catch up to me. I couldn't let that happen. My teammates would really get on me."

LSU 35 Michigan State 24 (9:20)

The Tigers soon got another turnover. The other end, James Gillyard, playing in his hometown, leaped and tipped Banks's pass at the line of scrimmage. Stansberry, who set an Independence Bowl record with 18 tackles, caught the deflection and returned it to the 14. It looked like the Tigers might have to settle for a field goal when an errant pitch on a flanker around play was recovered by Kennison for a loss of 13. But two snaps later, Tyler spotted Eddie running free past the cornerback and looped a pass to him in the back right corner of the end zone. "The plan was to take advantage of their defensive backs," explained Tyler. "They're good, but they were no match for Eddie. … We thought we were a lot quicker."

LSU 42 Michigan State 24 (7:13)

The rest of the game was anticlimactic. The Spartans lost their best offensive lineman, Flozell Adams, when he was ejected for unsportsmanlike conduct. Saban: "That's not how we would want to represent our university and how we would want our team to be represented. We'll have to work on the self-discipline we have as a team so that, hopefully, this won't happen again."

Gillyard took advantage of Adams' replacement to cause another fumble by Banks that LSU recovered. The fired-up Spartans gang-tackled Cleveland on the next play but continued to push him backward after the whistle before piling on top of him. That drew another 15-yard penalty. On third down, Tyler hit 6'7" 280-pound TE David LaFleur who barged to the 15. But Faulk's 6-yard loss took the steam out of the advance. So Andre Lafleur tried a 38-yard field goal that sailed wide left.

Gillyard registered two more sacks on MSU's next possession, and LSU got the ball back as the period ended with the Spartans gaining only 42 yards and just one first down.

LSU 42 Michigan State 24

FOURTH QUARTER

Tyler threw on the run to Kennison for 27 yards to the 24. But the Tigers bogged down, and Lafleur missed a 37-yard field goal. But another sack led to a punt to midfield. Four more carries pushed Faulk past 200 yards and set up a 48-yard field goal by freshman Wade Richey, who hadn't attempted one all year. That put the Tigers into a tie for the most points scored in an Independence Bowl.

LSU 45 Michigan State 24 (8:45)

The Spartans finally put together a sustained march, mostly through the air. They made four first downs to reach the 22. From there, Banks threw on the run toward the right sideline, but FS Clarence Litton made a leaping grab and went out of bounds at the one. After two runs and an incompletion, Kessler lined up in punt formation with the ball on the three. He took the snap and held the ball even though there was no appreciable rush. Then he jogged out the back of the end zone for an intentional safety.

LSU 45 Michigan State 26 (5:57)

The remaining minutes brought the Spartans' seventh turnover when Tory James cut in front of the receiver to snag an interception at the MSU 39. LSU ran out the clock from there.

Final Score: LSU 45 Michigan State 26

The Spartans outgained the Tigers, 448 yards to 436. But it's almost impossible to win when you have seven turnovers and allow six sacks.

Postgame

Offensive MVP Kevin Faulk, with 234 yards on 20 carries, said, "I owe it all to my blocking." Defensive MVP Gabe Northern said, "On my way up here, I told somebody I had a feeling I was going to win it. This was my last game, and I had some kind of determination that I was going to put us over the top." After guiding the Tigers to a fourth straight victory as the starting quarterback, freshman Herb Tyler was cheered by Tiger fans and asked to pose with their sons and daughters for pictures. "I never imagined it would be like this. This is just unbelievable. … We had some problems with our timing in the first half, but I knew it would come around in the second half."

Despite not catching a pass in the game, senior WR Sheddrick Wilson, LSU's leading receiver during the regular season, exclaimed, "I feel so good right now, man, I'm almost in tears. I'm trying to hold them back. The crowd was great. The atmosphere was great."

Coach Saban said his Spartans "could play better on special teams. We had a PAT blocked, gave up a kickoff return, and had another returned for good field position." But he praised the opponent. "They played a good game, made a lot of good plays, got seven turnovers on us, and ran the ball very effectively." Banks was disappointed that he played so poorly the second half. "This isn't the way that I planned on ending my college career. I had three picks in the Penn State game and three picks here. They weren't doing anything different in the second half, pass-rush wise, than they did in the first half. They were just a good team." MSU T Bob Denton said, "When they got that fumble for the touchdown, that just seemed to take our heart out."

Seventeen 1995 Tigers played pro football: OL Ben Bordelon, OL Alan Faneca, RB Kevin Faulk, CB Tory James, WR Eddie Kennison, TE David LaFleur, OL Todd McClure, DL Anthony McFarland, DL Arnold Miller, DL Kenny Mixon, DL Gabe Northern, K Wade Richey, TE Nicky Savoie, DB Denard Walker, LB Joe Wesley, DL Chuck Wiley, and WR Sheddrick Wilson. Alan Faneca was elected to the Pro Football Hall of Fame in 2021.

Peach Bowl vs. Clemson

Both coaches got the game they wanted

Georgia Dome, Atlanta, Georgia
December 28, 1996

LSU's Season

The 1996 Tigers proved that Gerry DiNardo's first season was no fluke. Invigorated by a Top 10 recruiting class, they finished 9–2, LSU's best record since 10–1–1 in '87. The result was a new school record for attendance—79,519 per game.

The Tigers won their first four games, starting with a great comeback against Houston. Five turnovers helped the Cougars build a 34–14 lead heading into the final period. Sophomore RB Kevin Faulk, who had an 80-yard touchdown run earlier, returned a punt 78 yards. With the defense shutting down Houston, the Tiger offense scored twice more to pull out the 35–34 victory. The next week, the Tigers upended Auburn in a game that was literally a barnburner. As flames from the old wooden gym, called "The Barn," rose above the upper deck, sophomore S Raion Hill returned an interception 39 yards for a touchdown and also ran back the two-point try in the last minute to turn a possible 17–17 tie into a 19–15 win.

Florida ended the win streak with a 56–13 romp. But victories over Kentucky and Mississippi State set up a showdown for leadership in the West against Alabama. Sophomore QB Herb Tyler left the game with a bruised nerve in his throwing arm in the first quarter. That helped the Tide cruise to a 27–0 triumph. LSU rebounded with victories over Ole Miss, Tulane, and Arkansas.

Freshman Rondell Mealey replaced Kendall Cleveland as Faulk's backup, adding 603 rushing yards to Kevin's 1,282. Tyler ran the option play adroitly and completed 58 percent of his passes to account for 1,933 yards of total offense. Faulk led the SEC in all-purpose yards (rushing, receiving, kick returns) with an average of 191.3 per game.

LSU earned a bid to the Peach Bowl. The Tigers had played in the first Peach Bowl in 1968 against Florida State but had not been back to Atlanta since.

The Opponent

Clemson won the mythical Lazarus Award for rising from the dead midway through the season. The Tigers shook off a 2–3 start and a spate of embarrassing off-the-field incidents to win five straight before losing to archrival South Carolina in the finale when

Matt Padgett's 37-yard field goal sailed wide left on the game's last play. Remember that name and the result. With a 6–2 conference record, the Tigers tied North Carolina for second in the Atlantic Coast Conference.

Some reporters commented on the similarities between the two Peach Bowl teams.

- Same team nickname and same stadium nickname: "Death Valley."
- Same coaching philosophy: Play physical football based on a strong running game and tenacious defense.
- Rely on a workhorse running back: Faulk rushed for 1,282 yards for LSU while junior Raymond Priester gave Clemson 1,194 yards. Each ranked second in his conference, and each team led its league in rushing.

When Clemson coach Tommy West watched LSU film, he saw the kind of team he wanted, built around the word "tough." He said of DiNardo: "I've got a lot of respect for the way he runs his program as far as the toughness part. I enjoy watching that. I think this game will turn into a very physical contest. It will be fun to watch." DiNardo also looked forward to the Peach Bowl. "There's a lot of history that makes this an interesting and exciting game. It will be fun to play in the Georgia Dome for our players, and it promises to be a tremendous experience for our fans."

The Game

The 63,622 spectators, including 15,000 LSU fans, saw each coach get the game he wanted. TV viewers who liked lots of scoring changed the channel early.

FIRST QUARTER

LSU's offense encountered heavy resistance, gaining only one first down on their first three possessions. Faulk provided most of the yardage on punt returns of 29 and 25 yards. Fortunately, Clemson wasn't moving the ball either, although they did take advantage of LSU's nickel defense on one series. With MLB Charles Smith out of the game, the ACC Tigers ran up the middle three straight times for a total of 31 yards. So LSU returned to its standard defense and forced a punt. Coach West explained, "We thought it would be hard to run the ball every play. We thought we had to hit them with some pass plays. [But] we didn't throw the ball very well" (6 of 20 for 66 yards).

The Clemson defense created the first break late in the period when DE Trevor Pryce sacked QB Herb Tyler, jarring the ball loose. LB Harold Means picked up the pigskin and rumbled to the nine. After two runs gained five, QB Nealon Greene rolled to his left but couldn't find anyone open. So he reversed field into the end zone.

Score: Clemson 7 LSU 0 (0:04)

SECOND QUARTER

LSU's offense finally started moving, driving 80 yards in seven plays to tie the score. Tyler was huge on the drive, rushing for 14 yards on the first play and hitting passes of 19 yards to Tyrone Frazier and 31 yards to TE Nick Savoie for a first down at the seven. Two Faulk runs put the ball in the end zone. Wade Richey booted the PAT. Tyler said, "Nicky

Allen Stansberry stops a Clemson drive (*Gumbo* Class of 1997).

made a great catch. I got good pass protection. All our hearts were in it to score on that drive."

Clemson 7 LSU 7 (12:43)

It didn't take LSU long to take the lead. On their next possession, the Bayou Tigers prowled 77 yards in ten plays aided by two Clemson penalties. LB Anthony Simmons drew a personal foul penalty for hitting Faulk out of bounds. One play later, CB Dexter McCleon was flagged for pass interference against Frazier to give LSU a first down at the Clemson 35. The march continued relentlessly inside the five. With fourth down and inches to go for a first down and less than a yard for a touchdown, Tyler sneaked across only to have the touchdown erased by an offside penalty. So DiNardo settled for a 22-yard field goal by Richey.

LSU 10 Clemson 7 (4:35)

Neither team threatened the rest of the half.

LSU 10 Clemson 7

THIRD QUARTER

With the Orange defense limiting Faulk to just 64 yards on 23 carries, LSU could not add to the lead and had to rely on the defense to hang on. On the Bengals' first possession of the half, they drove into Clemson territory and had only themselves to blame for not scoring. Tyler kept the drive alive early with a 15-yard third-down pass to Larry Foster. Then F-back Nicky Savoie made a diving 9-yard catch. After an offside penalty on the next third down moved the ball back to the 23, usually reliable TE David LaFleur dropped a wide-open touchdown pass. That forced Richey to try a 40-yard three-pointer, but Pryce came up with another big play—the first blocked kick against LSU as well as Clemson's first block all season.

The teams spent the rest of the evening pounding away at each other without putting any more points on the board. Clemson's "Sominex offense" (as one writer dubbed it) moved into LSU territory only to self-combust. As expected, Priester did the heavy lifting. He finished with 151 yards on 25 carries to become the school's leading rusher with 3,010 yards. He also broke the single-season yardage mark he set in '95 and added to his record for career 100-yard games with 12.

But Raymond needed more help from his mates. Clemson had ten possessions through the first three quarters, and half lasted just three plays, counting the short scoring drive. With such a pedestrian offense, Clemson couldn't afford any mistakes. Instead, a holding penalty stopped one drive, and false start and delay of game calls disrupted another series.

The ACC Tigers moved from their 10 to midfield on one drive, but DT Booger McFarland sacked Greene, and Cedric Donaldson stopped Priester for a loss. "We feel like no one can drive the length of the field on us," McFarland said afterward. "Every time they got going, we decided it was time for the defense to make a play. ... I always tell the secondary to give us three seconds. By then we know we can get pressure."

Punter Kevin Laird was Clemson's best weapon. He set a Peach Bowl record with seven punts inside the 20 to keep LSU backed up for most of the game. Another Clemson possession ended when Priester fumbled for the first time all season one play after setting the school career rushing record on a 13-yard gain. "There's not a whole lot to say," G Glenn Rountree said. "We just kept stopping ourselves, shooting ourselves in the foot."

LSU 10 Clemson 7

Fourth Quarter

The punting duel continued. Laird kept LSU bottled up when he boomed a 63-yarder that set a new Peach Bowl record. Later, Faulk muffed a punt to hand Clemson excellent field position at the LSU 39. Facing a third-and-one at the 30, the Orange Tigers were set back 5 yards by a procedure penalty. Then Greene's pass fell incomplete. That brought on Padgett to attempt the tying three-pointer from 52 yards out with 1:10 left. Padgett had never tried a field goal longer than 49 yards. He had missed a 37-yard attempt with 11 seconds left in the 30–27 season-ending loss to rival South Carolina. "Coach told me during the timeout that I was one of the luckiest people in the world to have a second chance," Padgett said. "Most people don't get that."

Still, he felt confident. "I wasn't really thinking about the South Carolina game. I hit it good. Whether it was low or not, I can't say. It felt like it had height to me." Padgett will never know whether his kick would have gone through the uprights because sophomore DE Aaron Adams blocked it. After nearly getting a piece of Padgett's extra point in the first quarter, Adams convinced special teams coach Jerry Baldwin to go to "rip switch" formation, which called for players on the right side of the line to rush the kick. At the last moment before the field goal snap, Adams switched his three-point stance by putting his left hand down instead of his right. "I made sure I was quick enough to beat the lineman to the gap," he explained. "I swung my body left, came through and got my left hand on the ball."

Final Score: LSU 10 Clemson 7

The victory gave LSU just its fifth season of ten or more wins. Also, the Tigers won bowl games in back-to-back years for the first time since 1967–68. Neither team reached the 300-yard mark for offense: LSU 297, Clemson 258. Tyler earned the Offensive MVP award after completing 14-of-21 for 163 yards while rushing for an additional 38. DT Booger McFarland won Defensive MVP.

Postgame

DiNardo seemed more relieved than exultant. "It was kind of typical of our year. We won ugly a lot this year. I felt on the sidelines that we should have played a lot better. If we had lost this game, it would have really bothered me." LSU defensive coordinator Carl Reese: "Being an old defensive coach, you like an ugly game because it means good defense. You don't like them because they're gut-wrenching and wear you out. A lot of the credit goes to the kids for their will to win and their intensity." He added, "I never thought we'd stop them cold, but we played hard enough and intense enough to win the game." He added, "Our passing defense won the game. They couldn't throw when they needed to."

Sophomore QB Tyler revealed his motivation. "I wanted to do it for the seniors. Getting ten wins this season is just outstanding. We had to overcome a lot of things to win."

Blocked-kick hero Adams had difficulty controlling his emotions after the game. He had been suspended for the Independence Bowl the previous year and had to work his way back onto the team. When lifted on the shoulders of LB Markeith Spears after the game, Adams was crying. "It's been a tough road for me. I've been through so much in this program. I've done a lot of praying. I'm glad God answered my prayers. I had a dream last night that I was either going to block a kick or recover a fumble on the kickoff. In fact, I was almost late for a meeting this morning because I was dreaming about the block."

Senior T Ben Bordelon said, "I'd give the game ball to the defense."

The loss dampened Priester's record-setting performance. "It wasn't enough to give my team a victory. This will stick with me until spring ball. But things happen. We didn't make the plays when we had the opportunity to."

LSU rose to #12 in the final AP poll, their highest ranking since 1987.

Nineteen 1996 Tigers played pro football: OL Ben Bordelon, K Danny Boyd, OL Alan Faneca, RB Kevin Faulk, WR Larry Foster, DB Raion Hill, TE David LaFleur, DB Clarence LeBlanc, OL Todd McClure, DL Anthony McFarland, RB Rondell Mealey, DL Arnold Miller, K Wade Richey, DB Mark Roman, TE Nicky Savoie, DL Mike Sutton, DB Denard Walker, LB Joe Wesley, and DT Chuck Wiley. Alan Faneca was elected to the Pro Football Hall of Fame in 2021.

Poulan Weed Eater Independence Bowl vs. Notre Dame

Second time's the charm

Independence Stadium, Shreveport, Louisiana
December 28, 1997

Coach Gerry DiNardo went three for three in taking LSU to bowl games.

LSU's Season

Tiger fans had great expectations for the 1997 season. LSU signed its second straight top-10 recruiting class. Eight offensive and seven defensive starters returned. For the first time since the SEC split into divisions in 1992, the media picked the Tigers to win the SEC West.

After a rent-a-win romp over UTEP, LSU began conference play at Mississippi State. The game marked the highly anticipated debut of RB Cecil Collins, who had gained a staggering 3,079 yards during his senior season at Leesville High School. With junior RB Kevin Faulk out with an injury, "the Diesel" plowed through the Bulldogs for 172 yards on 22 carries to spearhead the 24–9 victory. The game set the tone for coordinator Morris Watts' offense that would gain 62.5 percent of its yardage on the ground during the season.

Auburn came to Tiger Stadium for a slugfest that kept the national television audience glued to their seats until the end. Collins gave another spectacular performance—232 yards, the third-most in LSU history—and third string RB Rondell Mealey added 129 to more than make up for Faulk's absence. But the visiting Tigers scored with 30 seconds left to win 31–28. LSU tossed aside Akron before heading to Nashville for DiNardo's homecoming against his previous team, Vanderbilt. The fired-up Commodores shut down the Tiger offense, especially after Collins suffered a season-ending broken leg in the first half. LSU took a 7–0 lead and barely held on when DE Kenny Mixon blocked the tying-PAT try after Vandy's touchdown with 12 seconds left.

LSU had never beaten a No. 1 team in eight tries, although they did manage one tie. Their prospects didn't look good for breaking the streak against Florida, which had clobbered the Tigers 56–13 in '96. But the second largest crowd in Tiger Stadium history saw their heroes beat the Gators 28–21 thanks in large measure to four interceptions, including one returned for six by CB Cedric Donaldson. Steve Spurrier suffered his first defeat against LSU in 11 games as a player and coach. The triumph would prove to be the high point of DiNardo's five-year LSU tenure.

Would the #8 Tigers continue their good game-bad game trend against Ole Miss? DiNardo made the game a measure of his team's ability to handle success. His fears were realized when Ole Miss outscored the home team in the second half 22–0 to win 36–21.

Following a much-needed week off, the Tigers routed Kentucky 63–28 to set a school record for most points scored in a game. Faulk set another record with five touchdowns. The next week, LSU turned the tables on Alabama, gaining revenge for the 26–0 home loss in '96 with a 27–0 triumph in Tuscaloosa. Then came the renewal of the rivalry with Notre Dame, DiNardo's alma mater, which was having a mediocre season at 5–5. But the Irish gave the Tigers a dose of their own medicine, rushing for 260 yards to LSU's 121 in a 24–6 cakewalk in Tiger Stadium. For the second year in a row, the Tigers needed a team that defeated them to lose the Iron Bowl in order to win the West. In '96, Alabama won by a point. This time, Auburn eked out the win 18–17.

LSU ended the season with a 31–21 win over Arkansas to finish as SEC West Co-Champions and earn a berth in the Independence Bowl for the second time in three seasons. What might have been a ho hum trip to Shreveport turned into a chance to avenge a disappointing defeat.

The Tigers would have to beat Notre Dame without their defensive coordinator, Carl Reese, who resigned in early December to take the same position on Mack Brown's new staff at Texas. Reese's replacement was Lou Tepper, who had been fired in 1996 after five years as head coach at Illinois. Tepper had to learn the defensive terminology that Reese left behind. From his perch in the press box during the Independence Bowl, Lou would diagram what he wanted for the next play and an assistant would translate to the coaches on the sideline. DiNardo himself would signal the secondary on each defensive set.

The Opponent

Despite having a new coach following the resignation of Lou Holtz after the 1996 season, Notre Dame had high expectations heading into the 1997 season. Ranked #11 in the preseason polls, the Irish were led by fifth-year senior QB Ron Powlus, who threw for 2,078 yards. Junior Autry Denson provided balance by gaining 1,268 yards on the ground. But Bob Davie's first season as head coach after serving as defensive coordinator under Holtz produced a disappointing 7–5 record. The reason was not hard to find. While gaining 4,023 yards themselves, the Irish gave up 4,381. When the season started 1–4, fans took out their frustration on Davie and Powlus, even heckling Ron's wife and parents at games. A victory at Pittsburgh stopped the losing streak but was balanced by a home loss to USC the next week.

Unable to afford another loss to be bowl eligible, the Irish won their last four games, including the 24–6 road domination of #11 LSU. That victory, and another over #22 West Virginia the following week, were Notre Dame's only triumphs over ranked teams all season.

Their 7–5 record entitled the Fighting Irish to a bowl berth, but would they accept an invitation? They had stayed home in 1996 despite an 8–3 record. With no chance of playing in a major bowl and Holtz's resignation, the school administration decided not to accept any bowl bid. But this time they welcomed the invitation.

To have any chance of victory, LSU had to get a much better game from QB Herb Tyler, who threw three interceptions in the November loss to the Irish. And the defense had to stop Notre Dame's rushing attack. In the first game, LSU had often deployed only two linebackers with an extra defensive back. Now they would use a five man front much more, substituting a defensive back for a linebacker only when expecting a pass.

The Game

With a wind chill of 27 degrees and a 15 mph wind, 50,459 braved the cold, almost 2,000 more than LSU's visit to Shreveport two years earlier. A light snow fell two hours before kickoff, making the field a bit slippery.

LSU surprised their fans by taking the field in new uniforms designed by DiNardo— white helmets and pants and gold jerseys. Also three offensive linemen—All-America G Alan Faneca, All-SEC C Todd McClure, and G Ryan Thomassie—decided on a whim to shave their heads. Teammates tagged them the "Cueballs." The trio would play a vital role in the game.

FIRST QUARTER

Notre Dame started from their 20 against the wind and moved quickly to a first down when QB Ron Paulus hit FL Bobby Brown on third-and-seven for 10 yards to the 33. But two incompletions around a short run forced a punt that Kevin Faulk returned 23 yards to the LSU 45. Needing a strong start, QB Herb Tyler fired a quick pass to freshman SE Abram Booty at the ND 45. But two incompletions brought on the nation's #1 punter Chad Kessler, who pooch-kicked to the 13.

The Irish looked much sharper on their second possession. TB Autry Denson alternated carries with FB Ken Barry with only one pass mixed in on a march that bogged down at the 16. So Scott Cengia booted a 33-yard field goal.

Score: Notre Dame 3 LSU 0 (7:13)

LSU lost its leading ball carrier two plays into the next series. Faulk broke lose for a gain of 21 before being hit as he went out of bounds. He left the game with an ankle injury, never to return. So sophomore Rondell Mealey, who didn't have a single carry in the November game against Notre Dame, moved into the tailback slot and waited for his first carry while 250-pound freshman FB Tommy Banks banged through the line twice to midfield. Then Mealey toted the leather three straight times to the 37. An option keeper by Tyler made it fourth-and-one at the 33. DiNardo didn't hesitate—go for it. Rondell slipped but still managed to make enough to move the sticks. A sideline pass to Booty gained another first down. After Mealey's 3-yard gain, DE Brad Williams stopped the momentum by smothering Tyler as he rolled out to pass. When Herb failed to connect down the middle with Larry Foster at the goal line, Wade Richey tried a 42-yard field goal that hooked wide left. The period ended when Paulus ran out of the pocket to the 31 for a first down.

Notre Dame's Kory Minor (4) struggles to tackle Rondell Mealey. Alan Faneca (66) blocks in the background (*Gumbo* Class of 1998).

So far, the game had gone the same way as the regular season meeting. The Irish rushed for 81 yards on 12 attempts during the period. However, the Tigers buckled down and held Notre Dame to just 47 yards on the ground the final three periods.

Notre Dame 3 LSU 0

Second Quarter

The old-fashioned ground-and-pound slugfest continued, especially as the weather turned nasty. DE Arnold Miller made two straight outstanding plays, stuffing Denson and sacking Paulus, to force a punt. The Tigers gained two first downs before bogging down. Tyler hit Booty with another sideline pass to the 40. Then Mealey gained nine and Banks two. As rain fell, a delay of game penalty and a sack by LB Corey Minor brought in Kessler. Even against a strong wind, he hammered a 45-yard boot that Denson returned to the 23.

Junior QB Jarious Jackson took over with disastrous results. As he ran the option, LB Joe Wesley grabbed him as he tried to pitchout. S Mark Roman fell on the loose ball at the 24. Even though the Tigers gained only 4 yards in three plays, they were close enough for Richey to kick a 37-yard field goal into the wind.

Notre Dame 3 LSU 3 (7:11)

Paulus came back in and led the Irish to a go-ahead field goal in the last seconds of the half. Playing with confidence, the senior completed all three of his passes—two to SE Malcolm Johnson and the third to Joey Getherall for a total of 22 yards. But most of the territory was gained on seven runs by Denson and Barry to bring up first-and-goal at the four. At that point, Jackson came back in along with two new running backs. Led by DBs

Donaldson and Clarence LeBlanc, who were crashing from the edges, the Bandits stuffed three straight runs. So the Irish had to be content with Cengia's 21-yard field goal.

Notre Dame 6 LSU 3 (0:17)

With Tyler completing only three-of-nine passes, the Tiger offense gained only 97 yards in the first half and avoided a shutout only because of the fumble recovery. Fortunately, the LSU defense played much better than in the first game, holding the Irish to 152 yards.

The cold rain moved out during halftime and did not return.

THIRD QUARTER

The Tigers set the tone for the second half on the opening drive. With Faulk trying to loosen up

Chuck Wiley tackles Autrey Denson (*Gumbo* Class of 1998).

on the sideline, Mealey carried the ball eight straight times to move the ball to the ND 32. Finally, Tyler fired to Booty on a button hook to the 19. But the Irish stuffed Rondell for no gain, then Tyler slipped down while rolling out for a 6-yard loss. On third down, Herb threw too late to Foster down the middle. So Richey banged through a 42-yard field goal, his longest of the season.

Notre Dame 6 LSU 6 (9:17)

LSU got a break when Allen Rossum slipped down at the seven as he caught the kickoff. When the defense forced a three-and-out, Hunter Smith punted a line drive that Foster returned to the ND 49. After Tyler ran a keeper for 6 yards, Mealey carried four times in a row to move the sticks twice and set up third-and-three from the 16. Tyler turned the right corner and careened out of bounds at the 11 for a first down. After defensive star Kory Minor tackled Mealey for a yard loss, Herb faked a handoff to Rondell to freeze the secondary and fired a slant pass to Booty in the end zone.

LSU 13 Notre Dame 6 (4:05)

Notre Dame got a break when the kickoff went out of bounds, giving them the ball at their 35. Needing to make some first downs to run out the clock and get the wind for the fourth quarter, the Irish lost ground thanks to Miller's second sack. LSU had 2:18 with the wind to add to their lead, starting from their 40 after the punt. But after getting chewed out by defensive coordinator Greg Mattison, the Irish defense stopped Mealey a yard short on third-and-two. So pooch kicker Jeremy Witten tried to pin ND deep, but the ball backed up on him to the 23. Notre Dame moved to a first down at the 38 as the period ended with the Irish having run only eight plays.

LSU 13 Notre Dame 6

Fourth Quarter

With the wind now, the Irish could expect to overcome the seven-point deficit. But the LSU defense would nix that hope. First, though, a roughing the passer penalty gave Notre Dame a first down at the LSU 47. Then Paulus rolled right and reversed to the left with an empty field in front of him to the 20. But the Tigers buckled down and surrendered only three more yards. So Cengia kicked a 33-yard field goal.

LSU 13 Notre Dame 9 (13:10)

After the wind-aided kickoff into the end zone, Mealey made the play of the game with the assistance of his offensive line. He took a handoff over left tackle and raced 78 yards to the two before Rossum pushed him out of bounds. Any hopes of a goal line stand ended quickly as Rondell followed G Alan Faneca into the end zone.

LSU 20 Notre Dame 9 (12:47)

Two runs by Denton gave the Irish a first down at their 32. But Kenny Mixon got LSU's third sack, dropping Paulus for a 10-yard loss. After a substitution penalty, Ron backpedaled to throw a screen but had no chance as Booger McFarland roared through to drop him and send him to the sideline with an injury. Jackson must have thought, "Gee, thanks, coach," when asked to go in for third-and-26. He ran from the pocket and gained half the yardage needed.

After a punt exchange, Notre Dame started again at its 41. Paulus returned and threw the ball right into the hands of CB Cedric Donaldson, who dropped it to his great chagrin. Then Wiley got sack #4 to make it third-and-20. Under duress, the senior quarterback shoveled the ball forward to Denson to make it fourth-and-six. Coach Davie had no choice but to go for it. Wiley got LSU sack #5 to give the Tigers possession at the 35.

They moved from there to the clinching touchdown. Mealey ran for five, then four more. Banks pushed through the center for the first down. The defense won the next two snaps, holding Rondell to no gain and -3. Then he cut back over left tackle and sprinted to the one. Again, it took just one play for him to step into the end zone.

LSU 27 Notre Dame 9 (2:22)

Notre Dame padded its statistics with Jackson at the controls, reaching the LSU 30 when time expired. The Tigers got their sixth sack during the possession.

Final Score: LSU 27 Notre Dame 9

After gaining 222 yards and scoring two touchdowns, Mealey easily won the Offensive MVP Award while Arnold Miller won the defensive trophy for his seven tackles, including four for losses.

The rushing statistics were almost exactly reversed from the November game.
First meeting: Notre Dame 260 yards rushing, LSU 121 (a season-low)
Independence Bowl: LSU 265, Notre Dame 128

With the victory, LSU ended the 1997 season undefeated away from Tiger Stadium for the first time in ten years.

Postgame

Coach DiNardo explained the turnaround from the November game. "The biggest change was the way we tried to defense the run on first-and-10 with seven linebackers and defensive linemen instead of six. Then we used the plays we used all year."

Rondell Mealey joined Cecil Collins and Kevin Faulk as LSU backs who rushed for more than 200 yards in a game during the season. "My number wasn't called (for most of the season). When my number was called tonight, I responded. I just try to do the best I can all the time. … You can't let (not playing) frustrate you. If you get frustrated, you can't do your best job."

Coach Davie explained that "the difference today was we broke down on pass protection. That was the first time all year we weren't able to protect the passer."

Notre Dame G Mike Rosenthal praised the Tigers. "You have to give them a lot of credit for what they did tonight. LSU came out with a great game plan, and they executed it. They stacked things up front, and we couldn't get much going. We knew that they were going to make some adjustments after that last game, and they adjusted and executed." LB Kory Minor said, "The difference was we gave them some big plays tonight. The last time we played, we didn't do that. Tonight we had them and had them and then they would hit us with a big play."

Twenty 1997 Tigers played pro football: DB Fred Booker, K Danny Boyd, RB Cecil Collins, OL Alan Faneca, RB Kevin Faulk, WR Larry Foster, DB Raion Hill, OL Alcender Jackson, DB Clarence LeBlanc, OL Todd McClure, DL Anthony McFarland, RB Rondell Mealey, DL Arnold Miller, DL Kenny Mixon, K Wade Richey, DB Mark Roman, DL Mike Sutton, LB Joe Wesley, DL Chuck Wiley, and OL Louis Williams.

Chick-fil-A Peach Bowl
vs. Georgia Tech

"He makes you want to go to war"

Georgia Dome, Atlanta, Georgia
December 29, 2000

The LSU football program disintegrated quickly following the 1997 Independence Bowl victory over Notre Dame. The loss of defensive coordinator Carl Reese and the ill-advised hiring of Lou Tepper to replace him dropped the Tigers from first in the SEC in points allowed to ninth two years later. A similar decline occurred on offense, where another poor choice to replace Morris Watts as offensive coordinator led to a drop from fifth in the conference in '97 to eleventh in '99. Coach Gerry DiNardo tried to stop the bleeding by taking more and more responsibility on himself, which only made matters worse. Athletic Director Joe Dean ended Gerry's tenure as head coach with one game remaining on the '99 schedule after the Tigers had won only six of 15 games in DiNardo's last two seasons.

Dean started with a lengthy list of possible replacements, but all of them either chose to stay where they were or did not please new Chancellor Mark Emmert. Then Dean was put in touch with the agent of the Michigan State head coach who had lost to LSU in the 1995 Independence Bowl—48-year-old Nick Saban. Emmert was so smitten with Saban that he agreed to Nick's demand for improved facilities. On paper, the choice was puzzling. Nick had a so-so 34–24–1 record at Michigan State. But the results at LSU exceeded anyone's expectations.

LSU's Season

Instilling accountability that had been lacking the previous two years and improving the training regimen of the players, Saban led the Tigers back to a bowl game in his first year.

Picked to finish last in the SEC West, the 2000 Tigers didn't do anything in their first four games to silence the skeptics. After a 58–0 rout of Western Carolina, LSU jumped out to a 21–0 halftime lead over Houston only to see the Cougars dominate the second half before sophomore CB Damien James ran back a pick for the clinching score in the 28–13 victory. As expected, the Tigers lost at Auburn 34–17. But what happened the following week in Tiger Stadium was totally unexpected—a 13–10 loss to Alabama-Birmingham when QB Josh Booty threw an interception in the final minutes that led to the winning field goal.

With #11 Tennessee coming to town before a trip to #12 Florida, the Tigers seemed destined for another losing season. A *Knoxville News* article proclaimed that Tiger Stadium was no longer a fearsome place for visiting teams. The largest crowd for a football game in Louisiana history—91,682—helped the Tigers reestablish home field advantage with a stirring 38–31 overtime victory behind QB Rohan Davey. However, Florida brought LSU fans back to earth with a 41–9 thumping the next week.

After an easy 34–0 win at Kentucky, the Tigers hosted #13 Mississippi State. Again, the game went into overtime and again LSU pre-

Domanick Davis (*Gumbo* Class of 2001).

vailed, 45–38. If Saban still hadn't won over some of the Tiger faithful, what happened the following week completed the process. Alabama hadn't lost in Tiger Stadium since 1969, but LSU pulled out a 30–28 win to clinch a bowl berth.

The inconsistent play that frustrated Saban no end continued with a ho-hum road victory at Ole Miss followed by a dismal performance at Little Rock. An offense that had scored 30 or more points in four conference games was held to a field goal in Arkansas' 14–3 victory.

Saban didn't want just any bowl for his 7–4 Tigers. He had his sights set on the Chick-fil-A Peach Bowl, which would have the New Year's Eve time slot all to itself. In addition, Georgia was fertile recruiting territory. As luck would have it, Saban was friends with bowl president Gary Stokan, who recalled Nick's pitch to him. "We have to get to your bowl game. It's the best bowl game we can get to. We need to change the culture around here."

Peach Bowl officials were worried about LSU's reputation for tepid bowl-ticket sales. Tiger fans responded to Saban's urging by buying up the school's entire allotment of 21,000.

The Opponent

George O'Leary, in his sixth year as Georgia Tech head coach, won the Atlantic Coast Conference Coach of the Year Award for guiding the Yellow Jackets to a 9–2 record and a second-place finish. Their victims included five bowl teams and seven teams that finished with winning records. The highlights of the season were road wins over #5 Clemson 31–28 and the third straight win over archrival and #19 Georgia, 27–15.

Junior QB George Godsey got better as the season progressed. In the last four games, he threw for an average of 474.5 yards per game. He finished with 23 touchdown passes and only six interceptions. His favorite target was another junior, Kelly Campbell, who caught 59 passes—30 more than anyone else—for 963 yards and 10 TDs. One man also dominated the rushing statistics—sophomore TB Joe Burns with 942 yards. The offensive line was anchored by All-American LT Chris Brown.

The Yellow Jackets were justifiably proud of their rushing defense, which ranked 12th nationally (94.5 yards per game). Coordinator Ted Roof's crew also finished 21st in the nation in scoring defense (19.0). Tech also ranked second nationally in turnover margin at +1.64 per game, a new school record.

After the regular season ended, Offensive Coordinator Ralph Friedgen was named the head coach at Maryland. So O'Leary elevated running backs coach and fellow Irishman Bill O'Brien to the coordinator position for the bowl game.

The Game

A Peach Bowl-record crowd of 73,614, three-fourths of whom rooted for the Yellow Jackets, saw one team dominate the first half, and the other dominate the second.

First Quarter

After winning the toss and electing to receive, Tech came out throwing. Junior QB George Godsey hit WR Kelly Campbell for seven, then connected with Jonathan Smith for a first down at the 34. But two incompletions on the next series forced a punt. With junior Josh Booty at quarterback, LSU moved to one first down on a spot pass to FL Reggie Robinson, who ran to the 48. But they sputtered from there, and Donnie Jones punted into the end zone.

The Tigers got a break when Godsey fumbled the snap, and DT Chad Lavalais recovered on the 25. An incidental face mask penalty on first down moved the ball to the 19. Power-running TB LeBrandon Toefield smashed to the nine, but an unsportsmanlike conduct penalty after the play moved the pigskin back to the 24. A screen pass to 265-pound FB Tommy Banks made it first-and-10 at the 13. A short run, an incompletion, and a fumbled snap brought on John Corbello, who kicked a 32-yard field goal.

Score: LSU 3 Georgia Tech 0 (8:26)

The Yellow Jackets responded with an 80-yard drive. On third-and-seven, Godsey fired a quick pass to WR Nate Curry for a first down at the 43. TB Joe Burns rocketed to the LSU 44. RB Jermaine Hatch from Baton Rouge took an option pitch to the 37. Two plays later, WR Will Glover caught a pass at the 32 to move the chains. Then the slow progression ended suddenly when Burns steamed through left tackle and raced untouched down the sideline to pay dirt for only the third touchdown given up in the first quarter by LSU all season.

Georgia Tech 7 LSU 3 (5:32)

The Tigers quickly moved to two first downs on two runs by sophomore TB Domanick Davis and a look-in pass to sophomore WR Jerel Myers to the Tech 49. But that's when DE Greg Gathers from Reserve LA took matters into his own hands. He lined up against RT Brad Smalling, who was playing in place of Brandon Winey, out with a broken hand. Miffed that LSU considered him too small, Gathers pressured Booty into three straight incompletions. Smalling said afterward, "Gathers is a good player. He kept taking my hands away from me, and coach (Rick) Trickett teaches us to keep our hands up. I wasn't doing that."

Tech fans went wild when Godsey, seeing Campbell uncovered as the defense broke their huddle, called for a quick snap and threw the ball to him. Campbell juked a defender and ran down the sideline to the end zone. However, Godsey's haste cost him the touchdown because of a false start penalty. Another penalty helped force a punt as the quarter ended.

Georgia Tech 7 LSU 3

Second Quarter

LSU gained one first down on Booty's shot to Robinson on a slant to the 46. But the next three plays almost proved disastrous. Booty had to scramble and fumbled when hit from behind. Fortunately T Rob Sale recovered. With Gathers again applying pressure, Booty threw two straight incompletions. LSU punted but got the ball back right away when LB Bradie James pulled the ball loose from 5'7" Kelly Rhino on the return and also recovered on the Tech 44. James had lost his father on Christmas Eve and had returned to the team just the day before the game.

But LSU could not capitalize as Tech continued to own the line of scrimmage. Booty tried a play action pass but held the ball too long and was sacked for a loss of 7 yards. Obviously rattled, Josh took too much time getting the Tigers lined up and had to call timeout. Gathers, who moved around on the line from play to play, struck again to make it fourth-and-21. Rhino fumbled again on the punt return, but a Tech man fell on it.

Campbell took a reverse for 19 yards with a face mask penalty tacked on to put the ball on the 21. James tackled Burns on back-to-back plays that set up first-and-goal at the nine. Hatch then slanted over the left side to the pylon.

Georgia Tech 14 LSU 3 (8:17)

In desperate need of some offensive success before halftime, LSU started strong. Banks took a flat pass 16 yards to the 30. Blitzed out of the pocket, Booty fled to his right and threw on the run to Myers for 6 yards. But Davis was dropped for a 2-yard loss, forcing Josh to throw a third down pass that was almost intercepted. Jones, getting more work than he wanted, punted for the fifth time. When Rhino returned 14 yards to the 44 and held onto the ball, the Tech fans cheered.

Four straight runs put the Yellow Jackets on the LSU 26. But Godsey fumbled the snap, grabbed the ball, then lost it again when hit by blitzing S Lionel Thomas. The ball popped into James's hands at the 30. Four plays later, Jones launched punt #6. With time to add to their lead, Tech got a quick first down on a 13-yard pass to TE Russell Malvay to the 44. But LB Jeremy Lawrence snagged Godsey's short pass and set sail for the goal line. He might have gained big yardage had not the quarterback himself brought him down with a block tackle at the 32.

Instead of taking advantage of the field position, LSU went backward. Smalling was called for holding to put the Tigers behind the chains again. With less than a minute left, Jones punted into the end zone. The half ended with Lavalais sacking Godsey.

Georgia Tech 14 LSU 3

The Tigers were fortunate they were not further behind. Four turnovers kept the nation's #2 team in turnover margin from piling up a larger lead. But with the LSU offense in disarray, even an 11-point lead seemed insurmountable. But two halftime decisions changed everything.

Brandon Winey, dressed in his No. 68 jersey and slacks during the first half because of a broken left thumb, asked Saban if he could put his uniform on and give it a try. "The reason I didn't play at first was because I felt like I couldn't protect Josh on my inside. But I saw them hitting Josh, and I just couldn't take it. I take it personally when someone's hitting my quarterback."

With Booty only eight-of-19 for 110 yards, Saban decided to go with junior Rohan Davey for the second half. C Louis Williams said that the player the team voted the permanent team captain "came in, pulled us together, and we just went from there. He told us to put everything that had happened behind us, put it out of our mind, and just do what we do best. That's take the game over in the third and fourth quarter." Inspired, LSU went from Sleaux Tigers to Geaux Tigers.

THIRD QUARTER

After Davis returned the kickoff to the 30, the LSU fans in the end zone stood and cheered as QB Rohan Davey took the field. Unnoticed by most was the fact that Winey trotted out to play left tackle with a cast protecting his broken right thumb. Freshman Rodney Reed moved from left to right tackle. The changes sparked a complete reversal from the first half. With Gathers under control, LSU's offense began moving the ball, and the Tiger defense attacked the Tech offense.

Davey hadn't played since the Florida game because of an injured ankle. But he showed no signs of rust as he completed all five passes on a four-minute drive that produced a touchdown. Rohan felt FB Tommy Banks set the tone for the second half when he caught a flat pass and ran over a tackler for 10 yards. "The whole offensive line started jumping around, the receivers and backs. They said, 'Let's go, Ro. Let's win the game.'" Throwing quickly to blunt the rush, Davey completed two for 20 yards to All-SEC WR Josh Reed, who didn't catch a pass the first half after snagging 65 during the season. "In the first half, there were two people following me everywhere I went," said Reed. "I didn't really see anything different in what Georgia Tech was doing (in the second half). Maybe some other people were catching passes, and they were concerned about them." Myers caught another Davey aerial for 13. Finally, Banks was wide open in the end zone for the last pass from the three. It was the senior fullback's first career touchdown catch. However, Corbello's PAT try missed.

Georgia Tech 14 LSU 9 (10:59)

After gaining 115 yards rushing the first half, the Yellow Jackets found the going tough after the halftime adjustments. Plagued by penalties and another turnover, they ran only four plays in the period for a measly 13 yards against 157 for LSU.

Following a three-and-out by the fired-up Tiger defense, Davey hit Reed for 6 yards to the 44, then handed to Davis for eight, LSU's longest run since the first quarter. That's when Gathers exerted himself again, causing an incompletion on first down. After Davis gained four, Rohan moved up in the pocket to avoid the rush and threw down the middle off Reed's hands. Following Jones's eighth punt of the evening, the Tigers were right back in business when S Ryan Clark made a leaping interception on the sideline at the LSU 47.

After gaining 11 yards on two carries, Toefield took a short pass but fumbled while being tackled, and Tech recovered at the 27. LaBrandon argued that his knee was down first, and the replay backed him up. But there was no video review yet in college football.

A holding call and a personal foul penalty killed any chance Tech had of keeping the ball. So the Tigers embarked on a 53-yard drive to take the lead. It didn't start well when an illegal motion penalty and a batted down pass by a blitzer brought up third-and-seven. But with time to survey the field, Davey hit Reed in stride down the middle to the 33. With the Yellow Jackets giving ground grudgingly, the Tigers took three downs to move the chains to the 21. After a quick out to Reed to the 10, the period ended with LSU playing second-and-goal from the nine.

Georgia Tech 14 LSU 9

Fourth Quarter

With double coverage on Reed, Davey threw the ball out of the end zone. On third down, Rohan rolled right and threw to Reed again despite his being covered. Josh made one of the most remarkable catches in LSU history. He leaped high to snag the ball and came down with his right foot just inside the back line before his left foot landed behind the line. Josh explained, "The play is designed for the outside receiver to go a yard deep into the end zone and for me to go further. When Rohan was rushed, I broke to the middle of the end zone. I didn't think he saw me, so I waved my arms. He just lofted it up. When I saw I had it, I worried about getting my foot inbounds." Davey said, "Actually I saw him late. I was flushed out of the pocket, and that limited me. I was supposed to get it to him early. Then I did see him, and I threw the ball up there."

The Tigers went for two points and succeeded on another outstanding play by Davey and Reed. While being dragged down, the 240-pound quarterback flipped to Reed, who caught the ball at the one, spun around, and pushed through DB Jamara Clark into the end zone. "I was lower than him, and I just bulled my way in," Josh explained.

LSU 17 Georgia Tech 14 (14:47)

Tech's offensive woes continued against a defense that alternated blitzers from every direction. On first down, DE Jarvis Green recorded his eighth career sack for a loss of 12. Then Curry was hit immediately after catching a short pass and, while being spun down, fumbled, and Bradie James recovered. However, the Tigers were hit with an excessive celebration penalty to move the ball back to the 32. The exhausted Tech defense dug deep and forced three incompletions. So Corbello booted the longest field goal of his career, 49 yards.

LSU 20 Georgia Tech 14 (13:30)

The Tech offense got a huge cheer from their fans when they made a first down on a completion to WR Kerry Watkins for seven and a 5-yard run by Burns. Then they gained another one when Godsey connected with Campbell to the 43. But on the next third down, Lawrence and James met at the quarterback for a 10-yard sack to force a punt. LSU began a methodical 92-yard drive that put the victory on ice. Not playing it safe so deep

Tommy Banks celebrates his touchdown catch in the fourth quarter. No. 47 is Eric Edwards (*Gumbo* **Class of 2001**).

in his territory, Davey fired to Myers to the 21. Banks then caught a pass in the flat and barreled through two tacklers to the 47. LSU overcame an illegal motion penalty when Rohan found Robinson to the Tech 37. On third-and-seven, Davey hit—who else?—Reed between two white shirts to move the sticks to the 23. Then Toefield roared up the middle behind Sale's block to the four. After Banks gained one, Davey lofted the ball over a defender to the big fullback at the left pylon for the touchdown. Going for two again, Davey rolled right and threw to Robinson in the end zone.

LSU 28 Georgia Tech 14 (3:12)

The Yellow Jackets drove 77 yards in 13 plays before finally surrendering the ball on downs. The Tigers ran two plays, then started celebrating their fourth straight bowl win.

Final Score: LSU 28 Georgia Tech 14

The Yellow Jackets, who entered the game 18th in the nation in scoring with 33.8 points a game, were held to their lowest total of the year. The Tiger defense limited an offense that averaged 435 yards per game to just 317.

Davey was the clear choice for Offensive MVP after completing 17-of-25 passes for 174 yards and three touchdowns in just one half of play. Bradie James won the defensive award for his six tackles, including a sack, and two fumble recoveries.

Postgame

Coach Saban met the press with Davey seated next to him. When asked whether Winey's contribution in the second half was as big as Rohan's, Nick replied, "Brandon's not up here with me, so I don't want to get in trouble with this guy (Davey), but it was big. He helped us take the edge pressure off, and we were able to pass more effectively. Their defensive ends are probably their best players." But Nick didn't ignore Davey. "Rohan is one of the best leaders on the team, and he impacts his teammates even more than I can."

Davey was surprised when Saban told him he would start the second half. "I had no way of expecting it. Coach usually likes to stick with the starter, so I wasn't thinking about playing."

Offensive Coordinator Jimbo Fisher also praised the two second half newcomers. "Winey showed tremendous toughness. ... He did a great job, and so did Rohan. What we needed in the second half was an emotional lift, and Rohan is our emotional leader." Fisher added, "With Rohan, we were able to go to our quick passing game and do more play-action faking. Most of the time, Josh (Booty) made the right reads, but we just couldn't give him any protection."

Offensive line coach Trickett added, "Brandon knew we really needed him out there. A lot of football is mind over matter, and

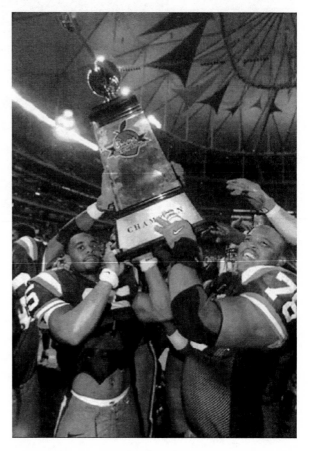

Tigers hoist the trophy (*Gumbo* Class of 2001).

the team was just lifted when he and Ro went in. You could see it in the other guys' eyes. They were going to get it done."

Tommy Banks, used mostly as a blocking back all season, had what he considered the best game of his four years with a career-high seven receptions for 71 yards. "Coach Fisher made an adjustment in the second half against their pressure, and we knew they would play zone defense. We threw more passes in the flat, and that got me more involved in the offense. To go out a winner and to have contributed to my final game, you couldn't ask for more."

Bradie James said he played on adrenaline after missing the last four days of practice for his father's funeral. "My teammates rallied around me. This (trophy) is for my father and my teammates and people at home. I just want to thank them. I did get tired a little bit early. But then I got emotional, and I just kind of got in a zone. I didn't know if I was tired or not."

LB Trev Faulk, who had eight tackles along with a forced fumble, said that LSU's goal was three turnovers. "I don't think they've been hit like we hit them tonight. We were hitting them real hard. They have a great offense, but we're not that bad ourselves on defense. We took offense to some of the things that were said about how much they were going to score."

S Ryan Clark sounded the same theme. "All week long people on TV and the papers, all they talked about was how they were going to score 40 points. We saw that as a slap in the face. Bradie made plays. Trev Faulk made plays. Jeremy Lawrence made plays." Ryan also praised Davey. "He makes you want to go to war. I've never been around a better person, never seen a guy look at you and give you a lift the way he does. It's just something he has inside. He comes into the huddle in the third quarter, and it was like turning on a light switch."

Coach O'Leary praised Davey. "He threw the ball where it was supposed to be thrown. I don't think the first guy did that." George added, "We were with our backs to the end zone the whole second half. You can't put a defense in that many bad situations and expect to win."

Twenty-two 2000 Tigers played pro football: DL Kenderick Allen, DB Fred Booker, DB Ryan Clark, QB Rohan Davey, RB Domanick Davis, TE Eric Edwards, LB Trev Faulk, DL Howard Green, DL Jarvis Green, WR Devery Henderson, DB Jack Hunt, LB Bradie James, P Donnie Jones, DT Chad Lavalais, DB Norman LeJeune, DB Adrian Mayes, OL Stephen Peterman, WR Josh Reed, TE Robert Royal, RB LeBrandon Toefield, OL Louis Williams, and OL Brandon Winey.

Nokia Sugar Bowl vs. Illinois

Two surprise conference champs meet

Louisiana Superdome, New Orleans, Louisiana
January 1, 2002

If ever an LSU season had its highs and lows, it was 2001.

LSU's Season

Nick Saban's second year started with great expectations. Slotted at #10 in the pre-season Associated Press poll, the Tigers were picked to win the SEC West. Yet after just four games, that seemed like a pipe dream.

They started with easy wins over Tulane and Utah State. Then the entire nation went into mourning following the 9/11 attacks in New York. As a result, all SEC games scheduled the next weekend were postponed until December 1 with the conference championship game delayed to December 8. Play resumed with the Tigers traveling to Knoxville. WR Kelley Washington set a Tennessee record with 256 yards on 11 receptions in the 26–18 victory that was not as close as the score indicates. Then #2 Florida came to Baton Rouge and, in the words of LSU S Ryan Clark, "kicked our tails," 44–15. With two conference losses, the Tigers' chances of winning the West hovered between slim and none, especially with two tough road games up next, starting with a make-or-break game at Kentucky. Senior QB Rohan Davey connected with freshman WR Michael Clayton with 13 seconds left to pull out a 29–25 victory. Tiger fans didn't have to bite their fingernails the next week—a 42–0 romp at Mississippi State.

Just when the team seemed to be hitting on all cylinders, Eli Manning followed in his father Archie's footsteps, leading Ole Miss to a come-from-behind 35–24 victory in Tiger Stadium. Callers on the postgame shows blasted LSU's multi-million-dollar coach. If two losses made the Tigers' chance of winning the West slim, three losses surely reduced the probability to next to nothing. Ole Miss, 3–1 in conference play, would have to lose three times since they held the tie-breaker over LSU. Auburn, at 4–1, would also have to lose twice, but LSU could take care of one of those defeats December 1 in the rescheduled game.

Continuing their pattern of losing at home and winning on the road, the Tigers scored the most points they ever tallied against Alabama. Davey torched the Tide for 528 yards on 35-of-44 passing. On his way to winning the Biletnikoff Award as the nation's best receiver, Josh Reed set SEC records for receptions (19) and yardage (293) in the must-have 35–21 victory.

Since Ole Miss lost their next three games after beating LSU, the Tigers could win the West by defeating Arkansas and Auburn, both at home. It isn't often you win a game in which your quarterback throws four interceptions, but that's what happened against the Razorbacks. Fortunately, Davey also threw for 359 yards and three scores as LSU took a 41–25 lead and held on to win 41–38.

That set up the showdown with Auburn, which was 5–2 in league play. When the visiting Tigers were flagged for unsportsmanlike conduct for stomping on the "Eye of the Tiger" logo at midfield, Saban called for an onside kick to start the game. LSU recovered and drove to a quick 7–0 lead that set the tone for the evening. The 27–14 triumph put LSU in the SEC championship game for the first time since its inception in 1992.

Their opponent would be the same Tennessee Vols that had smacked them in Knoxville. Philip Fullmer's club upset Florida in their postponed game to move to 10–1 and the #2 ranking in the Bowl Championship Series poll. Vol fans made their reservations for the Rose Bowl where the BCS championship game would be played. Who could blame them? They had beaten LSU 26–18 in September and just won at Florida, a team that had toyed with the West champs in October.

But the Tigers threw a monkey wrench into those plans, perhaps with intervention from on high from longtime coach Charley McClendon, who died two days before the game. LSU faced adversity early in the contest when Davey was knocked out of action with a broken rib. In came Matt Mauck, an unlikely hero if ever there was one. He was a 22-year-old redshirt freshman who had signed with Saban at Michigan State out of high school but decided to play baseball instead. After three years in the minor leagues, he contacted Nick, who had just moved to Baton Rouge. Matt had played little during the season, throwing only 26 passes. With Tennessee unprepared for his running, Mauck sparked the Tiger comeback from a 17–7 halftime deficit to stun the Vols 31–17. From clipboard holder to MVP—Matt's glorious evening.

As SEC champions, the Tigers became the host team in the Sugar Bowl.

The Opponent

Illinois won its first outright Big Ten crown since 1983, but with the Rose Bowl hosting the BCS Championship Game, the Illini had to settle for a trip to New Orleans. Their only loss of the season came at Michigan 45–20 in week four. Led by fifth-year head coach Ron Turner, whose expertise was offense, Illinois averaged 32.5 points per game, just a tenth of a point behind league-leader Iowa. The defense (23.8 points per game) ranked fifth in the conference.

QB Kurt Kittner, a four-year starter, led the Big Ten in passing yards (2,994) and in touchdown passes (23). His top targets were wideouts Brandon Lloyd and Walter Young, who combined for 104 catches. Like LSU, the Illini employed two running backs, junior Antoineo Harris (626 yards on 167 carries) and freshman Rocky Harvey (578/136). The O-line boasted two Big Ten first teamers and one second team selection.

With a new coordinator, the Illini defense improved from allowing 26.0 points per game in 2000 to 23.8 in '01. A big factor was the improved secondary led by All-American junior CB Eugene Wilson, the nation's leader in passes broken up. A big question going into the Sugar Bowl was whether the young but talented line could stop LSU's running game and put pressure on Davey to slow down the SEC's #2 offense (451.5 yards per game).

Aside from experience, Illinois' strength was tenacity. They came from behind to win against Purdue, Penn State, and Ohio State in consecutive weeks. The Illini came to the Crescent City with something to prove. As the Big Ten champion with only one loss, they were miffed that they were not chosen over one-loss Nebraska to face Miami in the Rose Bowl for the BCS championship. They also wanted to show that they didn't deserve to be a two-point underdog.

The Game

Eager to watch two surprise conference champions meet for the first time in their long football histories, 77,688 packed the Superdome.

FIRST QUARTER

Both offenses showed rustiness from their long layoffs, especially Illinois, which hadn't played since Thanksgiving. Facing defenses that liked to blitz, neither side moved far on their first possessions. LSU gained one first down on two runs by Domanick Davis, who would have to carry the rushing burden with LaBrandon Toefield sidelined with a knee injury. After the punt, the Tiger defense attacked, harassing Kurt Kittner into three incompletions on the Illini's first series.

On its second series, LSU should have converted on third down, but TE Joe Domingeaux dropped an easy pass. Thanks to two deflected passes, LSU quickly got the ball back at the Illinois 43 and moved in for the game's first points. Nimbly avoiding the blitz, 6'3" 240-pound QB Rohan Davey flipped the ball twice to freshman WR Michael Clayton on underneath routes for a first down at the 33. Then Rohan connected for 18 yards with his favorite target, Josh Reed, who was credited with having the finest season ever by a receiver in major college football. On second-and-eight, Davey fired a slant-in pass to junior WR Jerel Myers to the four. Davis covered the remaining distance on the next play. John Corbello added the PAT.

Score: LSU 7 Illinois 0 (7:22)

Illinois made its initial first down when Kittner found open space to his left for 15 yards. The chains moved again on an interference call on CB Randall Gay. But two more incompletions brought on P Steve Fitts, who put LSU in a deep hole at the four. The Tigers pushed out to their 44 with the biggest chunks of yardage coming on two passes to Reed and another to TE Robert Royal. But three straight incompletions led to P Donnie Jones pinning Illinois deep at the six.

The period ended with LSU outgaining Illinois 122–33. Coach Turner said afterward, "I felt like we came in a little bit tight. Maybe that has to do with not playing in a game of this magnitude."

LSU 7 Illinois 0

Second Quarter

Illinois' offense came alive for one three-play scoring drive, but they fell further behind as LSU set a Sugar Bowl record for points in a quarter. After Davis returned a punt 22 yards to the Illini 36, the Tigers staged a three-play march of their own. On second down, Davey hit Reed over the middle to the 25. Then Davis, faster than ever on the artificial turf, took a handoff and burst over the left side to the end zone. The PAT was blocked. Davey said afterward, "We tried to spread everybody out because Domanick is so shifty. We wanted to give him a lane, and he just picked a lane. They were very aggressive, and they love to pursue. Domanick did a great job of cutting back and finding the end zone."

LSU 13 Illinois 0 (13:29)

The Illini tried to get the running game going without success. On third and four, DT Chad Lavalais batted down his second pass to force another punt. The Tiger offense kept hitting on all cylinders, marching 69 yards as Davis scored his third touchdown in less than 20 minutes of playing time. Davey started by connecting with Myers to the Illini 45. The next three plays epitomized the frustration of the blue-shirted defense. While being tackled, Davey threw a pass that was almost intercepted. After a false start and an incompletion, LSU faced third-and-15. Davis got that and more when he sped through a big hole at right tackle all the way to the end zone. His three rushing touchdowns were a Sugar Bowl record and tied the record for most in a game by another Davis, LSU WR Wendell in 1987. But Domanick wasn't finished.

LSU 20 Illinois 0 (10:23)

The next Illini possession started strong when FL Brandon Lloyd took a reverse 14 yards to the 49. Then came a play that encapsulated Kittner's first half frustration. He tried to pass only to have leaping LB Jeremy Lawrence deflect the ball back into his hands. He wisely knocked it down to avoid taking another loss. The Tigers gained one first down—on a pass to Reed, of course—before punting to the 20. On second down, LSU got a big break from the officials. Lloyd caught a short pass just before being hit by Gay, who wrestled the ball from the 6'2" receiver while taking him down. Replay showed that Lloyd's knee touched before he lost control of the ball, but no whistle blew, and Randall ran to the five before being tackled.

With their backs against the wall, the Illini defense stuffed Davis for no gain, then forced Rohan to throw the ball away with everyone covered. But on third down, Davey found Reed open under the goal posts.

LSU 27 Illinois 0 (4:42)

Stifled for 25 minutes, the Illinois offense came alive and roared 75 yards on three plays in less than a minute. Kittner ran to his left to avoid the rush and threw on the run to RB Rocky Harvey, who somehow was being covered by 6'7" 285-pound DE Marquise Hill at the LSU 33. That 42-yard gain was followed by a 31-yard completion to SE Walter Young to the two. TE Brian Hodges blocked, then slid into the left flat to catch a pass that broke the scoring ice for Illinois.

LSU 27 Illinois 7 (3:47)

If the Illini could get a stop, they could go into halftime with some momentum. But that didn't happen. Clayton caught three passes for a total of 60 yards, the last reception putting the pigskin on the 10. On second-and-seven, the Illini came oh so close to ending the drive. Davey's pass over the middle bounced high and almost landed in Illini hands. But Royal turned defender and knocked it away. He was rewarded on the next snap when Davey spotted him in the back of the end zone for the touchdown.

LSU 34 Illinois 7 (0:18)

LSU ran 53 plays for 344 yards and set a Sugar Bowl record for points in a half. Davey said later that he was not surprised by his offense's performance. "All I did was get the ball to the people on our team who … have been making the plays all year."

Kittner had more passes batted down at the line of scrimmage (six) than completions (five).

Saban warned his team not to become complacent. He pointed to the Outback Bowl earlier in the day when South Carolina blew a 28–0 lead over Ohio State before winning on a late field goal. He also reminded the Tigers that Illinois had come from behind five times during the season.

THIRD QUARTER

The Illini played much better and outscored the Tigers in the period. They didn't show it on their first possession, a three-and-out. But after LSU did the same, Illinois went 72 yards in four plays. Taking a deeper drop, Kittner threw to Young, who took the ball away from 5'11" CB Demetrius Hookfin and ran to the eight A second-down sack by DE Kyle Kipps and a false start penalty made it third-and-goal from the 17. But with no pressure on him, Kittner waited for Lloyd to come open across the end zone and hit him for the touchdown.

LSU 34 Illinois 14 (10:35)

As they did after the previous Illinois touchdown, the Tigers came right back with one of their own. Davey made it look easy, throwing to Reed three straight times for 14, 21, and then 32 for the touchdown.

LSU 41 Illinois 14 (9:29)

Kittner stayed hot and answered back. First, he fired to FB Carey Davis down the seam for 23 yards. Then he threw high to Young, who at 6'3" easily outleaped 5'11" CB Damian James for the ball at the LSU 28. That gave the All-Big-Ten quarterback five completions in the second half, as many as he had the entire first half. Three snaps later, Kurt lofted a beautiful pass to WR Aaron Morehead that would have been a touchdown except that CB Travis Daniels grabbed the receiver from behind in the end zone. First-and-10 on the 13. After a 2-yard completion, Kittner hit Lloyd running underneath the coverage, and he reached the ball over the right pylon.

LSU 41 Illinois 21 (7:20)

Starting from their eight after a penalty on the kickoff, the Tigers gained four first downs, one on a pass to Davis, another on a Reed reception, a third on pass interference, and the last one on a completion to Myers. From the Illinois 39, Davey then flipped the ball to Davis, who made a diving catch and landed in the end zone. But a holding penalty negated the beautiful play. That led to a punt to the 13. S Ryan Clark sacked Kittner at the four, and LSU got the ball back on a punt.

LSU 41 Illinois 21

FOURTH QUARTER

The Fighting Illini lived up to their nickname, and Tiger fans couldn't breathe a sigh of relief until the final minutes. Kittner threw a long pass to Lloyd, but SS Norman LeJeune deflected it into the hands of Gay at the LSU 34. But the Big Ten champs soon had the ball back after sacking Davey and traveled 46 yards in six plays. The key gains were a quick slant-in to Lloyd to the 17, and Kurt's lovely loft to Young at the edge of the end zone over Hookfin.

LSU 41 Illinois 28 (11:33)

Needing to at least burn some clock, the Tigers did more than that. Davis got the ball rolling with a 29-yard kickoff return to the 36. When Davey needed crucial yardage, whom did he look to? Josh Reed, of course. On third-and-seven, Rohan had enough time to wait for Reed to make a double move and catch his beautiful throw to the 19. Then Josh, the former running back, lined up in the backfield, cut across to take a shovel pass, shook off a tackler, and ran to the three. Davis did the honors from there for his fourth touchdown—a Sugar Bowl record. The chart said go for two, but Davey's pass was intercepted in the end zone.

LSU 47 Illinois 28 (8:39)

A three-and-out by the defense sent LSU's offense back on the field. Clayton took a short pass on the run and headed into Illini territory until a smashing tackle from behind propelled the ball forward to the 25, where SS Bobby Jackson picked it up and scampered to the Tiger 40. The Illini then ran a trick play that worked to perfection. Lloyd took the ball on an end around and threw to Young who snagged the pass over the smaller defender in the back of the end zone. The two-point pass failed.

LSU 47 Illinois 34 (5:41)

With all his timeouts left, Coach Turner ordered a standard kickoff. The decision looked good when LSU started from the nine after a penalty on the return. But the strategy backfired thanks to an inspired performance by the LSU offensive line and backup RB Devery Henderson. With Davis exhausted on the sideline, the sophomore from Opelousas carried the ball nine times, the only interruption coming on a crucial third-and-five strike to another sophomore, WR Corey Webster, to the 22. Turner had to use all his timeouts until a final push by Henderson gained a first down at the Illini 38. Several kneel downs ended the three-hour-54-minute marathon and reduced LSU's total offense to 595 yards, but who cares? The Tigers won their fifth straight bowl game and their first Sugar Bowl since 1968.

Final Score: LSU 47 Illinois 34

The Miller-Digby Award for the outstanding player went to Rohan Davey, who completed 33-of-53 passes for three touchdowns with zero interceptions. The senior quarterback could easily have shared the award with Josh Reed, who snagged 14 passes for 239 yards, both Sugar Bowl records. His yardage was more than half of Davey's total of 444, which was also a record. Or the MVP award could have gone to Domanick Davis, who gained 266 all-purpose yards, and that didn't count his two big gains that were cancelled by holding penalties. The highest scoring Sugar Bowl in history included 595 yards of total offense, still another bowl record.

Postgame

Coach Saban said he was proud of the Tigers for winning their last six games after an up-and-down start. "We certainly proved we should be in a BCS bowl game, and we carried the mantle of the SEC proudly tonight."

Domanick Davis wasn't overwhelmed by the task of replacing LSU's leading rusher. "There was no pressure on me going into this game. Early in the week, I told my teammates I would go out and make the most of the opportunity. I really felt like I was in a zone. I basically went out there and just had fun. The offensive line, the receivers, everybody did a great job."

Davey wasn't surprised by Davis's performance. "All week long, the questions were if Domanick could replace Toefield. He can't replace Toe, but he's a variation of Toe. He's quick. He's elusive. His game tonight was a tribute to the way he prepared all week for the starting position." Rohan added, "As a group, we wanted to be remembered as a team that thrust LSU into the top 10, that thrust LSU into the national spotlight for next year. I was in a zone. There was no pressure on me. I was going to make the most of my opportunity."

Coach Turner praised the Tigers. "They have tremendous receivers and a very explosive offense, like we knew. The quarterback had a tremendous day."

Kurt Kittner's four touchdown passes allowed him to break the school single-season touchdown record. He agreed with his coach that the Illini were tight to start the game. "Obviously we were. I don't know for what reason. It's a big game and a big situation. Once we settled down, we played great football, but we were too far behind." WR Brandon Lloyd described the LSU defense as "ferocious. They kept coming 100 miles per hour and never relented. We found some offense in the second half, but it was too little, too late by then."

Twenty-seven 2001 Tigers played pro football: LB Eric Alexander, DL Kenderick Allen, DB Ryan Clark, WR Michael Clayton, QB Rohan Davey, RB Domanick Davis, TE Eric Edwards, LB Trev Faulk, CB Randall Gay, DL Howard Green, DL Jarvis Green, WR Devery Henderson, DL Marquise Hill, DB Jack Hunt, LB Bradie James, P Donnie Jones, DT Chad Lavalais, DB Norman LeJeune, QB Matt Mauck, DB Adrian Mayes, OL Stephen Peterman, WR Josh Reed, TE Robert Royal, DL Marcus Spears, RB LeBrandon Toefield, DB Corey Webster, and OL Ben Wilkerson.

SBC Cotton Bowl Classic
vs. Texas

"It's the hardest bunch for me to let go"

Cotton Bowl, Dallas, Texas
January 1, 2003

The Tigers had another up and down season in 2002.

LSU's Season

Despite the loss of their record-setting passing combo of Rohan Davey and Josh Reed, the Tigers were picked to win the SEC West for the second year in a row. LSU ranked 14th in the preseason AP poll but dropped fast after losing the opener at Virginia Tech, 26–8. Easy wins over The Citadel, Miami (OH), Mississippi State, and Louisiana-Lafayette cleared the decks for the visit to Gainesville, where LSU hadn't beaten the Gators since 1986. But without Steve Spurrier, now coaching the Washington Redskins, the Gators were no match for the Tigers, 36–7. However, the exultation was diminished by the loss of junior QB Matt Mauck for the season with a foot injury and RB LaBrandon Toefield indefinitely with a broken arm. That turned the spotlight on sophomore QB Marcus Randall. His first start went well, a 38–14 romp over South Carolina. But the tables turned the following week—a 31–7 debacle at Auburn. Through a quirk in scheduling, the Tigers visited Kentucky for the second year in a row. No LSU fan imagined the game could provide a more exciting finish than the Davey-to-Michael Clayton touchdown pass with 13 seconds left the year before. But they didn't count on the Bluegrass Miracle, a 75-yard Hail Mary pass from Randall to WR Devery Henderson as time expired to pull out the 33–30 victory.

But the inconsistent play continued as visiting Alabama dominated the Tigers 31–0. Still, LSU retained sole possession of first place in the West since the Tide were ineligible for postseason play because of NCAA probation. The Saban men stayed on top with a 14–13 squeaker over Ole Miss. The injury bug bit again as Henderson was lost for the season with a broken arm.

The season ended against Arkansas in Little Rock with the division title on the line. This time, LSU gave up the winning pass in the waning seconds. That threw them into a three-way tie for first place in the West with Arkansas and Auburn, both of whom had defeated the Bengals. So the 8–4 Tigers settled for their first invitation to the Cotton Bowl since 1966.

The Opponent

The Texas Longhorns started Mack Brown's fifth year as head coach with five straight victories, the most significant of which was a Big 12 Conference win over Oklahoma State. The good fortune ended the following week against Oklahoma, which dominated the second half to prevail 35–24. But the Longhorns bounced back with four more conference wins, including one in Lincoln that ended Nebraska's nation-best 26-game home winning streak. But the road was not kind to Texas the next week, a 42–38 loss to Texas Tech. UT ended the regular season on a high note, a 50–20 thrashing of archrival Texas A&M. That tied the Steers with Oklahoma atop the Southern Division with 6–2 records, but the Sooners played in the conference championship game against Colorado because of their head-to-head victory over the Longhorns. Coach Brown finished his 13th consecutive winning season and looked forward to his 11th straight bowl game.

Texas boasted a prolific offense that averaged 33.8 points per game, which ranked 16th in the nation. Senior QB Chris Simms completed 59.3 percent of his passes for 3,207 yards and 26 touchdowns against only 12 interceptions. His favorite receiver, 6'4" junior WR Roy Williams, gained 1,142 yards on 64 receptions. The leading rusher by far was sophomore RB Cedric Benson with 1,293 yards, more than three times the next highest total on the squad. The bowl game would pit the LSU offense against a familiar foe. Texas defensive coordinator Carl Reese occupied the same position in Baton Rouge under Gerry DiNardo before joining Brown's staff when Mack took over in Austin in 1998.

Though each team had been nosed out of a chance to win their conference championships, both squads were excited about playing in the 67th Cotton Bowl Classic. Brown said, "Our players will be excited about LSU because they know a lot of those guys. Because we're in the same region, we see a lot of their games on TV and vice-versa. A guy who can't get ready at Texas to play LSU probably shouldn't be playing college football." Nick Saban expressed similar sentiments. "This was the bowl game our staff, our players, our fans and everybody else was most excited about having the opportunity to play in."

The Game

Fans (70,817) got up early, or never went to bed, for the 10 a.m. kickoff in 52 degree weather to witness the first meeting between LSU and Texas since the 1963 Cotton Bowl. The outcome would be decidedly different this time.

FIRST QUARTER

LSU started strong in a weird quarter in which Texas ran only three plays and gained no yards, yet had a touchdown. The Tigers moved from their 20 to take a 3–0 lead. QB Marcus Randall completed three passes, all to WR Michael Clayton for 14, 14, and 15 yards. TB Domanick Davis added 26 yards on the ground. But the Longhorns stopped Davis shy of the first down after he caught a short pass. So John Corbello kicked a 27-yard field goal.

Score: LSU 3 Texas 0 (10:44)

The Cotton Bowl Stadium had not treated the Longhorns and their senior QB Chris Simms kindly. They lost the 2000 Cotton Bowl to Arkansas 27–6, then fell to Oklahoma in their annual Red River Rivalry game in that stadium three straight years. On third down, the southpaw son of retired New York Giants QB Phil Simms rolled left and threw a pass that was knocked down by S Jack Hunt, who was switched from offense midway through the season. So Brian Bradford rocketed a punt that bounded all the way to the LSU seven.

The Tigers immediately moved out of danger on a swing pass to Davis in the right flat to the 33. RB LaBrandon Toefield, recovered from the broken arm that sidelined him most of the season, found the going tough against the UT defense led by DE Cory Redding and LB Derrick Johnson. But a silly personal foul penalty on the Longhorns gave the Tigers a first down at the UT 46. It took four straight runs before LSU moved the chains again to the 36. But on third-and-10, lightning struck the Tigers when Redding knocked the ball out of Randall's hand as he tried to pass, and LB Lee Jackson scooped up the pigskin and ran 46 yards to the end zone.

Texas 7 LSU 3 (3:49)

Coach Brown said afterward, "Cory Redding made a great play to keep us in the

Adam Doiron tackles Domanick Davis (*Gumbo* Class of 2003).

ballgame. I don't think I've ever seen as lopsided a first quarter. LSU jumped right in our face. The Cory Redding play turned the momentum back."

Undeterred, Jimbo Fisher's offense got that touchdown back on an 87-yard drive that included five first downs. The first two came on Toefield runs. Then Randall saw Clayton get free from CB Nathan Vasher and hit him near the left sideline for 24 yards to the UT 37. On the next snap, Marcus fired to freshman WR Skyler Green in the right flat for 11 yards. On third-and-four, figuring Texas wouldn't pay much attention to a running back who caught only four passes all year, Fisher called a play he had put in for the game. Toefield lined up at right halfback and ran uncovered to the 10, where he caught Randall's pass and sped across the goal.

LSU 10 Texas 7 (0:04)

SECOND QUARTER

After a 13-yard run by Cedric Benson, Texas stalled, getting another good punt to the 10. On second down, Randall took off on a quarterback draw and raced all the way to the UT 15 before Vasher ran him down after a 75-yard gain. Davis gained five, then broke two tackles up the middle into the end zone.

LSU 17 Texas 7 (12:04)

Texas answered a big play with one of its own less than a minute later. Playing first-and-10 from the 49, Simms fired a strike to Roy Williams, who broke past CB Corey Webster down the middle and sprinted to pay dirt. Chris said after the game, "After the first big play to Roy, they never went to a single safety setup again."

LSU 17 Texas 14 (11:24)

The Tigers made one first down on a 12-yard swing pass to Toefield to the 44. But TE Eric Edwards dropped a third down pass for Randall's first incompletion after eight successes. That brought out Donnie Jones for his first punt of the day, a beauty to the nine.

The Steers moved the sticks once before having to punt. Bradford shanked the kick, which traveled only 10 yards to the 33. That set up a key sequence of possessions that changed the course of the game. Clayton made a great catch on a crossing route, grabbing a fast ball that was low and behind him to the 20 as LSU went over the 300-yard mark in offense to UT's 104. But the burnt orange defense stiffened, and Corbello missed from the 27, his first failure inside 40 yards all season.

In no time, Texas got its third long play of the half. Simms hit Williams who broke through attempted tackles by Hunt and Webster and roared to the five where LB Bradie James forced him out of bounds. James said, "We joked when I ran him out down on the sidelines. ... He's kind of scary when you look at him. He's the best player I have played against this year." Two runs by Benson gave the Longhorns the lead for good.

Texas 21 LSU 17 (3:11)

The Tigers took little time off the clock on their next possession, and Jones punted into the end zone. Using their timeouts, the Longhorns moved close enough to try a field goal. They overcame a 7-yard sack by senior DT Byron Dawson along the way when Simms fired to TE David Thomas for 19 yards. Finding his groove, Chris hit Benson out of the backfield to the LSU 29 with 0:37 left. When three plays gained only 3 yards, Dusty Mangum tried a 40-yard field goal that fell short.

Texas 21 LSU 17

LSU led in rushing 170–38, in first downs 17–8, and in time of possession 20:16–9:44. But Texas led in passing 202–143. Williams touched the ball only twice but gained 126 yards. Randall got treatment for heat cramps at halftime.

Texas defensive coordinator Carl Reese explained the adjustments he made at halftime. "We're a man-to-man defense, so they were running pick routes. So we ran some zone blitzes which made him (Randall) hesitate. When we started hitting him a little bit, the other stuff started working."

Third Quarter

The Tiger with the widest wingspan, 6'7" 295-pound DE Marquise Hill, disrupted the Texas attack to force a punt, wrestling Benson down for a 4-yard loss, then getting in Simms's face to cause an incompletion. When LSU couldn't move, Saban had Tiger fans shaking their heads when he called for a fake punt. LB Bradie James took the snap but gained nothing to give the Longhorns the ball on the LSU 42. Saban said afterward, "We were in a punt alert. However, Texas was not in the look we wanted. We should've punted and not run the ball. It was a mental mistake. But I know the competitor that Bradie is. He probably thought he could run it for 80 yards." But Texas couldn't take advantage of the gift. They gained one first down on a 13-yard burst by Young, but two incompletions to Williams led to a missed field goal from the 25.

With the Fox TV announcers wondering if Randall's passing was affected by a calf injury sustained in the first half, the sophomore quarterback overthrew a wide-open Jerel Myers down the middle. Vasher brought back the punt 18 yards to the 46. On third down, Hill struck again, knocking down Simms's pass. Starting from the 20, the Tigers went backward when a false start and an unsportsmanlike conduct penalty on Randall moved the ball to the eight. But Davis broke loose and meandered 44 yards to the UT 48. Aided by an offside penalty, LSU rode Toefield's battering ram runs to a first down at the 37. Then Fisher called for some razzle-dazzle that should have produced six points. Myers took a double reverse running to his right. Instead of planting his feet and making an accurate throw, he threw on the run and overshot Randall running behind the secondary. Then Randall fumbled on a draw, and Jackson made his second recovery for UT.

The Longhorns traveled 69 yards in just three plays. First, Simms faked a handoff and hit Williams to the 44. Then Benson burst over the left side to the Tiger 39. From there, Williams took an end around and wove his way through the defense to the end zone.

Texas 28 LSU 17 (4:08)

Down two scores for the first time, LSU needed to put points on the board. They moved smartly across midfield on two Toefield runs and a quick slant pass to Myers to the UT 44. The Tigers caught a break two plays later when a face mask penalty negated

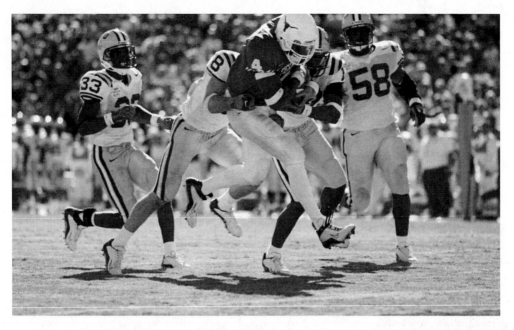

Roy Williams scores on an end-around as Jack Hunt (8) tackles him and Demetrius Hookfin (33) and Lionel Turner (58) arrive too late (Brian Bahr/2003 Cotton Bowl/*Getty Images*).

a sack to make it first-and-10 at the 24. But the Texas defense started attacking as they had all game when backed into their red zone. They dropped Toefield for a 3-yard loss. Then MLB Johnson cut in front of the receiver and took the interception to the LSU 44 to flip the field. The period ended after a 10-yard pass to FB Ivan Williams and SS Norman LeJeune's sack of Simms at the LSU 46.

Texas 28 LSU 17

FOURTH QUARTER

An all-out blitz on third down produced a sack by LSU freshman DT Melvin Oliver. After an exchange of punts, the Tigers drove into Texas territory thanks to a face mask penalty. Redshirt freshman RB Joseph Addai gained four, then took a flat pass for 12 more to the UT 33. Randall connected with Green to the 22, but the Tigers bogged down and Corbello booted a 40-yard field goal.

Texas 35 LSU 20 (7:41)

The Tigers tried an onside kick, and Hunt recovered at the LSU 38 after the ball was batted forward several times. Randall connected with Clayton again to move the chains to the UT 49. On fourth down, an offside penalty on Texas gave the Tigers another first down at the 39. But an incompletion on the next fourth down returned the ball to Texas. Neither side threatened in the last minutes, and LSU's five-game bowl winning streak went down the drain.

Final Score: Texas 35 LSU 20

Roy Williams won the Offensive MVP award while Cory Redding earned the defensive trophy.

Postgame

Coach Saban on his quarterback: "Marcus played extremely well in the beginning of the game. Texas does an outstanding job on loose-play downs of affecting the quarterback with their zone blitz and their pressures. He was a little confused at times, threw the ball to the wrong side of the formation at times on his reads, and he got hit a few times." Nick became misty-eyed as he talked about saying goodbye to his seniors. He didn't recruit them, but he became deeply attached. "I had a little bit of a tough time in the locker room. We had a real good senior bunch who have really done a lot for this program in three years. Some great character people who have played a lot of good football here. It's the hardest bunch for me to let go."

Randall: "We wanted to get things rolling early. We just couldn't get it rolling like we did in the second half. They made some adjustments, and we stopped making plays."

Michael Clayton caught a game-high six passes for 88 yards and made three tackles. He played 82 offensive plays as well as 16 defensive snaps and two special teams plays. "I was so excited. I just wanted to make a play."

Corey Webster had the unenviable job of covering Roy Williams. "Coach had told us that in a lot of bowl games, teams don't tackle well, and that's what happened to us. We didn't tackle real well, and that caused a couple of his big plays."

Coach Mack Brown praised his quarterback. "Chris is going to be a great pro player. Chris has matured as much as anybody I've seen. … He kept his class when people were critical of him."

Texas DE Cory Redding, who had four tackles for losses, on the LSU quarterback: "He was hot in the first half. We expected that. We saw it on film. He can beat you with his legs as well as his arm. We mixed things up a little bit in the second half. We were blitzing, disguising our coverage and having guys come out of nowhere to pressure him."

Randall praised Redding. "He gave us a lot of problems coming off the edge. He made a lot of big plays for their defense like the first sack."

Twenty-seven 2002 Tigers played pro football: RB Joseph Addai, LB Eric Alexander, DL Kenderick Allen, WR Michael Clayton, RB Domanick Davis, TE Eric Edwards, CB Randall Gay, WR Skyler Green, WR Devery Henderson, DL Marquise Hill, DB Jack Hunt, LB Bradie James, P Donnie Jones, DT Chad Lavalais, DB Norman LeJeune, QB Matt Mauck, DB Adrian Mayes, OL Rudy Niswanger, DL Melvin Oliver, OL Stephen Peterman, DB Ronnie Prude, QB Marcus Randall, DL Marcus Spears, RB LaBrandon Toefield, DB Corey Webster, OL Andrew Whitworth, and OL Ben Wilkerson.

Nokia Sugar Bowl vs. Oklahoma

BCS championship game

Louisiana Superdome, New Orleans, Louisiana
January 4, 2004

Tiger fans had long cried, "1958 and next year." Next year finally came.

LSU's Season

The Tigers were ranked #14 in the Associated Press preseason poll. But the players knew they were better than that. The 2002 team started 6–0 but lost QB Matt Mauck in game six to a season-ending foot injury. Yet that team almost won the SEC West, a last second touchdown pass by Arkansas denying them the crown. Coach Nick Saban also expected greatness from his fourth LSU squad. He recalled, "I don't know if I'll ever have an opportunity to coach a group of football players who have as much character as that team had. I think they thought they could win the championship long before I did."

After routs of Louisiana-Monroe and Western Illinois, with a surprisingly easy 59–13 victory at Arizona, the #11 Tigers hosted #7 Georgia, the defending SEC champions. LSU prevailed 17–10 on a touchdown pass from Mauck to WR Skyler Green with 1:22 left on the clock. No letdown occurred the following Saturday when the Tigers pummeled Mississippi State 41–6 at Starkville.

Then came the most puzzling game of the season. Florida was just 3–3, but freshman QB Chris Leak played the game of his life, and LSU scored its only points on Green's 80-yard punt return. The result was a stunning 19–7 upset in Tiger Stadium. The overconfident Tigers learned never to take anything for granted.

LSU took out its frustration on South Carolina the next week, 33–7 at Columbia. That set up a must-win battle with Auburn, which was 4–0 in the conference. Led by the nation's #1 rushing defense, the Bengals smashed the visiting Tigers 31–7.

After a 49–10 thrashing of Louisiana Tech and an open date, LSU traveled to Alabama as the #4 team in the Bowl Championship Series rankings. The Tigers dominated the Tide, 27–3. Since Bama had started the season with a 20–13 loss to #1 Oklahoma, reporters asked QB Brodie Croyle how LSU stacked up against the Sooners. "They're every bit as good," he said.

LSU hopes for a national championship rested on winning the SEC title. And that goal required beating Ole Miss in Oxford since the Rebels were 6–0 in conference play.

The Tigers held the potent Eli Manning–led offense to 27 yards on the ground and just 227 yards overall in a hard-fought 17–14 triumph. To win a championship, you need some luck. Ole Miss K Jonathan Nichols, that season's Lou Groza Award winner, missed two field goals including a 36-yarder that would have tied the score in the final period.

The year before, Arkansas had derailed LSU's ride to the SEC West title. But the Razorbacks were no match for these Tigers, falling 55–24. Rematches usually favor the team that lost the first game. But setting aside all talk of playing in the BCS championship game and focusing on the task at hand, the Tigers pounded Georgia in Atlanta 34–13.

Now the Tigers could focus on the BCS rankings, which were thrown into turmoil when Kansas State crushed #1 Oklahoma 35–7 in the Big 12 championship game. Which two of the one-loss teams, Oklahoma, LSU, and USC, would finish atop the final BCS standings? Because they had such a big lead in the computer rankings, the Sooners stayed on top, and the Tigers nosed out the Trojans for the second spot because of a slightly stronger schedule.

In 2001, LSU played in the Sugar Bowl because they were the SEC champions. Now they played in New Orleans because it was the Sugar Bowl's turn to host the BCS championship game.

The Opponent

If ever a #1 ranked team had something to prove in a bowl game, it was the 2003 Oklahoma Sooners. Critics of the BCS ranking system harped on the fact that OU, unlike LSU and USC, had not won its conference. They also pointed out that the Tigers' and Trojans' lone losses had come in game four by 12 and three points respectively.

The Sooners were ranked #1 in the AP poll the first 13 weeks of the season. No one questioned their prowess when they won at Alabama 20–13, clobbered UCLA 59–24, smashed Texas 65–13 and Oklahoma State 52–9, humiliated Texas A&M 77–0, and routed Baylor 41–3 and Texas Tech 56–25. The Sooners were ranked with the greatest teams in football history. The BCS Championship Game gave OU a chance to show that the shocking loss to K-State was an aberration.

The Sugar Bowl would provide a classic confrontation between the irresistible force and the immovable object. The Sooners averaged 45.2 points per game and 461.4 yards per game while Will Muschamp's LSU defense held opponents to 10.8 points per game—tops in the nation—and 259.5 yards per game.

OU QB Jason White won the Heisman Trophy in a close race over Pittsburgh WR Larry Fitzgerald. The senior passed for an astounding 3,744 yards in offensive coordinator Chuck Long's spread shotgun offense. White had 40 touchdown passes against only 10 interceptions in 451 attempts. Mark Clayton led the receivers with 79 catches and 1393 yards (17.2 ypc) with 15 touchdowns.

Like LSU, Oklahoma couldn't boast a 1,000-yard rusher but, also like the Tigers, did have two runners with over 500 yards: Kejuan Jones (866) and Renaldo Works (714). But head coach Bob Stoops, 55–10 in five years at Oklahoma, had made his reputation as a defensive coordinator at Kansas State and Florida. So his Sooners were no slouch on that side of the ball, 14.8 points per game (fourth in the nation) and 255.6 yards per game (first in the nation). If those numbers weren't impressive enough, consider the national awards OU defenders won: LB Teddy Lehman—Bednarik Award as best defensive player,

DT Tommie Harris—Lombardi Award as the best college player regardless of position, and CB Derrick Strait—Thorpe Award for best defensive back and Nagurski Trophy for best defensive player. Like LSU, the Sooners boasted a stout front four, rangy linebackers, and a fast secondary. Each team recorded 39 sacks. Mike Stoops, Bob's brother, and Brent Venables had been co-defensive coordinators all season. But Mike accepted the head coaching job at Arizona. LSU could expect even more blitzing from Venables.

Another similarity between the teams was their All-American kick returners, Antonio Perkins for OU and Skyler Green for LSU. Which one gave his team better field position could well determine the outcome of the game.

Because of gaudier offensive numbers, Oklahoma was favored by 6½ points.

The Game

The largest crowd to see a game in the Louisiana Superdome, 79,342, and the ABC TV audience witnessed a low-scoring slugfest.

FIRST QUARTER

LSU electrified their fans on the first snap of the game. Freshman HB Justin Vincent, who had ended the season with three straight 100-yard rushing games, bolted through the right side for 64 yards to the 16, where he was tripped up by DB Derrick Strait. That stop loomed large a few plays later. After Joseph Addai gained one, WR Michael Clayton caught two short passes to make it first-and-goal at the 1½ after a roughing the passer penalty on the second throw. But QB Matt Mauck fumbled the snap, and Strait recovered on the two.

The Tigers were right back in OU territory two plays later when White threw long to WR Will Peoples, who was double-covered by S Jack Hunt and CB Corey Webster. Webster intercepted, his 14th pick of the year, and returned 17 yards to the OU 32. LSU's first down snap showed the tightness of both teams on the big stage. Vincent fumbled when hit from behind, and OU recovered only to have the turnover negated because of an offside call on an overanxious end. After an incompletion, Vincent ran to the 24. On third-and-two, WR Skyler Green, a member of LSU's NCAA-champion relay team, lined up wide left but went in motion and took a reverse around the right side. Behind blocks by Addai and Clayton, Green turned the corner and tiptoed down the sideline to the end zone. Ryan Gaudet booted the extra point.

LSU 7 Oklahoma 0 (11:38)

The defenses continued to control play the rest of the period. On third-and-six, Webster was called for interference on White's short slant to WR Brandon Jones. But OU could not gain another first down and punted into the end zone.

After LSU went three-and-out, the Sooners ran their version of the end-around, Mark Clayton gaining 12 yards to the 48. But incompletions and a false start penalty forced another punt. The Tigers got a first down on a pass play thanks to a holding call that enraged OU Coach Bob Stoops. But nothing came of it, and OU had the ball on the LSU 38 when the period ended.

LSU 7 Oklahoma 0

Justin Vincent opens the game with a 64-yard run (The Historic New Orleans Collection, Gift of the Sugar Bowl).

SECOND QUARTER

Something had to give in this period. LSU outscored its opponents 154–16 in the second quarter while Oklahoma scored 212 points in that frame. The result was a stand-off—seven points each.

LSU was plagued by poor field position the first part of the period, which led to OU's tying touchdown. Blake Ferguson's punt nestled on the artificial surface at the LSU three.

Following three runs for a net of -1 yard, Antonio Perkins returned Donnie Jones's punt to the Tiger 35. But the Sooners squandered the excellent field position when Marquise Hill and Melvin Oliver sacked White for a loss of nine. A third down sack derailed LSU's next possession and brought out Jones to punt. Bob Stoops himself had worked with his special teams all week on punt blocking, and now it paid off. DB Brandon Shelby broke through untouched and made the first punt block against LSU all season. LB Russell Dennison recovered at the two.

The Tigers didn't give up points without a fight. First, they stopped Jones at the one. Then Webster ripped a pass out of Mark Clayton's hands in the end zone. After an offside flag moved the ball a half yard closer, Jones pushed over left tackle for the score. Trey DiCarlo added the PAT. LSU had outgained OU 204–50, but the game was tied.

LSU 7 Oklahoma 7 (7:35)

The Tiger offense, which had a net of -2 yards so far in the period, came to life behind Mauck's passing and the inspired running of Justin Vincent. Matt rolled left and threw on the run to WR Devery Henderson for 20 yards. A quickie to Clayton at the sideline added nine more. A confusing sequence of plays brought up third-and-seven at the OU 45. On one of the key plays of the game, Matt threw to TE David Jones on a delay pattern. He broke a tackle and got the first down at the 30. After a long incompletion to Clayton, Vincent gained 12 to go over the century mark for the fourth straight game and break Dalton Hilliard's school record for rushing yards by a freshman. Then Justin banged through left guard, stayed on his feet to thwart tacklers, and zipped into the end zone. Saban said afterward that the second scoring drive "was the turning point of the game. They blocked a punt and scored, and our offense came right back."

LSU 14 Oklahoma 7 (4:21)

Any hope that the Sooners had of answering right back were destroyed by DE Marquise Hill, who made three straight tackles ending with an 8-yard sack to force a punt to midfield. With a chance to add a field goal in the waning minutes, LSU was hampered by a holding penalty. On third-and-17, Mauck overthrown Clayton far downfield, and Perkins picked off the pigskin and returned to the 28. It turned out to be as good as a punt when an unsportsmanlike conduct penalty moved OU back to the 13.

The Sooners ran for a paltry 16 yards in the first 30 minutes. The Heisman Trophy winner completed only six-of-16 passes for a mere 28 yards. Coach Stoops told his team in the locker room that they were in good shape considering they had played about as poorly as they could and still were only a touchdown behind. "We told the guys not to panic," he said. "We told them if they'd just calm down, tackle better, and execute better, we'd have a chance."

THIRD QUARTER

The second half couldn't have started any better for the Tigers. DE Marcus Spears sacked White for a 3-yard loss to the 17. Then the former tight end from Baton Rouge dropped into coverage and snagged White's short pass and ran it back 20 yards to the end zone. "I dropped back, and it was like a gift," said Spears. "When I saw it coming, I said, 'Man, put your hands up and try to get the thing to the end zone.'"

LSU 21 Oklahoma 7 (14:13)

The Sooners tried a dipsy-do on the kickoff return. Clayton caught the ball in the end zone and lateraled to Mark Bradley. But Chad White wasn't fooled and smashed the ball carrier at the nine. The beleaguered crimson offense gained two first downs. The first came on White's best throw of the evening, a fastball to WR Travis Wilson to the OU 43. Then Mark Clayton took an end-around handoff to the left but, finding no opening, reversed his field to the LSU 42. MLB Lionel Turner slowed OU's momentum by stuffing a screen to Jones for no gain. Two plays later, Turner struck again, roaring up the middle untouched to smother White, who tossed the ball away while being tackled to draw a flag for intentional grounding.

Starting from their 17, LSU ate up most of the rest of the period with a 14-play drive that carried them inside the OU 10. On third-and-five, Mauck made a safe throw to Addai out of the backfield to the 35. Three snaps later, Green ran the same end-around play that scored the first touchdown of the game but to the opposite side to move the chains to the 47. Then Matt zipped the ball to Clayton over the middle to the 32. On third-and-six, Skyler took a short throw and ran to the five. But Oklahoma dug in and pushed the Tigers back to the 10. So Gaudet kicked a 27-yard field goal to seemingly give LSU a two-score lead. But not one but two LSU penalties on the play—holding and a personal foul— moved the ball back to the 35. Instead of punting, Saban kept the field goal unit on the field. With the TV announcers questioning whether Gaudet could kick a 52-yard field goal, holder Blain Bech got up and threw the ball to TE David Jones, who looked like he might score down the right sideline before OU closed and knocked him out of bounds on the six. Since it was goal-to-go, the ball went over to the Sooners but 14 yards closer to the OU goal line than it would have been on a missed field goal.

The OU offense continued to sputter. On third-and-six, White was flushed out of the pocket but made a good throw to Clayton who came back for the ball. However, an ineligible receiver downfield penalty negated the first down. White then made an errant throw from the end zone to bring out the punt team. The box score showed OU with only 79 yards of offense after three periods.

LSU 21 Oklahoma 7

Fourth Quarter

The way the LSU defense was playing, Oklahoma needed help to come back. And that's what they got on the first play. Mauck was flushed out of the pocket and threw off balance and late down the middle. The ball went right to S Brodney Pool who ran to the LSU 31. Matt admitted, "I just tried to force something. My read was basically on the back side, and I tried to pick up somebody coming across. I really should have thrown it away."

The Sooners took advantage of the short field although the Tigers made them work hard. A stuffed run and two incompletions made it fourth-and-11. As the O-line blocked the all-out blitz, Clayton cut across the middle a step ahead of Hunt, and White hit him for a first down at the 12. After Jones gained five, Jason rolled out and tossed to FB J.D. Runnels who was knocked out of bounds by Turner at the one. White slipped coming out from under the center, missed the handoff, then stumbled as he tried to run and fell at the five. Then he got the yardage back on a quarterback draw. OU sent in two tight ends to run a jumbo formation. Jones banged over left tackle for the score.

LSU 21 Oklahoma 14 (11:01)

LSU had answered OU's previous score after the blocked punt. But they weren't able to do so this time. Mauck made his second straight bad throw, rolling left and short arming a toss to TE Eric Edwards. When Matt had to call timeout before the next play, the Sooners danced on their sideline, and their fans roared. Vincent was dropped for a 4-yard loss as soon as he took the handoff. Then Matt was lucky to avoid the blitz and throw the ball away. So just like that the Sooners had the ball again on their 42 after the punt.

Needing to take control again, the Tiger defense got a break. Mark Clayton gained nine on an end around. Then a small twitch made a big difference. A false start penalty turned second-and-one into second-and-six. Clayton gained two on another end around before Hill made another big play, batting down a pass to force a punt into the end zone.

Trying to at least run off some time, the Tigers instead went three-and-out again. Mauck rolled out for 7 yards, but Vincent was hit before he could get started for a loss of two. Matt faded to pass, then headed up the middle for the first down only to stumble and fall 2 yards short. OU didn't rush the punt and took possession at their 39 with 5:45 on the clock.

Mixing Jones carries with short passes, the Sooners pushed through LSU's weary front line for four first downs, the last one putting the ball on the 13 after Webster was flagged for pass interference. But OU abandoned the run at that point and threw four straight passes. Coach Muschamp ratcheted up the pressure to force a first down incompletion. Then White rolled right and looked to throw back to the left to Runnels. But senior LB Dave Peterson stayed home to force Jason to throw the ball away. On third down, CB Randall Gay blitzed off the edge, causing a retreating White to overthrow Jones who was uncovered in the end zone. On fourth down, White sidestepped a blitzer and threw to Clayton in the middle of the end zone. Hunt tipped the ball, and it fell short and off Mark's fingertips. "It was fourth down, and I was trying to give one of our guys a chance to make a play," White explained. "It was a desperation play, and Mark Clayton almost caught it." Clayton said, "The ball was spinning, and I tried to get my hands under the ball. It fell faster than I expected, and I couldn't scoop it."

LSU took over at the 13 with 2:52 left. Make a first down, and you seal the game. Two runs forced OU to use its final timeouts. Then Coach Jimbo Fisher called a pass. Mauck faked a handout, then flipped over a rusher to Addai coming across. As he caught the ball and turned to run, Strait smacked him, causing him to drop the ball. Fumble or incomplete pass? Fortunately, the side judge ruled it an incompletion, much to the chagrin of Coach Stoops. A fair catch gave OU possession at their 49 with 2:10 remaining.

OU needed their Heisman Trophy winner to make plays, but he couldn't. Three straight incompletions made it fourth-and-10 with 1:56 to go. LSU called timeout to give the defenders a respite and plan strategy. With White in deep shotgun looking for an open receiver, Turner charged up the middle on a delayed blitz and knocked him down. Stoops later said, "I'm not going to second guess my coaches who make the calls. We probably should have made better decisions. Somewhere in there on first or second down, we probably should have run it. We were getting five or six yards. They were a little tired on that drive, and we should have stuck with it."

Three kneel downs weren't quite enough to kill the clock. So LSU let the play clock run down and took a delay penalty with 0:09 on the game clock. Saban used his last timeout to make sure the punt team was ready for an 11-man rush. Donnie Jones got the kick away, and, as the ball bounced to the 13, Tiger fans counted down the seconds to LSU's first national championship in 45 years.

Final Score: LSU 21 Oklahoma 14

Justin Vincent won the Most Valuable Player Award after gaining 117 yards on 16 carries with one touchdown.

Postgame

Coach Saban admitted that his defense "got tired at the end. But we played from the heart. We played with our identity. I believed in these guys, and they believed in each other. ... We're proud of what we accomplished. We're going to have 24 hours to enjoy what we've done here and then go on and try building for the future." He was proud of how the Tigers bounced back after the blocked punt. "When something goes bad in a game, it means nothing. They have tremendous identity, character, confidence, and they know how to compete. That's how you've got to compete. You've got to overcome adversity. That's why we won the national championship, because of the character and the ability of these guys and the attitude they played with."

The Tigers survived despite Matt Mauck's so-so performance. He completed 13 of 22 for 124 yards but threw two interceptions. "I was really upset with my decision on that last interception. That was an opportunity for us to go up by three scores, and it obviously turned the whole game around. So it is something I wish I could take back. But we won."

Skyler Green admired how Matt bounced back after the pick early in the second half. "Matt came out on the field, made a couple of mistakes but pulled himself together and calmed down. That's the great leader that he is. He controlled his offense, controlled us, and did what he had to do to win this game. Leadership is the biggest key that he gives us."

Coach Bob Stoops said, "I don't ever recall us having 11 penalties in a game. That was a major factor. Two penalties took away turnovers. We also had several on offense that put us in a hole. You can't win like that." Stoops was asked if the LSU defense was the best he had faced in his five seasons with the Sooners. "Yes, I'd say that's fair to say. ... I appreciate and admire the way their players play. Sometimes teams play better than you and coach better than you."

Giving credence to those who believe in the Heisman Jinx, Jason White finished 13-of-37 for 102 yards with two interceptions and five sacks. "They have a great defense. They didn't blitz as much as we planned on. They have great athletes all over the field. They out-executed us for most of the night. Give them credit." He added, "This dampens the season quite a bit. We won 12 games, which is extremely hard to do nowadays in college football, and we don't have anything to show for it."

C Vince Carter said he felt the Sooners were finally winning the battle at the line when they stopped running the ball in the last quarter. "We had pretty much taken control of the line of scrimmage. We were coming off on quick counts and running the ball better. We're out there to execute whatever plays were called. Toward the end, we just didn't do that."

Twenty-nine 2003 Tigers played pro football: RB Joseph Addai, LB Eric Alexander, WR Dwayne Bowe, WR Michael Clayton, DB Travis Daniels, WR Craig Davis, TE Eric

Edwards, CB Randall Gay, WR Skyler Green, WR Devery Henderson, DL Marquise Hill, DB Jack Hunt, P Donnie Jones, DB LaRon Landry, DT Chad Lavalais, OL Nate Livings, QB Matt Mauck, DB Adrian Mayes, OL Rudy Niswanger, DL Melvin Oliver, OL Stephen Peterman, DB Ronnie Prude, QB Marcus Randall, DL Marcus Spears, DB Corey Webster, OL Andrew Whitworth, OL Ben Wilkerson, DT Kyle Williams, and TE Keith Zinger.

Capital One Bowl vs. Iowa

"Somebody in an Iowa jersey has to catch this ball"

Florida Citrus Bowl, Orlando, Florida
January 1, 2005

LSU fans were excited when Nick Saban's 9–2, #12-ranked squad was invited to play New Year's Day in the Capital One Bowl in Orlando against the Iowa Hawkeyes, also 9–2 and ranked #11. But a Christmas announcement would dampen the enthusiasm.

LSU's Season

With fan anticipation at an all-time high after the Tigers won the 2003 BCS Championship, LSU was fortunate to win its opener against Oregon State 22–21 because the Beaver kicker missed two extra points. Also, a theme for the season started immediately as neither Marcus Randall nor JaMarcus Russell could play consistently enough to keep the starting quarterback spot.

After an easy win over Arkansas State, the Tigers lost on the road 10–9 to an Auburn team that would go undefeated. Then came a 51–0 rout of Mississippi State. Georgia got revenge in spades for the two defeats the Tigers hung on them in '03 by belting the Tigers 45–16 in Athens. The next week, Randall came off the bench to lead a 24–21 comeback win at Florida. That started a six-game winning streak to end the regular season: Troy 24–20, Vanderbilt 24–7, Alabama 26–10, Ole Miss 27–24, and @Arkansas 43–14.

Randall outperformed the more heralded Russell, completing 62.6 percent of his passes for 1,180 yards and nine touchdowns while JaMarcus's numbers were 47.3 percent, 925 yards, and seven TDs. Sophomore Alley Broussard carried the rushing load with 758 yards including a school-record 250 vs. Ole Miss. Junior Joseph Addai added 653 yards. The MVP of the championship victory over Oklahoma, Justin Vincent, battled injuries, gaining only 322 yards.

No receiver stood out from the others. A pair of sophomores topped the list—Craig Davis with 41 catches for 647 yards and Dwayne Bowe with 31/475.

Five LSU defenders earned All-SEC honors in the coaches' poll, led by two first-team selections, DE Marcus Spears and LB Lionel Turner. S LaRon Landry earned a second-team berth as did DT Claude Wroten and CB Corey Webster.

Coach Saban praised his men. "I think it's quite fitting for our team that struggled early, after tough losses at Auburn and Georgia, to come to a crossroad and finish with six consecutive wins."

The Opponent

Kirk Ferentz's #11 Hawkeyes did the Tigers one better by winning their last seven outings after suffering a humiliating early loss to Arizona State. It was amazing that Iowa became co-champions of the Big Ten with a 7–1 record (9–2 overall) considering they lost ten players to season-ending injuries, including four running backs. That greatly affected their ground game, which averaged only 74.9 yards per game—last in the entire nation. The Hawkeyes ranked 41st in passing offense with 235.8 yards per game behind sophomore QB Drew Tate. His team's performance despite the setbacks earned Ferentz the Big Ten Coach of the Year award.

While Iowa and LSU had never met on the gridiron, the opposing coaches served on the same NFL staff. Saban and Ferentz assisted Head Coach Bill Belichick with the Cleveland Browns in 1993 and 1994. Nick coached the defensive backs while Kirk handled the offensive line. The Browns made the playoffs in '94 behind the best defense in the league. Saban took the head coaching job at Michigan State in 1995 before coming to Baton Rouge four years later. Ferentz became Iowa's coach in 1999.

The focus on the Capital One Bowl changed Christmas day. Confirming rumors that had been flying, Saban announced that he was leaving LSU to coach the Miami Dolphins. His salary would be $5 million in a state with no income tax.

Discussion of Saban's successor crowded out the bowl game. By New Year's Day, the consensus came down to Les Miles of Oklahoma State. Nick refused to be sucked into the discussion other than to offer this: "I don't want to see somebody come in here and not continue it in a positive way. … If the politics of this institution come into play in making a decision about who the next coach is going to be, I would not think that would be in the best interest of the future." Athletic Director Skip Bertman insisted that he would make the final decision after receiving the recommendation of the selection committee.

Saban said there was never any discussion of someone else coaching the bowl game. Since the NFL season hadn't ended, Nick didn't need to start his tenure with the Dolphins right away. "I wanted to do it (coach the bowl game) out of respect for the players. I'm happy that I did do it, and I certainly want to do a great job for these guys on our team that have been the reason that we've had so much success…. This is their reward for having a great season. … I'm pleased with how the staff has tried to hang in there, but I think uncertainty affects a lot of things…."

The LSU players wanted to send their coach off with a victory. Senior DE Marcus Spears commented on the news of Saban's departure. "Everybody was still focused and said, 'Let's win this one for coach, the last one, and also for the seniors,' and I think everyone's committed to that."

Saban chose Randall to start in Orlando based on his "fantastic game" at Arkansas to end the regular season. Marcus threw for 173 yards and ran for 79, accounting for four touchdowns against the Razorbacks. Regardless of the quarterback, Iowa Defensive Coordinator Norm Parker, who served under Saban at Michigan State, thought stopping

Jimbo Fisher's offense would be a challenge. "They do a lot of the same things from different formations. … The quarterbacks are different, but they're both good in their own way; so it's like defending two different guys."

The Game

Before 70,229, JaMarcus Russell led a comeback destined to live forever in the annals of LSU football until a miracle finish enshrined the contest in Iowa's hall of memories.

FIRST QUARTER

Idle for over a month, the Hawkeyes showed no signs of rust as they took the kickoff and drove 69 yards. They scored on their sixth snap by burning a blitz. Clinton Solomon caught a short pass over the middle, shook off a defender, and sprinted to the end zone for a 57-yard score. The touchdown was the longest against the Tigers all season.

Iowa 7 LSU 0 (12:42)

LSU's offense started slowly, gaining a net of only 22 yards on their first two possessions. To make matters worse, Ryan Majerus blocked Chris Jackson's second punt to give the Hawks the ball on the LSU 27. But Melvin Oliver intercepted a first down screen pass and rumbled to the Iowa 31. When three plays netted -10 yards, Jackson punted into the end zone. After Iowa gained 19, Tate, under duress, threw another pick, this one by a diving Laron Landry on the 31. It was the sophomore safety's fourth interception of the season. LSU moved to the 12 as the quarter ended.

Iowa 7 LSU 0

SECOND QUARTER

Jackson kicked a field goal on the first play.

Iowa 7 LSU 3 (14:51)

After kicking off, the Tigers sacked Tate twice in a row, one by LB Kenny Hollis, the other by DT Claude Wroten. LSU gained great field position when Skyler Green returned the punt 16 yards to the Iowa 29. But seven plays later, the Tigers had to settle for another Jackson field goal, this one from the 37. Iowa 7 LSU 6 (9:26).

The teams then exchanged punts twice, and it looked like Iowa would take a one-point lead into halftime despite gaining only three first downs. But the Hawkeyes scored with 64 seconds left thanks to a special teams play. Miguel Merrick blocked Jackson's punt, and Sean Considine scooped up the ball at the seven and ran into the end zone.

Iowa 14 LSU 6 (1:04)

But the first half scoring still wasn't finished. After the kickoff return to the 26, redshirt freshman Matt Flynn took over at quarterback because a crushing sack had banged up Randall's ribs on. Matt was third-string all season but moved up the depth chart during the 14 days of pre-bowl workouts. Flynn took his first snap and handed to RB

Alley Broussard, who swept right, cut back, and zigzagged until he sprang loose down the right sideline to the end zone to complete LSU's longest play of the season. Jackson's PAT try went awry.

Iowa 14 LSU 12 (0:38)

THIRD QUARTER

LSU received the kickoff, and Randall returned to the huddle. But, after gaining 34 yards on two completions, Marcus threw an interception to CB Jovon Johnson, who returned 7 yards to the Iowa 38. Marcus didn't take another snap. Saban explained afterward, "Marcus convinced me he could play. The other guys out there thought he was really hurting." Using more rollouts and screen passes to blunt the LSU rush, Tate completed five of his first six passes to lead the Hawkeyes 60 yards in 12 plays to set up Kyle Schlicher's 19-yard field goal.

Iowa 17 LSU 12 (9:59)

Green returned the kickoff 58 yards to the Iowa 26. But after three plays failed to gain a first down, LSU lined up for an apparent field goal try. Holder Flynn took the snap and ran up the middle only to be stopped a yard short. After an exchange of punts, the Hawkeyes took possession on their 28. Take away Broussard's run, and LSU's other 47 offensive plays in the first three periods averaged just 2.5 yards.

Iowa 17 LSU 12

FOURTH QUARTER

Iowa took a commanding 12-point lead on Marques Simmons' 4-yard run to end the 10-play, 72-yard march. Tate hit three-of-four during the advance, including 20 and 21-yarders to TE Scott Chandler.

Iowa 24 LSU 12 (9:59)

With Flynn struggling (1-of-4 for 11 yards and a 14-yard sack), JaMarcus Russell came off the bench to drive the Tigers 74 yards in 11 plays. He completed five-of-seven passes, the last a picture-perfect 22-yard throw to Green on a skinny post pattern.

Iowa 24 LSU 19 (8:21)

The Tigers forced a punt after allowing one first down to get the ball back at their 31 at the 5:06 mark. Russell found Green again for back-to-back hookups to move to mid-field. The drive nearly ended when Early Doucet came up a foot short on a third-and-six pass. But the punt team watched from the sideline as Broussard slashed 8 yards to the 32. Russell then hit Dwayne Bowe for 18, scrambled for four, and dumped a pass over the middle to RB Joseph Addai to convert a third-and-six. After spiking the ball on first-and-goal at the three, Russell fired a laser that Green yanked down on a slant pattern before going out the back of the end zone. The two-point conversion attempt failed.

LSU 25 Iowa 24 (0:46)

LSU fans rejoiced over one of the greatest rallies in school history. But not so fast, my friend. Walter Belleus returned the kickoff 26 yards to the 29. Tate had two timeouts to work with as he tried to march the Hawkeyes into field goal range. He hit Ed Hinkel for 11 and Warren Holloway for nine. After the second completion, the Hawkeyes hurried to the line of scrimmage, and Tate spiked the ball. However, the referee ruled that they hadn't waited until he marked the ball ready for play. So a 5-yard penalty was marched off back to the 44.

Coach Ferentz, thinking the clock would not start until the next snap, failed to call a timeout. Tate and his offense huddled, not realizing the clock was running. Referee Hal Dowden stuck his head in to remind them the clock was moving. Tate called "all up," meaning the four receivers run vertical routes down the field. As the Hawkeyes broke the huddle, they realized the defense was confused. Tate took the snap and faded back but, seeing his first two options (Solomon and Chandler) covered and getting no pressure from the six-man rush, threw the ball down the right seam to Warren Holloway. The fifth-year senior was wide open because DB Ronnie Prude, thinking LSU was in a zone when man-to-man had been called, moved up to cover TE Chandler from the slot. Holloway snagged the ball in stride at the 10, escaped S Travis Daniels' arm tackle, and dashed into the end zone as time expired.

Iowa 30 LSU 25 (0:00)

Holloway recalled the winning TD for a 2018 article. "The play was supposed to go to the other side of the field. I guess that guy just wasn't as open as me." He looked back to see the ball sailing in his direction, but it was drifting so far to his right that he didn't

Warren Holloway catches the winning touchdown pass as Travis Daniels (29) chases in vain (The Register, *Des Moines Register* **via Imagn Content Services, LLC).**

think he could catch it. "I honestly didn't think he was throwing it to me." Since it was the last play, he ran toward the ball to be in position if it was tipped. "Somebody in an Iowa jersey has to catch this ball," he thought. But the ball seemed to hang up right over his head. He caught it, bounced off a defender, and instinctively put his hands over the ball, in case someone tried to jar it loose. "The last 15 yards felt like three steps. I hadn't seen that much green grass since high school." He realized immediately that he had completed a play that would be talked about for years to come. He ended up under a dogpile of dozens of teammates. Holloway had 32 catches and zero TDs before the game winner. It became a running joke in the family. "Every game it was, 'When are you going to get one?' My family was like, 'It's your last game, last chance to get a touchdown.'"

Final Score: Iowa 30 LSU 25

Postgame

Saban finished his LSU tenure with a 48–16 record. "You always dislike losing a game, especially losing a game like this. The last 14 or 20 seconds of this game somewhat tarnish the things that this team has accomplished in its four years. I only feel badly that I could not do more to help the players play better. ... I'm very proud of our players for the way they fought back in the game. ... Mental errors are a terrible way to lose, because that means the other guy didn't really physically beat you. You really beat yourself." On his LSU experience: "This has probably been the best experience I've ever had as a coach—the five years I spent at LSU. Call them golden years or whatever for me. I hope they were good years for everyone else."

LSU DT Kyle Williams: "The offense gave us the opportunity to win the ballgame, and we blew it. When you get a lead that late in the game, the defense has to stand up and protect it."

Spears refused to pin the loss on the distraction of the coach departing. "You couldn't tell he was going on to the new job. He was the first to arrive for meetings and the last to leave."

Ferentz: "I don't know if you could write a better script. Nobody would believe it if you did. ... We were playing for a field goal, needless to say. But nobody is complaining about the way it turned out." Concerning the clock mismanagement at the end: "I blew it not taking the timeout there. I didn't realize that after a penalty, they start the clock. It was my fault."

Holloway: "It really hasn't hit me yet. Maybe in a month or so. This is a dream."

Tate, who shrugged off a slow start to end with 287 yards passing (20-of-32) and earn the MVP award, discussed the final play. "That probably was the most time I had to throw all day. I thought I overthrew him. ... We ended up with an ESPN Classic."

Twenty-five Tigers on the 2004 team played pro football: RB Joseph Addai, WR Dwayne Bowe, DB Travis Daniels, WR Craig Davis, DL Glenn Dorsey, WR Early Doucet, QB Matt Flynn, WR Skyler Green, RB Jacob Hester, LB Ali Highsmith, DB Chevis Jackson, DB LaRon Landry, OL Nate Livings, OL Rudy Niswanger, DL Melvin Oliver, DB Ronnie Prude, QB Marcus Randall, QB JaMarcus Russell, DL Marcus Spears, DB Corey Webster, OL Andrew Whitworth, OL Ben Wilkerson, DT Kyle Williams, DL Claude Wroten, and TE Keith Zinger.

Chick-fil-A Peach Bowl vs. Miami

A season that began with hurricanes ended with the Hurricanes

Georgia Dome, Atlanta, Georgia
December 30, 2005

Following Nick Saban's departure to the Miami Dolphins, Athletic Director Skip Bertman hired Les Miles, who had compiled a 28–21 record in four seasons at Oklahoma State. His first season at LSU was like no other in school history.

LSU's Season

The 2005 season began with hurricanes and ended with the Hurricanes. Offensive coordinator Jimbo Fisher stayed at LSU, and Miles hired Bo Pelini from Oklahoma as his defensive mastermind. The coaches and players were heavily into preparations for the September 3 opener against North Texas when Hurricane Katrina smashed into south Louisiana August 29. Emergency plans went into action with LSU playing a pivotal role as a special-needs shelter and medical evacuation site for hurricane victims. On August 31, LSU Chancellor Sean O'Keefe cancelled the North Texas game. So the focus of the Tiger team shifted to September 10 and the home game against Arizona State.

Like so many LSU students, players crammed displaced family members and friends into their apartments. Some Tigers from the New Orleans area did not know where their families were or even whether they were alive or what happened to their homes. Players lost an average of seven pounds each because of the hectic off-the-field demands, steady practice routine, and shaky diet with normal food service disrupted. Squad members volunteered at refugee centers around Baton Rouge, gathering food and other supplies.

Through it all, Miles and his staff tried to maintain a sense of normalcy. The squad appreciated Les's different approach compared to his predecessor. "Saban screamed to get his point across," remarked LB Cameron Vaughn. "Coach Miles is more calmed down, and he'll talk to you to your face and tell you what you're doing wrong instead of screaming in your face."

After toying with the idea of relocating the game to a site within driving distance, AD Bertman accepted Arizona State's offer to host the game with the proviso that all profits go to Hurricane Katrina relief funds. Bertman expected the game to be a rallying point for Louisiana, a signal to the state and the world that Katrina's survivors would resume their lives and rebuild with pride. The Tigers came from behind to gain the most inspiring victory in school history, 35–31.

As if Louisiana hadn't suffered enough, Hurricane Rita came ashore south of Lake Charles the morning of the first home game against Tennessee. As a result, the game was postponed to Monday night. In a game fraught with emotion since it was the first home appearance after the catastrophe, the fired-up Tigers jumped to a 21–0 lead. But the disruption of training and conditioning regimens began to take its toll, and the Vols tied the game at 24 and won in overtime 30–27.

Just five days later, LSU traveled to Mississippi State and rolled to a 37–7 victory. Another road romp left Vanderbilt in shambles, 34–6. Then #11 Florida under new coach Urban Meyer came to Tiger Stadium. Many LSU defenders remembered how QB Chris Leak had led the Gators to the only defeat in their magical 2003 season. This time the Tigers registered five sacks and held him to 11 of 30 passing for only 107 yards to win 21–17.

The rivalry with Auburn had consistently produced intense games. The 2005 edition was no different as the Ghosts of LSU Past that some fans believe inhabit Tiger Stadium may have helped the Bengals. The lead changed hands four times until Colt David kicked a field goal with 1:40 left to tie the score. Then he booted another three-pointer on the first possession of overtime. On Auburn's possession, K John Vaughn hit the upright for his *fifth* missed attempt of the evening.

Breathers over North Texas and Appalachian State cleared the decks for the must-win road game against #4 Alabama (9–0, 6–0 in the SEC). With the LSU offense gaining just two first downs and 31 yards against the nation's #1 defense, the Tide led 10–0 at halftime. But the second half was a different story. The Tigers took the kickoff and marched 80 yards to cut the deficit to three, then tied the game with a field goal on the next possession. In overtime, Bama settled for a field goal. QB JaMarcus Russell found WR Dwayne Bowe in the end zone for the winning points. Miles thus became the first LSU coach to beat Florida, Auburn, and Alabama in the same season.

The Tigers sewed up the SEC West title with a 40–7 romp at Ole Miss and a 19–17 squeaker against Arkansas. After ten straight weeks without a break, the Tigers looked exhausted, especially on defense. They were no match for Georgia in the SEC Championship Game, 34–14.

That defeat dropped LSU down the bowl pecking order behind teams that they had beaten like Auburn and Alabama. The Peach Bowl president said, "The championship game loser should not fall to where they are not playing a top-ranked team." So he invited the Tigers to return to Atlanta to play #9 Miami in the first matchup of Top 10 teams in Peach Bowl history.

LSU would play the game without starting QB JaMarcus Russell, who was left home for disciplinary reasons.

The Opponent

Like LSU, the Miami Hurricanes were disappointed with the way their second season in the Atlantic Coast Conference ended. After an opening 10–7 loss to archrival Florida State, Larry Coker's squad reeled off eight straight wins to rise to #3 in the polls. But a dispiriting 14–10 home loss to Georgia Tech knocked them out of the ACC title game and dropped them to #10. They rose one notch following their 25–17 triumph over Virginia.

Miami's quarterback saw a silver lining in the Peach Bowl bid. Kyle Wright wanted to finish with a 10-win season and keep the Canes as the highest-ranked ACC team. "There's also a sense of pride," said the 6'4" redshirt sophomore. "I think people kind of lost confidence in us, especially down here and even around the country. … People lost respect for us." Wright finished the season with 2,303 yards passing, a 59.4 percent completion rate, and 18 touchdowns. LSU provided just the kind of opponent for regaining respect. "This is the best team possible that we could have played. I think it's going to be awesome, going up against LSU." Wright considered LSU's defense a huge challenge. "I'm very impressed with their front four guys. They do like to bring a lot of different blitzes…, but honestly they sometimes don't need to with the talent they have up front."

The major questions as kickoff neared were these.

Would first-time starting QB Matt Flynn be an effective leader for the LSU offense?

With Joseph Addai healthy again, would LSU regain its running game?

With three weeks to heal, would Bo Pelini's defense play with an aggressiveness that was lacking in the SEC Championship Game?

Would the Hurricanes, favored by seven points, be motivated for their second straight Peach Bowl?

The answers turned out to be Yes, Yes, Yes, and Not Very Much.

The Game

Near the end of pregame warmups, the Miami team in a mass huddle ran across to the LSU side of the field into a group of Tigers still warming up. The Hurricanes jumped up and down taunting the Tigers. The Big 12 officials moved in between them to make sure the situation didn't escalate. LSU responded in a big way before 65,620.

FIRST QUARTER

LSU began at its 35 following the out-of-bounds kickoff. The Canes employed an eight-man front to stop the ground game and force Matt Flynn to beat them through the air. Running the scripted plays prepared by Jimbo Fisher, the Tigers started with a toss sweep to Joseph Addai for 11 yards and a quick slant-in to Craig "Buster" Davis to the UM 36. But a short run and two incompletions led to a 50-yard field goal attempt by Chris Jackson that sailed wide left.

Coach Coker surprised the Tigers by using speedy WR Devin Hester at tailback. Starting from the 33, Miami moved smartly into LSU territory. After a short pass, Hester gained nine around right end for a first down at the LSU 49. After Jesse swept for four, QB Kyle Wright found him on a quick pass over the middle. Hit right after he caught the ball, Hester broke the tackle and continued to the LSU 26. Jesse lined up in the wildcat on the next play and took the direct snap around the right side for 11 more, but a holding penalty put the ball back at the 26. The Canes overcame the setback. Wright connected with TE Buck Ortega over the middle to the 11. Another quick throw to RB Tyrone Moss out of the backfield gained six. After a 3-yard run, the Hurricanes faced third-and-two for a first down and three for the touchdown. Wright called a pass play, but both safeties, LaRon

Landry and Jessie Daniels, blitzed up the middle and forced him to throw the ball away. So Jon Peattie booted a 20-yard field goal.

Score: Miami 3 LSU 0 (8:45)

After both offenses went three-and-out, the Tigers started from their 22. Determined to establish the run game, Fisher called three handoffs to Addai to the 37. Then Flynn demonstrated an ability he brought to the position that Russell didn't have when he went back to throw but, seeing a big hole to his right, ran all the way to the UM 39. On second-and-eight, WR Skyler Green took a direct snap and swivel-hipped his way around left end to the 20. Based on their SEC-best 92 percent scoring rate in the red zone, LSU seemed a good bet to at least tie the score, and that's what they did. When the next series gained only one, Jackson split the uprights from the 27.

Miami 3 LSU 3 (0:58)

The most penalized teams in their respective conferences combined for three flags on the kickoff—offsides on LSU and two holding calls on Miami. The rekick put the Canes in a hole when Hester was bottled up at the 12. But that changed quickly when HB Charlie Jones burst through a big hole at left tackle to the LSU 44. The period ended with Miami facing third-and-five.

ESPN announcers Brad Nessler and Bob Griese agreed that the game had gone as expected—good defense by both sides with some big plays by each offense. That analysis would change by halftime.

Jacob Hester just misses a touchdown pass beyond Kenny Phillips (Bill Feig, Baton Rouge *Advocate*).

LSU 3 Miami 3

SECOND QUARTER

Hester gained four to set up fourth-and-a half yard. Coker decided to go for it and inadvertently created a turning point in the game. Wright took the snap and rolled right on a bootleg. TE Greg Olsen, lined up on the left, ran wide open across the field behind the defense waving his arms futilely as Wright seemed intent on running for the first down. But DE Melvin Oliver fought off his blocker and knocked Wright out of bounds short of the line to gain.

Flynn immediately ran out of the pocket to the UM 49. Two snaps later, Matt hit Davis over the middle to the 41. Back-to-back penalties pushed the Tigers back 10 yards. But on third-and-12, Flynn, with excellent protection, threw long to Davis racing down the middle. Buster ran a shallow pattern as if going to the first down marker, then turned upfield to beat freshman CB Randy Phillips. The speedy junior hauled in the slightly underthrown pass inside the five and stepped into the end zone. Colt David converted.

LSU 10 Miami 3 (11:47)

The Tiger kickoff unit swarmed Hester at the 16. The Canes began the possession with two quick first downs on a Wright-to-Hill pass to the 28 followed by a completion to Hester to the 44. But after LSU stuffed Jones on a third-and-one run, Coker decided against taking another chance and sent in the punter. If you had told anyone that Miami would not make another first down the rest of the game, they would have called you crazy.

Flynn led an efficient drive that added three points to LSU's lead. Addai started with a 19-yard run. Matt then tossed to TE David Jones in the right flat to the 41. Joseph wiggled up the middle to midfield before Matt found Jones again to the 34. Two more Addai rambles moved the sticks to the 22. On third-and-eight, S Brandon Meriweather roared up the middle and sacked Flynn. So Jackson boomed a 47-yard field goal.

LSU 13 Miami 3 (4:57)

Miami went backwards thanks to a 9-yard sack by Oliver. Ending his LSU career with a bang, Melvin ran halfway across the field before leveling Wright from behind. With all three timeouts left, LSU started from its 30 with under four minutes to play. Flynn threw an arching pass to Bowe, who caught the ball between two defenders and raced to the UM 36. Three Addai carries the ball on the 22. Under heavy pressure, Flynn coolly threw the ball away on first down with 0:57 on the clock. The redshirt freshman then fired an out pattern to Bowe who made a lunging catch at the 11. After Davis took a short pass across the middle to the three, Miles took his first timeout. Hoping to hold LSU to a field goal, Miami stuffed Addai for no gain, forcing a second timeout at the 0:23 mark. Fisher came up with a great call. From the shotgun, Flynn faked a handoff to Green coming left and flipped to Addai coming out of the backfield to the right. Bowe took the cornerback into the end zone to free Joe to take the pass and score easily.

LSU 20 Miami 3 (0:18)

The halftime statistics showed LSU with a 310–150 yard edge in offense and 18 minutes of possession time to Miami's 12. Miles explained afterward what his staff talked about during the lengthy halftime. "We made some defensive mistakes in the first half,

Matt Flynn avoids the pressure of Glenn Cook (55) and Bryan Pata (95) (John Amis, Associated Press).

and we really tried to address those mistakes. Offensively, we wanted to continue what we were doing…."

Coker said LSU hadn't done anything surprising. But his team hadn't played with energy or enthusiasm. He told his players to make up their minds what they wanted to do. "Come out and either be embarrassed or be men and play up."

Third Quarter

The Tiger offense picked up where they left off in the first half as their ball carriers consistently gained more yardage after contact. Addai quick-footed twice for 13 yards and a first down. On second-and-12, the Flynn-Davis combo struck again to the 31. Then Joe followed FB Kevin Steltz through the middle, ran over a defensive back, and fought off three more Canes to the six. Flynn let Addai finish the 53-yard drive with a pitchout around the left side.

LSU 27 Miami 3 (11:54)

Needing to sustain a drive to stay alive, the Canes instead went three-and-out again. LB Ali Highsmith and Oliver tackled Wright after a 3-yard gain when he couldn't find a receiver. Highsmith had extra motivation to play well in the game. He grew up in Miami and dreamed of playing football as a Hurricane like his two cousins, Alonzo and Fred. Ali signed with UM in February 2003 but was declared academically ineligible and sat out that season before enrolling at LSU. During the two weeks of practice for the Peach Bowl, Ali wore his MIAMI sweatshirt. "I've been wearing it all year long, but nobody really paid attention to it until now," he said. "I wear it to keep me motivated," he claimed, but some thought he did it to fire up his teammates as well. "I just hoped that I would get a chance to play against them to let them see what they lost."

The Tigers extended their streak of scoring possessions to six with a nine-play drive starting from their 43. Facing third-and-two, Hester pushed for 7 yards to move the chains. Then Jacob knifed for 10 for another first down with a 15-yard face mask penalty tacked on to the 17. Two plays later, Flynn threw a pass to Jacob out of the backfield to the two. Miami finally showed some backbone and made the Tigers work for the remaining ground. Hester gained only 5' in two smashes. From a bunched formation, Flynn tried to sneak but went nowhere. However, Miami was called for lining up offside. So Hester dove over right guard into the end zone.

LSU 34 Miami 3 (5:27)

Following a sack by Claude Wroten, the Canes punted. LSU started a 69-yard scoring drive that continued into the fourth quarter. Hester roared around left end for 13 with another face mask violation moving the pigskin to the 49. Then the same play off the left side behind blocking by FB Steltz, T Andrew Whitworth, and TE Jones gained another 20 yards. When the next three rushes picked up a net of only 1 yard, Jackson set up for a field goal try from the 36. But it was a fake. Flynn took the snap and ran an option play to the left, pitching to Chris who ran for 12 yards to the 17. Hester picked up three as the quarter expired.

LSU held the Hurricanes to zero first downs during the period and outgained them 151–1. The Tigers increased their time of possession lead by controlling the ball for 11 of the 15 minutes.

LSU 34 Miami 3

FOURTH QUARTER

The Tigers drive bogged down, and Colt David booted a 35-yard three-pointer.

LSU 37 Miami 3 (13:59)

The only suspense was whether Miami would make another first down. They didn't do it on their next possession, and Green got loose on the punt return for 23 yards to the UM 46 and, for once, no flag fell. Facing third-and-six, Flynn dropped to throw but used his feet again for 21 yards up the middle to the 21. Two snaps later, Green zipped around right end past the first down marker but fumbled backward. Epitomizing Miami's evening, two Canes had a shot at the ball, but it went out of bounds at the 23. After Flynn was sacked for a loss of 10, Jackson tried his second 50-yarder of the evening, and this time hit it to extend LSU's scoring possession streak to eight.

LSU 40 Miami 3 (8:20)

Sacks by two backups, DT Glenn Dorsey and LB E.J. Kuale, forced another punt. But two short runs and an incompletion led to LSU's first punt since the first quarter. Only they didn't punt. Craig Steltz took the direct snap but got only half the 6-yard needed to give Miami the ball in LSU territory for the first time since their opening drive of the game. Previously, they had not gone past their own 29 in the second half. Even with an offside on LSU, the Canes couldn't attain the coveted first down. CB Jonathan Zenon intercepted at the 22 for the first turnover of the game. As the Tigers ran out the clock, Les Miles received a Gatorade bath on the sideline.

Final SCORE: LSU 40 Miami 3

The victory margin was LSU's largest in a bowl game and Miami's worst bowl defeat. Three points were the Canes' fewest in a game since a 47–0 shutout in 1997 against Florida State.

Flynn was voted the offensive MVP. He went 13-for-22 for 196 yards and two touchdowns and no interceptions against the No. 1–ranked pass defense. He also picked up 59 yards on four scrambles.

LSU had 468 yards of offense to just 153 for the Hurricanes. Miami went the final 41 minutes of the contest without a first down and gained just 2 yards in the second half. LSU held a 26–6 edge in first downs and controlled the ball for 39 minutes to 21 for the Canes.

Skyler Green's 46 yards in punt returns gave him 1,064 for his career to rank second in LSU history behind Domanick Davis's 1,126.

Postgame

Coach Coker reported that two of his players were knocked unconscious shortly after the game. "I don't know what happened, and I don't condone it. That's not how we operate. Obviously it detracts from the bowl game and what the spirit of college football is all about."

LSU WR Dwayne Bowe ignited the altercation when, moments after the game, he took a football from a young Hurricanes ball boy and started running. About 20 UM players chased him, pouring into the tunnel leading to the LSU locker room. There was shouting and pushing as police with riot control wands moved into the tunnel to try to quell the melee. A Miami official said Bowe took his helmet off in the tunnel and swung it at UM lineman Andrew Bain, hitting him in the helmet. LSU fans in the stands above the tunnel threw ice and cups on the UM players during the scrum as assistant coaches from both teams tried to separate the teams.

LSU's Jacob Hester said trash talking, some involving Bowe, began as good-natured fun. "We had a guy who was from Miami (Bowe) who was kidding around with one of his boys. Miami thought it was something serious. They came in the tunnel, and they were swinging, but it was just a joke between friends." Miles said the incident made for a messy ending to the game. "It really did surprise me to find out there was a problem. I saw a lot of sportsmanship during the game. It was unfortunate that a game that was played so well had something like that happen."

Les changed to a more pleasant topic. "I am so happy for this team with everything they went through this season. They come into the final game of the season with a new quarterback, a very capable, confident young man. ... No way did we think this would be an unusual outing for him. We saw the throws he made all year. We never doubted for a minute he would have a calm and a comfort under center. ... I thought our offensive line put together a great game." As for the defense, "I anticipated that our defense would give Miami fits. ... The way our defense was playing, there was no way they were coming back."

Flynn praised his teammates. "It's easy when it's always second-and-two, third-and-short. The offensive line made that possible. ... Once I got my feet under me, I was just trying to get the ball to the athletes around me. ... After those first couple of drives, we knew we could move the ball on them. We started finishing those drives."

Coach Coker lamented, "This could have been a great game. LSU met their part of the bargain, and we didn't. We didn't play the whole game." On Matt Flynn: "We knew he was a good player. He didn't have experience, but he had a month to practice as a first-team player."

Having lost control of his team, Coker would not last the entire 2006 season as Miami's coach.

Twenty-four 2005 Tigers played pro football: RB Joseph Addai, LB Darry Beckwith, WR Dwayne Bowe, WR Craig Davis, DL Glenn Dorsey, WR Early Doucet, QB Matt Flynn, WR Skyler Green, RB Jacob Hester, LB Ali Highsmith, DB Chevis Jackson, DE Tyson Jackson, DB LaRon Landry, OL Nate Livings, OL Rudy Niswanger, DL Melvin Oliver, DB Ronnie Prude, QB JaMarcus Russell, DB Craig Steltz, DB Curtis Taylor, OL Andrew Whitworth, DT Kyle Williams, DL Claude Wroten, and TE Keith Zinger.

Allstate Sugar Bowl vs. Notre Dame

"The seniors came to play"

Louisiana Superdome, New Orleans, Louisiana
January 3, 2007

Several controversial calls/non-calls cost the Tigers a shot at the national championship.

LSU's Season

Les Miles brought in a Top Ten recruiting class to fill the vacancies left by the most successful senior class in LSU history—41 wins in five years, two SEC titles, and a BCS championship. The spotlight shone on the quarterback position. Which junior would be the starter? JaMarcus Russell or Matt Flynn? The answer was Russell, the 6'6" 260-pound behemoth from Mobile.

The first challenge for the #6 Tigers came in Week 3, a trip to #3 Auburn after identical 45–3 routs of ULL and Arizona. The 7–3 defeat ranks high on LSU fans' "Robbed by the Officials" list because of four controversial calls or non-calls, the last being a flag for interference against WR Early Doucet at the Auburn three that was picked up with 2:43 remaining.

Easy home wins over Tulane (49–7) and Mississippi State (48–17) preceded the next big road challenge against #5 Florida. Another questionable call burned the Tigers. Jacob Hester appeared to score when he rolled over a defender at the goal line, but he was ruled down at the one. Russell fumbled the next snap, and Florida recovered. Freshman QB Tim Tebow threw two touchdown passes as the Gators won a key game on their journey to the BCS championship, 23–10.

As they had done following the Auburn loss, the Tigers blasted their next two opponents, Kentucky (49–0) and Fresno State (38–6). Would they falter on the road again, this time at Tennessee? The game demonstrated both the exhilaration that Russell's breathtaking talent could evoke and the frustration that his careless throws could produce. He threw three interceptions, including a pick six, but he also threw the winning touchdown pass to Doucet with nine seconds left to pull out the heart stopping 28–24 victory.

Alabama had once made 14 consecutive visits to Tiger Stadium without tasting defeat. But for the first time since 1948, the Tigers defeated the Tide at home for the second straight time, 28–14. Then Ed Orgeron's Ole Miss Rebels came to Baton Rouge and nearly handed Miles his first defeat at LSU against an unranked opponent in 14 tries.

256

It took a Russell fourth-down strike to WR Dwayne Bowe to tie the game with 14 seconds left. Then the defense got a fumble recovery in overtime that set up a field goal that snatched victory from the jaws of defeat, 23–20.

Arkansas, 7–0 in conference play, had clinched the division title, but the Tigers were determined to show that they were really Best in the West. Sparked by Trindon Holliday's 92-yard kickoff return, LSU won 31–26 in Little Rock.

The following week caused a frenzy among the LSU faithful over the possibility that the Tigers might be chosen for the Rose Bowl if either the Pac-12 or Big Ten champion finished first or second in the Bowl Championship Series final standings. Tiger fans pledged money to buy 40,000 tickets for the Pasadena game if LSU were selected. Ohio State beat Michigan to clinch the top BCS spot, but USC lost to UCLA. Florida defeated the Razorbacks in the SEC Championship Game to earn the other berth in the BCS Championship game. The Rose Bowl then chose Michigan to face USC in the Rose Bowl. So the Tigers, as the next highest SEC team at #4, took the SEC spot in the Sugar Bowl.

The Opponent

Charlie Weis's second Notre Dame squad, ranked #2 to start the season, defeated Georgia Tech and Penn State before getting thumped by Michigan in South Bend, 47–21. The Fighting Irish then ran off seven straight wins in which they averaged 36 points per game. The season ended with a 44–24 loss to USC that dropped the Irish from sixth to 11th in the polls.

As you'd expect from a team coached by the former offensive coordinator of the New England Patriots, Notre Dame fielded a potent offense led by senior QB Brady Quinn, holder of 36 school passing records. He completed 63.4 percent of his passes for 3,278 yards and 35 touchdowns, with only five interceptions. The leading rusher, Darius Walker, gained 1,139 yards on 233 carries for a robust 4.89-yard average. Quinn had two senior receivers to target. 6'5" Jeff Samardzija had 70 receptions for 958 yards and 11 TDs, and Rhema McKnight caught 64 balls for 885 yards and 15 TDs.

As a student of Patriots coach Bill Belichick, Weis wanted his defense to take away the opponent's offensive stars. That would be a challenge against the deepest and most physical receiving corps the Irish had faced all season. Charlie also played the underdog card to the hilt, telling his team that no one believed they could cope with the speed of the Tigers.

Sugar Bowl officials couldn't have been more thrilled with the pairing of America's Team with the local favorites as their annual classic returned to New Orleans after a year in the Georgia Dome while the Superdome was refurbished after Hurricane Katrina.

LSU senior S LaRon Landry, from nearby Ama, Louisiana, spoke for his teammates, "After the disaster of last year, playing in the city of New Orleans, it would be great if we come out with a win in the first Sugar Bowl back here. My goal is just to give it all back to the city and state."

LSU was favored by 8½ points to hand Notre Dame its ninth straight bowl defeat.

The Game

The 77,781 fans in attendance saw a back-and-forth game until LSU pulled away in the second half.

FIRST QUARTER

LSU had outscored opponents 122–20 in the first quarter, and Notre Dame was 7–0 when scoring first. Which trend would prevail? The Irish gained one first down on two runs by Darius Walker, but an unsportsmanlike conduct penalty against WR Jeff Samardzija after he caught a pass was too much to overcome. So the punt team lined up on fourth-and-three from the 34. But Coach Weis made a decision that would be second-guessed by Irish fans. The ball was snapped to the upback who was stopped by S Curtis Taylor 2 yards short of the first down marker. First-and-10 LSU at the ND 35. It took only two plays for the Tigers to score. QB JaMarcus Russell flipped a long pass to WR Early Doucet who made a leaping catch at the four. TB Keiland Williams took it in from there. Colt David kicked the PAT.

Score: LSU 7 Notre Dame 0 (11:16)

Notre Dame's second possession mirrored the first. One first down on a holding penalty against LSU on a passing play before two incompletions led to a punt. The Tigers drove 80 yards in nine plays to double their lead. Doucet took a quick pass in the left flat and gained 8 yards, with 15 added on for a late hit. Russell repeated that play on third down to move the chains to the ND 44. JaMarcus overcame a false start penalty by running a draw up the middle to the 15. After senior TB Justin Vincent gained four, Russell fired a strike to Bowe across the middle in the end zone. It was Dwayne's 12th TD catch, a school record.

LSU 14 Notre Dame 0 (6:03)

Vincent explained LSU's early offensive success this way. "I think we surprised them a little bit with a lot of the shifts we did, moving the running backs out to wideout, a lot of motioning."

The next Irish possession started badly with a 9-yard sack by sophomore MLB Luke Sanders. But just when it looked like the rout was on, the Irish finally got going. Quinn hit Walker out of the backfield for 21 yards to the 42. Then an end around to Samardzija coupled with a face mask penalty moved the ball into LSU territory for the first time at the 40. A run by Quinn and two by Walker gained another first down on the 25. Brady then made a beautiful throw to WR David Grimes between S LaRon Landry and LB Jason Spadoni at the left pylon.

LSU 14 Notre Dame 7 (1:26)

On the last play of the period, the Irish were back in business at the LSU 21 when Russell fumbled while being sacked, and DT Travis Leitko recovered.

LSU 14 Notre Dame 7

SECOND QUARTER

Notre Dame couldn't take advantage of the turnover. Two incompletions and a 5-yard run caused Carl Giola to try a 34-yard field goal that sailed wide right. LSU made one first down before punting. Notre Dame moved the chains three times, twice on Walker runs and on a pass to Rhema to the LSU 39. Quinn threw long to Samardzija, but CB Jonathan Zenon leaped and intercepted the ball on the four. Or did he? A review of the play resulted in a questionable reversal based on Zenon not retaining possession to the ground. But poetic justice prevailed two plays later when Quinn evaded LB Ali Highsmith's blitz and threw on the run right to Jonathan who ran to the 41.

Russell fired to Bowe on a crossing pattern to the 29, then tossed to FB Jacob Hester to the 17. But the Irish dug in and forced a field goal try that David missed from the 21.

Momentum from the defensive stop carried over to the offense. Notre Dame marched 80 yards in eight plays to tie the score. An incompletion preceded five straight runs, four by Walker and one by Quinn, who ran out of the pocket for 12 yards. Then the Irish attacked the flanks. Darius broke loose down the right sideline for 45 yards and zipped around left end for 15 more before taking a breather. Freshman James Aldridge gained four before Quinn started sending Samardzija against Zenon again. The first try failed; then Jeff got past the sophomore from Breaux Bridge to grab the ball in the end zone.

LSU 14 Notre Dame 14 (2:25)

The Fighting Irish seemed to have momentum going into halftime, but the Tigers took it away by charging 82 yards in five plays. After Justin Vincent bolted for 19, Russell lofted a pass to Doucet on the run behind two defenders. Early caught it at the 17 and ran to the five. Two plays later, JaMarcus crashed his 260-pound body into the end zone on a draw. "That (touchdown) right before the half got our morale down," said Irish CB Mike Richardson after the game.

LSU 21 Notre Dame 14 (1:15)

The Irish led in time of possession 19:31–10:29.

LSU made halftime adjustments to stop Walker, who gained 125 yards in the first half but would get only three in the second.

Third Quarter

A review two plays after the kickoff resulted in another reversal of a call. Russell threw quickly to Doucet near the left sideline. As Early fought for yardage, CB Ambrose Wooden wrestled the ball away and grabbed it as he went out of bounds. But did he have possession? After a lengthy review, LSU retained the ball at their 32. Given new life, the offense ripped off three first downs in three plays, all passes—17 yards to Davis, 11 to Vincent, and another strike to Davis to the 28. But on third-and-two, the Irish stuffed Russell on a draw. So Chris Jackson lined up for a 33-yard field goal. But repeating what he had done in the 2005 Peach Bowl, holder Matt Flynn ran an option play to the right, pitching the ball to Jackson. The former high school quarterback scurried for a first down at the 16. Vincent took a pass for 8 yards. But the Irish drew the line there. So Colt David booted a 26-yard field goal.

LSU 24 Notre Dame 14 (9:34)

The Irish gained one first down on a pass to FB John Carlson. On third-and-three, Samardzija lined up opposite Zenon and ran a slant in. Jonathan reached in front and knocked the ball away.

Starting from the 21 after a penalty on the punt, the Tigers gained yardage on six straight plays. Keiland Williams ran three times for 31 yards. Bowe caught two passes for 24 yards. But an errant third-down pass to Bowe brought David in for a 37-yard field goal.

LSU 27 Notre Dame 14 (3:49)

With the LSU front four retaking control of the line of scrimmage, Notre Dame went three-and-out. The Tigers then traveled 73 yards in five plays to extend their lead. The touchdown came when WR Brandon LaFell got behind freshman CB Darrin Walls on his first play after replacing the injured starter to complete a 58-yard strike.

LSU 34 Notre Dame 14 (0:18)

Notre Dame DB Chinedum Ndukwe said, "We never felt like we were out of the game until that big play. We've made big comebacks this season. They were throwing deep balls all over the place by then."

FOURTH QUARTER

With the issue no longer in doubt, play became sloppy with four penalties in the first minutes, including two unsportsmanlike conduct calls against LSU. LaRon Landry got an interception, but Notre Dame got a pick of their own when Russell threw into double coverage in the end zone.

When the LSU offense got the ball back, they made their head coach, a Bo Schembechler disciple, immensely proud by driving to a final touchdown with all but 11 of the 76 yards gained on the ground. Williams carried the mail six times for 63 yards, including the final 20 on a beautiful cutback run to go over the 100-yard mark for the first time in his career.

LSU 41 Notre Dame 14 (7:27)

Both teams put in their backup quarterbacks in the final minutes.

Final Score: LSU 41 Notre Dame 14

The victory gave Miles the SEC record for most victories in his first two seasons as a coach—22. His reward was a Gatorade bath when the game ended.

Russell won the MVP award for leading the LSU offense to 577 yards and 31 first downs. He finished 21-of-34 through the air for 332 yards with two passing touchdowns and another one on the ground.

Postgame

Coach Miles praised a senior class that compiled a 44–8 four-year mark to break the record set the previous year. "The seniors came to play. They played early, and they played late." He added, "The receiving corps blocks extremely well. It takes a toll on the defense—big, strong men imposing their will on others." He didn't neglect his other unit. "Our defense was stingy all day. It was dominant in the second half."

LSU offensive coordinator Jimbo Fisher explained the game plan. "We wanted to be diverse, try to keep them off balance, give them a lot of different looks and a lot of different personnel because we thought we could get some personnel matchups."

Charlie Weis pointed to the third LSU touchdown as the turning point. "We gave up that big play before the half, which is never good. And then they really laid the wood to us in the second half. They were in control, and we played crummy."

Irish S Tom Zbikowski: "They ran a little bit more than we expected, and Russell's a hard man to bring down on those sprint draws. They had a lot of weapons, and they used them all."

DB Chinedum Ndukwe praised the Tiger receiving corps. "We play some of the best receivers in the country, and those guys are up there. ... You just have to tip your hats. They came to play, and we didn't." As for Russell, "he definitely shocked us by pulling it down and running it because we didn't expect him to run it as much. He has a great arm.... He made a lot of throws you don't think he can make."

Twenty-four 2006 Tigers played pro football: LB Darry Beckwith, WR Dwayne Bowe, LB Jacob Cutrera, WR Craig Davis, DL Glenn Dorsey, WR Early Doucet, QB Matt Flynn, DB Chris Hawkins, RB Jacob Hester, LB Ali Highsmith, WR Trindon Holliday, DB Chevis Jackson, DE Tyson Jackson, DT Rickey Jean-Francois, RB Quinn Johnson, WR Brandon LaFell, DB LaRon Landry, DB Danny McCray, LB Perry Riley, QB JaMarcus Russell, DB Craig Steltz, DB Curtis Taylor, RB Keiland Williams, and DL Al Woods.

Chick-fil-A Bowl vs. Georgia Tech

What a second half explosion!

Georgia Dome, Atlanta, Georgia
December 31, 2008

The 2008 Tigers found it impossible to follow in the footsteps of the '07 team that won the BCS Championship in the Superdome against Ohio State. (The BCS separated the championship game from the bowls starting with the 2006–07 season.)

LSU's Season

Four starters on the '07 offense, including QB Matt Flynn and RB Jacob Hester, were lost to graduation as were eight defensive starters, led by T Glenn Dorsey and DBs Craig Steltz and Chevis Jackson. To make matters worse, defensive coordinator Bo Pelini became the head coach at Nebraska. So coach Les Miles replaced him with co-defensive coordinators Doug Mallory and Bradley Dale Peveto. The Tigers went from allowing 19.6 points per game in '07 (which included two triple overtime games) to 25.9 points per game in '08 with two games (Georgia and Florida) in which the opponent scored more than 50 points. Evidence of the defense's decline was the fact that only two Tiger defenders, T Rahim Alem and LB Darry Beckwith, made all-SEC first or second team.

'08 was supposed to be the Year of Ryan Perrilloux who was considered the #1 quarterback prospect in the recruiting class of 2005. After redshirting that season, he saw limited duty in '06. Senior Matt Flynn beat him out for the starting quarterback job in 2007, although Ryan started the second game when Matt was injured. Perrilloux replaced the injured Flynn in the SEC Championship Game and, eliciting memories of Matt Mauck coming off the bench in 2001 against Tennessee, led the Tigers to a 21–14 victory over that same opponent. Ryan was the heir apparent for '08, but off-field transgressions led Miles to dismiss him from the team in May.

Redshirt freshman Jarrett Lee earned the starting spot over true freshman Jordan Jefferson. But Lee was inconsistent, completing just 53.2 percent of his passes and throwing only 14 touchdown passes against 16 interceptions.

Still, LSU won the first four games and split the next four. Then an overtime loss to Alabama sent the Tigers into a tailspin. They had to rally from a 31–3 third quarter deficit to beat Troy 40–31. Miles and offensive coordinator Gary Crowton decided to start

Jefferson, a better runner than Lee but not as good a passer, the last two games. LSU lost to Ole Miss 31–13 at home and Arkansas 31–30 on the road. The result was a 7–5 record and no Top 25 ranking to end the regular season for the first time since 2000. LSU was fortunate to receive a bid to the Chick-fil-A Bowl (formerly the Peach Bowl) to play #14 Georgia Tech.

Durable junior Charles Scott carried the ball on 44 percent of LSU's rushing attempts and gained 1,174 yards to earn all-SEC honors. Another all-conference performer, junior Brandon LaFell, led the receivers by a wide margin with 61 receptions for 903 yards.

Jefferson did enough in the last two games to get the nod for the bowl. A few days before the game, JJ—as he was known—asked to address the team. He promised, "I will not let you down."

The Opponent

Despite having the youngest team in the Atlantic Coast Conference, Georgia Tech went 9–3 under new coach Paul Johnson, who came from the Naval Academy where he implemented his "flexbone" offense. Derived from the wishbone, the flexbone featured a quarterback under center with a fullback lined up directly behind the quarterback. Two smaller slotbacks lined up just behind and outside of the tackles with a wide receiver further out on each side. The option offense required a good runner at the quarterback position. The Yellow Jackets ran the ball an average of 49 times a game and passed only 13 times. They ran for over 400 yards in three games during the season. The leading ball carrier was FB Jonathan Dwyer, the ACC Player of the Year, who gained 1,328 yards on 190 carries. The LSU coaches watching film never saw anyone catch him from behind. So it would be imperative to get a body on him before he could get up a head of steam. The second highest ground-gainer, as is typical in an option offense, was QB Josh Nesbitt (156/631 yards). Nesbitt threw the ball only 99 times all season, completing 46 for 958 yards—an impressive average of 20.8 ypc.

On the other side of the ball, the key matchup would be LSU OT Ciron Black against DE Michael Johnson. Black led the Tigers with 68 knockdown blocks while Johnson had 15 tackles for loss, including seven sacks. The 6'7" senior also broke up seven passes.

The Yellow Jackets tied Virginia Tech for the top spot in the Coastal Division of the Atlantic Coast Conference, but the Hokies played in the championship game because of their 20–17 victory over the Yellow Jackets in Week 3.

Georgia Tech had impressive wins over Clemson (21–17), Florida State (31–28), Miami (41–23), and the one that thrilled Tech fans the most—their first victory in eight years over archrival Georgia (45–42), which beat LSU 52–38 in Tiger Stadium October 25. What he accomplished largely with players inherited from a different system made Johnson ACC Coach of the Year.

The game promised an intriguing clash between Tech's rushing offense, third in the nation, and LSU's 17th-ranked rushing defense. The Tigers had not faced a triple option team like Georgia Tech in many years. However, the defense had a month to prepare. The staff had the scout team run the Tech plays without a football to better simulate the speed with which the Jackets executed the triple option. "I think we're a better football team than we've been," said Les Miles the day before the game. "We needed the extra time." His team's performance would bear that out.

The Yellow Jackets were favored by 3.5 points. That would turn out to be one of the worst betting lines in the history of bowl games.

The Game

The 12th consecutive sellout crowd for the Chick-fil-A Bowl, 71,423, and the ESPN audience saw the Tigers explode in the second period on their way to a decisive victory.

First Quarter

LSU came out firing on all cylinders. Starting from the 40 after the kickoff went out of bounds, the Tigers got first downs on their first three plays. Charles Scott roared through left tackle past DE Michael Johnson for 14 yards. QB Jordan Jefferson, the first true freshman to start at quarterback for LSU in a bowl game since Herb Tyler in the '95 Independence Bowl, rolled right and hit WR Jared Mitchell for 11. Next, Jefferson connected with WR Terrence Toliver for 11 yards to the 24. After Keiland Williams gained two, Jefferson threw to TE Richard Dickson at the nine. Jordan ran around right end to the two. Scott stepped through left tackle into the end zone. Colt David booted the PAT.

Score: LSU 7 Georgia Tech 0 (11:58)

Knowing the Tigers would be tough to run on, Tech had been working on their passing game. QB Josh Nesbitt faked to RB Jonathan Dwyer who then ran through the line wide open and took a pass 40 yards to the LSU 40. Next, Nesbitt threw deep to WR Demaryius Thomas in the end zone, but S Chad Jones knocked the ball away. A short run and another incompletion made it fourth-and-eight. Amid confusion, Coach Johnson sent out the field goal unit, but when Tech was penalized for delay of game, he decided to punt.

The second LSU possession was decidedly different from the first. Tech's top rusher Johnson lined up at left end and came through untouched to sack Jefferson for a 9-yard loss. The Tigers gained only 11 on the next two plays. So Brady Dalfrey punted to the Tech 33.

Running mostly at LSU's left side, the Yellow Jackets launched their longest drive of the season in terms of time of possession (7:05) and number of plays (13). Roddy Jones ripped off 19 yards to the LSU 48. An offside penalty on the Tigers and runs by Nesbitt and Jones made it first-and-10 at the 35. Even a chop block penalty couldn't stop the march as Nesbitt connected with Thomas for a first down at the 23. Then Nesbitt kept the ball around right end to the 12. On third-and-five, Nesbitt threw a slant-in pass that freshman CB Patrick Peterson broke up in the end zone. So Scott Blair kicked a 24-yard field goal.

LSU 7 Georgia Tech 3 (1:03)

Second Quarter

"Dominate" is too weak a word to describe what the Tigers did to Tech this period. Aided by offside and roughing the passer penalties against the Yellow Jackets, the Tigers completed a 76-yard drive that featured Jefferson's running and passing as well as his improvisation. First, he escaped trouble and threw on the run to Dickson to the Tech 41.

After Scott rammed through his favorite left tackle slot for the first down, JJ again fired on the run, hitting LaFell in stride to the 16. On the next play, Jefferson ran off the right side and, while being tackled, through an underhand pass with his left hand out to Scott, who rumbled to the four. Charles then zipped through left tackle for the score.

LSU 14 Georgia Tech 3 (12:08)

Riverboat Gambler Miles called for an onside kick that was successful. But nothing came of it—at least right away, and Dalfrey punted. The Tech receiver tried to catch the ball on the run but was hit by Peterson before he could secure the ball, and Ron Brooks recovered at the 19. JJ ran to the 10, then handed to Scott four straight times, Charles prancing into the end zone from the one for his third touchdown of the evening.

LSU 21 Georgia Tech 3 (8:27)

Facing its largest deficit of the season, Tech's offense was not designed to come from this far behind, and they quickly faced fourth down on their 22. In panic mode, Coach Johnson called for a fake punt that didn't fool Brooks, who chopped down the upback, 270-pound DE Derrick Morgan, on the 24. The Tigers' waltz to another touchdown was almost derailed by a holding penalty that made it first-and-20 at the 25. But JJ made it look easy by hitting Dickson on a crossing pattern at the nine. The 235-pound tight end shrugged off a tackler and ran into the end zone. ESPN analyst Bob Griese, a Pro Football Hall of Fame quarterback, said, "You're seeing Jordan Jefferson grow up right in front of your eyes."

LSU 28 Georgia Tech 3 (5:21)

But LSU wasn't finished. On third-and-two, DE Rahim Alem poured through to drop FB Lucas Cox for a 4-yard loss. Speedy Trindon Holliday, a world class sprinter made even faster by the artificial turf, returned the punt 18 yards to the Tech 42. Four runs, two by Williams and two by Jefferson, increased the lead, Keiland doing the honors from the 18 to put LSU in a tie for the Chick-fil-A bowl record of 28 points in a quarter.

LSU 35 Georgia Tech 3 (1:27)

The Jackets made their initial first down of the period on a screen pass to Dwyer, then got another on a pass to Thomas. A neat middle screen to Dwyer put the ball at the LSU 48. With time running out, Nesbitt threw long, but CB Chris Hawkins looked like a receiver, snagging his third interception of the season while running toward the goal line alongside the intended receiver.

LSU 35 Georgia Tech 3

Jefferson completed 11 of 12 passes for 129 yards to seven different receivers. LSU didn't have an overwhelming lead in offense, 214–157, but the Tigers took advantage of the belated Christmas gifts from the Yellow Jackets.

THIRD QUARTER

The highlight of the period was Tech's goal line stand. The Yellow Jackets took the kickoff and reeled off two first downs with a late hit tacked on. They soon faced fourth-and-six at the LSU 46, but Nesbitt, under pressure as he was most of the evening, misfired on a pass.

The Tigers started moving just as they had in the second quarter. Two Scott runs gained a first down. Following a short pass to Demetrius Byrd, Sir Charles zipped 18 yards to the 17. On third down, Jefferson kept for 11 yards to make it first-and-goal from the one. The next play was a no brainer—give the ball to Scott. But Tech was expecting it, and he met a stone wall at left tackle. JJ threw too high to Dickson in the end zone, then swept left end for the pylon. He was ruled out at the one. On fourth down, he tried to sneak behind 6'7" 385-pound LG Herman Johnson, but DT Vance Walker slanted inside and stuffed JJ for no gain.

LSU was knocking on the door again when Holliday returned the punt 18 yards to the 22. But a chop block penalty made it first-and-25. The Tigers got a break when Jefferson was hit as he threw. The ball squirted forward and was picked up by a blue shirt and run to the end zone. But the officials ruled it an incomplete pass. So David tried a career long 53-yard field goal that sailed through the uprights with room to spare.

LSU 38 Georgia Tech 3 (1:56)

The period ended with Nesbitt completing a long pass to Marcus Wright for 46 yards to the 16.

LSU 38 Georgia Tech 3

FOURTH QUARTER

Determined to keep the Jackets out of the end zone, the Tiger defense yielded only three yards on three snaps. On fourth-and-seven, DT Lazarius Levingston sacked Nesbitt. Jefferson showed off his arm strength on the first play, throwing a long pass that LaFell took in stride into the end zone for an apparent 86-yard touchdown. But LSU was flagged for holding and Tech for roughing the passer. So the Tigers started moving in smaller chunks. Holliday took an end around handoff for 12 yards and two plays later, ran from tailback for a first down at the 41. JJ tried the long one to LaFell again but overthrew him at the 10. On fourth-and-five, Dalfrey came out to punt. But in a move that provoked boos from the Tech fans, the punter threw a pass to Chad Jones, who ran to the Tech 33. Two penalties set the Tigers back, and this time Dalfrey punted to the 17.

Facing backups, Tech moved deep into LSU territory when Dwyer took a pitchout 39 yards to the 19. The Tigers dug in and on fourth-and-one, Nesbitt fumbled, and DE Kirston Pittman recovered at the six. LSU's third-down play epitomized Tech's frustrating evening. Jefferson, passing from the end zone, was hit and fumbled. But RB Richard Murphy picked up the ball and ran out to the nine. That allowed Dalfrey to punt out of danger.

Final Score: LSU 38 Georgia Tech 3

LSU held Tech's vaunted rushing attack to 164 yards, 118 below their average. The 35-point loss was Tech's worst in bowl games.

The victory was LSU's 700th and ran Coach Miles's bowl record at LSU to 4–0 and the Tigers' record in Peach/Chick-fil-A Bowls to 5–0. The defense also extended its streak of touchdown-less quarters in Chick-fil-A Bowls to ten.

Jefferson was voted the offensive MVP after completing 16-of-25 for 142 yards. The defensive award went to LB Perry Riley, who had eight tackles—five more than any other Tiger—and three assists.

Postgame

Coach Miles gave a positive send off to his much-maligned co-defensive coordinators, both of whom were leaving—Peveto to become head coach at Northwestern State and Mallory to become defensive coordinator at New Mexico. "I really give great credit to the game plan they drew up. We're going to miss them. ... My hat's off to our defensive team. You must tackle every play and play with great intensity from the first to the end. I can't tell you how proud I am." Les said he didn't regret not getting Jefferson on the field sooner during the season. JJ agreed. "We had a lot of time to prepare for this game. I worked on my footwork and my accuracy. Even though we weren't ranked, we had something to prove here to get our respect back."

Coach Johnson was asked if the failed fake punt in the second quarter was the turning point. He answered with a chuckle. "I think the turning point was when we lined up and kicked off to start the game." He continued, "What happened is we got so far behind, it took us out of the realm where we could really do anything offensively. We were overpowered on both lines of scrimmage, more so on offense than defense. Clearly, we weren't ready to play, and that comes back to me. But clearly, they were bigger and faster than us, too." He added, "This is probably the worst special teams play I can remember."

DE Derrick Morgan expressed his team's disappointment. "We let down the fans— all the fans throughout the city. Playing in your home city, you're supposed to come out and represent. We didn't get the job done." S Morgan Burnett praised LSU. "Those guys looked like a defending national champion."

Twenty-one 2008 Tigers played pro football: T Joseph Barksdale, LB Darry Beckwith, LB Ron Brooks, LB Jacob Cutrera, DB Chris Hawkins, WR Trindon Holliday, DE Tyson Jackson, DT Rickey Jean-Francois, RB Quinn Johnson, WR Brandon LaFell, DL Lazarius Levingston, DB Danny McCray, DL Drake Nevis, DB Patrick Peterson, RB Stevan Ridley, LB Perry Riley, LB Kelvin Sheppard, DB Brandon Taylor, DB Curtis Taylor, RB Keiland Williams, and DL Al Woods.

Capital One Bowl vs. Penn State

A sloppy game on a sloppy field

Florida Citrus Bowl, Orlando, Florida
January 1, 2010

The Tigers finished the regular season 9–3, with all three losses to SEC foes.

LSU's Season

Les Miles hired John Chavis as his defensive coordinator. Chavis came from his alma mater, Tennessee, where he had led the defense for 14 seasons until Philip Fulmer resigned as head coach. Chavis was named the Assistant Coach of the Year by the American Football Coaches Association following the 2006 season. "Chief" had a reputation for developing linebackers.

LSU entered the '09 season without a quarterback controversy. Jordan Jefferson's outstanding performance in the Chick-fil-A Bowl against Georgia Tech cemented his hold on the position over fellow sophomore Jarrett Lee.

The Tigers began the season with five wins, starting with a 31–23 victory at Washington. Included were three in the SEC—Vanderbilt 23–9, at Mississippi State 30–26, and at #14 Georgia 20–13. As a result, LSU moved up from #11 in the AP Poll to #4 in time to welcome #1 Florida to Tiger Stadium. Chavis's defense held QB Tim Tebow and the Gators to 13 points, but the Tiger offense could score only three.

The Tigers bounced back with a 31–10 thumping of Auburn and a 42–0 romp over Tulane before losing at #3 Alabama 24–15. After a tougher-than-expected victory over Louisiana Tech 24–16, the Tigers traveled to Oxford for a game that ended in controversy and ignited a firestorm of criticism of coach Miles. The 25–23 defeat ended with LSU on the Ole Miss one, unable to get off a final play because of botched clock management on the final drive.

The following week in Tiger Stadium, LSU showed they had learned their lesson from Oxford. Arkansas scored with 1:18 left in regulation to take a 30–27 lead. The Tigers then executed an efficient drive to set up Josh Jasper's 41-yard field goal to send the game into overtime. Jasper kicked another field goal on LSU's possession, and the Razorbacks missed their try.

Injuries at the running back position plagued the Tigers. By the end of the season, they were down to fourth-stringer Stevan Ridley. Charles Scott, who gained 1,174 yards in

2008, gained only 542 in '09. LSU averaged over 40 yards per game less on the ground in '09 than the year before.

The 9–3 Tigers, ranked #12, accepted an invitation to play #9 Penn State in the Capital One Bowl.

The Opponent

Eighty-three-year-old Joe Paterno's 44th Penn State team breezed through their first three games against non-conference foes to rise to #5 in the AP poll. But a home loss to Iowa dropped the Nittany Lions to #15. Five wins in a row, including a 35–10 blowout at Michigan, set up a showdown with Ohio State for sole possession of first place in the Big Ten. But once again, PSU was not equal to the task, losing 24–7. Victories against Indiana and Michigan State completed the 10–2 season.

Senior QB Daryll Clark had another outstanding season. Having already set school records as a junior for career touchdown passes and passing yards in a season, he broke his own record by throwing for 2,887 yards and 24 touchdowns to earn first team All-Big Ten honors for the second straight season. The Tiger ends would have to keep him contained when he ran his trademark bootleg off play-action. Another first team all-conference player, Evan Royster, had run for nearly 3,000 yards in his three-year career. He posed a problem for the LSU defense, which allowed 714 yards on the ground in the final four games (177.5 yards per game).

Paterno, with an NCAA record 23 bowl victories, bristled at the suggestion that Penn State needed to beat LSU to salvage a "disappointing" season in which the Lions lost to all the good teams they played. "You start off with the wrong assumptions. We're a good football team playing against a very good football team, and hopefully we can play well." Miles relished the challenge of playing a team "you're not necessarily familiar with. I think it's exciting. … And a game that will create a curiosity, probably throughout the country, to see how Penn State and LSU match up."

Unfortunately, the game is remembered for the disgraceful field conditions. Eight high school state championship games had been played at the Citrus Bowl stadium in recent weeks. The turf was replaced immediately after the last games on December 19, but the Champs Sports Bowl, played ten days later, tore up the new turf. The grounds crew worked diligently over the next three days to get the field in shape for the Capital One Bowl but ultimately failed. As a result, this was the last Capital One Bowl to be played on grass as artificial turf was installed several months later. To make matters worse, a driving rain the morning of the game made the footing even worse. Tom Bradley, Penn State's defensive coordinator, admitted after the game that the rain was bad. "But I was one guy that wasn't saying, 'Rain, rain go away.' I was OK with it." He knew the conditions would negate the Tigers' speed advantage.

The Game

A sloppy game that produced a Capital One Bowl record 15 punts was witnessed by 63,025 who braved the weather conditions.

First Quarter

LSU S Chad Jones partially blocked Penn State's first punt, which traveled to the LSU 34. Jordan Jefferson immediately hit WR Brandon LaFell for 15 yards to the 49. That would be the only Tiger offensive highlight of the entire period. With neither team able to move the ball, the contest descended into a punting duel. The wet ball and sloppy field—divots flew whenever a player cut—contributed to the poor play. PSU QB Daryll Clark said, "If (the football) wasn't wet, it had some mud on it. If it didn't have mud on it, it was wet."

The Tiger defense kept missing opportunities to gain turnovers. The Nittany Lions would fumble four times during the game—three of them on center snaps—and recover every one of them. LSU LB Harry Coleman had a pass bounce off him that he might have returned for a touchdown. Another throw ricocheted off FS Danny McCray's helmet.

Penn State struck suddenly for the game's first points. Staring at a fourth straight punt and second straight three-and-out, Clark zipped a third-and-10 pass to WR Graham Zug for a 21-yard gain to the LSU 37. Then Daryll rolled to his left, evaded one rusher, and lobbed a touchdown pass to WR Derek Moye, who was wide open on an out-and-up pattern at the two behind sophomore CB Patrick Peterson. Clark explained, "Peterson jumps a lot of routes. He's a very aggressive corner. If we had a regular out pattern called, he would have had it covered. He drove on the out, just like we thought he was going to do. I wanted to put it out there not too far. I didn't want to underthrow it because Peterson has good make-up speed as well."

Score: Penn State 7 LSU 0 (1:54)

The Tigers finally got a big play when Jefferson rifled a short pass to LaFell. Brandon got away from the cornerback and raced 36 yards down the sideline to the 11. But two plays went backward as the period ended.

Penn State 7 LSU 0

Second Quarter

When JJ connected with Terrence Toliver for only 8 yards, Josh Jasper kicked a 25-yard field goal.

Penn State 7 LSU 3 (14:15)

After Derek Helton shanked a punt, the Lions started a 10-play, 46-yard drive that got the three points back. McCray missed a chance to get the ball back when he dropped a deflected pass again. Clark twice converted on third down, hitting TE Andrew Quarless for 23 and Moye for eight to the 17. On third-and-three, Clark tried a quarterback draw but gained only a yard. So Collin Wagner booted a 26-yard field goal.

Penn State 10 LSU 3 (5:29)

The Tiger offense was unable to make even one first down. The low point came when they were penalized for holding and intentional grounding on the same play. After that, Jefferson threw a long pass to WR Reuben Randle, who was double covered. One defender got his hands on the ball but succeeded only in hitting the ball into the air. Randle was in position to catch it with no one between him and the goal line, but he dropped it.

On the Tigers' next possession, Jefferson's pass bounced off Toliver's hands to CB A.J. Wallace at the 22. RB Evan Royster broke loose to the seven. On third-and-goal, LB Jacob Cutrera was called for holding to give the Lions a first down. But the Tigers held their ground and forced an 18-yard field goal by Wagner. Penn State 13 LSU 3 (:04).

LSU ended the half with only 67 yards of offense and two first downs, both on passes to LaFell. They ran 12 times for -2 yards.

THIRD QUARTER

The offenses floundered until PSU got their second turnover inside the LSU 25. LB Sean Lee scooped up Stevan Ridley's fumble and ran to the 21. PSU gained a first down at the nine before bogging down again. So Wagner banged through his third field goal.

Penn State 16 LSU 3 (2:27)

After a poor kickoff, the Tigers started at the PSU 47. Jefferson found Toliver to the 32. JJ fired a third-and-two pass to LaFell, who caught it at the 10, evaded a tackler, and ran into the end zone. Jordan explained that offensive coordinator Gary Crowton "noticed some things from the (press) box in the second half, and we were able to be more productive. At the end, it came a little easier for us, and we found some rhythm."

Penn State 16 LSU 10 (0:13)

FOURTH QUARTER

The turf was so chewed up that the bowl logo at midfield was unrecognizable.

LSU started from their 49 after Holliday's 37-yard punt return and marched to the go-ahead touchdown. Trindon darted 11 yards to the PSU 40. After gaining nothing on two plays, Jefferson uncorked a long pass to Toliver, who snagged the ball at the 11 and carried it to the one. Ridley plunged over on the next play. LSU 17 Penn State 16 (12:49).

An intentional grounding penalty against Clark was too much for PSU to overcome, and LSU soon had the ball back. But the Tigers couldn't sustain a drive to at least run time off the clock.

Ron Brooks returns a punt as Chase Clement (88) and John Williams (31) try to block (*Gumbo*** Class of 2010).**

Before taking the field with 6:54 remaining for what might be PSU's last possession, Clark told his teammates, "We are not losing this game, no matter what." He backed up his words by engineering a 12-play, 65-yard march that ate up 5:57 and resulted in the go-ahead field goal. Clark went three-for-three for 34 yards and ran four times for 13 yards. He lost 2 yards on the last play intentionally to give Wagner a better angle. The 21-yard three-pointer was the junior kicker's fourth of the game. "I thought Daryll Clark did a great job late in the game keeping the ball in his hands and making some runs that were key," said Miles.

Penn State 19 LSU 17 (0:57)

LSU needed a big return, and Holliday gave it to them, dashing 26 yards to the 41. Jefferson scrambled for 10 yards and got out of bounds at the PSU 49 to stop the clock with 39 seconds left. That's when things went haywire. LaFell grabbed a slip screen pass in the middle of the field and gained 4 yards to the 45. As the rest of the Tigers scrambled up to the new line of scrimmage, LaFell couldn't get up because LB Navorro Bowman pinned him to the soggy turf. "I was looking right at the ref," said Brandon, "and he was telling that dude to get off me. He told me later he was trying to spot the ball, but I don't know how he was trying to spot the ball when the guy was laying on top of me." When LG Lyle Hitt grabbed Bowman's shoulder pads and lifted him off LaFell, he was called for a personal foul, the Tigers' tenth and most costly penalty. Bowman wasn't flagged for delay of game. Navorro said afterward he didn't think Hitt deserved a flag. "I thought the flag was against me at first for laying on him." Instead of getting closer to Jasper's field goal range, the Tigers were set back to their 40. A long heave to LaFell fell incomplete and a desperation throw to Randle against the prevent defense produced only 25 yards.

Final Score: Penn State 19 LSU 17

It was Les Miles' first loss to a non-conference opponent in his five years as LSU coach. The Tigers ended the season without a win against a team that would finish ranked in the Top 25—another first for Les's tenure.

Postgame

Miles was asked about the penalty against Hitt in the last minute. "Our player was trying to help (Bowman) up to get him off the pile so we could (spike) the ball. I don't know that lifting a guy off the ground could possibly be misconstrued as a personal foul." LSU LB Kelvin Sheppard refused to blame the terrible turf for the loss. "It slowed down our speed. But Penn State was out there on the same turf, so you can't for one second use that as an excuse."

Coach Paterno said he was glad no one suffered a significant injury in the game. "I don't want to gripe about it (the field). But it was tough." After being criticized during his career for not winning big games, Clark won the MVP award after throwing for 216 yards and a touchdown and leading the clutch drive to the winning field goal. "I'm more overjoyed than satisfied or relieved. I put this team before myself.... I made it clear to everyone that it's not about me. This football team did not come down here to win for Daryll or for Daryll's legacy. That's not what this is about. We bonded together to get a big-time win for this program."

Twenty 2009 Tigers played pro football: T Joseph Barksdale, LB Ron Brooks, DB Morris Claiborne, LB Jacob Cutrera, DT Lavar Edwards, DB Chris Hawkins, WR Trindon Holliday, WR Brandon LaFell, DL Lazarius Levingston, DB Danny McCray, DL Drake Nevis, DB Patrick Peterson, WR Rueben Randle, RB Stevan Ridley, LB Perry Riley, WR Russell Shepard, LB Kelvin Sheppard, DB Brandon Taylor, RB Keiland Williams, and DL Al Woods.

AT&T Cotton Bowl Classic
vs. Texas A&M

Game of his life in his home state

Cowboys Stadium, Arlington, Texas
January 7, 2011

The 2010 Tigers certainly played their share of thrilling games.

LSU's Season

The continuing saga of Les Miles's sixth Tiger team was the quarterback controversy. Jordan Jefferson started eight games while Jarrett Lee started four times and relieved in six other contests. Yet the Tigers won their first seven games to rise to #6 in the polls.

The season opened with North Carolina in the Chick-fil-A Kickoff Game in Atlanta. The Tigers led 30–10 early in the fourth quarter thanks to an 87-yard punt return by Patrick Peterson, a 50-yard TD run by Russell Shepard, and a 51-yard TD pass from Jefferson to sophomore WR Rueben Randle. But the Tar Heels cut the margin to 30–24 and reached the LSU six in the last minute, forcing the Tigers to bat down two passes in the end zone to secure the victory.

The next two games were not close—27–3 over Vanderbilt in Nashville and 29–7 over Mississippi State at home. Peterson returned another punt for a touchdown, this one for 60 yards, to spark the 20–14 home victory over West Virginia in the first-ever meeting between the two schools.

The game against Tennessee in Tiger Stadium invoked another outburst of criticism of LSU's clock management like the one that erupted after the 25–23 loss at Ole Miss in 2009. But this time the Tigers lucked out. With LSU alternating quarterbacks throughout the game, the Vols took their first lead, 14–10, early in the fourth period. In the final minutes, Lee led a drive that reached the UT two. Jefferson came in and ran for a yard instead of throwing the ball away to stop the clock. LSU then sent in new personnel, which caused Tennessee to make hurried substitutions. With the clock running out, the ball was snapped before JJ was ready, and he fell on the loose ball with 0:00 showing. As booing fans started leaving, the referee looked at a replay that showed the Vols had 13 men on the field. So LSU received an untimed down at the one. Stevan Ridley banged through left tackle into the end zone to snatch victory from the jaws of defeat.

Lee and Jefferson alternated again at Florida in a game that cemented Miles's "Mad Hatter" reputation. Trailing 29–26 in the final period, LSU faced fourth-and-three at the Gator 36. Josh Jasper lined up to kick a field goal, but instead holder Lee took the snap and flipped the ball over his shoulder to Josh who gained five to keep possession. The drive ended with Jarrett tossing to Terrence Toliver in the end zone with 0:06 on the clock for a memorable road victory.

In a battle that would determine the SEC West champion, Auburn defeated LSU on the strength of a 49-yard touchdown run by eventual Heisman Trophy winner Cam Newton. The Bengal Tigers bounced back the following week to defeat Alabama 24–21. Both quarterbacks contributed big plays. Jefferson hit Randle on a 75-yard pass-and-run for a touchdown to put LSU ahead 10–7 in the third quarter. Trailing 14–13 in the fourth period, LSU faced a fourth-and-one at the Bama 26. Instead of kicking a field goal, the Tigers ran a reverse to TE Deangelo Peterson for 23 yards to the Bama three to set up the go-ahead touchdown. Late in the game, with LSU ahead 24–21, Lee connected with Randle on third-and-13 from the LSU 20 to deny the Tide another possession.

In another thriller, the Tigers outlasted Ole Miss 43–36. Then came the most disappointing game of the season—the finale in Little Rock. Three long scoring plays, including an 80-yard TD reception as the first half ended, propelled Arkansas to the 31–23 victory that dropped the Tigers to 10–2 for the season and gave the Razorbacks the SEC berth in the BCS Sugar Bowl. LSU got a spot in the SEC's next highest bowl, the Cotton Bowl.

In his final season at LSU, junior Patrick Peterson won the Jim Thorpe Award as the best defensive back in the nation and the Chuck Bednarik Award as the best defensive player.

The Opponent

Mike Sherman, the former head coach and general manager of the Green Bay Packers, started his third year at Texas A&M on the hot seat. The Aggies went 4–8 in his first season but improved to 6–7 the next year, losing to Georgia in the Independence Bowl. His 2010 squad started 3–0 against non-conference foes but lost their next three—at Oklahoma State (38–35), Arkansas in Dallas (24–17), and Missouri (30–9). But just when it looked like Mike might not survive the season, A&M won six straight conference games down the stretch, including a 33–19 triumph over Oklahoma and the 24–17 finale at archrival Texas.

The Aggies' 6–2 conference record put them in a three-way tie in the Big 12 Southern Division with Oklahoma and Oklahoma State. Since none of the three had beaten both the others, Oklahoma played in the conference championship game because they were rated highest by the BCS.

A big reason for A&M's mid-season turnaround was a quarterback change. With senior Jerrod Johnson struggling, Sherman made the somewhat unpopular decision to go with Ryan Tannehill, who had been starting at receiver. The 6'4" junior completed 65.3 percent of his passes for 1,434 yards with 11 touchdowns against only three interceptions. LSU Defensive Coordinator John Chavis praised the A&M signal-caller. "The one thing I have seen on the field is tremendous offensive execution. Tannehill makes a lot of great decisions, and he can run with the ball when he needs to. He executes the run-zone scheme better than most quarterbacks we have seen."

The Aggies deployed a balanced attack, averaging 281.7 yards per game through the air and 165.8 on the ground. Chunky junior RB Cyrus Gray edged over the 1,000-yard mark by 33 (5.7 yards per carry).

LSU's SEC-best pass defense would have to contend with two outstanding receivers, who were 1–2 for most catches in a season in school history. Junior Jeff Fuller caught 65 balls for 983 yards for a whopping 15.1 yards per catch. Sophomore Ryan Swope snagged 67 for 789 yards (11.6 ypc).

LSU LB Kelvin Sheppard was impressed with A&M's no huddle offense. "This is the fastest team we've played all year. I would compare them to Auburn, how they just came back up to the ball and got the play from the sideline. It seems like they have 10 plays already called."

The unquestioned leader of the Aggie "Wrecking Crew" defense was senior LB Von Miller, the Butkus Award winner who had 9.5 sacks and 14.5 tackles for losses. He was the heart of a unit that allowed only 117 yards per game rushing, 15th best in the nation. LSU T Joseph Barksdale said of Miller, "We've got to know where he is every play." The Aggies used more zone coverage and zone blitzes than LSU had seen during the regular season.

The #18 Aggies were excited about playing the Tigers. "A victory would be monumental for the A&M program," said senior center and LSU transfer Matt Allen. "Beating a team like LSU, who … has always showed up at the bowls prepared, would be huge for A&M. It would put us back on the map and show the nation that we can play in these types of games."

Would the #11 Tigers match the Aggies' enthusiasm? How would the LSU offense fare against A&M's 3–4 defense, which no SEC team used?

The Game

Packing the state-of-the-art stadium known as "Jerry World," 83,514 fans watched the game along with a national television audience that had the Friday prime time slot to itself.

FIRST QUARTER

Not only had the LSU defense not allowed a touchdown on the opponent's opening drive all season, no opponent had crossed midfield on their first possession. But the fired-up Aggies ended both streaks. DB Coryell Judie took the kickoff and streaked 69 yards to the LSU 31. QB Ryan Tannehill hit WR Uzoma Nwachukwu for a first down at the 19, then found WR Kenric McNeal to the 10. Cyrus Gray, who had six straight 100-yard games to end the season, ran for the first down at the six. Tannehill then threw over the middle to Uzoma at the one, and he extended the ball over the goal line.

Score: Texas A&M 7 LSU 0 (13:01)

The LSU offense gained six on two runs by Stevan Ridley, who had been cleared to play by the NCAA a week earlier after an investigation of an alleged academic violation. But Jefferson threw behind Terrence Toliver to bring out the punt team. Derek Helton dropped the snap but that turned out to be a blessing as he was hit right after he got the kick away to draw a 15-yard penalty. Given new life, the Tigers moved quickly into A&M

territory on a 9-yard pass to WR Rueben Randle and an option keeper by Jefferson around right end to the 45. Attacking the middle of the defense, Ridley gained seven, then Spencer Ware added 11 more. But on third-and-seven, Judie intercepted JJ's pass at the two. Jefferson explained later, "They were in the two-tail coverage. Rueben ran right past the cornerback. … After my play-action, I thought I would be able to get the ball over the corner, the safety wouldn't make the play. The ball fell kind of low on me. I really couldn't let that turnover really define us as a team. That turnover would mess up everything for us. I had to overlook that, come out the next drive, make sure we put points on the board."

Despite the bad field position, the Aggies drove far enough to pad their lead with a field goal. The big gains came on Tannehill's 32-yard scamper out of the pocket and Gray's 18-yard sweep. But two high throws brought out Randy Bullock for a 39-yard field goal.

Texas A&M 10 LSU 0 (5:03)

The Tigers answered with an 80-yard drive. Runs by JJ and Ridley earned the initial first down. On third-and-six, Jefferson rolled left and threw past blitzing LB Von Miller to Randle in the flat to the 45. Then JJ ran out of the pocket to the Aggie 42. The plodding drive suddenly ended when Jefferson looped a beautiful pass down the middle to Toliver running behind the defenders in the end zone. Josh Jasper converted.

Texas A&M 10 LSU 7 (1:48)

After another good kickoff return to the 34, the Aggies needed only two plays to enter Tiger territory again—Gray's 11-yard run and Tannehill's pass to WR Ray Swope to the 39. Fuller became the first A&M receiver to reach the 1,000-yard mark when he gained five to the 24. Freshman CB Tyrann Mathieu blitzed from the left side and hit Tannehill as he tried to throw. T Jake Matthews, who missed the block on Mathieu, recovered the fumble for a loss of 11.

Texas A&M 10 LSU 7

SECOND QUARTER

The Tigers seized control of the game during this period, thanks largely to two turnovers.

The Aggie possession ended with Bullock's 52-yard field goal try hitting the right upright.

Jarrett Lee had been relieving Jefferson on the third possession of many games, but JJ stayed in and engineered a 65-yard drive to take the lead. After two Ridley runs and a penalty moved the sticks, FB Spencer Ware spun away from tacklers twice during a 24-yard gain to the 23. Facing third-and-11 moments later, JJ ran out of the pocket to the 11. Steven then took a delayed handoff within 1 yard of the goal. Jordan then rolled right to the pylon.

LSU 14 Texas A&M 10 (7:44)

The lead didn't survive the next Aggie possession, which covered 78 yards in seven plays. Fuller and CB Patrick Peterson were waging a competitive one-on-one duel, and the receiver won the next two rounds, gaining 15, then 19. Gray carried twice for a first down at the 27. With the other cornerback, Morris Claiborne, out with an injury, Tannehill picked on the replacement, freshman Tharold Simon, completing a slant to Brandal

Spencer Ware fights for yardage. #35 is FB James Stampley, and #72 is T Alex Hurst (Matthew Visinsky).

Jackson to the 14. Gray started right, then surprised the Tigers by throwing to Nwachukwu in the end zone.

Texas A&M 17 LSU 14 (7:44)

But that lead didn't last long either as the Tigers zipped 67 yards in seven plays. On third-and-four, Ware tore through the line behind LT Joseph Barksdale for 26 yards to the A&M 35. Two plays later, JJ fired a strike to the 19 to Toliver, having a great game to end his LSU career. After gaining two on first down, Ridley started left, then angled around right end to the end zone.

LSU 21 Texas A&M 17 (4:43)

But LSU wasn't finished. They got the ball back when Tannehill and Judie got their signals crossed. The receiver cut short, and Ryan threw long right to Simon on the LSU 30. It was Tannehill's first interception in 127 pass attempts.

The Tigers went three-and-out for the first time and punted into the end zone. Tannehill threw his second interception, and this one was on him. S Eric Reid stepped in front of an ill-advised pass down the middle and scampered 34 yards to the two. Ryan explained, "My first read on the right side got jammed up pretty bad. Came across to my second read. The guy (Reid) just made a great play and undercut the throw."

Miller broke through and dumped Ridley for a loss of one. After Jefferson gained that yard back, LSU took a timeout. Offensive coordinator Gary Crowton called a formation that isolated 6'5" Toliver on another Terrence, 5'10" CB Frederick. JJ took the snap and lobbed the ball toward the left edge of the end zone. In a play reminiscent of his winning TD catch at Florida, Toliver snatched the ball over the top of the defender and got one foot in bounds.

LSU 28 Texas A&M 17 (1:27)

The Aggies had slight edges in first downs, 15–14, and total offense, 259–253, but also led in turnovers with two. As a result, the Tigers dominated time of possession 18:31–11:29.

THIRD QUARTER

Coach Sherman characterized his squad as "a second half team," but they didn't show it this night. LSU, which had wisely deferred on the opening coin toss, drove 67 yards to extend their lead. Jefferson continued to frustrate the Wrecking Crew. He threw pinpoint passes in a tight window to covered receivers. When the Aggies had everyone covered or brought a heavy rush, JJ ran to open space for sizeable gains. An example came on the third play of the drive after Miller's sack made it third-and-19. JJ eluded a furious rush and ran untouched for 32 yards to the A&M 44. Two plays later, the junior from Destrahan High teamed with Toliver for a carbon copy of their first TD hookup—a lovely pass down the middle that Terrence caught a step behind the defenders inside the five and took into the end zone for his third touchdown of the game. After throwing just four touchdown passes all season, JJ now had three in a little over a half.

LSU 35 Texas A&M 17 (12:06)

The Aggies tried to answer back. Mixing passes with Gray runs, they gained four first downs to the LSU 29. But on third-and-five, sophomore LB Ryan Baker sacked Tannehill at the 32. Instead of trying a field goal, A&M pooch punted to the 14.

The Tigers ate up the remaining five minutes of the period by pounding the Aggies on the ground. Ridley, Ware, and Michael Ford took turns toting the pigskin, with Spencer gaining the most on a 12-yard carry and a splendid diving catch for 18 more to the A&M 29. But the Aggies finally rose up and stopped Ware 3 yards short on third-and-nine. They were rewarded when Jasper's 44-yard field goal attempt sailed wide right.

LSU 35 Texas A&M 17

FOURTH QUARTER

The Aggies pulled within 11 with the help of a strange penalty against LSU. A&M got back-to-back first downs on Tannehill's keeper to the 49 and his pass to Fuller to the LSU 40. But two incompletions led to a punt to the two. But a booth review of the play revealed that LSU had 12 men on the field. The Aggies took advantage of the break, although it wasn't easy. After two Gray carries, Tannehill hit Swope, who was hit immediately by Brooks a yard short of the first down. On fourth down, Ryan foiled the all-out blitz by tossing to TE Michael Lamothe to the eight. On third-and-goal from the four, Tannehill lofted the ball to WR Kenric McNeal, who outleaped Mathieu for the ball in the back corner of the end zone.

LSU 35 Texas A&M 24 (10:04)

The rest of the game was all LSU. Starting from their 48 after the onside kick went out of bounds, the Tigers moved close enough for a field goal thanks to two third-down conversions. First, Jefferson hit Toliver who made his fifth catch despite tight coverage over the middle to the 37. Then Ware went around left end to the 33. From there, Jasper boomed a 50-yard field goal to tie for the longest in Cotton Bowl history.

LSU 38 Texas A&M 24 (6:12)

Judie took the kickoff and was smashed at the 14 by sixth-year walk-on Daniel Graff, who led the Tigers in special teams tackles after missing two years of his college career because of Hurricane Katrina. After Tannehill ran out of the pocket for eight, Mathieu made a spectacular diving interception at the 28. It was Ryan's third pick after he threw just four in the regular season. The Tigers continued their third down success when Jefferson connected with TE Tyler Edwards to the 13. After two runs, JJ had to throw the ball away when everyone was covered in the end zone. So Jasper booted another field, this one from the 16 to end the season with 28, a new LSU high.

LSU 41 Texas A&M 24 (3:04)

On A&M's first snap, the player who would become known as "The Honey Badger" in 2011 struck again. Just as TE Hutson Prioleau took a short pass, Tyrann hit him and wrestled the ball away and scampered down the sideline for an apparent touchdown. But a senseless unnecessary roughness penalty negated the score but not the turnover. Mathieu's great game—six solo tackles, one assist, one sack, a fumble recovery, and two interceptions—served as a preview of his outstanding 2011 season when he would finish fifth in the Heisman voting. Ware went over the 100-yard mark in rushing, and the Tigers converted their ninth third down in 16 tries to enable them to run out the clock.

Final Score: LSU 41 Texas A&M 24

Postgame

Coach Miles praised his team. "Our football team is a very close-knit group of men. … I think tonight was just really a number of great performances to cap a year that they achieved greatly. A team that's beaten the teams they've beaten and played as well as they have, this was a fitting game." He singled out what is usually every successful team's unsung unit. "I think our offensive line came to play. … (They) said this is a challenge they wanted. I think they played to that challenge." Les also lauded the defensive MVP of the game, Tyrann Mathieu. "He is a special athlete. He's learning how to make those plays in the confines of a defense."

The offensive MVP went to Terrence Toliver from Hempstead, Texas, whose three TD receptions tied a Cotton Bowl record. "I took visits to A&M. I chose to go a different way. Since I've been at LSU, I always wanted to play a Texas school, whether it was Texas A&M, Texas. Just play a good game, have a game of my life in my own home state."

After criticism during the season for inconsistent play, Jordan Jefferson revealed his motivation for the Cotton Bowl. "I just came into this game with the mindset (of) showing the critics that I can do what I need to do on the field to be noticed as a good quarterback."

Sherman offered no excuses. "I thought we prepared extremely well for the football game, but without question, LSU was the better team. I take my hat off to them. They really played well…. (We) turned the ball over three times which doesn't help against a team like that."

Twenty-six 2010 Tigers played pro football: T Joseph Barksdale, LB Lamin Barrow, RB Alfred Blue, DT Michael Brockers, LB Ron Brooks, DB Morris Claiborne, DT Lavar Edwards, RB Michael Ford, WR Brandon LaFell, DL Lazarius Levingston, DL Bennie Logan, DB Tyrann Mathieu, DL Barkevious Mingo, LB Kevin Minter, DE Sam Montgomery, DL Drake Nevis, DB Patrick Peterson, WR Rueben Randle, DB Eric Reid, RB Stevan Ridley, WR Russell Shepard, LB Kelvin Sheppard, DB Tharold Simon, DB Brandon Taylor, RB Spencer Ware, and WR James Wright.

Chick-fil-A Bowl vs. Clemson

For want of a first down

Georgia Dome, Atlanta, Georgia
December 31, 2012

LSU's 2012 season began with the head coach on the hot seat despite a 13–1 SEC championship year in 2011. If the 2007 Tigers were the beneficiaries of a lucky sequence of events that propelled them into the BCS Championship Game, the 2011 team was the victim of an unlucky sequence of events that led to the ruination of what many commentators called the finest regular season in college football history.

The '11 Tigers defeated #3 Oregon on a neutral field and won at #16 West Virginia to rise to the top spot in the AP Poll. They defeated seven SEC opponents by a combined margin of 271–61. The only close contest was the "Game of the Century" at #2 Alabama. In a game that featured 14 future NFL defensive players on each side, the Tigers prevailed 9–6 in overtime.

Undefeated Oklahoma State moved up to #2 but were upset by Iowa State 37–31 in double overtime in a game that was played the day after a plane crash killed eight passengers involved with the OSU women's basketball team. The Cowboy kicker missed a 37-yard field goal that would have won the game on the last play of regulation. With no team undefeated except LSU, Alabama moved back into the #2 spot, giving the Tide a second chance at the Tigers in the BCS Championship Game. Using a revamped offensive game plan from the first meeting, the Tide dominated the Tigers, who didn't deploy any new offensive wrinkles. What had been the greatest season in LSU history crashed and burned on the artificial turf of the Superdome. Ironically, the score was identical to the humiliating rematch with Ole Miss in the 1960 Sugar Bowl, 21–0.

LSU's Season

The 2012 Tigers suffered a blow before the season began when Coach Les Miles dismissed 2011 Heisman Trophy finalist Tyrann Mathieu from the team for repeated drug test failures. Nevertheless, coordinator John Chavis fashioned a Top Ten defense. A big reason for the Tigers' success was their +15 turnover ratio, including 31 takeaways, 18 of which were interceptions. That helped them limit opponents to 16.9 points per game and slightly under 300 yards per game. Junior LB Kevin Minter led with 111 tackles.

Transfer QB Zach Mettenberger threw for 2,489 yards with 11 touchdowns against six interceptions. He had two outstanding sophomore receivers in Jarvis Landry (52 catches for 536 yards) and Odell Beckham, Jr. (40/673). The workhorse running back was 6'2" 235-pound freshman Jeremy Hill (130 carries for 631 yards).

The Tigers' chance to defend their SEC championship came down to a single play against #1 Alabama at Tiger Stadium that illustrated fans' frustration with Coach Miles's offensive philosophy. Leading 21–17, the Tigers faced third-and-10 at the Alabama 32 with 2:28 to go. Get one more first down and, at the least, force the Tide to use up their time-outs. Landry had caught eight passes and Beckham four. But LSU ran the ball and tried a field goal that missed. Alabama then drove to the winning touchdown.

LSU's only other loss was at Florida 14–6. The victories included a home squeaker over Steve Spurrier's South Carolina Gamecocks, ranked #3 at the time, and a 24–19 triumph at new SEC member Texas A&M led by their sensational freshman QB Johnny Manziel.

The Opponent

Known as an excellent recruiter, 39-year-old Dabo Swinney became the interim Clemson head coach midway through the 2008 season. He finished that season 4–3 and was named permanent head coach. His '09 Tigers went 9–5, finishing first in the Atlantic Division of the ACC. After a 6–7 record in '10 that put Swinney's job in jeopardy, Clemson won the 2011 ACC championship, the school's first since 1991. That earned the team their first major-bowl appearance in 31 years and Swinney the Bobby Dodd Coach of the Year Award.

His 2012 Tigers went 10–2, but one of the losses was to Florida State, which cost Clemson the Atlantic Division crown. The other loss came to South Carolina in the annual finale.

#9 nationally in total offense, Clemson gained 61.6 percent of their yardage through the air. Junior QB Tajh Boyd completed ⅔ of his passes for 3,550 yards and 34 touchdowns with only 13 interceptions. His 4,083 yards of total offense set a school record. WR DeAndre Hopkins also set school records for career receiving yards and touchdown receptions with at least one score in each of the last 11 games. The biggest factor in South Carolina's upset victory in the Palmetto Bowl was holding Hopkins to just one catch, a 43-yard touchdown. Senior RB Andre Ellington passed the 1,000-yard mark in the final game against the Gamecocks. The next closest rusher was Boyd with 492 yards.

Clemson's defensive coordinator was Brent Venables, who had fulfilled that same role with Oklahoma in the 2003 BCS Championship Game against LSU. He said the SEC Tigers' offense likes to "pound you into oblivion" with its ground game. Asked his reaction to that description, Les Miles replied, "I take that as a compliment."

#8 LSU and #14 Clemson met two common opponents during the season. The ACC Tigers prevailed over Auburn 26–19 in the Chick-fil-A Kickoff game to open the season, and LSU eked out a 12–10 victory at Auburn in Week 4. The Bayou Bengals edged South Carolina 23–21 while Clemson lost to the Gamecocks 27–17. LSU was installed as a four-point favorite to extend their Peach/Chick-fil-A Bowl record to 6–0. LSU hoped to continue its amazing 19-game winning streak against ACC opponents.

Sweeney summarized his feelings this way. "These guys are top 10 in defense. We're top 10 in offense. So it's pretty easy to get excited about that."

The Game

LSU let victory slip from their grasp in the final period as witnessed by the 68,027 in attendance.

FIRST QUARTER

The stars of the opening minutes were the defensive left ends on each side. LSU junior Barkevious Mingo roared through on second down to hit WR Sammy Watkins just as he took the handoff. S Craig Loston recovered the fumble on the 23. Watkins, who led Clemson in receptions and yardage in 2011 but had been plagued by injuries and illness during the 2012 season, was finished for the evening with an ankle injury. LSU, which scored 31 percent of its points off turnovers, capitalized. RB Jeremy Hill gained two, then popped through the right side 21 yards to the end zone. Drew Alleman added the PAT.

Score: LSU 7 Clemson 0 (14:05)

Clemson responded immediately, driving 75 yards in 11 plays. Crucial third down conversions came on Tahj Boyd's pass to Andrew Ellington out of the backfield and a strike down the middle to DeAndre Hopkins to the 19. After Ellington gained eight up the middle, Boyd kept over the left side and slipped past several tacklers to pay dirt.

LSU 7 Clemson 7 (9:46)

Now it was DE Malliciah Goodman's turn to disrupt the opposing offense. On third-and-seven, he burst past freshman RT Vadal Alexander to sack Mettenberger. With punter Brad Wing suspended for a violation of team rules, another Australian, freshman Jamie Keehn, boomed a 51-yarder to the 30. CB Tharold Simon knocked down Boyd's third down pass to give LSU possession at their 40 after Odell Beckham's 12-yard punt return. The first play was a repeat of LSU's last snap before their punt as Mettenberger, not the nimblest of quarterbacks, had no chance as Goodman dumped him for a loss of eight. Two plays later, the senior end struck again, causing Zach to earn an intentional grounding penalty. So Keehn launched a 53-yard kick to the nine.

All-American S Eric Reid was flagged for a high hit to move the ball to the 40. But a block in the back penalty on Clemson put them back to the 30. That's when Mingo rose up again, smothering Boyd for a 6-yard loss. LSU's next possession started strong when Hill popped outside for 8 yards and Zach, rolling out to blunt the rush, threw to Jarvis Landry for a first down at the Clemson 40. Then a blitz up the middle gave the orange-shirt Tigers their third sack of the period.

LSU 7 Clemson 7

SECOND QUARTER

Mettenberger improvised on the first play, throwing sidearm on a middle screen to RB Spencer Ware to gain 11 yards. When a roughing the passer penalty moved the ball to the 12, 272-pound junior FB J.C. Copeland came in and led Ware up the middle to the seven and again for just one yard. Then Zach lobbed to Landry in the end zone.

LSU 14 Clemson 7 (13:12)

Jarvis Landry catches a touchdown pass (*Gumbo* Class of 2013).

Clemson gained two first downs, but Mingo wreaked havoc again to force an errant third down throw. Following LSU's three-and-out, Clemson drove to their second touchdown. Keeping his composure in the face of constant pressure, Boyd connected with TE Brandon Ford and Hopkins for third down conversions to the LSU 28. RB Roderick McDowell popped up the middle to move the sticks again to the 18. Three snaps later, Hopkins broke across the middle and went low to grab Boyd's ankle-high pass in the end zone. DT Bennie Logan got a big mitt on the PAT attempt.

LSU 14 Clemson 13 (5:43)

The action continued fast and furious the rest of the half without changing the score. Clemson had the best chance for points when they marched to the LSU 34 on the strength of the fourth and fifth completions to Ford, a swing pass to Ellington, and missed tackles by the secondary. Finally, Sweeney said go for it on fourth-and-nine at the 38 with under two minutes left. Boyd ran up the middle to avoid Mingo coming around the edge and was dropped a yard short.

Clemson got the ball right back. After Beckham gained 26 yards on a pass and run to raise LSU hopes of kicking a field goal in the waning moments, freshman LB Travis Blanks snared a pass that Mettenberger forced into coverage. To make matters worse, a personal foul penalty advanced the ball to the LSU 46. But MLB Kevin Minter blitzed up the middle for his 13th tackle of the half, dropping Boyd at the Clemson 47. The ACC

Tigers used two timeouts to try to get into field goal range, but Mingo and SS Micah Eugene ended that hope with another sack.

LSU 14 Clemson 13

Every halftime statistic favored Clemson except the score: Total plays 54–24, First downs 18–6, Rush yards 71–11, Pass yards 248–106, Sacks 4–2. LSU led because of the short drive following the turnover at the beginning of the game.

Third Quarter

Right out of the locker room, it was freshman Hill who again provided the spark. He ran through the right side behind C P.J. Lonergan's block, stiff-armed the safety, and rumbled 57 yards to the end zone.

LSU 21 Clemson 13 (14:43)

The game settled back into a defensive slugfest the rest of the period. After several punts, Sam Montgomery pulled the ball away from Ellington, and Reid recovered at the Clemson 29. Hill broke loose to the nine to set up two plays that had a major impact on the outcome. First, Jeremy gained only 2 yards up the congested middle instead of a possible touchdown through the big hole at left tackle. Then CB Garry Peters knocked away a quick pass to Landry in the end zone. So LSU settled for Alleman's 20-yard field goal.

LSU 24 Clemson 13 (4:49)

Clemson gained two first downs before two false start penalties led to a punt. Then LSU also had to kick because Hill couldn't gain 2 yards on third down.

LSU 24 Clemson 13

Fourth Quarter

The 15-round heavyweight fight went down to the wire with both sides expending their last ounce of energy. On the first of a number of crucial plays he made during the period, Boyd converted a third-and-one by a foot on his 21st carry. Then he overcame a sack by firing a strike to Hopkins on a slant-in for 21 yards to the LSU 43. While dodging the rush with his "gifted feet," Tahj flipped a shovel pass to Ford to the 28. Boyd threw incomplete to Hopkins on third-and-six, but CB Jalen Collins was called for interference at the 10. But LSU dug in and stopped Boyd on the next third down on Clemson's 80th offensive play. So Chandler Catanzaro kicked a 26-yard field goal.

LSU 24 Clemson 16 (9:26)

Needing to make some first downs to give their weary defense some rest, the LSU offense went three-and-out when Goodman and NG Grady Jarrett sacked Mettenberger. That gave Goodman 3½ sacks after just four all season. Clemson then started another relentless drive. On third-and-one at the 32, Boyd kept for three. After a defensive delay of game call moved the chains, offensive coordinator Chad Morris called for a hook-and-ladder play that succeeded to the 23. Tahj converted yet another third down by flipping a pass to Ford just beyond SS Micah Eugene to the 14. Two plays later, Boyd fired a bullet to Hopkins a step ahead of Reid at the back of the end zone. Because of the

S Craig Loston makes a tackle (*Gumbo* Class of 2013).

missed extra point in the first half, Clemson had to go for two to tie, but Minter blitzed up the middle, forcing an incompletion.

LSU 24 Clemson 22 (2:47)

Visions of the last minutes of the Alabama game danced in LSU fans' minds. With all three timeouts left, Clemson pooch-kicked, Beckham returning to the 39. Needing to get first downs to force Clemson to use its timeouts, Mettenberger started with an 8-yard pass to Kadron Boone. Then came a puzzling play in which Zach rolled right and threw badly on the run to Landry. Not only did the play fail to gain, but the incompletion stopped the clock. Surely Miles will want a run on third-and-two? No, another pass, which was batted down at the line of scrimmage. Keehn's punt was a tad too long and bounced into the end zone to stop the clock at 1:39. The disastrous offensive sequence used up less than a minute and left Clemson with all their timeouts. Miles explained afterward why three passing plays were called. "We were not running the football. They were in a position where they outnumbered us in the run."

If ever LSU needed Mingo, it was now. But he was on the sideline with a stomach ailment. After two incompletions, Montgomery recorded LSU's fifth sack to set up the play of the game. On fourth-and-16, Hopkins made a sliding catch at the 40 beyond Reid, who might have deflected the ball had he turned around. "We thought if we stayed on top of the routes, we'd get the ball to come out early with some pressure," explained defensive coordinator John Chavis. "Sometimes you live by the sword and die by the sword. We thought it was the right call at the right time." The agonizing drive continued, interrupted by more defenders leaving the field with injuries.

> 0:52—7-yard pass to Hopkins at the sideline to break the bowl record for receiving yards. Montgomery left the game.
>
> 0:45—Incompletion to Hopkins but a questionable interference call on Reid, who stayed down.
>
> 0:42—Quick pass to Ford for 3 yards to the LSU 39. Timeout Clemson.
>
> 0:37—With the LSU secondary playing off the receivers, pass to Hopkins, his 13th catch for 13 yards to the 26.
>
> 0:30—Slant pass to Adam Humphries in front of the cornerback for 9 yards. Loston injured, stopping the clock.
>
> 0:25—On Clemson's 100th play, Boyd takes a loss of three to position the ball in the middle of the field. Clemson lets the clock run down and calls timeout.
>
> 0:02—Catanzaro kicks a 37-yard field goal as time expires.

Final Score: Clemson 25 LSU 24

To no one's surprise, Tahj Boyd won the MVP award for completing 36-of-50 passes for 346 yards and two touchdowns and rushing 29 times for 22 yards and one TD.

Postgame

Coach Miles praised the Clemson quarterback. "Tajh Boyd was phenomenal. I did not expect the heroic, if you will, efforts that he had." Miles cited the inability of his offensive line to protect Mettenberger as the undoing of his offense. "When you can't protect your passer, it becomes hard to run. If we protect the passer a little bit, the running game comes to life. ... The reality of it is, one team played a hundred plays on defense and one team played 50." Les praised his middle linebacker. "Kevin Minter is an all-in guy. Just a great leader, a great player. Instinctive." He finished with 19 tackles despite missing plays in the second half because of leg cramps. That gave him 130 for the season, the most since Bradie James in 2002.

Minter had nothing but kind words to say about the Clemson quarterback. "There's a reason why Tajh Boyd is an All-American. We hit him pretty hard, we came after him and brought the heat. I can't say enough about that guy." RB Jeremy Hill gained 124 of LSU's 219 yards of total offense against a team that surrendered 411 yards per game during the season. "They made it tough for us by stacking eight or nine guys in the box. ... But we left some plays out there. We didn't convert third downs and put our defense on the spot. Late in the game, we had good position but just didn't execute."

Dabo Sweeney exulted, "It's been 31 years since Clemson's won 11 ball games. It's been a steady progress. ... These guys fought every frickin' play. They fought for every patch of grass. They overcame adversity. They played with a lot of love and toughness. ...

You can't win a national championship until you learn how to win games like this. This was a landmark win." Dabo didn't fault Miles for throwing the ball on LSU's last possession. "I think he was trying to win the game. I know he felt he needed to get a first down."

Catanzaro said the blocked extra point in the second quarter didn't cause him to doubt his chance to make the winning field. "I was ready when the opportunity came to me. It was next-kick mentality. I was so thankful for the opportunity."

Thirty-two 2012 Tigers—the most in school history for any team—played pro football: LB Kwon Alexander, OL Vadal Alexander, LB Lamin Barrow, WR Odell Beckham, DB Jalen Collins, OL La'el Collins, DT Lavar Edwards, DT Ego Ferguson, LS Reid Ferguson, RB Michael Ford, RB Jeremy Hill, DE Danielle Hunter, DT Anthony Johnson, LB Deion Jones, WR Jarvis Landry, DL Bennie Logan, DB Craig Loston, RB Terrance Magee, DB Ronald Martin, QB Zach Mettenberger, DB Jalen Mills, DL Barkevious Mingo, LB Kevin Minter, DE Sam Montgomery, DB Eric Reid, WR Russell Shepard, DB Tharold Simon, LB Corey Thompson, G Trai Turner, RB Spencer Ware, P Brad Wing, and WR James Wright.

Outback Bowl vs. Iowa

"Old school football"

Raymond James Stadium, Tampa, Florida
January 1, 2014

A coaching change improved the Tiger attack for the 2013 season.

LSU's Season

Still being criticized for his offense, Coach Les Miles hired an old friend as his offensive coordinator for 2013. Malcolm "Cam" Cameron had been an assistant with Les at Michigan in the 1980s. Most recently the offensive coordinator for the Baltimore Ravens, Cam brought an NFL flavor to the Tiger attack. Passing improved from 200.5 yards per game in 2012 to 265 yards per game. The Tigers increased their per game rushing yardage from 173.7 to 202.3 for a total offensive improvement of 59 yards per game—LSU's best statistics since the 2007 BCS Championship Team. The points per game average went from 29.8 (59th in the nation) to 35.8 (23rd). The Tigers led the nation in third down conversions at 58.6 percent.

Senior Zach Mettenberger had one of the finest seasons for a quarterback in LSU history. He improved from a 58.8 completion percentage in 2012 to 64.9, from 12 touchdown passes to 22, and in Passer Rating from 128.3 to 171.4. The 2013 Tigers became the first team in Southeastern Conference history to feature a 3,000-yard passer—Mettenberger, two 1,000-yard receivers—Odell Beckham, Jr., and Jarvis Landry, and a 1,000-yard running back—Jeremy Hill. Beckham won the Paul Hornung Award as the nation's most versatile player. He led the SEC and was third nationally in all-purpose yards with 185.2 per game. Odell needed 175 yards in the bowl game to shatter the SEC single-season record of 2,396 yards set by Kentucky's Randall Cobb in 2010.

Unfortunately, the defense retrogressed in large measure because of the loss of many stalwarts to the NFL—DT Bennie Logan, DE Barkevious Mingo, LB Kevin Minter, DE Sam Montgomery, S Eric Reid, and CB Tharold Simon. The 2013 Tigers gave up 143.2 yards per game on the ground compared to 101.6 in '12 and 22.0 points per game compared to 17.5. The game at Georgia epitomized the 9–3 season. The Tigers scored 41 points but gave up 44. The other two losses also came on the road at Ole Miss (27–24) and Alabama (38–17). On the positive side, LSU handed SEC champion Auburn their only defeat of the season, 35–21, in the rain at Tiger Stadium. Also John Chavis's defense held Texas

A&M QB Johnny Manziel and his offense to their lowest offensive output in Kevin Sumlin's two seasons as head coach.

Mettenberger would miss the bowl game because of a torn ACL he suffered in the fourth quarter of the final game against Arkansas. True freshman Anthony Jennings would make his first start in the Outback Bowl after leading LSU on a 99-yard game-winning drive against the Razorbacks in the final two minutes.

The Opponent

Like LSU, Iowa was led by an experienced head coach, Kirk Ferentz in his 15th season. He had been voted Big Ten Coach of the Year in 2002, 2004, and 2009, putting him in the elite company of Hayden Fry, Bo Schembechler, and Joe Paterno as the only three-time recipients.

When Iowa sat at 5–4 with three games left, two of which were on the road, the Hawkeyes were in danger of not bowling for the second straight season. But they won all three—at Purdue 38–14, Michigan 24–21, and at Nebraska 38–17.

The Hawkeyes boasted the #7 defense in the nation, allowing only 18 points per game. A unit can't rank that high without having outstanding linebackers, and Iowa's trio finished 1–2–3 in tackles. MLB James Morris made first team All-Big Ten and was a finalist for the LOTT Impact Trophy presented annually to the defensive player of the year in college football. Anthony Hitchens led the team with 102 tackles, four more than Morris, including 13 behind the line. Christian Kirksey had 97 tackles with four for losses.

The offense averaged 190 yards per game on the ground. TB Mark Weisman gained 937 yards on 208 carries for a 4.5 average. Sophomore QB Jake Rudock completed 60.2 percent of his passes for 2,281 yards and 18 TDs. His favorite target was WR Kevonte Martin-Manley, who caught 39 passes for 384 yards. Martin-Manley led the Big Ten in punt returns with a 16.2-yard average and two touchdowns.

LSU fans bought just 7,000 of the school's allotted 12,000 tickets. Would the football team have more enthusiasm for the game than the fans? The oddsmakers thought so, making #14 LSU a 7.5-point favorite over the unranked Hawkeyes.

Heavy rains in the morning evolved into intermittent showers the rest of the day, making the field slippery.

The Game

The 51,296 fans in attendance saw a game that featured, in the words of ESPN commentator Jon Gruden, "old school football."

FIRST QUARTER

Following their game plan built for the young quarterback, LSU ran the ball eight straight times in a 77-yard drive to a touchdown. They started with a play that would work time and time again. QB Anthony Jennings pitched back to 230-pound Jeremy Hill, who followed FB Connor Neighbors through a big hole at right tackle opened by blocks from RT Jerald Hawkins and pulling RG Trai Turner for 42 yards to the Iowa 33. Aided by an offside penalty, the Tigers soon reached the three. From there, Jennings ran an option to the left side. Seeing OLB Christian Kirksey staying wide to cover the pitch man, Hill, Anthony scampered into the end zone.

LSU 7 Iowa 0 (10:59)

The best thing that happened for Iowa on their opening possession was S Jalen Mills' late hit penalty on a third-down incompletion that gave the Hawkeyes a first down at their 36. QB Jake Rudock then hit All-Big Ten TE C.J. Fiedorowicz for another 10 yards. But the next three plays lost two, forcing a punt into the end zone. Fiedorowicz said, "Their alignments were a little different than … they had done the whole year. That makes it tough, especially when you game plan."

An exchange of punts following three-and-outs put the Tigers at their two. Jennings completed his first pass, a quick throw to Jarvis Landry for a first down. But a penalty and a sack set LSU back, and Jamie Keehn, an Aussie feeling right at home in the Outback Bowl, punted 54 yards to the 38. The Hawkeyes ended the period with only 22 yards of offense on 14 plays.

LSU 7 Iowa 0

SECOND QUARTER

After a holding penalty derailed the Tiger advance, Iowa gained two first downs, both on passes to tight ends. But the advance stopped when freshman CB Tre'Davious White intercepted an underthrown pass on the seven. Oddly, the Iowa defense forcing a punt led to a break for LSU when Kevonte Martin-Manley dropped the ball, and WR James Wright recovered at the Iowa 39. On third-and-13, Jennings rolled right and threw to senior RB Alfred Blue, who carried to the 25. The rest of the yardage was gained on the ground—Blue for six, then one; Hill for four and then the final 14 behind LT La'el Collins.

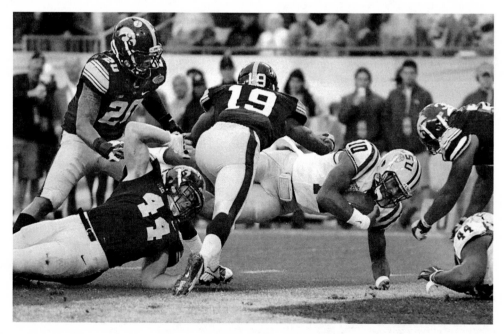

Anthony Jennings dives ahead for more yardage (Baton Rouge *Advocate*).

LSU 14 Iowa 0 (7:23)

Neither team made a first down the remainder of the quarter. A poor kick gave LSU fine field position at the Iowa 36 with time to add to their lead, but they couldn't take advantage.

The Hawkeyes ended the half with just 73 yards on 31 plays, including five three-and-outs. They were a pitiful one-for-nine on third downs.

LSU 14 Iowa 0

Third Quarter

Iowa came out with more fire in the belly, taking the kickoff and driving into LSU territory. Two third-down strikes to WR Jacob Hillyer gained first downs to the 21. But the Tigers built a wall there, and Mike Meyer missed a 35-yard field goal.

Beckham made one of his fantastic one-handed catches that he became known for in the NFL when Jennings looped a pass that Odell snared with his right hand behind the defender to the Iowa 48. But two plays later, the entire complexion of the game changed when Jennings, with plenty of time, threw too high down the middle into the hands of DB John Lowdermilk, who motored down the sideline 71 yards for a touchdown. Or did he? Replay took several minutes to determine that he dropped the ball just before he crossed the goal line. The ball bounced into the end zone, but no one from either team claimed it. So the six points were taken off the board, and Iowa given possession at the ½ line. The Tigers dropped Wiseman at the two and forced a throw away before the 235-pound halfback banged over right tackle into the end zone.

LSU 14 Iowa 7 (5:52)

How would the freshman Jennings react to his interception? Miles said afterward, "He was tight as heck. This was his first interception of note, and he came to the sidelines just sick. He has to drop it. It's the middle of the game. There were some lessons that he learned that will benefit him as he goes forward." To take the pressure off, Blue ran twice and Hill once for a first down at the 38. On third-and-two, Jennings flipped a short pass to FB Neighbors to move the sticks to midfield. But on the next third down, Jennings held the ball too long and was sacked.

LSU 14 Iowa 7

Fourth Quarter

With Rudock sidelined with an injured knee, redshirt freshman C.J. Beathard quarterbacked the Hawkeyes the rest of the way. RB Jordan Canzaneri pulled off Iowa's best run of the afternoon—13 yards. Starting with third-and-one, the Big 12 officiating crew confused everyone, including themselves, with their calls. Beathard sneaked for the first down, but the play was nullified because LSU was not given time to match an offensive substitution even though the livid Iowa staff said they hadn't substituted. When the play was run again, LSU was ready and stopped Beathard short. The referee wrongly signaled LSU's ball until his crew corrected him. Boos rained down from the Iowa side. When the Hawkeyes punted, a flag was dropped on LSU for an illegal substitution. Replay showed the 12th Tiger got off the field before the snap. Given new life, the Hawkeyes tried

Odell Beckham, Jr., stiff-arms a would-be tackler (*Gumbo* Class of 2014).

a double pass, and S Craig Loston hit the receiver just as the ball arrived. No flag. Boo! So Ferentz ordered a fake punt, but LB Tahj Jones stopped Wiseman a yard short.

LSU couldn't make a first down, giving Iowa the ball on their 20 after a touchback. How much gas was left in the Tiger defense's tank? Needing to convert on third-and-one, Beathard swept right end for a first down at the 40. Then he hit TE Fiedorowicz for 34 yards to the 26. Facing fourth down and less than a yard, Iowa tried to surprise the Tigers with a rollout pass, but sophomore LB Deion Jones broke through and hurried Beathard into a bad throw that Loston intercepted. A penalty on the runback put the ball at the eight. "They covered the pass. They covered the run," said Coach Ferentz about the Tiger defense. "They're not a finesse outfit."

Needing to control the ball, LSU got more than that as they replicated their first drive of the game. Back to back Hill runs gained 28 and 20 yards. After taking a breather for two plays, Jeremy came back in and outdid himself, breaking through right tackle, bursting through two tacklers, and sprinting 37 yards to the end zone.

LSU 21 Iowa 7 (2:02)

Just when the LSU fans thought they could start celebrating, Jordan Cotton returned the kickoff 96 yards to the four. Then came another controversial play. Jermauria Rasco hit Beathard as he tried to pass, and DT Quentin Thomas recovered the loose ball. But replay review ruled it an incomplete pass. Beathard then tossed a touchdown pass to Hillyer.

LSU 21 Iowa 14 (1:42)

With the Tiger faithful wondering else could go wrong, the onside kick went right to Neighbors.

Final Score: LSU 21 Iowa 14

Hill won the MVP award for gaining 216 yards, the most by an LSU back in nine years. "I just took it on my shoulders that I needed to make plays to win this football game," said Jeremy. "Our O-line and our fullbacks did a great job, and it was just up to me to make a few guys miss."

Postgame

The smash-mouth contest evoked fond memories for coach Miles. "I certainly did enjoy it like it was 20 years ago." He called his defensive unit's play "spectacular. There was no question they were going to play like this." Les also praised his punter, who had a 46.9-yard average with four punts downed inside the Iowa 20. "How about Jamie Keehn? … He always could hit the ball like that but, bang!, he hit another one. We needed him, and he came through big-time." Asked about his young quarterback's performance, Miles replied, "He did some things that he would like to have back. But he managed the game and came away with a victory."

Jeremy Hill ended the season with 1,401 yards rushing, second best in school history behind Charles Alexander (1,686 yards in 1977). He too was asked to comment on Jennings' game. "I think Anthony did a great job finishing the game, making the right checks at the line and clock management and not giving Iowa a chance to get back on the field." Odell Beckham agreed. "We cut the playbook down a little bit so Anthony could make the plays, and I thought he did a great job of managing the clock and getting the offense going." Connor Neighbors added, "It's hard for someone like that to step in and lead a team. But every time we were in a huddle, he'd tell us to shut up, because we'd be jawing, but he'd take control of the team and lead us to victory."

Thirty 2013 Tigers played pro football: LB Kwon Alexander, OL Vadal Alexander, LB Lamin Barrow, WR Odell Beckham, LB Kendell Beckwith, RB Alfred Blue, LB Tashawn Bower, DB Jalen Collins, OL La'el Collins, DT Ego Ferguson, LS Reid Ferguson, OT Jerald Hawkins, RB Jeremy Hill, DE Danielle Hunter, DT Anthony Johnson, LB Deion Jones, WR Jarvis Landry, DB Craig Loston, RB Terrance Magee, DB Ronald Martin, QB Zach Mettenberger, DB Jalen Mills, DE Lewis Neal, OL Ethan Pocic, LB Duke Riley, CB Rashard Robinson, LB Corey Thompson, G Trai Turner, DB Tre'Davious White, and WR James Wright.

Franklin American Mortgage
Music City Bowl vs. Notre Dame

*A disappointing end
to a disappointing season*

LP Field, Nashville, Tennessee
December 30, 2014

A disappointing season ended with a disappointing bowl loss.

LSU's Season

With the south end zone expansion increasing Tiger Stadium's capacity to 102,231, the Tigers continued their slide down the SEC standings. Since 2011's 8–0 record and conference championship, LSU had gone 6–2, 5–3, and now 4–4 in SEC games. The overall record stood at 28–11 since the loss to Alabama in the 2012 BCS Championship Game.

For the second year in a row, LSU had more underclassmen declare for the NFL Draft than any other team. Included were QB Zach Mettenberger, WRs Odell Beckham, Jr., and Jarvis Landry, and RB Jeremy Hill. Hill was replaced by New Orleans freshman Leonard Fournette, ranked the #1 running back in the 2014 recruiting class. He didn't disappoint, gaining 905 yards (5.1 avg) with eight touchdowns. He might have gained more had the passing game been more efficient, but finding a replacement for Mettenberger proved difficult. The Tigers averaged 163.9 passing yards per game compared to 251 in 2013. Sophomore Anthony Jennings, who managed the victory in the Outback Bowl when Mettenberger was injured, started 11 of the 12 games but completed only 48.8 percent of his passes for 1,460 yards. As a result, one writer described LSU's style of offense, which gained 57 percent of its yardage on the ground, as "clock-churning, run-heavy."

The season started with a stirring come-from-behind victory over Wisconsin in Houston. After routing Sam Houston State and Louisiana-Monroe, the Tigers saw their 14-game winning streak against Mississippi State come to an end as Louisiana native Dak Prescott led the 34–29 victory in Tiger Stadium. A rent-a-win preceded a disastrous trip to Auburn, which clobbered LSU 41-7, the Tigers' worst defeat since 2002's 31-0 loss to Alabama. But the Tigers bounced back with a thrilling 30–27 last-minute victory at Florida on Colby Delahoussaye's 50-yard field goal with three seconds left. Two home wins followed, an easy one over Kentucky and a tight one over Ole Miss. Then #4 Alabama had to kick a tying field goal in the last seconds to get a chance to win the game in over-time. The tough loss led to another one the next week in frigid Fayetteville as the desul-tory offense managed only 123 yards in the 17–0 defeat. The season ended with another head-scratching performance as the offense, displaying some new wrinkles, gained nearly 500 yards in the 23–17 win at Texas A&M in a game that was not as close as the score indicated. Fournette had his most productive outing of the season—146 yards on 19 attempts (7.7 ypc).

The victory extended LSU's streak of winning at least eight games to 15 years—the longest stretch by any Power Five conference team. Through all the ups and downs of the offense, the bedrock of the team was the defense, which finished first in the SEC in pass-ing yards allowed and in total yards allowed. The Tigers ended the season #22 in the AP poll and #23 in the Coaches and CFP rankings.

Before bowl preparations started, Les Miles faced the same situation that confronted him at the end of the 2011 regular season. Michigan fired Brady Hoke after three years, provoking another Miles-to-Michigan rumor mill. But Les was never on his alma mater's radar screen. Their target was San Francisco 49ers coach Jim Harbaugh, a "Michigan Man" who agreed to leave the NFL in mid–December. The uncertainty cost LSU a coach, but it wouldn't be Les Miles.

The Opponent

Notre Dame didn't enter the bowl game with momentum, having lost five of their last six games after a 6–0 start. The Fighting Irish welcomed back dual-threat QB Ever-ett Golson after a year away because of academic issues. He didn't throw an interception in the first three games but put the ball in enemy hands 14 times in the next nine contests, including four picks in the devastating 55–21 loss at Arizona State that started the spiral of four straight losses to end the season. When Golson struggled in the 49–14 loss at USC to end the season, coach Brian Kelly replaced him with sophomore Malik Zaire late in the first half. Ranked #5 when they were 6–0, the Irish fell out of the Top 25 after ten games. Golson ended the season #2 in the FBS in turnovers.

Another reason for the late season decline was a slew of injuries on the defense the likes of which coordinator Brian VanGorder had never seen. Only three starters played in all 12 games. Injuries beset 14 defenders, with 11 out for the season.

Sophomore Tarean Folston led the Irish in rushing—816 yards, 5.3 ypc. Folston was next highest in yards gained with 526. But under NCAA rules, his 249 yards in sacks low-ered his net yards. Another sophomore, Will Fuller, had by far the most receptions, 71, for 1,037 yards. The next highest was sophomore Corey Robinson with 40/539.

The game was likely to come down to which team could get more consistent play from the quarterback position.

In the last days before kickoff, rumors surfaced that Texas A&M had contacted LSU defensive coordinator John Chavis about the Aggies' coordinator vacancy. Adding fuel to the fire was the fact that Chavis had not signed the contract extension that had sat on his desk for weeks. He was reportedly upset by a clause that stipulated he would be com-pensated for just six months should Miles leave for another school. Chavis would accept A&M's offer the day after the bowl game.

The Game

This game made the 60,419 watchers wonder why LSU was an 8½ point favorite.

FIRST QUARTER

Coach Kelly started southpaw sophomore Malik Zaire at quarterback. Using Zaire's running ability and giving him easy throws to get comfortable, the Irish marched 66 yards in 15 plays to a touchdown, using up almost eight minutes. The four first downs were achieved by a rollout strike from Zaire to WR C.J. Prosise, a quarterback keep up the middle to the LSU 40, a run by Tarean Foster to the 29, and—the killer—Zaire's run out of the pocket on fourth-and-nine to the 18. The touchdown came on third-and-four on a wide receiver screen to Will Fuller, who had an open highway to the end zone. It was the first TD pass of Malik's career.

Score: Notre Dame 7 LSU 0 (7:04)

Showing nothing new, LSU failed to gain a first down. So the Irish got the ball right back on their 18 and began moving immediately as Zaire ran up the middle to the 44. Then he found Prosise to the LSU 29. But the defense stiffened and stopped Zaire a yard short on third down. Kelly rolled the dice on fourth down, but DE Tashawn Bower forced Malik deep as he tried to round left end, allowing sensational freshman S Jamal Adams to dump him for a 4-yard loss.

Seeing how much trouble Notre Dame had with USC's no huddle spread attack, LSU unveiled the hurry up offense Cam Cameron had installed for the game. The result was an 8-play, 76-yard drive that took only 2:36 to tie the game. After Darrel Williams gained 16 yards on two carries, the Tigers ran their version of the "fumblerooski." They lined up in a bunch formation with WR Travin Dural crouched down next to QB Anthony Jennings behind the center. Dural took the handoff, delayed as the line pulled to the right, then swept left for 24 yards to the ND 31. Leonard Fournette rambled for 18, then five more. After an incompletion, Leonard stepped to the right, then took a pitchout around left end to the end zone.

Notre Dame 7 LSU 7 (0:05)

SECOND QUARTER

Senior Everett Golson directed a drive deep into LSU territory. He completed a crucial third-and-eight pass to WR Chris Brown to the 23. After Everett kept for six, Zaire replaced him and two plays later ran up the middle for a 7-yard touchdown.

Notre Dame 14 LSU 7 (11:04)

It took just 12 seconds for LSU to tie the game. Fournette took the kickoff on the goal line, rocketed up the middle, swung to the right, and raced to the end zone.

Notre Dame 14 LSU 14 (10:52)

Good news: LSU tied the game. Bad news: The Tiger defense took the field with no respite. Starting from the 41, Zaire directed another scoring drive. Defensive holding gave the Irish a first down at the LSU 40. On third-and-seven, Golson entered and was creamed on a blitz by DE Jermauria Rasco just after he threw the ball up for grabs. But the luck of the Irish kicked in as the ball landed in the hands of WR Will Fuller for a first down at the 26. Reenter Zaire, who converted third-and-11 with a pass to Fuller to the five. After Rasco dumped him for a loss of one, Malik handed to Folston who followed his quarterback across the goal line at the left pylon.

Notre Dame 21 LSU 14 (6:12)

LSU used up the rest of the half with a ponderous drive that ended with the game's most controversial play. The big gains were a 17-yard pass to TE DeSean Smith to the ND 45, a 6-yard run on third-and-one by Terrance Magee, and a 6-yard carry by Darrel Williams to make it first-and-goal at the five. LSU took a timeout with 30 seconds left to set up the most crucial sequence of the game.

Jennings wanted to pass but was sacked for a loss of two. Timeout LSU at 0:24.

Jennings kept to the three. Timeout LSU at 0:17.

Jennings threw to WR John Diarse, who went out of bounds at the two.

The Tigers set up for a field goal but instead ran a play they had practiced for weeks. Holder Brad Kragthorpe took the snap and tried to score through the left side. He disappeared into a pile of tacklers at the goal line. The officials ruled he did not score. A lengthy review showed that Brad extended the ball over the goal line, but no angle gave a clear view of when his knee went down. So the call on the field stood. After the game, Miles said, "The guy that carried the ball said he absolutely scored. Kids will be kids, but this guy's going to tell the truth."

Notre Dame 21 LSU 14

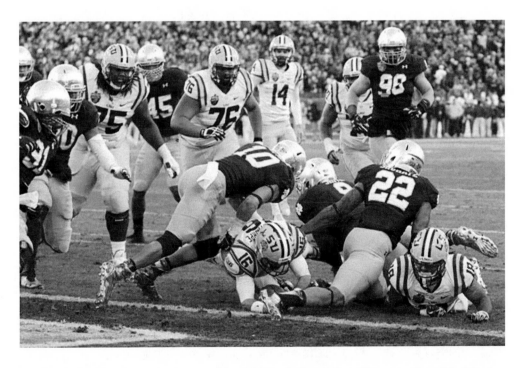

Brad Kragthorpe tries to score on a fake field goal play. Other Tigers are Evan Washington (75), Josh Boutte (76), Trent Domingue (14), and Terrence Magee (18) (Baton Rouge *Advocate*).

Talking to the ESPN sideline reporter before the kickoff, Miles said his defense would make adjustments to stop the quarterback runs. He also implied he had more trick plays up his sleeve.

Third Quarter

On LSU's first play, Jennings took the ball in shotgun formation, took several steps as if to run, then lobbed a pass to Diarse running behind the secondary for a 75-yard touchdown—the longest passing play in Music City Bowl history.

LSU 21 Notre Dame 21 (14:46)

Zaire led the Irish to two first downs, one on a pass to Brown, the other on a Folston run to the LSU 45. But a loss of four on a screen pass led to a punt to the nine. The Tigers moved smartly across midfield as Cameron called one of the new plays he put in for the Texas A&M game, a jet sweep by Dural for 15 yards. Then Jennings hit TE Smith to the ND 49. But a botched exchange between Anthony and Fournette produced a fumble that Notre Dame recovered at their 45.

When three plays gained only two, LSU received the punt at the 11. That's when Fournette struck again. From his deep tailback position, he took a handoff and with the aid of blocks by LT La'El Collins, LG Vadal Alexander, and FB Connor Neighbors, tore through the left side into the clear for the longest run in bowl history. "They blocked," Leonard said. "I saw everybody was on the ground. I saw the gap, and I took it. I was tired at the end."

LSU 28 Notre Dame 21 (6:14)

The Fighting Irish answered back, going 67 yards in four plays. The touchdown came on another long play—Prosise's 50-yard scamper around the right side.

LSU 28 Notre Dame 28 (4:15)

Each offense went backwards on their next series, and the period ended with Dural running another jet sweep to the LSU 37.

LSU 28 Notre Dame 28

Fourth Quarter

Which young quarterback would make the key plays that produce victory? Jennings passed to Smith for a first down at the ND 42. Kenny Hilliard ran twice for 11 yards as LSU inched into field goal territory. But the Tigers soon faced fourth-and-two at the 23. Sophomore Trent Domingue came in to try the field goal. He had attempted just three during the season, making two, the longest being 31 yards. He booted a line drive that had no chance, bouncing off the blockers.

LSU stopped Zaire for no gain on third down to get the ball back at their 20. The Tigers' cause was hampered when Fournette limped off after gaining eight. Magee replaced him and got the first down. Jennings kept on third-and-three but was stopped a yard short. The Irish started from their 15 with 5:41 left after the punt. Zaire found WR Amir Carlisle for nine, but Adams dropped Folston for a 2-yard loss. On third-and-three, Malik looked for a receiver, then ran out of the pocket for a first down at the 30. Since his helmet came off when he was tackled, he had to leave for a play. Golson stayed in for two plays, the second one being a pass thrown with authority to Fuller after a false start penalty to make it third-and-one at the 39. Boos rang out from some Notre Dame fans when Zaire returned to the field. He kept for 3 yards and another first down. An incompletion brought Golson back. Coach Kelly explained his thinking. "It was a feeling of what I believed they could execute in a very crucial situation of the game. That's how I called the game the last series, fit it with plays I thought they felt comfortable with." An incompletion brought up third-and-10 with 1:44 on the clock. Could the LSU defense get a stop and send the game to overtime? With no pressure, Golson found his secondary receiver, TE Ben Koyack, to the LSU 46 for ND's 11th third-down conversion in 17 tries. Then Folston took a pass over the middle to the 31. A wide receiver screen to Brown gained eight. Following an LSU timeout with 0:40 on the clock, Zaire, the better runner, gained another eight to the 14. Then he ran again for no gain but put the ball on the left hashmark and called timeout with four seconds left. LSU used its last two timeouts to ice the kicker to no avail. Senior Kyle Brindza had missed six of nine field goal attempts in the last five games, but he came through, booting the 32-yarder through the uprights as time expired.

Final Score: Notre Dame 31 LSU 28

Postgame

Les Miles praised his freshman running back. "Leonard Fournette distinguished himself in this game today. Very special player." Asked about John Chavis, Les replied, "I could tell you John Chavis was very productive for us. He's had a great career at LSU. That's all I'm going to say." But then he added, "We understood he was unsigned. We understood why. Again, as far as I'm concerned, I'm going to try to pitch him again. We like Chief."

Leonard Fournette established the single-season LSU freshman rushing record in a performance that many called a Heisman Trophy launching party for 2016. "It's exciting, but we didn't get the 'W,' man. It kind of hurts right now that the seniors went out like that." He added, "I'm really not worried about the Heisman. Just getting better for next season. We have a long way to go."

Asked by the sideline reporter to evaluate Zaire's play, coach Kelly said, "He did what we asked him to do. We controlled the clock and kept Fournette off the field." Later he added, "We wanted to be challenged. We were disappointed in the way we played obviously at the end of the year, and our guys wanted the opportunity to finish the season the right way."

Malik Zaire won the game's MVP award. "I felt like I could contribute to the team. Life is about these opportunities that we get each and every day and taking advantage of them. … It's a blessing that I got that opportunity, and I didn't want to ruin it for this football team. Coming off the losses that we had, it was important to take advantage and do whatever it took to win."

Twenty-two 2014 Tigers played pro football: DB Jamal Adams, LB Kwon Alexander, OL Vadal Alexander, LB Kendell Beckwith, LB Tashawn Bower, DB Jalen Collins, OL La'el Collins, WR Malachi Dupre, LS Reid Ferguson, RB Leonard Fournette, DL Davon Godchaux, OT Jerald Hawkins, DE Danielle Hunter, LB Deion Jones, RB Terrence Magee, DB Ronald Martin, DB Jalen Mills, DE Lewis Neal, OL Ethan Pocic, LB Duke Riley, DB Tre'Davious White, and RB Darrel Williams.

AdvoCare V100 Texas Bowl
vs. Texas Tech

"We just kept running it down their throat"

NRG Stadium, Houston, Texas
December 29, 2015

After the disappointing 8–5 record in 2014, Les Miles made changes to his coaching staff.

LSU's Season

Former Alabama defensive coordinator Kevin Steele replaced John Chavis, who would now compete against the Tigers at Texas A&M. Former Ole Miss head coach Ed Orgeron became the new defensive line coach following Brick Haley's departure for Texas.

LSU lost only three underclassmen to the NFL, which was a decrease from the 11 lost in 2012 and seven in 2013. For the third consecutive season, LSU signed a top-ten recruiting class. Most importantly, RB Leonard Fournette returned for his sophomore season after gaining 1,034 yards as a freshman despite sharing carries with two other backs.

The Tigers began at #14 in the AP poll and advanced to #4 after starting 7–0. Running behind an offensive line in which four of the five starters were drafted by the NFL, Fournette rose to the top of the list of Heisman candidates by gaining at least 150 yards in all seven victories.

- 159 yards in the 21–19 road victory over #25 Mississippi State and their dynamic QB Dak Prescott.
- 228 yards in the 45–21 rout of #18 Auburn.
- 224 yards in the 34–24 victory at Syracuse.
- 233 yards in the 44–22 pasting of Eastern Michigan to become the first SEC player to rush for 200 yards in three straight games.
- 158 yards in the 45–24 win over South Carolina in a game moved to Tiger Stadium because of massive flooding around Columbia, South Carolina.
- 180 yards in the 35–28 win against #8 Florida.
- 150 yards in the 48–20 shellacking of Western Kentucky.

Being able to hand the ball to Fournette made the job easier for QB Brandon Harris, who beat out Anthony Jennings for the starting position. Taking every snap in the seven victories, the sophomore from Bossier City completed 58.5 percent of his passes for 1,098 yards and an excellent touchdown to interception ratio of 9:0.

The stage was set for the trip to Alabama, ranked #4 because of a loss to Ole Miss in Week 3. Not only did LSU's hope of winning the SEC West crash and burn, but so did Fournette's Heisman hopes. The Tide held him to just 31 yards net in 19 carries. The Tiger offense that had averaged 466 yards, 21.3 first downs, and 38.9 points per game gained a mere 182 yards and made just 12 first downs in the 28–12 defeat. Fournette would finish sixth in the Heisman voting.

Coaches always preach: Don't let one defeat turn into two. But the wounded Tigers not only lost to unranked Arkansas at home 31–14 but also fell at Ole Miss the following week as well, 38–17. Rumors spread that key boosters had lost confidence in Miles.

Amid talk of LSU wooing Florida State coach Jimbo Fisher, the Tigers faced Texas A&M in what would "probably" be the last game of Miles's 11-year career at LSU. That was such a foregone conclusion that the players carried Les off the field on their shoulders at the end of the lackluster 19–7 victory. However, the post-game news conference took an expected turn. Instead of announcing Miles's firing, Athletic Director Joe Alleva said Les would return for the 2016 season. Chancellor F. King Alexander added that the decision was made at halftime and admitted that concerns about the $15 million buyout of Miles's contract was a factor at a time when Alexander was lobbying the state legislature to increase the university's funding. No one seemed more surprised by the decision than Miles himself.

The Opponent

LSU's first appearance in the Texas Bowl would feature an interesting duel between contrasting offenses. Behind the first running back in SEC history to gain 2,000 yards in a season, the Tigers, #20 in the final BCS rankings, led the SEC and ranked #9 nationally in rushing. The 7–5 unranked Texas Tech Red Raiders finished second nationally in scoring average (46.5), passing offense (391.3), and total offense (588.1). Sophomore QB Patrick Mahomes threw for 4,283 yards, more than twice Brandon Harris's total, and 32 touchdowns, 20 more than Harris. The Second Coming of Johnny Manziel, Mahomes also gained 484 yards rushing. In addition, Tech boasted a 1,000-yard rusher in senior DeAndre Washington (1,455 yards) and a 1,000-yard receiver—5'7" senior Jakeem Grant (1,143 yards). He also set Tech's career kickoff return record—2,068 yards (24.9 average) with four touchdowns.

Thirty-six-year-old Kliff Kingsbury was finishing his third season as head coach at his alma mater where he threw for 12,423 yards and 95 touchdowns over four seasons in head coach Mike Leach's "Air Raid" offense. That no-huddle scheme called for passes twice as often as runs. The quarterback could audible on any play based on what the defense showed him at the line of scrimmage. Another feature was the wider splits of the offensive linemen, which allowed easier blitz lanes but also forced the edge rushers to cover more ground to reach the quarterback, who could throw quick, short passes to speedy receivers running free into open areas to offset any blitz.

The Red Raiders had to win their last two games against Kansas State (59–44) and

Texas (48–45) to finish 7–5. Tech had no victories over ranked FBS teams but did win at Arkansas, which later defeated LSU.

It didn't take an Einstein to figure out the Tigers' bowl strategy. Turn Fournette loose against a defense with seven starters whom he outweighed, including three of the four linebackers, thereby keeping Mahomes on the sideline. On the other side, Patrick expressed his offense's goal like this. "Our job is to get out there, jump on them early, and speed the game up."

LSU needed a good performance by Harris to compete with Mahomes. So at Brandon's request, offensive coordinator Cam Cameron moved from the press box to the sideline during the game to work more closely with the players, especially the quarterback.

LSU was a seven-point favorite. One near certainty for the game was that Fournette would get the MVP award if LSU won, and Mahomes would take home the honor if Tech prevailed.

The Game

A record Texas Bowl crowd of 71,307 were entertained by the highest-scoring game in the bowl's ten-year history.

FIRST QUARTER

LSU NG Davon Godchaux put his stamp on the game immediately, sacking Patrick Mahomes for a 5-yard loss and tackling DeAndre Washington for no gain. Then Mahomes threw to Jakeem Grant, who dropped the ball just as CB Jalen Mills hit him. The no-huddle offense used up only a minute and 15 seconds, including the punt. Starting from the 34, Leonard Fournette gained four, then set the tone for the evening by running over DB Keenon Ward for 35 yards to the TT 27. After losing a yard, the sensational sophomore from New Orleans threw an errant pass to WR Malachi Dupre, but Tech was called for pass interference to make it first-and-10 at the 13. Given a chance to pass, QB Brandon Harris nearly killed the drive when he rolled left and threw to TE Foster Moreau in the end zone. Moreau had to knock the ball away from the defender. Then Dupre took a quick pass in the right flat and ran to the two to set up Fournette's 19th touchdown of the season, an LSU record. Trent Domingue converted. LSU 7 Texas Tech 0 (11:47).

Tech couldn't recover from a tripping penalty and a 13-yard sack by Kendell Beckwith. The Tigers overcame a holding penalty when Harris's pass to freshman RB Derrius Guice gained 10 to the 47. With Tech stacking as many as 10 men within 7 yards of the line of scrimmage, Fournette began to find heavy sledding. When he gained nothing on third-and-three, LSU punted to the 10.

If LSU's defense didn't appreciate Mahomes' scintillating skill set from watching him on video, a real-time demonstration removed any doubt. He was almost more dangerous fleeing the pocket than in it. If defenders hung back, he kept running. If they came up, he threw over them. He could throw accurately running to his left as well as to the right. He and his receivers improvised plays in real time.

The nation's total offense leader completed three straight passes while on the move to put the pigskin at the LSU 45. On third-and-11, with good protection, Mahomes threw down the left sideline to Grant, who had broken past one of the best DBs in the

Patrick Mahomes tries to elude Deion Jones (45) and Arden Key (nola.com).

land, Tre'Davious White. Jakeem caught the ball on the dead run inside the five and continued into the end zone. Tech lined up quickly in a "muddle huddle" to go for two, but the pass failed.

Score: LSU 7 Texas Tech 6 (0:53)

The Tigers answered Tech's long strike with one of their own. Harris faked to Fournette up the middle and handed to WR DJ Chark who tore around the left side, then sped back across the field for a 79-yard touchdown, dragging a defender into the end zone the last 5 yards. Amazingly, it was Chark's first touch—run or pass—in his two seasons at LSU.

LSU 14 Texas Tech 6 (0:29)

The Raiders reached the LSU 46 to end the action-packed quarter.

LSU 14 Texas Tech 6

SECOND QUARTER

The game settled down as the defenses held sway the first half of the period. The Tech drive reached the LSU 36 before several incompletions forced a punt to the 10. Harris did his best Mahomes imitation, fleeing the pocket to his left and throwing on the run to TE Colin Jeter. Two plays later, Brandon fired a low dart to Dupre, who made a sliding catch at the 38. Then an interference call put the ball on the TT 41. But the Tigers bogged down and punted to the five.

Kevin Steele's defense had their best series so far, forcing three incompletions, and

LSU got good field position when White returned the punt 16 yards to the TT 42. Harris let the rush come in and flipped a screen pass over them to Fournette, who got good blocks to pick up a head of steam that carried him 44 yards to the end zone.

LSU 21 Texas Tech 6 (6:41)

The Raiders responded with a 90-yard scoring drive. Mahomes had misfired on his last five passes after completing the previous six. Running plays almost faster than their descriptions could be typed, he started by handing to Washington for a 22-yard gain, then tossing a flare pass to him for three more. The future Super Bowl MVP then ran through the vacant right side for a first down at the 47. He threw sidearm to Cameron Batson to the LSU 35. Snapping the ball before the defense was set, Patrick threw a quick screen to Grant to the 15, then found Washington for 12 more to the three. After DE Arden Key stopped DeAndre for no gain, Tech lined up quickly, and Grant caught a pass in the left flat and ran untouched into the end zone.

LSU 21 Texas Tech 13 (3:38)

Trying to at least hold the ball the rest of the half, LSU quickly faced third-and-two. Fournette time, right? No. Cam Cameron called for Harris to roll out to his left and throw downfield. The ball landed far short of the receiver.

The time on the clock of 1:26 was more than enough for Tech to get at least a field goal. But LB Deion Jones chased down Mahomes as he ran out of the pocket for a

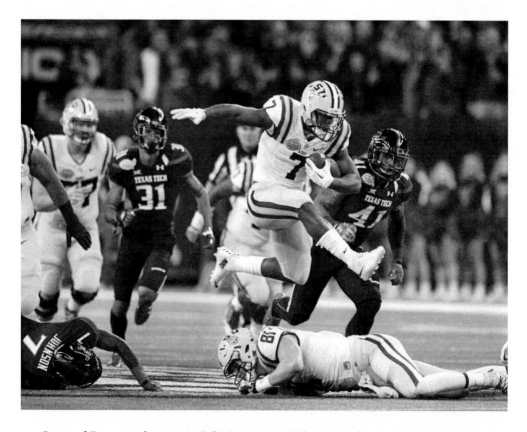

Leonard Fournette leaps over Colin Jeter. #77 is Ethan Pocic (Baton Rouge *Advocate*).

loss of three. After a holding penalty on LSU made it first-and-10 at the TT 44, Jones blitzed and leaped in the face of Mahomes, forcing a throw away. Then Key brought third-down pressure from the edge, and freshman CB Donte Jackson knocked down the pass. After the punt, Fournette gained eight to bring his first half total to 81 yards. Harris went eight-for-11 for 103 yards.

LSU 21 Texas Tech 13

The Tiger defense held the Air Raid offense to its fewest first half points of the season. Tech was just 1–17 under Kingsbury when trailing at the half because their defense would wear down in the final 30 minutes.

THIRD QUARTER

Tech would pull within a point before a sequence of big plays allowed LSU to take control of the game.

Two LSU incompletions gave the ball to the Red Raiders at their 26. A 9-yard sack by Godchaux on third down produced a punt to the LSU 20. Once again, Harris twice passed unsuccessfully in three plays. The second misfire was snagged by LB Dakota Allen at the LSU 31. The Tiger defense continued to dominate on the first two plays, both incompletions. When a Tiger jumped offside, Mahomes knew he had a free play. So he threw long to Reginald Davis in the end zone despite tight coverage by CB Kevin Toliver, who had his back to the quarterback. The ball sailed past Toliver into Davis's hands.

LSU 21 Texas Tech 20 (10:28)

Having gotten off script in the first two possessions of the half, LSU went back to their strength against the 125th-ranked rushing defense. Playing with a chip on their collective shoulder, the Raider defense stuffed Fournette for no gain, then held him to 2 yards. That set up Big Play #1 for LSU. John Diarse was tightly covered, but Harris threw a beautiful back shoulder throw that only his receiver could catch. John broke free of the defender and raced 30 yards to the TT 43. Fournette then hit left tackle, broke into the secondary, and scored his third touchdown of the evening.

LSU 28 Texas Tech 20 (8:17)

Tech started moving immediately on one of their patented short pass/long run plays to Washington for 28 yards to the 42. On third-and-five, the Tigers chased Mahomes out of the pocket, but he stopped and hit Washington to the LSU 35. Seconds later, Brad Pearson was on the receiving end for 18 yards. DE Tashawn Bower stopped Mahomes after a 1-yard gain to set up Big Play #2. Mahomes threw down the left sideline to the goal line only to have White deflect the ball high into the air into the hands of FS Ricky Jefferson, Jordan's younger brother, who ran out to the 22. Coach Kingsbury later pointed to Jefferson's interception as "a big turning point."

Harris threw a long pass up for grabs. 6'4" Dupre outleaped the defender to snag the ball, then secured it as he hit the ground after bobbling it twice. On Big Play #3, Harris launched a beautiful pass down the middle to WR Trey Quinn running behind two defenders for a 46-yard gain to the four. Guess who scored his fourth touchdown on the next play.

LSU 35 Texas Tech 20 (4:07)

The Tigers had one more touchdown in them before the period ended. LB Kendell Beckwith, lined up at left end, was a one-man wrecking crew on the next Tech possession. First, he stopped Washington for no gain. Then he sacked Mahomes for a loss of six before teaming with Bower for another sack for -7. White returned the punt 13 yards to the LSU 36.

Chark took a double reverse for 11 yards through weary defenders to the 43. Fournette gained 10, then 21 to the 26. That set up the touchdown as Harris put the ball in Leonard's belly on the zone read, pulled it out, and ran through a huge hole off the right side.

LSU 42 Texas Tech 20 (0:09)

FOURTH QUARTER

Over the first three periods, LSU hit Mahomes on 11 passing attempts, hurried him 20 times, and sacked him six times. But he kept competing and led the Raiders to another touchdown. Escaping pressure to his left, he twisted and threw back to the right to Ian Sadler for a first down at the 31. Later, on fourth-and-15 at the 36, Patrick sprinted to the right and hit Grant in stride to the nine. After a throw away when no one was open, the Raiders lined up quickly, and Grant took a throw in the left flat and found a crease between defenders into the end zone.

LSU 42 Texas Tech 27 (12:20)

LSU answered back with a fourth straight TD drive. It started with Guice returning the kickoff angrily to the 35. Fournette burst up the middle for 30 yards. Harris lofted a lovely third-down pass to Dupre running behind the defender to the 18. After Brandon kept for nine, a face mask penalty on Fournette's run moved the ball to the three. Following an incompletion, Superman leaped into the end zone for his fifth touchdown to tie an NCAA bowl record.

LSU 49 Texas Tech 27 (8:16)

Three incompletions later, the exhausted Tech defense was back on the field staring at big #7 across from them. Fournette gained 10, eight, and 16. Guice took over and ran for 21, then eight more to the two. FB Darrel Williams did the honors from there.

LSU 56 Texas Tech 27 (4:24)

The game ended with LSU staging a goal line stand. The Raiders converted three third downs. First, Justin Stockton broke loose for 30 yards to the Tiger 25. Then Mahomes hit Jonathan Giles for 12 yards to the 13. Finally, Cameron Batson took a pass and may well have scored as he was knocked down by Jackson at the goal line, but the official put the ball inside the one. The proud Tiger defense played the next series as if the game was on the line.

First down: Finding no one open, Mahomes throws the ball out of the end zone.

Second down: Jefferson knocks Demarcus Felton out of bounds as he tried to sweep right end.

Third down: Patrick tries to run, but S Jamal Adams stops him for no gain.

Fourth down: Mahomes doesn't see his tight end running free into the right flat and throws instead into a crowd in the end zone.

Final Score: LSU 56 Texas Tech 27

Leonard Fournette won the Most Valuable Player award for gaining 212 yards on 29 carries, including four rushing touchdowns and one receiving. He finished the season just 47 yards shy of the magic 2,000-yard mark. It was also the tenth time he had run for more than 100 yards in a season, tying the school record set by Charles Alexander in 1977.

Postgame

Coach Miles was proud of the way his team finished the season. "When you have a string of losses, they could say, 'Forget this year.' They didn't forget this year. That's character. That to me is maybe the strength of this program." Les said Cam Cameron calling plays from the sideline was "exactly the right thing." Cam agreed. "There's nothing like being in the action. It was good to be able to communicate with the receivers, running backs, coaches, and O-line. Being able to sit there and get more thoughts from Brandon. I could look in his eye."

Leonard Fournette said, "Tonight was productive. Our focus was to win the game and boost us for next season, and we did an excellent job." Speaking of the Tech defense, he added, "You could see they were kind of getting tired. They were smaller than us, and we just kept running it down their throat."

LSU's swarming defense held Tech to 399 yards, nearly 200 under their season average. LB Deion Jones said, "We knew they passed the ball pretty efficiently. Our guys were going 100 percent and giving max effort on every play."

Twenty-four 2015 Tigers played pro football: DB Jamal Adams, OL Vadal Alexander, LB Kendell Beckwith, LB Tashawn Bower, WR DJ Chark, OL Will Clapp, WR Malachi Dupre, LS Reid Ferguson, RB Leonard Fournette, DL Davon Godchaux, RB Derrius Guice, OL Jerald Hawkins, DB Donte Jackson, LB Deion Jones, DE Arden Key, DB Jalen Mills, TE Foster Moreau, DE Lewis Neal, OL Ethan Pocic, LB Duke Riley, LB Corey Thompson, DB Kevin Toliver, DB Tre'Davious White, and RB Darrel Williams.

Buffalo Wild Wings
Citrus Bowl vs. Louisville

"You give Coach Aranda more than a week,
it's going to be hard for you"

Camping World Stadium, Orlando, Florida
December 31, 2016

The year 2016 brought a bizarre season which saw the star running back miss numerous games because of injury, the head coach get fired after four games, and a road game end up being played in Tiger Stadium in place of another scheduled home game.

LSU's Season

After coming within a whisker of being fired at the end of the 2015 regular season, Coach Les Miles promised offensive changes for 2016. However, LSU renewed the contract of offensive coordinator Cam Cameron, the target of the ire of LSU fandom, when it expired at the end of March. Les said the spring practices would "emphasize" the passing attack, adding, "If you do the same thing you've always done, it will be the same thing you've always been. We're going to change spring. It's going to be different."

The AP poll voters put the "hat" on the Mad Hatter when they ranked LSU #5 in the preseason poll. That meant the talent was there after four straight seasons of Top Six recruiting classes.

The season opened with an intriguing game that pitted new defensive coordinator Dave Aranda against his previous team, the Wisconsin Badgers, at Lambeau Field in Green Bay. LSU fans expecting to see a more imaginative offense were disappointed as Tiger linemen heard the Badger linebackers calling out the plays before the snap. Despite 176 yards of total offense from junior Heisman candidate Leonard Fournette, the result was a 16–14 loss in which seven of LSU's points came on Tre'Davious White's interception return. The Tigers had a first down at the Wisconsin 30 with a minute to play, but QB Brandon Harris threw an interception that sealed the defeat, which was Miles's first in 43 games against non-conference foes in the regular season.

Junior Purdue transfer Danny Etling took over at quarterback and started every game the rest of the season. He didn't have as strong an arm as Harris or Brandon's running ability, but he was more reliable and consistent, throwing only five interceptions all season with 11 touchdown passes. After a rent-a-win against Jacksonville State, the Tigers nearly blew a 20-point lead against Mississippi State but held on to win 23–20.

The trip to Auburn for Game 4 proved to be the last straw for the Les-Must-Go forces in the LSU hierarchy. The defense kept the Plainsmen out of the end zone, but the six field goals were enough to win 18–13. What sealed Miles's fate was the way the game ended. Trailing 18–13, Etling led a drive that reached the two on an 8-yard completion to Malachi Dupre. But the play was nullified by an illegal shift penalty. With no timeouts and only a second left on the clock, the Tigers lined up quickly and Etling threw an apparent winning touchdown pass. But replay ruled that time expired a split second before the ball was snapped. The frustrating ending evoked memories of previous games in which poor clock management in the last minutes cost victories.

Defensive line coach Ed Orgeron was named interim head coach for the rest of the season. A Louisiana native who always dreamed of being LSU's head coach, Orgeron had been Ole Miss's head coach from 2005 to 2007, compiling a dismal 10–25 record, including 3–21 in the SEC. He was more successful as interim coach at USC, going 6–2 after Lane Kiffin was fired in 2013. Orgeron chose not to retain Cameron, replacing him as offensive coordinator with tight ends coach Steve Ensminger, a quarterback at LSU from 1976 to 1979. Ed immediately changed almost all aspects of the program from shorter practices to how meetings were conducted. "Coach O did everything like an NFL team did, and we loved it," recalls G Will Clapp.

The offense that had scored just 84 points in the first four games exploded for 125 in the next three—42–7 over Missouri, 45–10 over Southern Mississippi, and 38–21 over Ole Miss in a game in which Fournette set a school record with 284 rushing yards.

Then came the annual test against Alabama. The game earned the dubious distinction of being the only FBS game all season that was scoreless after three periods. Bama pushed across 10 points in the final period to earn their fifth straight victory over the Tigers. As in 2015, the Crimson defense bottled up Fournette, holding him to 35 yards on 17 carries.

Leonard gained 98 the following week in the 38–10 romp over Arkansas. That set up the game with Florida that had been postponed from October 8 because of Hurricane Matthew. LSU agreed to replace the home game against South Alabama November 19 with the Gators, who also had a non-conference home contest scheduled that Saturday. The Tigers led at halftime 7–3, but the game turned on back-to-back plays in the third quarter. First, a botched snap foiled a 19-yard LSU field goal attempt. On the next play, the Gators completed a 98-yard touchdown pass to take the lead. Trailing 16–10, LSU drove to a first-and-goal at the seven with 0:50 on the clock. What happened next made LSU fans wonder if LSU's offense had really changed under Orgeron-Ensminger. Derrius Guice, replacing Fournette who left the game with a recurrence of an ankle injury that had plagued him all season, ran twice to put the ball on the one. A fullback plunge gained nothing. After a timeout, Guice went the wrong way on a pitchout and tried to fumble the ball into the end zone to no avail.

LSU finished the campaign on a high note, smashing the defenseless Aggies in College Station 54–39 despite missing four starters, including Fournette. Guice more than took up the slack, breaking Fournette's recent single-game rushing record with 285 yards.

Two days later, AD Joe Alleva announced that Orgeron would become LSU's permanent coach in 2017, ending speculation that Houston's Tom Herman would take the job.

The Opponent

The Citrus Bowl against Louisville would be LSU's second straight postseason game against a dynamic dual-threat quarterback—in this case, Lamar Jackson. The youngest Heisman Trophy winner ever at age 19 accounted for an incredible 4,928 yards of total offense—3,390 passing and 1,538 rushing. That was a prodigious 79 percent of Louisville's total offense!

Bobby Petrino, whom LSU had faced during his four years as Arkansas, became Louisville's head coach for the second time in 2014, when the Cardinals joined the Atlantic Coast Conference. He had brought them to a bowl each season, and a win in the Citrus Bowl would give him a 10–3 record, his best during his current tenure at the school.

Jackson catapulted into the national spotlight in the first three games of the season—a 70–14 rout of Charlotte, a 62–28 pasting of Syracuse, and an attention-getting 63–20 romp over Florida State. The sensational sophomore accounted for 18 touchdowns in that span—eight passing and 10 rushing.

The big test came two weeks later at Clemson, which boasted the best defense the Cardinals would meet in the regular season and a dynamic offense led by another dual-threat quarterback, junior DeShaun Watson. The battle between the nation's #2 and #3 teams ended with a Clemson defender knocking the Cardinal pass receiver out of bounds at the three to preserve the Tigers' 42–36 victory.

Five straight conference victories followed, the closest being 32–25 at Virginia. Then Louisville traveled to Houston for a Thursday-night matchup with the Cougars, who were coached by Tom Herman, the man who was rumored to be in line for the LSU job. If the game was an audition, he passed it with flying colors as his unranked squad held Jackson to his lowest output of the season—244 yards with only 33 on the ground—to upset the Birds 36–10. Another unranked team, Kentucky, beat the Cards in the annual finale the following week, 41–38. That dropped Louisville to #13 in the final College Football Playoffs rankings. That was seven spots ahead of 7–4 LSU.

On December 5, Fournette announced his intention to enter the 2017 NFL Draft. Coach Orgeron told him to skip the bowl game because he was injured and couldn't practice. Leonard thus finished his three-year career with 3,830 yards, which was fourth in school history, and 40 rushing touchdowns, tied for third. MLB Kendell Beckwith would also miss the bowl game because of an injury sustained in the Florida game. Orgeron held only 12 of the allotted 15 practices, but that was enough for Aranda to install an excellent game plan against Jackson.

The Game

In varying stages of alertness, 46,063 showed up for the 11 a.m. kickoff on a sunny morning.

FIRST QUARTER

LSU's first possession started well when QB Danny Etling lofted a pass to WR Malachi Dupre for 36 yards to the UL 37. TB Derrius Guice gained 11 on two carries for another first down. But two incompletions brought on Colby Delahoussaye for a 39-yard field goal try that missed.

The Cardinals started with a 12-yard run by HB Brandon Radcliff. But 6'6" All-SEC OLB Arden Key began his outstanding game with two straight stops on Jackson to force a punt that skipped all the way to the LSU five. The poor field position eventually led to a Louisville field goal. The Cardinals received the ball at their 38. Jackson threw long on first down to WR James Quick for 53 yards to the nine. But the Tigers bowed their backs and allowed only 2 yards on three downs. So Blanton Creque booted a 24-yard field goal.

Score: Louisville 3 LSU 0 (7:14)

Once again, Etling connected with Dupre on first down for 26 yards, this time to the UL 49. But Louisville's best defender, OLB Devonte Fields, tackled Etling for a 15-yard loss, and the Cards soon had the ball back on their 25. Freshman ILB Devin White roared through and sacked Jackson for a loss of 19 to start a three-and-out possession. After senior DB Tre'Davious White returned the punt 12 yards to the LSU 48, the Tigers drove to the one as the quarter ended. Etling hit Dupre again for 18 yards. Three Guice runs plus an offside put the pigskin on the 16. Danny then flipped to Guice on a middle screen to the four before Derrius smashed to the one on his tenth carry.

The first quarter tally showed that the Tiger defense hurried Jackson on three of his seven pass attempts, hit him twice, and sacked him once.

Louisville 3 LSU 0

Derrius Guice gets upended by S Chucky Williams (Baton Rouge *Advocate*).

SECOND QUARTER

On the first play, TE Colin Jeter faked a block and slipped out into the end zone to take Etling's pass for the touchdown. Delahoussaye added the extra point.

LSU 7 Louisville 3 (14:54)

The Tiger defense continued to dominate. Jackson twice could not find an open receiver and had to run, being sacked the second time by LB Tashawn Bower, who said he stayed up until 3 a.m. studying for the game. The team wakeup call came just 3½ hours later. "I was up last night watching a lot of film to pick apart these guys. We mixed things up, gave them some different looks. Everyone did their job."

The Cardinals continued to do a good job of containing Guice, but two great catches spearheaded another touchdown drive. Twice, Etling connected with Dupre on third down with Malachi plucking the second one out of the air with one hand. Danny said afterward, "I let it go a little early, just to give him time to run underneath it, and he made a great play." Dupre explained, "It's a read route for me. I could take it high up the middle, or I can break it off. As soon as I got my head around, the ball was in front of me. I didn't have any time to get second hand on it." Then Etling did his best Jackson imitation by running out of the pocket for 10 yards. On third down, WR DJ Chark made a spectacular catch while falling backwards on the two because of pass interference. After the Cards stopped Guice twice, Etling rolled right and tossed to Derrius just inside the right pylon.

LSU 14 Louisville 3 (7:14)

After the teams traded three-and-outs, LSU junior S Jamal Adams demonstrated his incredible speed and tackling ability. Jackson tried to run around left end, but Adams came from the other side of the formation to run down the fleet quarterback for a loss of two. Etling hit Dupre again for a gain of 13 to midfield. But LSU could go no further, and a holding call on the punt set the Cardinals back to their nine with 1:21 to go.

Coach Petrino didn't play it safe, and it cost him two points. On third-and-10, Key tackled Jackson in the end zone.

LSU 16 Louisville 3 (1:08)

Same question for Ed Orgeron. Run out the clock after receiving the free kick on the 23? His answer was no, and it cost the Tigers points. Etling tried to pass, but as a blitzer reached him, Danny tried to throw the ball out of bounds but fell short. S Zykiesis Cannon intercepted as he went out of bounds at the 33. The Tiger defense partially bailed out their quarterback, holding Louisville to a 47-yard field goal to end the half.

LSU 16 Louisville 6

The nation's #1 offense had snapped the ball 26 times in the first half. Fifteen plays resulted in no yardage or negative yardage. The Cardinals had a mere 38 yards of offense, thanks to -24 rushing because of sacks. Louisville had zero third-down conversions.

THIRD QUARTER

Louisville wanted to roll out Jackson more to either pass or run. On the first play, Key tackled him for a 7-yard loss as he tried to come around his end. Two plays later,

Lamar Jackson is upended by Tre'Davious White (Baton Rouge *Advocate*).

Jackson was ruled to have the first down when he fell forward to the 23. But replay moved the spot back half a yard.

After LSU went nowhere, Jackson kept on two straight zone reads for 14 yards to the 32. Two snaps later, he held the ball too long and was sacked by DE Davon Godchaux, who said he watched so much film of Jackson he could anticipate his moves. When White broke up a long pass, LSU started from their 18 after the punt and took only two plays to increase their lead. Guice ran off left tackle to the 30. Then he zipped through right guard, veered to the outside, and ran down the sideline to the end zone.

LSU 23 Louisville 6 (8:48)

Excessive celebration caused LSU to kick off from their 20. But even then Louisville couldn't get good field position because the returner let the ball bounce past him, and he could return only to the 12. On third down, Jackson finally targeted his leading receiver, Cole Hikutini, who dropped the ball.

Aided by a roughing the passer penalty, the Tigers drove to a field goal. With

Louisville crowding the line of scrimmage, a pass to Chark gained a first down. When Guice fell short of the marker on third down, Delahoussaye split the uprights from the 32.

LSU 26 Louisville 6 (3:04)

Louisville started a scoring drive that carried into the final quarter. Hikutini finally got his first reception for a first down. Jackson moved the chains on a keeper to the LSU 44, then hit Quick for 19 yards to the 25. On fourth-and-two, Petrino had no choice but to go for it. Jackson faked a handoff and threw to TE Keith Trowbridge to keep the drive alive.

LSU 26 Louisville 6

FOURTH QUARTER

On third-and-10 from the 13, a Cardinal receiver dropped a pass for the fourth time on this drive alone. So Creque kicked a 40-yard field goal.

LSU 26 Louisville 9 (14:43)

The Tigers got the three points back with an eight-play drive. Penalties for interference and holding aided the advance. On third-and-eight from the 15, Etling set sail for the first down marker, but his dive fell a yard short. So Delahoussaye kicked a 25-yarder.

LSU 29 Louisville 9 (10:41)

That ended the scoring but not the excitement. The Tiger defense provided it with a goal-line stand. The Cardinals converted two third downs, the first when Jackson found WR Jamari Staples for 22 yards to the LSU 48. Then the future NFL MVP moved the chains with his feet, scampering 13 yards to the 32. An interference penalty on S John Battle in the end zone put the ball at the two. Bower burst through on first down and forced Jackson to throw the ball away while being tackled. Lamar was flagged for intentional grounding to make it second-and-goal at the 14. A 5-yard completion and a quarterback keeper brought up fourth down at the 5. Jackson completed a shuttle pass to Charles Standberry, but Adams tripped the runner at the four.

LSU used up four minutes before punting. Jackson suffered a final ignominy when he fumbled, Duke Riley recovering for the Tigers.

Final Score: LSU 29 Louisville 9

Incredibly, the 220 yards Louisville gained was the least given up by LSU all season. The Cards were only two-of-16 on third down, a big contributing factor to the Tigers holding the top offense in the country to 36 points below their average.

Postgame

Coach Orgeron praised Derrius Guice, who churned out 138 yards with two touchdowns to earn the MVP award. "He stepped in for (Leonard Fournette) and didn't blink an eye. He's one of the best players in the USA." Derrius explained why he ran better the second half. "As a running back, you've just got to be patient. You can't get upset. You can't get mad when things don't always go your way. … The second half, I just waited for things to set up and develop, and I was able to hit a long run."

Arden Key's two sacks gave him 13 for the year to break Gabe Northern's 1994 mark of 12. Key credited his defensive coordinator. "You give Coach Aranda more than a week, it's going to be hard for you. If you don't change your offense, and you run the same thing you've been running all year, Aranda's going to make something happen."

Louisville Coach Petrino summarized the game this way. "I think we hurt ourselves early in the game with negative plays, either assignment errors or good pass rushes and not being able to get the ball out and throw it away. When you're going backward, and you get behind the sticks, it's really hard to make first downs against them. I did think we came back in the second half and executed better and made some plays. Still couldn't get the ball in the end zone, and that really hurt us."

Lamar Jackson lamented, "There were a lot of mistakes each and every one of us made out there. LSU was a great team. The defense was just being good. They were working hard. We just had to step up, and we didn't."

Twenty-four 2016 Tigers have played pro football: DB Jamal Adams, LB Kendell Beckwith, LB Tashawn Bower, WR DJ Chark, OL Will Clapp, WR Malachi Dupre, LS Blake Ferguson, RB Leonard Fournette, WR Russell Gage, DL Davon Godchaux, RB Derrius Guice, DL Frank Herron, DB Donte Jackson, DE Arden Key, DL Rashard Lawrence, TE Foster Moreau, DE Lewis Neal, OL Ethan Pocic, LB Duke Riley, TE Stephen Sullivan, DB Kevin Toliver, LB Devin White, DB Tre'Davious White, and RB Darrel Williams.

Citrus Bowl Presented
by Overton's vs. Notre Dame

Notre Dame did it by the book

Camping World Stadium, Orlando, Florida
January 1, 2018

Ed Orgeron hired a new offensive coordinator for his first full season as head coach.

LSU's Season

Matt Canada came aboard in December 2016 after first choice Lane Kiffin became the head coach at Florida Atlantic. Canada had been a finalist for the Broyles Award honoring the nation's top assistant coach after his 2016 offense at Pittsburgh became the most prolific in school history, averaging 42.3 points per game, 14.1 more than the year before his arrival. QB Nathan Peterman set career highs in both passing yards and touchdowns as well as passer rating. Steve Ensminger, the interim coordinator in 2016, stayed on the LSU staff as tight ends coach.

However, the 2017 Tiger offense essentially was no better than 2016's in the most important statistic, points-per-game—28.1 in '17 compared to 28.3 in '16. Without Leonard Fournette, the rushing offense decreased from 233.1 yards per game to 210.8. With senior Danny Etling returning at quarterback, the passing offense improved from 190.1 yards per game to 201.3.

As in 2016, a game was moved to a different venue. Because of extensive flooding in the Houston area, the opener against Brigham Young was played in the Superdome and resulted in an easy 27–0 LSU victory. The home opener the next week produced a 45–10 rout of Chattanooga.

The trip to Starkville shook the confidence of many Tiger fans in Orgeron's ability to lead LSU back to greatness. Mississippi State dominated the line of scrimmage on both sides of the ball to run up their largest margin of victory over the Tigers in the 111-game rivalry, 37–7. The Tigers bounced back the following week to defeat visiting Syracuse 35–26 after taking a 28–10 lead in the third quarter. Orgeron's seat got red hot the next week when Troy won a shocking victory in Tiger Stadium 24–21. Ed admitted afterwards that he broke a promise by inserting himself into the offense and eliminating much of

Canada's presnap movement in favor of formations similar to those used in 2016. The head man promised to stay out of the way the rest of the season.

The players took the embarrassing loss as a wakeup call. The defense began watching more film and taking practice more seriously. Leaders like sophomore LB Devin White, TE Foster Moreau, and RB Darrel Williams called "Come to Jesus" players-only meetings. The Tigers responded by winning six of their last seven games, the only loss coming at Alabama.

The first victory came in a tough place to play, The Swamp. LSU sacked Florida QB Felipe Franks five times and held him to 108 yards passing to squeak by 17–16 thanks to a missed extra point by the Gators. Two of Canada's jet sweeps gained 30 yards each, including a touchdown.

When Auburn raced to a 20–0 lead in Tiger Stadium the next week, the visiting fans chanted, "We want Troy!" But not so fast, my friends. With Dave Aranda's defense shutting down RB Kerryon Johnson after his strong start, DJ Chark's electrifying 75-yard punt return at the start of the final period pulled LSU within 23–21. Two Connor Culp field goals clinched the 27–23 victory.

The Tigers' second trip to Mississippi produced happier results than the first one—a 40–24 thumping of Ole Miss. After an off week, LSU hit the road again—to Tuscaloosa. Canada's offense scored 10 points—10 more than LSU tallied at home the year before—but the #1 Tide won by 14 on their way to the College Football Playoff Championship.

The Tigers finished the season with a flourish—three victories in which the offense totaled 108 points: Arkansas 33–10, @Tennessee 30–10, and Texas A&M 45–21. It was the first time that LSU closed out a season with three victories over SEC opponents by 20+ points each.

Junior RB Derrius Guice topped the magic 1,000-yard mark for the second year in a row, although his 1,153 yards in '17 (before the bowl game) was less than his 1,387 total in '16. The Tigers boasted another physical back in Darrel Williams, who gained 776 yards, topping the 100-yard mark twice, including the Ole Miss game in which he added 105 receiving yards. Steady but unspectacular, Etling completed 60.3 percent of his passes for 2,234 yards and 14 TDs against only two picks. Chark was the top receiver with 35 catches, averaging 23.2 ypc.

All-SEC sophomore LB Devin White, a fast 248-pounder, anchored the defense with 127 tackles (33 solo), twice as many as the next highest LSU player and more than any other SEC defender. Freshman Andraez "Greedy" Williams also topped the conference with five interceptions. The Tigers tied an NCAA record with only eight turnovers during the season—four interceptions and four fumbles lost.

The Opponent

Notre Dame finished 4–8 in 2016, missing a bowl game for the first time in Brian Kelly's seven seasons as head coach. He responded by hiring seven new members of his staff, including two coordinators, Chip Long for offense and Mike Elko for defense. The result was one of the biggest turnarounds in college football in 2017.

After dispatching Temple 49–16, Notre Dame hosted Georgia. The Bulldogs eked out a 20–19 victory on a field goal with 3:39 remaining. The Irish rebounded with a win at Boston College, 49–20, in the first of their annual five games against Atlantic Coast

Conference foes. Notre Dame was outgained at Michigan State but never trailed as the defense forced three turnovers in the first half to spearhead the 38–18 victory.

Wins over Miami (OH) and North Carolina preceded the annual clash with USC. The Irish ground attack proved unstoppable, totaling 377 yards in the 49–14 pasting of the #11 Trojans. The winning streak reached seven with triumphs over North Carolina State and Wake Forest to vault ND to a #3 ranking. But they didn't stay long in that heady atmosphere. Miami, ranked only #7 despite their 8–0 record, extended the nation's longest winning streak to 14 games with a 41–8 thrashing of the visiting Irish. Dropping to #8 in the AP poll, the Fighting Irish beat Navy 24–17 before losing the finale at Stanford, 38–20.

Notre Dame's junior quarterback, Brandon Wimbush, was a better runner than passer. His poor performance in the final three games—45 percent completions with four picks—contributed to the two losses. Coach Kelly admitted that his squad wore down late in the season, which included nine games against teams ranked in the Top 25 when the Irish played them. Still, Notre Dame's 9–3 record earned them the opportunity to play LSU in a bowl game for the fourth time.

Like LSU, the Irish followed the old coaching mantra: To be successful, you must be able to run the ball and stop the run. Notre Dame ranked seventh nationally at 279.1 yards per game rushing behind one of the country's best offensive lines with a pair of Associated Press All-American selections in LT Mike McGlinchey and LG Quenton Nelson. "There's a lot of different offenses we have to defend," said Coach Orgeron. "Their quarterback runs, their power game, big offensive line coming right at you." Making matters more difficult for LSU were injuries on defense. Three linebackers, Arden Key, Corey Thompson, and Donnie Alexander, would miss the bowl game, replaced by a combination of freshmen. But the Irish had problems of their own. Two wide receivers were suspended, and another had a shoulder injury.

Amid speculation that he might follow the course of Leonard Fournette the year before and not play in the bowl game before turning pro, Derrius Guice suited up for the Citrus Bowl. "I really want to compliment him for playing this game," said Coach Orgeron. "Obviously other people may make other choices, which I don't think is right. I think you need to finish with your team if you're healthy, and Derrius is healthy. He's ready to go."

Meanwhile, reports surfaced that Canada might be coaching his final game with the Tigers because of philosophical differences with Orgeron. How much impact would that have on LSU's bowl performance?

The Tigers were rated a three-point favorite. Whereas the previous season's Citrus Bowl had been played on a sunny day, this one took place in overcast 60 degree weather with intermittent rain.

The Game

The 57,726 fans watching saw the Tigers let victory slip through their fingers in the last minute.

FIRST QUARTER

Despite the steady drizzle, both teams started their possessions with passes. Brandon Wimbush threw to WR Equanimeous St. Brown for 35 yards to the LSU 40. Facing third-and-six, Wimbush hit TE Durham Smythe who was stopped a yard shy of the first down. The Irish lined up quickly and went for it, but MLB Devin White dropped RB Josh Adams for a 3-yard loss.

Danny Etling, who grew up a Notre Dame fan in Indiana, also passed on first down but overthrew WR DJ Chark. After Darrius Guice gained five, Danny connected on two straight, 15 yards to WR Russell Gage and 11 to Stephen Sullivan to the ND 35. A false start penalty helped slow down the drive. So Josh Growden pooched a punt that was downed on the two.

Running mostly behind their All-Americans on the left side, the Irish pushed into LSU territory. The big plays were Adams' 11-yard run to the 23 and Wimbush's scamper for 31 yards to the LSU 46. But the Tigers drew the line there to force a punt. Chark, who

Derrius Guice carries the ball over T Toby Weathersby (66) (Baton Rouge *Advocate*).

had returned two punts for touchdowns during the season, foolishly fielded the punt on one hop at the one and was downed immediately. But Guice erased the mistake on the first play, bursting through right tackle to the 34 to become the fifth LSU player to rush for over 3,000 yards in his career. The defense tightened up, and Zach Von Rosenberg punted the Irish into a hole again at the 13.

Chark almost made another costly error when Notre Dame punted back, letting the ball go through his arms, but Tory Carter bailed him out by recovering at the LSU 45. Like Wimbush, Etling was having accuracy problems, and his third down incompletion brought in Growden, who punted to the 10. DE Rashard Lawrence tripped Adams for a 6-yard loss on second down, and St. Brown was stopped 3 yards short to force a punt as the period ended.

LSU 0 Notre Dame 0

SECOND QUARTER

The long layoffs before bowl games often affect the special teams more than any other unit. This quarter would illustrate that and cost LSU the game when they twice drove deep into Notre Dame territory and came away with no points. Gage started LSU rolling by taking a reverse jet sweep 15 yards to midfield. Then Etling rolled right and threw a screen pass back to the left to TE Foster Moreau, who ran to the ND 36. Darrel Williams gained five, then took a middle screen for four more. Danny sneaked for a first down at the 23. On third-and-four, Etling ran out of the pocket to the right and fired a low fast ball to Moreau to the 10. When Williams zipped to the one, it looked like LSU would take the lead. Darrel took a handoff but was hit immediately and fell a foot from the goal. On third down, Etling tried a sneak that turned into a rugby scrum. Officials ruled that he didn't penetrate the goal line, and video review upheld the call. The Tigers lined up to go for it, but FB Tory Carter rocked forward in his stance to draw a 5-yard penalty. So Connor Culp came in for a chip shot field goal only to have the Notre Dame leprechaun blow the kick just outside the right upright.

A minute later on the clock, LSU had the ball back at their 34 and drove into Notre Dame territory again. Etling converted two third downs, hitting WR Dee Anderson for 30 yards to the ND 42 and Chark to the 19. But the Irish rose up and stopped Guice for no gain and tackled Derrick Dillon for a loss of eight on a jet sweep. Etling moved the field goal point 7 yards closer on a pass to DJ. Since Culp had missed four of his last five attempts, sophomore Jack Gonsoulin came out to try a 37-yard FG from the left hash mark. The ball sailed wide left.

With 2:00 left, Coach Kelly made a decision that changed the game. He replaced the ineffective Wimbush with Ian Book. Managing the clock like an NFL veteran, the California sophomore led a drive that produced the game's first points. The first crucial play came on third-and-19 after sacks by Michael Divinity, Jr., and Ed Alexander. Expecting to get the ball back, Orgeron called a timeout with 1:02 left. But Book fled the pocket and ran 21 yards to the 47 to keep possession. So Kelly stopped the clock. Finding no one open, Book ran out of bounds at the LSU 47. Then he fired to WR Miles Boykin at the sideline for 18 yards. Remember that name Boykin. Book wasn't finished throwing to him. Ian flipped to Adams who ran out of bounds at the 23. The defense won the next two plays as White hurried Book into an incompletion, and NT Greg Gilmore got a 6-yard sack. So Kelly called timeout with 10 seconds left and sent out the field goal unit. Justin

Yoon showed the LSU kickers how to do it, booming a 46-yarder through the uprights. Cheers, many of them sarcastic, cascaded from the Notre Dame crowd.

Notre Dame 3 LSU 0

The Tigers won the time-of-possession battle 18:42 to 11:18. But the squandered opportunities in the red zone left them trailing.

Third Quarter

With both defenses shutting down the run, which quarterback would make big plays? Or would the special teams bug strike again? After an inept possession, Von Rosenberg punted into the wind. The ball bounced into a Notre Dame blocker, and long snapper Blake Ferguson pounced on it at the ND 43. The Tiger offense came to life, charging to a touchdown in only five plays. After Guice ran for four, Etling executed his favorite play, rolling right and hitting a receiver on the sideline—Chark to the 26. A quick pass to Anderson gained five before Guice added one more to the 20. Would the Tigers bog down in the red zone again? No, because Etling threw a delay pass to Guice over the middle, and Derrius took it all the way, diving into the end zone between two defenders.

LSU 7 Notre Dame 3 (11:37)

The Irish almost botched another kick but managed to secure possession at the 25. Not surprisingly, Kelly handed the keys to the offense to Book, who passed his audition at the end of the first half. Using misdirection to confuse LSU's freshmen linebackers and mixing runs with passes, the Irish moved swiftly into Tiger territory. Alternating bootlegs and rollouts to avoid the rush, Ian completed his first four passes, none for more than 9 yards. Adams ran four times for 18 yards, and Book gained 12 with his feet. But on first-and-15 at the 30 after an illegal shift penalty, Ian lobbed a pass that fell short of the receiver into the hands of CB Greedy Williams at the eight.

The Irish sacked Etling on third down to get excellent field position at the LSU 49 after the punt. With his receivers blanketed downfield, Book took off for 15 yards, then threw three straight drop offs to backs that netted just 3 yards. So Yoon booted a 49-yard field goal.

LSU 7 Notre Dame 6 (2:47)

Etling once again rolled right and threw a beautiful pass down the sideline, this time to Moreau who made a lunging catch just before going out of bounds for a 26-yard gain to the ND 43. Darrel Williams then burst up the middle to the 31.

LSU 7 Notre Dame 6

Fourth Quarter

The Tigers continued their march to the end zone. Another roll right pass to Chark to the 24. Etling keeps and makes the first down by inches at the 21. With the cornerback hanging back, a quick throw to Chark to the 13. Guice hit at the 10 but pushes to the three. First-and-goal. Guice goes airborne to the 1' line. Then LB Nyles Morgan stuffs Derrius at the two. With the defense massed to stop the run, Etling rolls right and flips to Guice slanting out of the backfield into the end zone.

LSU 14 Notre Dame 6 (11:13)

The Irish came right back thanks to several clutch plays. After Dexter Williams darted through a big hole off the left side to the LSU 39, Ed Alexander roared through to smother Book, who tried to get rid of the ball as he was hit. The officials ruled intentional grounding to make it second-and-23. Two plays later, Book executed clutch play #1 with a beautiful pass over Greedy Williams to that man Boykin again for 29 yards to the 19. Book kept for nine, and Adams gained three. First-and-goal at the seven. Ian kept for one, then rolled right and threw back to the left. Freshman LB Ray Thornton batted the ball away in the end zone. Next came clutch play #2. Ian bought time with his feet to survey the field and fire a strike to WR Michael Young in traffic at the back of the end zone to make it 14–12. The two-point try consisted of a shovel pass to Adams who pushed his way into the end zone. He was originally ruled short, but replay showed that he clearly broke the plane.

LSU 14 Notre Dame 14 (7:49)

The Tigers almost botched the short kickoff, Clyde Edwards-Helaire catching the ball on the bounce at the 23 just before getting creamed. Two Guice runs moved the chains to the 35. Then Etling got blasted just after throwing to Sullivan on a crossing pattern to the 48. Following Guice's 4-yard run, Danny avoided a sack and ran out of bounds at the ND 41. A defender clearly hit him from behind when he was beyond the boundary, but it was on the Notre Dame sideline, and no flag was thrown. The Tigers shifted into the wildcat, and Williams took the snap and knifed over right tackle for another first down at the 31. Following a 4-yard run by Darrel, Etling bootlegged and threw to Moreau for 10 more. It was Danny's ninth completion in 11 second half passes. That set up the series that drove the last nail into Canada's coffin as offensive coordinator. Guice gained one, then pushed to the three. Notre Dame used its first timeout. Canada called a shovel pass to Guice who fell inches short of the goal line. After the second ND timeout, Orgeron sent in Gonsoulin for a 17-yard field goal from a sharp angle to the right. Jack came through this time.

LSU 17 Notre Dame 14 (2:03)

Book had engineered a field goal drive in the last two minutes of the first half. Could he do that again? The Tigers went to a zone defense after playing man-to-man the whole game. After an incompletion, Book connected with WR Chris Finke for 18 yards to the 45. Next came the play that put Ian's name in the Book of Notre Dame's Greatest Plays. He threw long down the right sideline for 6'4" 225-pound WR Miles Boykin, who was closely covered by 5'11" 175-pound Donte Jackson. Boykin speared the ball with his outstretched right hand at the 33, pushed Jackson aside, ran through the tackle of S John Battle, and sprinted to the end zone. "Ian put it in a place where only I could reach it," said Boykin.

Notre Dame 21 LSU 17 (1:28)

Kelly had told Boykin during a practice earlier in the week that the junior would be named the most valuable player. After the game, Brian said, "One of the things that was really important in this game was to get him the ball in a position where their defensive backs, who were outstanding, couldn't make a play on the ball. It looked like a top-10 play, and it was, obviously, but that's something he and the quarterbacks work on, and it was successful today."

WR Miles Boykin makes a one-handed catch in front of DB Donte Jackson and continues for the winning touchdown (Associated Press).

LSU had one last chance, but the Irish stayed aggressive, blitzing and in no way playing a prevent defense. On third-and-10, Etling ran for a first down to the 34. But four straight incompletions sealed a devastating defeat for the Tigers.

Final Score: Notre Dame 21 LSU 17

Postgame

Coach Orgeron defended his decision to kick the field goal with two minutes to play. "Your defense has played well. I didn't think they were going to score. I thought we could stop them and give our team the chance to win. We went for it on fourth-and-one (in the first half), and we had a penalty, and we missed a field goal. So I wasn't going to do that again." Ed praised his senior quarterback. "I thought he made some tremendous plays. Some of those third down conversions, some of those passes were good. He scrambled. He got hit. He got up. Tough, you know, typical Danny Etling."

Derrius Guice said he planned on meeting with Orgeron about entering the NFL draft. "We're going to have a deep conversation about it and see where it goes."

Coach Kelly praised his team's defense inside the 10-yard line. "We fought for every inch. And, quite frankly, it became a game of inches down there where we were able to hold them to the field goals. That was the difference in the game. It's a mentality that we've developed within our football program. It's a mentality that we lacked last year, that we didn't fight for every inch."

Asked about the winning touchdown, Boykin replied, "It was really almost just a blur. We talk about situations like this all the time, and it's not often that you get to be in one like this. It's an extremely humble moment for me, to be able to go out there and help make a play for my team."

Postscript

Guice entered the NFL draft and was picked in the second round by the Washington Redskins.

As expected, the Matt Canada experiment ended January 5 after a lower buyout of his contract was negotiated with the university. Steve Ensminger was reinstated as the offensive coordinator for the 2018 season.

Twenty-three 2017 Tigers (through the 2020 NFL season) have played pro football: LB K'Lavon Chaisson, WR DJ Chark, OL Saahdiq Charles, OL Will Clapp, OL Lloyd Cushenberry, RB Clyde Edwards-Helaire, LS Blake Ferguson, WR Russell Gage, RB Derrius Guice, DL Frank Herron, DB Donte Jackson, WR Justin Jefferson, DE Arden Key, DL Rashard Lawrence, TE Foster Moreau, LB Jacob Phillips, LB Patrick Queen, TE Stephen Sullivan, LB Corey Thompson, DB Kevin Toliver, LB Devin White, RB Darrel Williams, and DB Andraez Williams.

PlayStation Fiesta Bowl
vs. Central Florida

One man can make a big difference

State Farm Stadium, Glendale, Arizona
January 1, 2019

The Tigers benefited greatly from the NCAA rule that allowed a player who had completed his degree at a university to transfer to another school without losing a year of eligibility.

LSU's Season

Joe Burrow, a redshirt junior at Ohio State who had been a four-star prospect out of high school in The Plains, Ohio, announced he had chosen LSU over Cincinnati. He moved to Baton Rouge in June and began extensive workouts with his receivers during the summer. Having thrown just 39 passes in his three years at Columbus, it took Joe a while to get comfortable in Steve Ensminger's offense which, compared to previous years at LSU, featured more shotgun formations, a fullback only on rare occasions, and four wideouts most of the time.

Burrow's performance in the early season was notable more for what he did *not* do than what he did do—no interceptions in the first five games, all victories, with six touchdown passes. Joe won over the LSU faithful with his performance at Auburn in Game 4. He led the comeback from a 21–10 third quarter deficit by connecting with WR Derrick Dillon on a 71-yard pass-and-run touchdown. Another graduate transfer, Cole Tracy from Division II Assumption College (MA), booted three field goals, including the 42-yard winner on the last play of the game.

The Tigers had started the season ranked 25th but immediately jumped to #11 with a 33–17 upset of #8 Miami (FL) at Arlington, Texas. LSU rose to #5 after the Auburn victory, then climbed another notch with a 45–16 pounding of Ole Miss in which Joe displayed his running ability with 96 yards on nine attempts with one TD. The winning streak ended the following week when he threw two interceptions in the 34–19 loss at Florida. But the #13 Tigers bounced back with a dominating home performance against #2 Georgia, 36–16. Joe threw no TD passes but also no picks. He went 15-for-30 for 200 yards and added 66 more on the ground. The defense took center stage the next week in a 19–3 triumph over Mississippi State.

ESPN College GameDay came to Baton Rouge for the clash between #1 Alabama and #3 LSU. Tiger fans hoped their revamped offense would make them more competitive with the Tide, but the game proved LSU still had a long way to go to hang with Bama, which pitched a second straight shutout in Tiger Stadium, 29–0. Fortunately, the next two opponents were unranked teams. A lackluster 24–17 victory in Fayetteville was followed by a 42–10 romp over Rice.

The annual finale with Texas A&M produced the most memorable game of the 2018 college football season, a contest that caused the NCAA to change its overtime rules. Aided by controversial calls and non-calls, the Aggies prevailed in *seven* overtimes, 74–72. Burrow accounted for six TDs, three through the air and three on the ground.

Joe finished the season 198-of-345 passing for 2,500 yards and 12 touchdowns against just four interceptions. He was also the team's third-leading rusher, carrying the ball 119 times for 375 yards and seven touchdowns. His favorite target was sophomore WR Justin Jefferson, who hauled in 50 passes for 788 yards and four scores. No other receiver caught more than 20 balls. With Derrius Guice in the NFL, senior Nick Brossette shouldered the rushing workload to the tune of 922 yards rushing (4.8 ypc average) and 14 touchdowns.

The #11 Tigers earned their 19th consecutive bowl invitation and their first to the Fiesta Bowl.

The Opponent

The Central Florida Knights came to the Fiesta Bowl with an amazing 25-game winning streak, with all but one of the victories by double digits. The 2017 team finished the regular season 13–0 after defeating Memphis 62–55 in double overtime for the American Athletic Conference championship. That earned the #12 Knights, as the highest ranked Group of Five team, the automatic bid to play in a CFP New Year's Six bowl. Despite losing coach Scott Frost to his alma mater, Nebraska, CFU upended Auburn 34–27 in the Peach Bowl. Afterward, the school displayed a national championship banner since the Knights were ranked #1 by the Colley Matrix, an NCAA-recognized selector of national champions.

Under new coach Josh Heupel, darned if the Knights didn't go undefeated again in 2018. Their only Power Five Conference victim was Pittsburgh, which they clobbered 45–14 in Orlando. Their greatest triumph came in the American Athletic Conference Championship Game against Memphis. Despite the loss of star QB McKenzie Milton to a gruesome knee injury the week before, CFU overcame a 38–21 halftime deficit behind an outstanding performance by a redshirt freshman QB from Hawai'i named Darriel Mack, Jr.—348 yards passing, 59 yards rushing, with four TDs on the ground and two more through the air.

The Knights boasted a 1,000-yard rusher in sophomore Greg McCrae. His backfield companion, Adrian Killins, was no slouch with 698 yards.

Count Ed Orgeron among the admirers of the CFU Knights. "It's unbelievable that they've got that done, especially through a coaching change. They must have a great culture out there. Guys believe in winning. They know how to practice. They know how to compete. They know how to win. I know (defensive coordinator) Randy Shannon. I know what type of coaches those guys are. A tremendous football team. This will be a challenge for our football team."

Coach Heupel also had words of praise for LSU. "Through the years, having seen LSU, they are going to be long and athletic. They're going to run really well. They're going to be powerful and explosive up front. They pose a lot of issues defensively. I have a tremendous amount of respect for LSU, their program, and their football team this year."

LSU prepared to face the team ranked #3 nationally in total offense without four defensive starters—DE Breiden Fehoko (injury), NT Ed Alexander (skipping the bowl game for the NFL draft), and CBs Greedy Williams (NFL draft) and Kristian Fulton (injury). To make matters worse, LB Jacob Phillips would sit out the first half because of a targeting violation against A&M. Two seniors, Stanford transfer Terrence Alexander and starting nickel back Kary Vincent, Jr., would start at CB. Devin White, expected to be a first-round draft pick after winning the Butkus Award as the nation's best linebacker, would play in the game.

The Game

At 11 a.m. local time, 57,246 gathered to see if David could KO another Goliath.

First Quarter

RB Clyde Edwards-Helaire got LSU off to a great start when he took the opening kickoff, broke away from tacklers at the 20, and raced 77 yards before being pulled down at the CF 16. RB Nick Brossette started right, then reversed field for 11 yards to make it first-and-goal. But UCF, which had an excellent red zone defense all year, protected their goal line with the aid of a false start penalty. So Cole Tracy booted a 24-yard field goal.

LSU 3 UCF 0 (12:38)

The Knights moved 69 yards in six plays against the depleted Tiger defense to take the lead. QB Darriel Mack handed to WR Marlon Williams, who turned and threw back to Mack, who scampered to the LSU 43. On third-and-one, Mack kept on the run-pass-option (RPO) and gained nine to the 25. Then HB Greg McRae took a handoff and ran untouched off the left side to the end zone behind great blocks by two wide receivers.

UCF 7 LSU 3 (10:59)

The LSU possession started promisingly when QB Joe Burrow hit freshman WR Ja'Marr Chase on a crossing pattern. With a facemask penalty added on, the ball was placed on the CF 46. Finding the going tough on the ground, Burrow converted a third-and-10 with a beautiful throw to WR Justin Jefferson on the left sideline to the 29. It took three runs by Brossette to move the chains again to the 17. On third-and-eight, Burrow threw to the right sideline to Derrick Dillon, who was manhandled by CB Brandon Moore. The result was a 75-yard interception return. As Moore started down the LSU sideline, 313-pound DT Joey Connors blindsided Burrow, who stayed on the ground for several minutes. With Coach Orgeron yelling for a targeting call, the play was reviewed and allowed to stand.

UCF 14 LSU 3 (6:39)

With Burrow crumpled on the ground as his team fell behind by 11, it wasn't hard to imagine the Knights knocking off another band of Tigers from the SEC. But, as TV commentator Brian Griese observed, "If there's one word you can use for Joe Burrow, it's 'tough.'" Burrow said afterward, "The only reason I didn't get up right away is because I got the wind knocked out of me. I didn't really think too much about the hit after I got up. It hurt for a second, and I got right up and went on to the next play." He showed his mettle by leading the Tigers on a 11-play 67-yard touchdown drive against an aggressive defense that was covering the receivers tightly. He hit WR Stephen Sullivan on a crossing pattern for 15 yards to midfield, then escaped the rush and ran off the left side for 11 more. He was hit a yard out of bounds, but no flag was thrown, increasing the ire of Tiger fans against the ACC officiating crew. On third-and-12, the Knights stopped the advance by sacking Joe for a loss of six. But freshman DE Randy Charlton spiked the ball in celebration—15 yards for unsportsmanlike conduct and a first down at the 32. Another UCF penalty, for offside, helped the Tigers, who needed four runs by Brossette, including the Knights' fifth tackle for a loss in the period, to get another first down. Nick's last carry was a fourth-and-one lunge that barely made the line to gain. Then Joe lobbed a gorgeous pass to Jefferson streaking down the left sideline. He caught the ball over his shoulder behind two defenders just before stepping out of the end zone.

UCF 14 LSU 10 (1:27)

QB Joe Burrow hands off to RB Nick Brossette (Baton Rouge *Advocate*).

UCF tested CB Terrence Alexander, who grabbed the receiver as he broke past him for an obvious interference call to the 44. Mack ran an RPO keeper but lost the ball when hit by All-SEC MLB Devon White, and junior LB Michael Divinity recovered. After the play, Alexander was ejected for throwing a punch at the wide receiver who continued to block him after the whistle.

UCF 14 LSU 10

Second Quarter

The Tigers capitalized on the turnover to take the lead. Burrow ran out of the pocket for a first down at the 48. On third-and-seven from the UCF 49, he hit Derrick Dillon in stride flying across the middle. A missed tackle allowed him to turn down the sideline to the end zone.

LSU 17 UCF 14 (12:59)

After UCF went three-and-out, the Tigers embarked on their third straight scoring drive. Joe went four-for-four, hitting Sullivan over the middle for 19, Chase for nine on a

Justin Jefferson pulls in a touchdown reception as DB Nevelle Clark (14) defends (Baton Rouge *Advocate*).

leaping catch and getting a foot down inbounds on the sideline, Edwards-Helaire in the flat for eight, and finally a 33-yard touchdown to a wide-open Jefferson behind the confused defenders.

LSU 24 UCF 14 (7:11)

The Tigers lost another member of the depleted secondary when All-SEC S Grant Delpit was called for targeting on a pass receiver to give UCF a first down at the LSU 36. Defensive coordinator Dave Aranda compensated for a depleted secondary by dialing up blitzes. S JaCoby Stevens sacked Mack for a loss of six. Two plays later, the Knights went for it on fourth-and-five, but Stevens deflected the pass.

The Tigers used only 50 seconds on their possession before punting, but LB Patrick Queen's 22-yard sack of a stumbling Mack produced another three-and-out. Burrow started sharply, finding Jefferson for 15 yards and Chase for 14 more to the CF 38. But three incompletions brought in Josh Growden for a punt to the five.

With only 1:57 on the clock, the Knights couldn't go 95 yards, could they? Yes, they could, unleashing their lightning fast two-minute drill. They even overcame a Rashard Lawrence 9-yard sack, lining up so fast two plays later that Rashard was caught offside. That helped convert a third-and-four on McCrae's 12-yard run to the LSU 44. Gabriel Davis caught a slant pass to the 28. After UCF used its final timeout with 0:17 left, LSU used one of theirs. Lawrence then sacked Mack again. "Last month and toward the back end of the season, I've been really been working on my pass rush and just trying to have a good get-off," explained Rashard. "So today they kind of got me isolated with some one-on-one situations, and I took advantage of it." However, the Knights got off another play, and Mack threw a perfect pass to Davis a half-step behind third-string CB Mannie Netherly at the back of the end zone.

LSU 24 UCF 21 (0:04)

"We went in at halftime," Coach O said afterward. "The team had their head down. We got after it in the locker room. We had some great talks in the locker room, had some great adjustments, great leadership. And our team came out in the third quarter. ... I think that was the change in the game, us dominating the third quarter."

Third Quarter

LSU's beleaguered defense got much needed assistance from LB Jacob Phillips' return from suspension. He made his presence felt on the first play, tackling Adrian Killins after a gain of seven. A 1-yard run and an incompletion brought on the punter. It took the Tigers only three plays to increase their lead. Burrow hit TE Foster Moreau over the middle for 16 yards to the 44. Brossette got loose for his best run of the day, 24 yards to the CF 32. Joe then threw to Chase, who did a stop-and-go to break behind the defender and gather in the perfect pass in the end zone.

LSU 31 UCF 21 (12:38)

Divinity and Phillips led the charge that forced another three-and-out. With LG Garrett Brumfield, C Lloyd Cushenberry, and RG Damien Lewis taking over the line of scrimmage, the Tigers used up 6:35 off the clock on an 11-play drive that ended with a 28-yard Tracy field goal. Burrow converted a third-and-six with a 14-yard strike to Chase to the 39. Brossette overcame a false start penalty by regaining the 5 yards, then six more. Two plays later, the Tigers snapped the ball quickly, and Joe ran for seven to the CF 45. He then threw long to Jefferson, who was grabbed from behind by the defender to prevent a sure completion. First-and-10 at the 30. Brossette's 11-yard carry moved the sticks to the 14 and put him over the 1,000-yard mark for the season. An illegal formation penalty stopped the momentum temporarily, but Edwards-Helaire ran for 11 to make it fourth-and-one at the five. The Tigers lined up to go for it, but another false start penalty canceled that plan. So Tracy hit a chip shot from the 18.

LSU 34 UCF 21 (5:18)

The UCF possession illustrated the adage that sometimes it's better to be lucky than good. The Tigers were so short on DBs that sophomore WR Jontre Kirklin was pressed into service. Davis ran past him so far that Jontre's dive to trip him fell short. Mack's pass came down into the receiver's hands, but he dropped it. The breaks evened out, though, when Jefferson back-pedaled to take Mac Loudermilk's 54-yard punt. Just as the ball arrived, JJ's back foot slipped, and he fumbled as he hit the ground. UCF's Jacob Harris ran the ball into the end zone. But you can't advance a muffed punt. Still, the Knights were in business at the 20. Two incompletions and a false start forced UCF to settle for Matthew Wright's 37-yard field goal.

LSU 34 UCF 24 (3:01)

LSU's next possession was prolonged by a gutty play by Dillon. He took Burrow's third down pass and was hit short of the first down line but bulled his way through two tacklers into the clear for a 34-yard to the CF 34. Inspired, Edwards-Helaire also was hit short of the line to gain but, aided by a push from FB Tory Carter, kept going for 15 yards to the 19.

LSU 34 UCF 24

Fourth Quarter

Showing second and even third effort, Edwards-Helaire gained six to the 13. A quick slant-in to Chase put the pigskin on the three. Then things went awry. First, Burrow bobbled the snap, then fumbled it as he turned to handoff. He was lucky to fall on the ball at the eight. Next, Brossette was smothered for a 2-yard loss. Finally, Joe looped a pass to Jefferson in the back right corner of the end zone, but he dropped the ball. So Tracy tied the LSU record for field goals in a season with his 28th three-pointer.

LSU 37 UCF 24 (12:09)

Mack started by targeting Kirklin again and getting another interference call. First-and-10 at the 40. But a 2-yard run and two throwaways under pressure led to a punt to the 14. The Tigers then took 7:12 off the clock with a 12-play, 78-yard march that ended with another Tracy field goal. Needing 2 yards on third down, Brossette got 10 to the 32, then gained 13 on two carries to move the chains again. The big play came on the next third down when Burrow hit Sullivan in stride down the right seam for 42 yards to the 10. After three rushes against the massed defense gained just two, Tracy sent a 26-yarder through the uprights to break the NCAA all-division record of 96 field goals in a career.

LSU 40 UCF 24 (4:12)

With the Knights in desperation mode, the Tigers gave them a break when Ray Thornton and Phillips sacked Mack only to have two penalties called on the play—face mask and unnecessary roughness. Suddenly, UCF was at midfield. With LSU braced for the pass, Otis Anderson carried twice for 20 yards. Then the Knights overcame a false start penalty on 11 and 22-yard runs by McCrae to the two. The Tigers made it tough, stuffing McCrae for no gain, then blitzing Stevens to force another throwaway. Finally, Taj McGowan slammed into left tackle and fell on the goal line. The Knights went for two and succeeded on a pass to Anderson.

LSU 40 UCF 32 (2:24)

The Tigers barely eluded disaster on the onside kick. The ball bounced off Jefferson and was up for grabs for a second before Moreau fell on it just before two Knights could get it. With UCF having only a single timeout, the Tigers could run out the clock with just one first down. But three Brossette carries—giving him 29 for the game—fell a yard short. So Growden punted to the 12.

After Notre Dame's miraculous touchdown in the last minute in the Citrus Bowl a year earlier, Tiger fans couldn't breathe easy until the clock showed 0:00. Mack was hit as he threw, and the ball fell incomplete. Then he overthrew the receiver on what was intended to be a hook-and-ladder. Finally, he threw downfield into a crowd. Todd Harris deflected the ball, and it landed in the hands of Stevens to end the season with 10 victories for the first time since 2013.

Final Score: LSU 40 UCF 32

Burrow was the obvious choice for the MVP award after completing 21-of-34 for 394 yards and four touchdowns in what would turn out to be a preview of his sensational 2019 season.

Postgame

Coach Orgeron raved about his quarterback. "We've been proud of Joe. He's smart. Joe's an excellent quarterback. We believe in him. He's exactly what we feel an LSU quarterback ought to be." Turning to the defense, which recorded five sacks, Ed said, "The difference was the pressure on the quarterback. We had more pressure on the quarterback than we had all year." He complimented the Knights. "They had an excellent football team. They were well-coached. What a heck of a football game." Then Coach O looked ahead to 2019. "We have a tradition to uphold. We blocked out the noise (from the dire preseason predictions), but it galvanized our team. We should have been 11–1…. We're going to learn from that next year."

Burrow explained that UCF was "kind of sitting on our short routes so we had to start throwing it deep. We hit a couple and got them to back off so that opened up the underneath game. We really had it clicking on all cylinders in the passing game."

Devin White revealed the Tigers' motivation for the game. "They were too cocky. Our coaches told us they were cocky. We just wanted to shut them up, and we shut them up."

Perhaps thinking of the unsportsmanlike penalty that prolonged LSU's scoring drive after UCF went up 14–3, Coach Heupel said, "We didn't handle the emotional part of the game as well as we needed to early and combine that with an early turnover when we got things going. We stubbed our toe enough early that we weren't able to change the way the game was played." He added, "Were there opportunities in this football game that we missed? Absolutely. I think that's what's special about this game. I mean, you only get one opportunity to walk out on the field."

Sixteen 2018 Tigers (through the 2020 season) have played pro football: QB Joe Burrow, LB K'Lavon Chaisson, OL Saahdiq Charles, OL Lloyd Cushenberry, RB Clyde Edwards-Helaire, DL Breiden Fehoko, LS Blake Ferguson, WR Justin Jefferson, DL Rashard Lawrence, OL Damien Lewis, TE Foster Moreau, LB Jacob Phillips, LB Patrick Queen, TE Stephen Sullivan, LB Devin White, and DB Andraez Williams.

Chick-fil-A Peach Bowl
vs. Oklahoma

*"Is there an award higher
than the Heisman Trophy?"*

College Football Playoff Semifinal

Mercedes-Benz Stadium, Atlanta, Georgia
December 28, 2019

"There is no way I could have written a better script," is how Coach Ed Orgeron described LSU's magical 2019 season.

LSU's Season

It isn't often that a coaching hire for a subordinate position makes a major difference in the outcome of a season. But one of those times was LSU's hiring Joe Brady, a 29-year-old offensive assistant for the New Orleans Saints in 2017–18. He became the Tigers' passing game coordinator and wide receivers coach and contributed so much to LSU's success that he won the 2019 Broyles Award as the best assistant coach in college football.

With Brady working hand-in-glove with Offensive Coordinator Steve Ensminger, the LSU no-huddle offense enjoyed the greatest season in school history and arguably the best in NCAA history. With senior QB Joe Burrow performing at a level that won him the most first place votes and the largest margin of victory in Heisman Trophy history, the Tigers averaged an astounding 47.8 points per game against a regular season schedule that included five teams in the top 12 of the preseason AP poll. Burrow also won the Maxwell, Walter Camp, Johnny Unitas Golden Arm, Davey O'Brien, and Manning Awards and was named Player of the Year by the Associated Press and *The Sporting News*.

The two Joes weren't the only national award winners. Sophomore Ja'Marr Chase won the Biletnikoff Award as the best wide receiver. S Grant Delpit was honored with the Jim Thorpe Award as the top defensive back. Freshman CB Derek Stingley was a consensus All-American. The offensive line won the Joe Moore Award. And Ed Orgeron won four coach of the year awards.

336

LSU, and Burrow in particular, first caught the nation's eye when they defeated Texas in Austin 45–38 on a primetime telecast in Week 2. However, many Tiger fans' fondest memory of the '19 team will be the 46–41 victory over Alabama in Tuscaloosa that ended the demoralizing eight-game losing streak to the Crimson Tide. Forty-six points against the program that had held LSU to a combined 10 in the three previous meetings! Even the wariest skeptics among the faithful began to think, "This just may be our year!" One of the heroes of that triumph was junior RB Clyde Edwards-Helaire, who had a banner year—1,319 yards rushing and another 399 receiving.

The Tigers were never behind in the fourth quarter in any of the 13 regular season games. The last contest in which they trailed in the second half was October 26 against Auburn, which led 13–10 before LSU rallied to win 23–20—the tightest margin of the year.

Another game that gave LSU fans immense joy was the 50–7 drubbing of Texas A&M. It was sweet revenge for the Aggies' seven-overtime officials-aided win the year before, after which Aggie fans stormed the field and roughed up some LSU players and staff members. Burrow delighted Tiger fans before the game when he trotted out during Senior Night introductions wearing a jersey that read "JOE BURREAUX" on the back.

The defense became a concern the week after the Alabama ecstasy when Ole Miss ran up 37 points and gained 614 yards (exactly 100 less than the Tigers). LSU dropped from the top spot in the CFP rankings to second behind Ohio State. But after the A&M rout and the 37–10 domination of Georgia in the SEC Championship Game, the Selection Committee returned the Tigers to #1, which gave them the closer semifinal site, Atlanta, and the #4 opponent, Oklahoma.

The Opponent

Like LSU in 2018, the 2019 Oklahoma Sooners received a shot in the arm when QB Jalen Hurts transferred from Alabama for his senior season after losing the starting job to Tua Tagovailoa. Hurts had no trouble adapting to the no-huddle spread offense that Head Coach Lincoln Riley had installed when he was offensive coordinator because it resembled the one he ran at Alabama. In his first game as a Sooner, Jalen shattered the school single game yardage record, accounting for 396 yards of total offense. Hurts produced 4,889 yards of offense, including 1,255 on the ground to lead all Sooner rushers. His favorite receiver, junior CeeDee Lamb, a Biletnikoff finalist, caught 58 passes for 1,208 yards, an impressive 20.8 ypr. Jalen finished a distant second in the Heisman voting and was also a finalist for the Maxwell and O'Brien Awards.

The Sooners also received a boost on defense, not from a player but from a new defensive coordinator, the aptly named Alex Grinch. OU improved from allowing 453.8 yards per game and 33.3 points per game in 2018 to 330.6 yards per game and 24.5 points per game.

The Sooners won their first seven games, including the annual Red River Showdown over Texas, 34–27—the same margin by which LSU beat the Longhorns. Then a 48–41 upset at Kansas State dropped OU from #5 to #9 in the AP poll. But that was the only bump in the road. The Sooners won their remaining four games to qualify for the conference championship game where they beat Baylor for the second time to claim their fifth straight Big 12 title. The Sooners were chosen for the College Football Playoff for the third straight time and fourth time in five years. But they had yet to win a playoff game.

The teams' offensive statistics portended a high-scoring game. Incredibly, their yards per game differed by a mere tenth.

Offense	Points per Game	Yards per Game
LSU	47.8	554.3
Oklahoma	43.2	554.2

The oddsmakers, no doubt thinking that LSU's defense would gain more stops than OU's, installed the Tigers as 12.5-point favorites. The Sooner defense would play without two starters. S Delarrin Turner-Yell broke his collarbone the week before the game, and DL Ronnie Perkins was suspended.

Just hours before kickoff, LSU received the devastating news that the daughter-in-law of offensive coordinator Steve Ensminger died in a plane crash on the way to the game. Orgeron, who told Steve the sad news, said afterward, "It was tough. I didn't want it to affect the mindset of the football team, the energy of the football team. Neither did Steve. We tried to keep it from them." With a heavy heart, Steve went to the press box and called the game of his life.

The Game

A Peach Bowl record crowd of 78,347 saw the Tigers shred the OU defense to the tune of 49 first-half points.

FIRST QUARTER

The game started perfectly for LSU: OU three-and-out, touchdown drive, OU three-and-out. Starting from the Oklahoma 42 after a shanked punt, it took the Tigers only three plays to reach the end zone, all passes to different receivers. TE Thaddeus Moss for 17. WR Terrace Marshal for six. Slant-in to WR Justin Jefferson who dragged a tackler close enough to the goal to stretch the ball across. Cade York converted.

Score: LSU 7 Oklahoma 0 (12:03)

After forcing a three-and-out on LSU's second possession, the Sooners drove 69 yards in five plays to tie the score. QB Jalen Hurts opened up the passing game by running twice, for five and 12 yards to the 48. WR CeeDee Lamb lined up in the slot, forcing S JaCoby Stevens to cover him. Stevens stayed right with him but couldn't stop the All-American from catching the pass at the three. RB Kennedy Brooks powered over on the next play.

LSU 7 Oklahoma 7 (7:34)

The Tigers took the lead for good on their next possession, traveling 75 yards in nine plays. Burrow hit JJ twice for a total of 32 yards to the OU 43. Then it was Marshall's turn for eight. Freshman Chris Curry, starting at RB for Clyde Edwards-Helaire, who had not practiced for weeks with a strained hamstring, got the first down at the 30. On

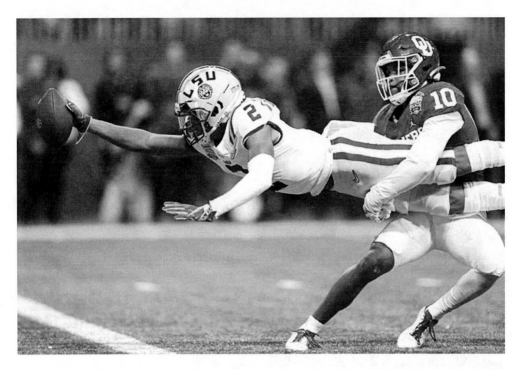

WR Justin Jefferson stretches out for a touchdown as Oklahoma S Pat Fields tries to make the stop (Baton Rouge *Advocate*).

third-and-two, Clyde made his first appearance and showed he was just fine by bulling over two tacklers for 14 yards to the eight. Two plays later, Joe did his best Tom Brady imitation, moving to his left to avoid the rush and flipping on the run to Marshall running across the end zone.

LSU 14 Oklahoma 7 (4:24)

LSU got a big break on third down when freshman All-American CB Darryl Stingley got away with an obvious interference that the ACC officiating crew missed on the OU sideline. On the first third down of LSU's possession, Burrow created another "Heisman moment" except that he had already won the Heisman. Running from the pocket to his right, it appeared he would throw the ball away just before going out of bounds, but instead he lobbed it over the defender into the hands of Marshall just inside the boundary for a 24-yard gain. OU challenged that Terrace had gone out of bounds and come back, but replay ruled that he had been forced out. Curry zipped to the OU 35 before Jefferson dropped a pass as he turned to run. But he made up for his mistake on the next play when Burrow made a gorgeous throw that JJ took on the run just beyond the left pylon. An OU defense that had allowed only 42 points in the first quarter all season had now allowed half as much.

LSU 21 Oklahoma 7 (1:16)

SECOND QUARTER

LSU batted 1.000 in the period—four possessions, four touchdowns. Burrow made the first two first downs of the initial drive with his feet, rushing for 11 yards on a play when OU's defense lost another player for targeting, then 12 more to the 42. From there,

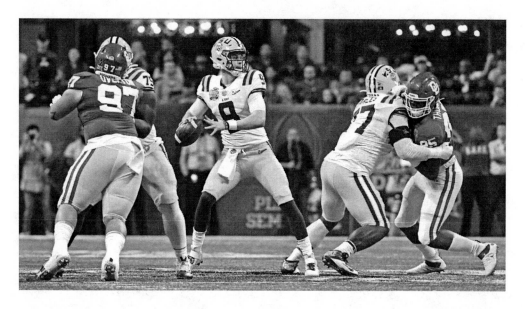

Joe Burrow drops back to pass as Lloyd Cushenberry (79) and Saahdiq Charles (77) block (Baton Rouge *Advocate*).

Joe avoided the rush and threw long to Jefferson, who had gotten past the replacement for the ousted defender.

LSU 28 Oklahoma 7 (12:13)

The Sooners tried a flea-flicker, but S Kary Vincent wasn't fooled and intercepted at the LSU 45. Burrow went five-for-five, finding Moss for 11, JJ for 10 and 12, Ja'Marr Chase for 22, and Jefferson again for 30 yards and his fourth touchdown of the half.

LSU 35 Oklahoma 7 (9:17)

OU put together their best drive so far, traveling 75 yards in 10 plays with all but 13 coming on runs. On third-and-goal at the six, CB Kristian Fulton was called for interference in the end zone to put the ball on the two. After the Tigers stuffed Kennedy Brooks for no gain, Hurts ran a nifty option play, faking the pitch and stepping into the end zone untouched.

LSU 35 Oklahoma 14 (4:45)

The Tigers got those points back quickly. On the second play, OU defenders played Alphonse and Gaston with Thaddeus Moss. Spotting the opening immediately, Burrow fired to Randy's son running free as a bird. A 190-pound safety caught up with him at the 10 but could only slow down the 250-pound tight end, who fell into the end zone.

LSU 42 Oklahoma 14 (4:18)

On the LSU sideline during the possession, sophomore LB K'Lavon Chaisson gathered the defense and told them to cut out the pushing and shoving after the whistle and anything else that might get them ejected and miss the first half of the championship game.

The next Sooner possession netted -5 yards and took only 1:24 off the clock. That gave Burrow a chance to tie the record for TD passes in an *entire* bowl game before the first half ended. He ate up most of the yardage by connecting with Chase for 39 yards to the 10. After Ty Davis-Price's 6-yard gain and a penalty put the ball on the two, the Tigers lined up in a bunch formation. Marshall delayed, then sneaked into the end zone where he caught Joe's seventh TD pass.

LSU 49 Oklahoma 14 (0:50)

The LSU offensive machine ended the half with an astounding 495 yards. Burrow was 21-of-27 for 403 yards with more touchdowns than incompletions! The fans gathered in Arizona for the other CFP semifinal could head to the stadium knowing which team would face the Clemson-Ohio State winner in the finals.

Third Quarter

The biggest question for the second half was, How long will Joe play? He directed a workmanlike 13-play, 74-yard march for LSU's eighth touchdown in nine posses- sions. Jefferson and Marshall caught third-down passes for the initial first downs. On fourth-and-two at the OU 17, Chase took an end-around handoff for five to keep the drive alive. Then Curry ran three times to set up first-and-goal at the two. Joe then bur- rowed into the end zone.

LSU 56 Oklahoma 14 (10:11)

Hurts ran or passed the ball on 12 of OU's 13-play drive that covered 75 yards. On fourth-and-nine at the 12, Jalen ran out of the pocket and dove at the pylon with the ball extended for the score.

LSU 56 Oklahoma 21 (4:19)

Surprisingly, Burrow came out for the next drive, which carried into the final period. It started with three passes to Jefferson to the OU 46. Throws to WR Stephen Sullivan and FB Tory Carter followed by a Davis-Price run for eight made it first-and-10 at the 29.

LSU 56 Oklahoma 21

Fourth Quarter

The first play made LSU fans gasp as visions of losing their beloved quarterback for the championship game flashed through their heads. A fierce rush forced him out of the pocket as his head was twisted around without a facemask penalty being called. When hit from behind, he fumbled, but G Ed Ingram recovered at the 28. So York tried a 46-yard field goal that hit the left upright.

Hurts went five-for-five on a 9-play, 77-yard scoring drive. The key play was a 19-yard pass to the one to WR Drake Stoops, son of the former Oklahoma coach. RB T.J. Pledger scored from there.

LSU 56 Oklahoma 28

Redshirt sophomore Myles Brennan took over at quarterback and directed a nine-play TD march that covered 75 yards. He hit on all three of his passes. Senior WR Derrick Dillon caught two for 22 yards, and junior Racey McMath the other for 17 yards to the OU six. Freshman John Emery covered the remaining ground to score standing up.

LSU 63 Oklahoma 28 (3:59)

Final Score: LSU 63 Oklahoma 28

An Atlanta sportswriter wrote, "Is there an award higher than the Heisman Trophy?

What LSU QB Joe Burrow did—493 yards passing, seven passing touchdowns, one more touchdown by foot—should be of some interest to the Nobel committee." Burrow set an FBS record by being responsible for eight touchdowns in a bowl game and tied the record for passing TDs in a bowl (seven). He also tied LSU and SEC single-game records for passing touchdowns and broke four College Football Playoff records. Jefferson also claimed two with his four receiving touchdowns and 227 receiving yards, and LSU as a team broke three—49 points in a half, 63 total points, and 692 yards of total offense.

Postgame

Coach O gave the game ball to Steve Ensminger. "Great job by Steve, who went through a tragedy today to calling a game. He's the MVP right now." He added, "What a tremendous job by everybody. One team, one heartbeat. Everybody in our organization. We got tremendous play by Joe Burrow and have a great coaching staff."

Burrow offered a surprising comment after completing 29-of-39 for 493 yards and seven TDs to earn the MVP award. "To be honest, it wasn't my sharpest game. This guy (Justin Jefferson) was bailing me out on a couple throws that I missed. Guys like Terrace (Marshall) and Ja'Marr (Chase) were bailing me out on misreads and being late with the football. That's the kind of team we have. Someone doesn't have their best game; the other guys step up."

Thaddeus Moss told a story about the team's leader. "Joe said at breakfast this morning he wanted to go for 70 (points). Knowing Joe, he was upset scoring 63. He wanted to go for 10 touchdowns."

Coach Riley: "I felt like if we played well, we would be able to stand in there and trade blows with them, I really did. And we did early. But when you start making mistakes, combination of that and a talented team playing well, they go on a run like they like to do."

Postscript

Sixteen days after the semifinal, LSU won the school's fourth national championship by defeating the defending champions from Clemson 42–25. Incredibly, the final game in all four championship seasons (1958, 2003, 2007, and 2019) was played in New Orleans.

The 2019 Tigers performed a feat that had never been done before and may never be seen again. They defeated four of the five teams that were ranked ahead of them in the preseason AP poll: #1 Clemson, #2 Alabama, #3 Georgia, and #4 Oklahoma. And Clemson defeated #5 Ohio State in the other semifinal game before losing to LSU. It's no wonder that so many commentators across the nation ranked LSU's 2019 season as the greatest in college football history.

No matter how long college football is played—50, 75, 100 years—every outstanding team will be measured against the 2019 LSU Fighting Tigers.

Fourteen 2019 Tigers (through the 2020 season) have played pro football: QB Joe Burrow, LB K'Lavon Chaisson, OL Saahdiq Charles, OL Lloyd Cushenberry, RB Clyde Edwards-Helaire, DL Breiden Fehoko, LS Blake Ferguson, DB Kristian Fulton, WR Justin Jefferson, DL Rashard Lawrence, OL Damien Lewis, LB Jacob Phillips, LB Patrick Queen, and TE Stephen Sullivan.

Bibliography

Books

Dietzel, Paul F. *Call Me Coach: A Life in College Football.* Louisiana State University Press, 2008.

Finney, Peter. *The Fighting Tigers II: LSU Football, 1893–1980.* Louisiana State University Press.

Fitzgerald, Francis J., ed. *Greatest Moments in LSU Football History.* Capital City Press, 1998.

Hardesty, Dan. *The Louisiana Tigers: LSU Football.* The Strode Publishers, 1975.

Johnson, Bud. *The Perfect Season: LSU's Magic Year—1958.* Gulf South Books, 2007.

King, Sam. *Tiger Beat: Covering LSU Sports for 35 Years.* Acadian House Publishing, 2013.

Mulé, Marty. *Eye of the Tiger: 100 Years of LSU Football.* Longstreet Press, 1993.

Mulé, Marty. *Game of My Life LSU: Memorable Stories of Tigers Football.* Sports Publishing, 2006.

Rabalais, Scott. *The Fighting Tigers 1993–2018: Into a New Century of LSU Football.* Louisiana State University Press, 2008.

Newspapers

Atlanta *Journal Constitution*
Augusta (GA) *Chronicle*
Baton Rouge *Morning Advocate*
Baton Rouge *State Times*
Dallas *Morning News*
Houston *Chronicle*
Miami *Herald*
New Orleans *Times-Picayune*
Orlando *Sentinel*

Index